Copyright © 2025 by Kitty Stitt

All rights reserved.

No part of this book may be reproduced in any form or by any electronic or mechanical means, including information storage and retrieval systems, without written permission from the author, except for the use of brief quotations in a book review.

Living Evolved

write here
write now

Kitty Stitt
Author & Storyteller

✉ kitty@bykitty.net
🌐 www.bykitty.net
📞 +61 433 827 532

@bykitty1   ByKitty1   @bykitty2

I would like to acknowledge the Wiradjuri people as the traditional custodians of the lands in which I live, write and learn. I pay my deepest respects to the Elders – past, present and emerging – for sustaining this land, the culture and the songlines.

I dedicate my life's story to all the versions of SELF that turned up along my path to guide me home to my true SELF. Living evolved feels aligned, authentic and abundant.

CONTENTS

EPIGRAPH	ix
1. Igniting universal creative power	1
2. Unhooking society's corset self	11
3. Talking to spirits self	16
4. Loving unconditionally self	20
5. Opening Pandora's Box self	37
6. Having telepathic perception self	53
7. Manifesting a miracle self	68
8. Rebirthing in the desert self	77
9. Learning how the Buddha meditated self	93
10. Realizing, whatever happens, is the perfect happening self	115
11. Surrendering self	128
12. Making babies self	152
13. Hearing the Earth Mother's call self	170
14. Adding tools to the toolbox self	185
15. Inviting spirits to give me information self	205
16. Finding the lightworkers' path self	210
17. Forgiving self	220
18. Journeying with the Native American Clan Mothers self	229
19. Grieving lost children self	235
20. Assisting a child transitioning to the spirit world self	240
21. Visioning the void self	260
22. Embracing discomfort self	280
23. Seeing the world is what I think it is self	286
24. Calming the COVID-19 chaos self	291
25. Feeling locked and loaded self	297
26. Claiming my creator self	301
27. Experiencing a Kundalini awakening self	311
28. Changing self	316
29. Answering the call self	332

30. Returning to work after a retreat self	336
31. Activating superpowers self	341
32. Healing childhood trauma self	345
33. Breaking society's molds self	355
34. Leaving my job self	363
35. Accessing multidimensional me self	372
36. Acknowledging I'm frequency self	380
37. Being SELF	389
38. Expressing mySELF	401
SELF	405
Appendix 1	409
Appendix 2	413
About the Author	427

EPIGRAPH

As I interpret the Course [A Course in Miracles] our deepest fear is not that we are inadequate. Our deepest fear is that we are powerful beyond measure. It is our light, not our darkness, that most frightens us. We ask ourselves, Who am I to be brilliant, gorgeous, talented, fabulous? Actually, who am I not to be? You are a child of God. Your playing small doesn't serve the world. There's nothing enlightened about shrinking so that other people won't feel insecure around you. We are all meant to shine, as children do. We were born to make manifest the glory of God that is within us. It's not just in some of us; it's in everyone. And as we let our own light shine, we unconsciously give other people permission to do the same. As we're liberated from our own fear, our presence automatically liberates others.

A Return to Love: Reflections on the Principles of 'A Course in Miracles' by Marianne Williamson

1
IGNITING UNIVERSAL CREATIVE POWER

When I was 38 years old, I had a vision where humans manifested their dreams to be self-realized, allowing humanity, too, to achieve its dream to awaken. This book explains how each of us can turn this vision into reality.

Together we are awakening our universal creative power, the power needed at this time to ignite a global shift in consciousness. This mass evolution is up to us because individual amplification creates it. Human consciousness is expanding exponentially, and each of us can harness this expansion.

Do you ever think *Life should be easier and more joyful?*

Do you ever ponder *There must be more to life and more to my relationships?*

Do you ever wonder *Am I more than just this physical body?*

Do you ever get the feeling *Maybe I am here for a reason?*

I felt this, too, and it sent me on a quest to discover our true self. I experienced self-realization awakenings that proved our true self is not our mind, breath, sense perceptions, thoughts, body, ideas, or identifiers. Instead it is the omnipresent awareness before anything has taken form.

I call our true self SELF (upper case). You might call it *God, oneness, love, Higher Self, Biyaami, Tao, Spirit, Divine, 'I am' presence, pure consciousness, Great Central Sun, Buddha Nature, the Universe, Allah, Christ Consciousness, one heart, supreme self* or just plain *home*. You are welcome to use your term whenever I use the word SELF. Whatever you call it, know it is your natural state of being and it does not need a name to know what it is.

WHAT DOES SELF feel like to you? My acronyms are

- Spacious/Still/Silent/Spiritual/Surreal
- Expanded/Essence/Everlasting/Effortless/Empty/Enlightened
- Latent/Lifeforce/Limitless/Love
- Formless/First/Forever/Frequency

Using your word, could you make an acronym for what I call SELF? Have a play, write it on the bookmark. For example God might be: Supreme Eternal Loving Father. Doing this helps you connect to the word I use throughout the book.

Every human is expressing their version of SELF in every moment. We have a choice: *I can express mySELF aligned to SELF (mySELF Expressing Love Frequency) or misaligned to SELF (mySELF Expressing Low Frequency).* More examples in Appendix 1.

I bring to you tools to align to SELF throughout your day. I come to you as a fellow traveler who has evolved enough to guide others to evolve themselves intuitively. We continue evolving until our last breath and beyond because our consciousness is infinitely expanding.

When I contemplated why I lived out of alignment for so long, I knew it had something to do with being human. It felt as though when I came into physical form in this 3-Dimensional (3-D) reality, I agreed to forget where I came from and what I came to do. However, throughout my life, experiences allowed me to remember my origin and reason for being.

Each catalyst highlighted my misaligned habitual thoughts and programs, which I learned from society. Our 3-D world consists of duality which is the opposite of SELF which is oneness. I realized that if I signed up to experience this contrast, I would have to discover how to awaken within the polarities because there was no escaping them. Do I think it is possible to awaken instantaneously and bypass all the life lessons? Yes, I do. But, for me, this was not the case. I had to lovingly bumble around on the edges of my true potential for years, experiencing mini-awakenings before stepping fully into my light. There is no way of knowing when you will awaken to your truth. But one thing is for sure, once you achieve this liberation, it ripples out to your family, friends, country, and ultimately our planet.

This book is your call to action, so your awakening might be now.

Millions of us are living evolved, and you can live that way too. By realizing SELF, aligning to it and eventually embodying it, we raise our frequency and Planet Earth's frequency.

We write humanity's story by embodying SELF in the now

Change is inevitable if everyone embraces their unique expression in their little piece of the world because each holds a part of the puzzle, creating the whole together.

You are loved, seen, and heard. You are where you need to be. Everything that is happening to you right now is OK. You are safe.

Each time we embody SELF, we access a more evolved timeline that exists now as a parallel timeline (everything exists in the now). To break it down, at any given moment, we can be on a timeline that is low frequency with lower potential or on a timeline that is high frequency with higher potential. I know which one I would rather be on!

The higher timeline, which I also refer to as the new, is immediately available. It can be what we see and experience. Imagine that another version of you has evolved and is on that timeline. You can step onto that timeline any moment you choose. At first, you allow your evolved self to guide you by pausing and making deliberate choices *mySELF Expressing Love Frequency or mySELF Expressing Low Frequency*. Eventually, you become your evolved self and remain in the new reality all the time. Here, you glide through life, allowing it to unfold effortlessly. You trust that whatever you think, say, and do flows from SELF and is for the good of all.

I appreciate the complexity of what I am explaining. Therefore, this book will act as a roadmap, taking you through my SELF-realization process from the beginning. I gathered my knowledge through transformative events, not through beliefs. Beliefs are learned intellectually from other people and books, whereas inner knowing and truth are learned experientially through personal experiences.

Every word in this book is my truth. However, some phenomena can not be scientifically proven because they are beyond the visible world, so if skepticism arises, I invite you to explore these concepts yourself. Rather than believe them out of respect for me, I encourage you to gain direct experience to see if they resonate with you. As you live your life, you confirm them or discover something else. This makes them your truth. Each experience is perfect for your SELF-realization because each of us uniquely expresses our version of SELF. This is the beauty of SELF-expression. This book is just one example of the infinite ways we can express ourSELF.

Rewrite the past

WE EXIST IN A MULTIDIMENSIONAL, quantum reality; how we think about the past changes the vibration of those stories in the now. This elevated vibration attracts what is in alignment with it and creates a new, higher-frequency reality. We no longer have to live a life aligned to our old stories' lower frequency. Instead, we can write the past, the present, and the future in the now.

After you read a chapter, I invite you to reflect and think about times in your life when you may have had a similar experience. Then, choose one of your stories and write it down, explaining how it acted as a wake-up call for your SELF-realization. This process makes you an empowered participant in the book rather than an inactive consumer. Writing down your stories allows you to celebrate and claim what you are doing instead of focusing on what you are not doing. It replaces *I should do this* with *I am already doing this!*

Another way to use the book is to rewrite your stories with a new ending. The body does not know the difference between real and imagined, which means you can give yourself pseudo awakenings and evolution catalysts in the now (even if it happened years ago). Writing your account with a different ending changes things energetically, not literally. You can not change the physical manifestations created by your choices. You did the best you could with the knowledge you had at the time. Still, by rewriting your story from an evolved perspective, you change its vibration now, which aligns you to your highest frequency timeline. You then experience people, things, and events that match that elevated frequency. In these moments, you are embodying SELF, living evolved and creating the new.

When you know yourSELF as SELF you realize you are the creator of your reality. Therefore, you take full responsibility for your story, including all the thoughts, words, and actions of everyone involved. Yes, that means you and those that wronged you. Instead of thinking *Why did that happen to me?* You think *I created the experience to learn from it, so it met my needs at the time, but now I can practice forgiveness of self and others.* You can even advise your past self, which is really your parallel self (all timelines exist in the now). So next time you are in a similar situation, you can do what your evolved self would do. This shifts the frequency of your story, moving you from the victim to the creator. So, in a way you energetically rewrite your story, humanity's story, and history.

Write the future

We have the power to write our story our way. What we do now writes the future. What will we write?

We can be a new, evolved character; in an evolved setting with evolved co-stars. By embodying SELF, we transform the world. We focus on unity instead of division, which causes our priorities to change. We begin to value community and develop empathy and genuine care. Our desire to evolve equals our desire for others to grow because we realize it benefits everyone. As more and more people evolve, we leave behind the old and create the new.

Like bees cooperate to preserve the colony, we will band together to sustain Planet Earth. We will spark a peaceful revolution. We can do this. There are enough of us awakening. A revolution is simply a willing of the unimaginable into existence.

Write the present: The first step is to imagine a new world vision

---

Each of us will express ourSELF by embodying SELF, living evolved, and creating our dreams, thereby raising the frequency of the planet and igniting humanity's vision to awaken human consciousness. The collective will hold the idea of a new world in their vibrational fields until it becomes our reality.

I invite you to imagine our evolved world where every living being on Earth is free. A place where abundance springs from love and manifests instantly like a blooming flower. Pristine nature (fully rejuvenated) is tended by Mother Earth's caretakers, who are intuitive, compassionate, and telepathic. The planet's ecosystems are sustained, and animal species have returned to their pre-agricultural revolution level. Renewable energy is the only source of power. The carbon dioxide problem has been solved. Patriarchal institutions and tyranny have dissolved, and wars have ceased. Humans exist in peace and harmony, in sync with the law of nature, free from prejudice, religious dogma, and personal, political, and corporate dominance. A world where individuals are viewed as equal and respected regardless of race, religion, sexual orientation, gender identity, and age. Shared communal resources have replaced old greed-fueled profiteering. Small communities provide for members' needs without corporations such as supermarkets and large chains. As a result, corporate power has been dissolved, and wealth is evenly distributed. Poverty has been eradicated, and everyone has enough food. People no longer need pharmaceutical drugs as they know they are the medicine and plants can restore and maintain their health. Money has been replaced with a barter system. Living in groups means people feel connected, supported, and valued. Hierarchy and competition have been replaced by cooperation. Unearned white supremacy and colonial systems that benefited a privileged minority have been abolished. History books contain true stories about the First Nations people. Individuals have a balanced service-to-others/service-to-self mindset and healthy relationships. The planetary media that kept the lower vibration of fear, anger, and separation alive have been extinguished, replaced by honest reporting rooted in love.

It may be hard for you to imagine Earth as a place like this because, at the moment, it is not our experience. However, if we agree with the current paradigm, we will stay within existing limits. But, on the other hand, if we imagine a new reality, we will create something beyond the present-day Earth.

As Albert Einstein said in 1931, "Imagination is more important than knowledge. For knowledge is limited, whereas imagination embraces the entire world, stimulating progress, giving birth to evolution."

I acknowledge the new world is a tremendous change to imagine. However, as more and more people put their energy into it and hold the vision in their awareness (as if it has manifested), momentum builds, and the chance of it succeeding increases.

As high-frequency humans, who know themselves as creators, we manifest whatever we dream is possible. As dream weavers, our choices impact the world today, tomorrow, and future generations.

The second step is to ask ourselves *What can I do to make the new world vision a reality? How can I express mySELF by embodying SELF, living evolved, and creating my dreams?*

Firstly, we must determine how our body shows us that something we are thinking, saying, or doing is out of alignment with SELF. Then, every time we notice this misalignment, we replace the old thought with a new one until we create new habits (fake it until you make it). By training the brain to remain as SELF we no longer identify with triggered false selves and false narratives. We turn our back on other people's expectations regarding how we should be and start being ourSELF. We begin to break free of old patterns. Life does not become perfect, but our evolved perspective allows us to live fully anchored in the present moment. Here we confidently claim whatever arises as perfect for us, regardless of what it looks like. We see it as an opportunity to realize SELF.

When we truly know life happens for us, not to us, we replace resistance with allowance. We help humankind evolve, one choice point at a time, until it is no longer a conscious choice but an evolved way of being. Then, life starts to flow spontaneously. This moment-to-moment existence cultivates the creative energy necessary to foster our gifts, figure out our calling, live purposefully, create our dreams, and contribute to the collective awakening vision. At this point, humanity's highest timeline story writes itself through us.

The good news is, we do not have to light up and then change the world; us lighting up automatically changes the world.

As we let our light shine, everyone sees their original light in us, inspiring them to shine. Imagine the global frequency created by humans celebrating and accepting the endless ways to light up. This union would activate our universal creative power and evolve human consciousness.

Some know change is possible, but some ask, "It all seems so dark. How can we get there?"

We do not need to know precisely how it will happen.

We can trust that darkness is part of the transformation. A butterfly emerges from its chrysalis with a whole new perspective. This perspective was previously unimagined. For humans to achieve a similar metamorphosis, we must uncover our dormant capabilities. When the butterfly was a caterpillar, it had the potential to fly, but it could not fly because it did not know how. First, it had to go within, surrender to the change process and courageously take flight powered by blind faith.

It is the same with human evolution. The whole process is within us; it simply needs to be realized. Everyone reading this book is capable of doing this. So, no matter how far removed from SELF you feel right now, know this book reveals your innate perfection. It guides you home, to you—to yourSELF.

You are the one you are looking for. You already have the answers to all your questions.

I allowed this book to be written through me. It feels like it has been called forth by humanity, for humanity, to bring us home to SELF.

Everyone's journey to find SELF is different. My story might inspire you to follow your path of SELF-realization.

Together we raise human consciousness and evolve as a species to support Mother Earth and preserve our planet.

We write the new in the now. So what story will we write; write here, write now?

2

UNHOOKING SOCIETY'S CORSET SELF

Looking back now, I see I developed true and false senses of SELF at different stages of my life. Each belief, true and false, formed my character and created patterns of thoughts and behaviors. At any given moment, I was expressing my true self (mySELF Expressing Love Frequency) or my false self (mySELF Expressing Low Frequency). The true:false ratio depended on my experiences on all timelines. Often false senses of self formed unconsciously to protect me from people, places and things in my environment. I was forced to give meaning to perceived threats, which formed my identity. I identified with these imagined aspects of SELF for so long that eventually, I believed they were me. Before embarking on my journey of SELF-realization, I had no idea these senses of SELF were untrue because they were ingrained ways of being. I just kept on doing the same things over and over without realizing my thoughts (aligned and misaligned) were creating my reality.

Infancy

I WAS ATTACHED to my mother's umbilical cord when I was born. Therefore, I believed I was her and she was me. The cord was cut, but I remained close to her, and stress rose if we were apart. I thought we were still one person. She was my sense of SELF, and I was my needs. I required nutrient-rich liquid to nourish and hydrate me, warmth, and comfort to make me feel safe. These were imperative to my survival and my voice was my survival mechanism. When my parents responded promptly, I felt loved, and my attachment bond to them strengthened. Luckily, the carers in my life were physically, psychologically, and emotionally capable. They detected their evolutionarily hard-wired impulse to stop my crying and successfully supported me to stop. Thus, my brain did not atrophy from an overproduction of cortisol. Instead, I could use the energy I saved to develop neural pathways to grow and communicate (smiling, babbling, and cooing). The more successful I was at communicating, the more empowered I felt. I was beyond surviving; I was thriving. My sense of SELF was: *I am secure.*

However, I still experienced trauma. For example, the nurses taught Mum to leave me to cry myself to sleep. Mum often got the timing right, but surely she occasionally got the timing wrong. At these times I felt unheard. My sense of SELF was: *I am unworthy.*

At around nine months of age, I realized I existed separately. I observed Mum physically leaving me. I worried she might never come back and felt separation anxiety. After months of her consistently returning, this anxiety subsided. At this stage, I developed the concept of a separate self. I formed an identity or a picture in my head of how mySELF looked/sounded, and felt. My sense of SELF was: *I am separate.*

Toddler

I IDENTIFIED with false senses of SELF such as *I am my body, my thoughts, and my possessions*. As a toddler, a toy was *my toy*. It was an extension of me, and if someone took it away, I felt physically violated and upset. My sense of SELF included everything within reach—fingers, bed, book, Dad, pencil, and bike. Sharing was not an option; it would be like asking me to share my heart—*How could I? It's mine!* I developed a strong ego to protect my sense of SELF, so I behaved egocentrically. The world revolved around me because I did not have an expanded perspective. I only knew my limited surroundings. I was not only my needs but also my wants, my interests, and my plans. The foot-stamping tantrums and the overuse of the word *mine* helped me meet my increased needs. I believed *If I don't have what's mine, I won't exist*. At these times, my attachment to what I could not have was so intense that I was incapable of self-soothing. Instead, I relied on skillful, patient adults to teach me. Luckily they were stable, and my behavior did not trigger their unresolved trauma too much. I want to add that no matter how emotionally intelligent and securely bonded our carers are, there is no way of shielding us from pain; it is part of being human. As we grow up we experience personal and collective trauma, for example: death, disease and disconnection.

Childhood

AROUND THE AGE of five or six, I began to realize that I existed in a community. What was happening to the people around me affected me. I started to develop empathy skills. I began to understand that caring for others satisfied my needs too. I learned rules within my family, local playground, and school that required sharing and taking turns. Adults explicitly taught me these rules, allowed me to practice them, monitored my progress with positive reinforcement, and retaught skills when necessary. The rules were consistent across all settings, and I had effective role models. Therefore, I saw the behavior I was trying to learn. My sense of SELF was: *I am a good rule follower.*

Living in a group required me to master resilience strategies. I needed to bounce back from challenges. I began to succeed in situations that required negotiation and problem-solving. I realized that it felt good when another's needs were met, as well as mine. When faced with a conflict, I began to mediate with group members to reach favorable outcomes for all involved. When I could not achieve a win-win outcome I was flexible enough to move on without resentment. With chameleon-style ease, I changed myself depending on different groups' expectations and acted accordingly. My sense of SELF got conditioned by the people I interacted with and I began to play roles to feel accepted. Adapting this way is normal child development behavior. My sense of SELF was: *I am a daughter/friend/neighbor/student/team member/child.*

Adolescence

AS A TEENAGER and in my early 20s, my sense of SELF was affected by how I thought others viewed me. I observed my parents, coaches, teachers, community members, and the media to learn what my society valued. I learned I was valued if I was pretty, thin, rich, smart, and sporty. I developed a belief that I was not pretty enough, not thin enough, not rich enough, not smart enough, and not sporty enough. My resilience became shaky and I would make things mean more than they needed to mean. I refused to get over things because it felt good being *poor me*. Why? It satisfied a need; it justified my belief *I am unworthy*. I would wallow in self-pity, create drama, and turn the situation into a story that confirmed my sense of SELF which was: *I am not enough.*

This became a habit. My parents let me get away with it because they also identified with this narrative. Therefore, my behavior appeared quite normal.

Adulthood

WHEN I BECAME AN ADULT, catalyst after catalyst pointed me to a realization that I was viewing my world through false filters (fear, lack, victim) and from unrealistic perspectives (white privilege, elitist school, prestigious university). It occurred to me that my habitual thoughts were limiting me, my relationships and my life. Eventually my false selves were running the show and creating a world I did not want to live in. So, I went on a quest to discover my true SELF. To realize SELF I had to ignore all the false selves I had identified with along the way. These guys were loud and demanding so it was not easy, but I did it!

I share my journey of remembering, aligning to, and embodying my true SELF with you, hoping that it makes your journey smoother.

3

TALKING TO SPIRITS SELF

18 years old

Tuesday, August 1st

A rare school-night sleepover at Lysa's mum's Darling Point, Sydney apartment. Her mum was home in the country so we were there alone.

The room where we were sleeping lit up completely with a bright blue light.

That's weird. I thought, *There's nothing there that could be shining a light.*

The curtains blew horizontally, but there was no wind.

It was bizarre. I was in my last year of high school, old enough to know something was not right.

A man in a Dry As A Bone coat and an Akubra hat appeared at the doorway. He was shrouded in the blue light.

I immediately knew it was Lysa's dad. He had died nine years earlier, and they were very close.

I tried waking Lysa by shaking her.

"Please wake up. Please wake up." I felt completely panicked, short of breath, and heart racing.

She was a limp doll. Her body bounced lifelessly on the double bed. I shook her shoulders a couple more times in disbelief. *How could this be happening?* I was terrified.

Her father then sat up out of her body and was sitting in the bed with me.

I pressed my back up against the cold wall. I could taste fear.

I decided I had no choice but to talk to him, "I will always love your daughter. I will always look after her. I promise you. I won't let you down. I will look after your daughter for the rest of my life." My hands were in a prayer position.

Time stood still.

It felt like an eternity.

Then just like that, he was gone. His body disappeared from her back. The blue light went off, and the wind stopped. I was sitting there trembling.

When I was a child, I had an imaginary friend who told me things I could not have known. Then growing up, floating spirits visited my bedroom. This was the first time, though, that a spirit was in human form. I knew exactly who he was. I could see him vividly as if he were physically standing there looking at me; the only difference was his body was transparent instead of solid.

In the morning, I told Lysa the whole story.

"Well, it's funny you should say that. A few months ago, Tony was sleeping over. There were bunk beds in here then. I got out of bed to go to the toilet. When I came back in, he exclaimed, "As soon as you stepped out of the room, the bunk bed started shaking. That painting over there looked like it was going to fly off the wall!" I replied, "That's not a painting, Tony; that's a picture of my dad.""

Seeing Lysa's dad was a SELF-realization catalyst that confirmed: SELF is eternal.

That day we skipped school. Not just any school. A Sydney, Eastern Suburbs Independent Girls' School. In those days, if you took a day off school for a holiday or to play a representative sport, the principal gave away your place. She did not tolerate non-attendance.

When I got off the bus in Randwick, dressed in my school uniform, Mum was waiting at the bus stop. She had never done this before.

Oh no! I'm in so much trouble. The school has called Mum and Dad, I'm going to get killed by my parents. Guilt and regret filled the pit of my stomach.

Mum engulfed me in her arms. I'm so sorry." she said, "Are you Ok? You must be so upset. I'm so upset. It's just dreadful."

My ear pressed against her chest. *I have not been here for a while. What is she talking about?*

"What, Mum?" I muttered.

"The school didn't tell you. But, of course, they told you. It's all over the news." Her sharp mind raced. "A swimming mum was murdered yesterday in her home," she explained.

A beautiful mother of three daughters was dead, just like that.

Even as a teenager, I was an empath. Perhaps too sensitive to have received this news in assembly. I will never forget the grief that followed. The girls returned to school the next day. Their father came to talk to us at a Memorial Service a few days later. He said, "Please don't avoid us. I know you're unsure what to say, but please don't walk away from us. We need you now."

As Vice-Swimming Captain, I took these words on board and spent countless hours checking in on the girls. I would ask, "What are you feeling right now?"

One answered, "Some days I can think about her, and some days it's like there is a sign up saying *Not Today*."

So many things happened the year I finished school but losing one of our swimming mums had the most significant impact. It exposed me to human vulnerability. A loving woman returned home and interrupted an intruder. A paroled criminal who had worked there two years earlier had copied their key and entered their home. She did nothing wrong except recognize him. As her three daughters waited patiently for her at our school gates, they never imagined not seeing her again.

I realized that there is no way of knowing what is around the corner.

Her husband and daughters clung tightly to each other at her funeral as Bette Midler's *Wind Beneath My Wings* sang out across the packed St Mark's Church in Darling Point. As I looked down at them from the balcony, I thought they looked unified and strong, arm in arm in the front row, where you never want to be sitting at a funeral.

This event taught me how to be of service to grieving people, and to this day, I never shy away from offering support. It also inspired me to be grateful for my parents. I still gave them hell as a teenager but I tried to verbalize my love for them, and give them compliments. Sometimes this felt awkward, but I knew they deserved to hear these words because their last breath could be later that day.

I found this quote pinned up at my friend Katrina's family home in Bunbury, Western Australia.

Let me be aware of the treasure you are. Let me learn from you, love you, bless you before you depart. Let me not pass you by in quest of some rare and perfect tomorrow. Let me hold you when I may, for it will not always be so. One day I shall dig my fingers into the earth, or bury my face in the pillow, or stretch myself taut, or raise my hands to the sky. And want more than all the world for your return.

4

LOVING UNCONDITIONALLY SELF

23 - 25 years old

Friday, January 20th

Stitty and I were set up at a dinner party at Lysa's mum's Darling Point apartment when I was 23 and he was 24. He had just returned from traveling overseas and apparently there were sparks between us but we only crossed paths a couple of times the following year.

Monday, January 15th

TWELVE MONTHS LATER, Lysa had bought a place in Bondi and hosted a second dinner party to set us up again. I was considering traveling to South America with a couple of guy friends Paul and

Ben. Stitty and his travel buddy Jim (Lysa's flatmate) were invited to share their South America tips, having spent 7 months there. They dressed in traditional costumes they had picked up on their trip, what legends! Stitty purposefully left his car at home, knowing I would offer him a lift, just before he hopped out, he kissed me, I panicked, screeched away and almost drove over his foot.

Background

WE WERE SET up by mutual friends who were a couple back then; Lysa was one of my best friends from school and Nick was an old family friend who became best mates with Stitty when they lived in the same residential college at The University of Sydney (USYD). Stitty's family was from Forbes in Central West NSW, so he went to boarding school. He and I were in the same crowd at school and attended the same parties but never spoke (I even have a picture of him at 16 years of age where I spelled his name Peter Stit - with one t). I arrived at USYD a year after Stitty, so we were unknowingly brushing shoulders again. Lysa, Nick, and Stitty spent a lot of time together while living in London after their university days.

Nick says, "We set you two up because you are both as 'all or nothing' as each other. It was a no-brainer!" (We both came to the relationship with national medals in swimming and rowing).

My mum, Penny, grew up in Bathurst, a country town just two hours east of Forbes where Stitty's Dad, Brian, grew up. When Mum was at boarding school in Sydney, she dated Brian's cousin, and then Mum met Brian at the picnic races when she visited her aunt and uncle who had a property in Forbes. After Mum finished school, she met Stitty's Mum, Patti (before Patti met Brian). Mum and Patti lived together at Tremayne, a boarding house for country girls working in the city, at Kirribilli overlooking Sydney Harbour. They were 19 years old.

For these reasons, dating Stitty was like dating the guy next door, which was incredibly random since Mum had traveled the world after she left Tremayne. She met and married Dad (an American) in London (he had three children—Janet 18, Judy 16, and Bill 10). Eli Lilly, the pharmaceutical company Dad worked for, gave him a promotion to open a new office in Rome, Italy, and be in charge of Italy and the Middle East. My younger brother, Patrick, and I were born in Rome. Two years later, Dad was put in charge of Europe, so we moved to Paris, France. Two years after that, when I was four, Dad became one of the Eli Lilly Vice Presidents in charge of Central and South America and went to head office in Indianapolis, Indiana, United States of America (USA). We lived there for six years before Dad took early retirement from his employer Eli Lilly, of 32 years, to move to Sydney and work as a pharmaceutical consultant. Mum was 41 years old. She never expected to be living in Sydney again.

Dating

LYSA AND NICK'S second dinner party set-up worked! Five days later Stitty and I went on our first date to The London Hotel, a pub in Paddington. Six days after that, Stitty took me to an Australia Day (January 26th) dance party at *Club 77* on William Street in Sydney's Kings Cross. I loved it.

The following day I noticed how generous Stitty was. He offered me a sip before he had a drink himself and was attentive to my needs and happiness. He seemed to think of me before himself, and when his friend Andrew called, he said, "we." I heard Andrew joke, "We!

So are you going to marry her?" I thought it was such a weird thing for a guy to say but perhaps he witnessed a parallel timeline.

I mentioned a music track to Stitty that I enjoyed the night before and rattled off a couple of vague notes. A few nights later, he put a record on his turntable in the bedroom of his rented Paddington apartment (next to The Lord Dudley Pub). Sure enough, it was *The Night Train* by Kadoc, the song I loved on Australia Day. *He is psychic as well! I could fall for this guy.*

Stitty loved doing exciting things to make memories. For example, one night, he dragged his mattress into the living room and we camped out on his apartment floor. We watched one of his all-time favorite movies, *Taxi Driver,* with Robert De Niro and Jodie Foster. Stitty was into picnics and passionately kissing on the grass or at the beach. We loved to kiss.

Self-sabotage

YOU WOULD THINK I would be happy with a guy like Stitty but I wasn't used to being treated with respect. His consistent, reliable nature was unfamiliar territory. I was used to being rejected, used or overlooked. When faced with an emotionally intelligent man capable of expressing his feelings and making me feel loved I panicked. *Where was the chase, games, and mystery?*

I said to my brother and best friend Patrick, "Do you think Stitty might be boring?"

He replied bewildered, "God no! What are you talking about?"

I realize in hindsight I was bored because there was no drama. For years I had identified with a false sense of SELF *I am unworthy and not enough.* I did not believe I deserved devotion *so* I went after boys who would confirm this limiting belief. When they let me down,

I would think *I knew he wouldn't go for me, no one wants a fat girlfriend* or *Maybe if I sleep with him he will like me* or *He's been unfaithful but I don't deserve love anyway so I'll take him back.* I was that girl who always went after unavailable guys not capable of loving me. The ones everyone else knew would treat me badly and guess what, surprise, surprise—they did. One night stands, boys with girlfriends—I did all the 'bad girl' things.

When I started dating Stitty It took me a while to ignore these loud and demanding *I am unworthy and not enough* false selves. They tried their hardest to sabotage my relationship by saying outrageous things like *Stitty is boring*. But eventually their voices faded and I began to feel worthy.

Sunday, February 25th

THE DAY I realized I was falling in love.

I was floating on my back, salty aquamarine Pacific Ocean lappy rhythmically on my lips. Admiring the expansive cobalt blue sky and noticing how it became lighter on the horizon. *It doesn't get any better than Sydney's Icebergs ocean pool on a stellar summer's day! I get to live in this city! How lucky am I?* I skillfully tilted my body to stand, rough concrete on soft feet. Pools are my domain; I grew up unaccompanied at the Highland Country Club, in Indianapolis, Indiana, USA. Joyfully communicating underwater with imaginary dolphins and mermaids. However, soon play turned to purpose, and by the time I was eight I was the Indiana state champion. I playfully bounced along the Bondi ocean pool's recreational lane with supreme confidence accompanying my every move. Bombarded by a kaleidoscope of beachside sounds consisting of children squealing, idle chatter, and waves gently crashing. I noticed Stitty laughing with his old boarding school mate, Shane. They were sitting side-by-side on the 1920s Art Deco-inspired glaringly white platform stairs. The lines are sleek and geometric, perfectly suiting the style of this famous landmark. Stitty's eyes, as blue as the sky, are twinkling from a recently shaved head. The scene is a postcard, capturing this quintessentially iconic Aussie snapshot.

He has the most honest face I have ever seen. With that thought came an unexpected stomach somersault that ended in a limp flop. *Shit, where did that come from? I think I'm falling in love. It's only been a month, but I feel like we've loved each other for lifetimes. Is this actually happening?*

Sunday, March 16th

STITTY RETURNED from a trip to Byron Bay with a card and a present, a handbag. In the card he wrote

> This week has made me realize how strong my feelings are for you, and they are growing stronger daily. Every time I see you, there is something new that I see in you that I like. You have the <u>exact</u> qualities that I look for in a girl. You are kind, considerate and caring, and so motivated and energetic!! I enjoy being with you very much. You have re-motivated me at a time when my life was becoming flat. So here's to spending some more quality time together and getting to know each other.

A card writer, a present giver! I think I've met my equal. I had given him a card too. I explained that he was unselfish and considerate and made me feel happy. I pointed out that he was strong enough to achieve anything he put his mind to. I shared that I admired his work ethic and quoted James Michener, "Talent is very common, disciplined talent is very rare."

Our cards were self-expression vehicles, allowing us to reflect each other's values and character to one another. Thus, the more we looked for qualities to admire, the more those traits were amplified. It was a self-fulfilling prophecy. It was like we rose to the occasion by raising our standards to confirm the expectations of the other. We were very similar types, so we brought out the best in each other and extended beyond our original selves. This transformation was effortless because it was for the common good.

My connection to the unseen world inspired me to look for signs Stitty was *the one.* While we watched the movie *Mask,* I noticed how moved he was by Rocky, the main protagonist's death. Rocky was a teenager with a facial deformity called craniodiaphyseal dysplasia (CDD), also known as lionitis. When Rocky's classmates bullied him, I saw a tear in Stitty's eye, which showed me he was empathetic. Afterward, Stitty walked me from his new rental in Rushcutters Bay, Sydney, to my car down the dead-end road. It was a stormy evening, and I saw a big stick blocking our path. I imagined the scene from one of my favorite movies from the year I left school *Say Anything.* Lloyd (John Cusack) and Diane (Ione Skye) were leaving a Seattle, Washington area 7-Eleven when Lloyd spotted some broken glass on the ground. He instinctively brushed it out of Diane's way to protect her from walking through it.

If he moves this stick, he's the one.

"Oh, be careful, Babe, let me move that for you," He said, and right on cue, the legendary *Say Anything* theme song started in my head *In Your Eyes* (Peter Gabriel), filling my body with sentimental nostalgia. Imagining Lloyd holding the ghetto blaster above his head serenading his love Diane. Hearing those familiar lyrics I once dreamed were for me. *In your eyes I am complete... The resolution of all the fruitless searches... I want to touch the light... I see in your eyes.*

I stepped into the Age of Chivalry alongside a *Knight in Shining Armour*. I did an internal jump for joy. I felt honored, respected, and cherished. I knew, right then and there, he would always defend me.

We became regulars at *Club 77*. The unpretentious, dingy basement city club hosted *Jus' Right* (Not Too Heavy, Not Too Light) Friday night dance parties run by resident DJ Sugar Ray. Stitty had discovered dance music while living in London. It made him feel something he could barely articulate. The beats connected him to everything all at once. He had bought himself turntables and taught himself to mix vinyl records together into a continuous set. Our little crew felt at ease at *Club 77*, bonded by our love of music and commitment to the cause (especially the boys). We would recline on the sofas in trainers and t-shirts, wearing our eclectic style with confidence. It was here I learnt from Stitty and our old mate Max the art of backpacking. They had traveled the world and possessed an open-minded, cruisy, and curious nature. They invited strangers to join us, allowing us to meet people from all over the planet. Being in the presence of backpackers and clubbing together has a feel that crosses all borders. It inspired a fearless approach to life. We would welcome newcomers to the family, knew all the DJs by name, and could pick their favorite tunes after just a few beats.

The feeling of dancing in a group facing the DJ box, to music that took us on a journey of SELF-discovery, was beyond this world. I felt connected to a universal frequency of love. The dance floor in the mid-'90s was pure freedom. I talked, smiled, and danced with everyone throughout the small club. Everyone was equal. Gender identity, sexual preferences, ethnicity, age, and social status merged into one. The music was so beautiful, so inclusive, and so expansive. The deep beats took us back to past/parallel lives when we drummed in tribal groups and to our mother's heartbeat in the womb. I felt comfortable expressing myself through dance for hours! My naturally high energy could be shared and appreciated by others. I was filled with gratitude, overflowing with abundance and radiating joy. Utilizing my imagination, I pretended I was a powerful angel able to spray love and healing energy onto everyone in the venue and beyond to everyone in the world. There, eyes closed, under the strobe lights, in the smoke machine, I believed I could lead the world to peace. I believed if everyone could feel this pure love, there would be no violence, inequality, or suppression. My mind was extraordinarily present in each beat. Dancing became like a meditation where my heartbeat unified with the heartbeat of all—connecting me to my ancestors and future generations. We were a microcosm of society, a melting pot of souls who remembered how to play. We discovered how much fun it is to let go and trust our bodies to move to our instinctive primordial beat.

I whistled and cheered to get people excited for the track's crescendo. It would peak, and so would we. Euphoric joy would ignite. These moments gave me hope for our often divided planet. Our connection identified our potential; we experienced harmony. We were our true SELF. The space we shared felt more real than the world outside. This was our tribe and our vibe.

On Saturdays we partied at other Sydney dance venues hosting Australian and international DJs. The techno electronic music era was in full swing. These events were fun. We spent hours dancing, and I was always right at the front, clapping and encouraging the DJ with an acknowledging nod when I loved what I was hearing. I would applaud their music and encourage other dancers to do the same.

Sunday, April 6th

AFTER A BLUE MOUNTAINS camping trip with Nick and Lysa, we had a night alone at the Blackheath Motor Inn. After watching a random, out there episode in the *Nowhere Man* series on television we walked to dinner, hand-in-hand, arms swinging. Out of the blue, like he was talking about the weather, Stitty told me he had a serious disease, severe ulcerative colitis. It was April, and we had been together for four months. I was hook, line, and sinker in love and I had no idea he had an illness with the potential to kill him.

My mouth dropped open then I stammered, "What the hell is ulcerative colitis?" He explained that it is a disease characterized by inflammation and micro-ulcers in the superficial layers of the large intestine, which causes bloody and painful diarrhea. He was honest and said the illness could be fatal, explaining that his twin friends' lost their sister to this disease at the age of 25. Stitty shared that he had been diagnosed four years prior, the cause unknown. Since that time, he had: managed rigorous USYD Bachelor of Civil Engineering (Honors) studies; rowed for NSW; lived in a wild residential college; traveled overseas to developing countries; lived, worked, and partied in London; started his career in Sydney as a civil engineer doing crazy hours and making stressful decisions. He had diarrhea at inconvenient times like on the bus traveling to work. He was trying to do a massive construction job with one eye on the public toilet sign, poised, ready to run in that direction at any moment. He explained that going out to a dance party took strategic planning to empty his bowel to avoid multiple toilet trips. For example, if he were going out Friday night, he would have to stop eating Wednesday night. I had not noticed this, probably because we were not living together (I was living at home with Mum and Dad in Randwick, also in Sydney's Eastern Suburbs).

He admitted being on 35 tablets a day, including anti-inflammatory agents, corticosteroids, and immunosuppressants, all with different side effects. He told me six of Sydney's best specialists had helped in various ways but could not cure him. Some recommended, "Cut out the bowel and get a colostomy bag." He said he had just recently discovered Dr. Thomas Borody, a gastroenterologist in Five Dock, Sydney, who he really liked.

This news was a lot to process. My first thought was *Do I really want to marry a sick man? Do I want to have children with someone who might die on us? No, I don't.*

At that moment I had three choices. Option 1: leave Stitty immediately, Option 2: stay with Stitty and try to heal him or Option 3: stay with Stitty and love him as if he were well.

I did not consider Option 1 because we were in love. Option 2, on the other hand, seemed like the easiest choice because my *fix it self* aka *the school teacher* in me would thrive in control mode. This option would look like me micromanaging his life, attending doctor's appointments, encouraging him to see healers, changing his diet, and putting his health problems in the spotlight. This option would sound like *I guess I'm destined to be the carer of a sick man, this is my narrative, my reality.* This option would feel like *I have to make him well. If I can't make him well I've failed.*

I do not know how but somehow, I knew to choose Option 3. Loving him as if he were well felt counterintuitive and left me feeling vulnerably out of my comfort zone. Sitting back patiently and letting him do his own thing was an act of surrender foreign to me. In hindsight, I think perhaps my evolved self whispered *You can love him, but you can not heal him. Trying to control his behavior will make him feel like a helpless child instead of an empowered man. If you focus on his sickness you will inadvertently create more sickness. Your annoying interference and his fierce independence will clash and result in 'bye-bye boyfriend.' Allow your higher self to connect with his higher self on your highest potential timeline. See your future together as abundant, healthy, and prosperous. Realize Stitty is already perfect and whole on a soul level, just not on a physical level—yet! Look beyond his disease's symptoms to his potential. You don't need to know how he will reach this potential; you just need to trust he will. Only he can figure out how to bring his body into balance. But don't worry, you can trust him because he loves you and your future children enough to heal himself. So be the woman he'll want to heal for. Remember, if you try to change him your vibration will not match his future healed self because the evolved Stitty will be energetically matched with a woman who does not try to change him.*

Option 3 was by far the hardest choice to navigate, especially when his face became red and swollen from the steroids, and he was extremely skinny from malnutrition. However, somehow I managed to trust the process. To this day, I still do not know how I stuck with Option 3. I can not believe I had the foresight to not get involved in his dying story. How did I do that? It helped that he was the most self-disciplined person I had ever met, so when he told me it was all under control I believed him.

Monday, August 27th

HE COMPLAINED to me for the first time in August about being sick. We had been out partying, and he felt depleted.

I wrote him a card the next day.

Dear Babe,
I want you to know that I love you so much and that if you really want to choose to do everything you

can to get better, I will support you. We will do it together, but if you don't want to accept it and do all you can, I will still love you, but please don't talk to me about it because it hurts me too much. I don't feel it's fair to talk to me about your pain when you are down and then see you blocking it out the next day when I continue to worry. I don't want to feel frustrated when you don't do all you can to improve your situation. As I said, Babe, I will love you regardless. Your life and what you do with it is up to you, but either decide to improve your quality of life or let me love you without having to worry about you. I will always love you.

    Katie XXO

THE NEXT DAY I received this card from him.

Katie,

    I just want you to know that I love you very, very much. I will always love you dearly regardless of what happens in the future. When I act like a rubber band, I still love you whether I am stretched or relaxed. It may not appear that way, but I do.

    Babe, if I were the only person affected by my actions, I would put up with pain and suffering. In my arrogant, stubborn way, I would convince myself it *would go away. I am very tough! But I have now realized my actions really affect you, and this means a lot to me. I hadn't sat down to think about this before. Because I love you, I want you to know that I'm really going to make a 100% effort to look after myself. I am a very determined, positive person most of the time, and this is the time for it.*

I am still going to enjoy myself, but I'm just going to be a little more rational, realistic and honest with myself.

I appreciate so much what you do for me, Babe. Without you, I would well and truly be lost.

I have always been so independent that I got annoyed if anybody ever worried about me or fussed over me. But I have accepted that you do worry, and it's unfair of me to make it worse for you.

No promises, Babe, just actions. Have faith in me.

Love forever.

Stitto

THAT WAS THAT. I continued to love him unconditionally. But every night, when he fell asleep, I would put my hands on his belly and imagine my health going from my body into his body. I was intuitively doing Reik/biofield therapy before I had heard of it.

Monday, September 30th

WHILE ON HOLIDAY in Queensland with Weenie (Andrew's girlfriend), I wrote Stitty a postcard

> *I love the way we want each other to be happy and that every decision we make is based on the desire for us both to be happy. By considering each other, everything is so easy. I love that we trust each other so we can be happy apart. I love that we never try to change each other. I love that we don't upset each other by having stupid fights and saying horrible things we'll regret. I love the way we don't have any psychological disorders or bad hang-ups. I love the way you drive, your voice, your cuddles, your humour, your music, your mouth, your smile—and these are just a few of the things I thought about while I was away in Noosa!*
>
> *Love, your beautiful Babe forever xxo*

(I thought about these things while Weenie and I played the song *Children* by Robert Miles full boar and on repeat).

After I wrote this card, I reflected on my behavior with my previous boyfriend Simon. With my ex, I displayed psychological disorders and hang-ups because I was unconsciously acting out conditioned patterning in the form of a lack mentality. I was in the habit of looking for things that were missing to confirm my belief: *I am lacking*, so I expected him to fill that hole. I identified with my false selves and indulged in misaligned emotions such as disappointment and judgment. I blamed Simon for making me feel the way I did. I also manipulated and controlled my environment to try and create the happiness I yearned for. I was passive-aggressive when things did not go my way and would sulk for hours (one time because he mashed the potatoes wrong while we were on a yacht cruising the islands of the Whitsundays). Why would I do that? Because this behavior was modeled to me by my Mum and to her by her Mum and so on.

I valued myself so little that when I found out he was unfaithful to me with seven different women I forgave him. *Ouch!* If I could give my young 21 year old self advice from my evolved self, I would say *See Simon as a mirror and inquire with curiosity. What is he reflecting in you that needs your attention? What are your limiting beliefs? What unresolved trauma is he triggering? This situation has less to do with him and more to do with your reaction to him. Letting him disrespect you shows you don't respect yourself. You have given him two years too many. Break up with him right now and fall in love with yourself.* Luckily, when I forgave him, he ended it anyway, saying he had fallen out of love with me. *Ouch again!*

I realized that with Stitty, I was a completely different person. He never asked me to change but I had changed because I felt worthy. In our relationship, my prior psychological disorders and hang-ups were no longer relevant. Firstly, that old conditioned love behavior did not reflect Stitty's behavior or his view of me, so I never did it. Secondly, I finally loved mySELF, and felt seen and heard. So my old programmed thoughts upgraded to thoughts aligned to true reality. I was no longer delusional, therefore I could embody our true SELF. I swapped out destructive traits like anger, control, and paranoia for playfulness, humor, and ease and my relationship became effortless.

At the end of the year, I had planned to travel to India with Lysa. I was too scared to resign from my teaching job because I had a highly sought position at a private girls' school in Sydney's Eastern Suburbs. I was employed there for seven years: four years as a sports coach while I did my degree at USYD followed by three years as a kindergarten—year 12 Personal Development and Physical Education (PDHPE) teacher after I graduated. I had worked hard, so hard that the principal nominated me for a state-wide award, which I won. *The NSW Teachers' Guild Excellence in Teaching Award* for teachers in their early years of teaching. In her recommendation letter, she referred to my *exceptional contribution and leadership*. Instead of resigning I decided to request a year's leave without pay which my principal granted with the words, "You go and travel. We'll see you back here in a year's time?"

Before I knew it, it was time to go traveling. I made Stitty a beautiful scrapbook with our memories from the previous 12 months. It was in diary entries with photos, newspaper clippings, club tickets, cards, quotes and funny memories. The last page had a photo of me in a pretty summer hat SO WHAT'S A NICE GIRL LIKE THIS…and a picture of him making a weird face DOING WITH A GUY LIKE THIS?

Underneath, I wrote SHE IS MADLY IN LOVE WITH HIM.

When I look back on our first year together, I know every obstacle I encountered was created by me, for me, as a catalyst for SELF-realization.

Falling in love with a dying man gave me a choice *I can choose a low vibration timeline (make everything about his illness), or step courageously onto our highest potential timeline. I can be mySELF Expressing Low Frequency or mySELF Expressing Love Frequency.*

I chose the latter and wrote the future.

The rest is history!

5

OPENING PANDORA'S BOX SELF

25 - 26 years old

Friday, January 17th

Sydney Airport, waiting to fly to Mumbai, India.
I rang an old school friend, Alex, "I'm terrified."

"Kits, pretend you are taking a group of students on a school excursion. Don't think too far into the future; just focus on the tasks at hand. Feel confident. Stitty will be fine. You will see him when he meets you in London at the end of July," Alex assured me.

Stitty stayed in Sydney to finish his civil engineering job constructing the new Sydney Harbour Casino. He was very supportive of my traveling because he loved backpacking. Three years prior, he had spent two years visiting around 40 countries. He encouraged me to travel as he felt it would shake off any remaining residue of private school privilege. He knew that experiencing developing countries rich in culture, religion, and tradition would expand my mind, expose me to the thrill of the unknown and undoubtedly toughen me up! I had led a sheltered Sydney Eastern Suburbs life, and he sensed that my Pandora's Box of life-changing experiences was ready to be cracked open.

He was right.

More than 25 years ago, India was the perfect place to start. I spent five months traveling (first with Lysa, then alone, then with another school friend Milly) from Bangalore, in the south, to Rishikesh in the north, and then to Nepal. Days were full of catalysts, each one leaving me changed forever. First, I had to contend with the smell, an assault on the senses. Then, my heart got ripped out by the beautiful beggar children living in makeshift shacks made of metal offcuts. Then, there was so much disorganization, such as chaos in Government offices and the lack of services forcing men to defecate on train tracks (no idea where the women went). Indians had no concept of things we take for granted in the West, like lining up and waiting your turn. I had to see beyond the shockingness of poverty to its magic.

Indians take pride in their appearance; they are always clean, with scrubbed feet. Men wear immaculate white shirts, and women wear exquisitely beautiful pleated sarees in vibrant colors. People with nothing are happier than people in Sydney with everything. The Hindu/Buddhist faith in karma (actions have consequences) and the Muslim faith in good reaps rewards allows a billion people to exist crammed together like sardines. Indians are the most caring, helpful people I know. Your problem becomes their problem, and they will go out of their way to make sure it is solved, even if ten people are already helping you, all offering contradicting advice!

I discovered India's beauty by nestling into her heart, listening to her patient pulse, and learning her lessons (big and small). Her ability to teach me how to shift my perspective caused me to fall head over heels in love with her. To use a local Indian term, I became "Same, same, but different." I was still the same person having the same experiences but was changed unimaginably. For example, physically—traveling for ten hours on a train seated on my backpack squashed between Indian families taught me to endure discomfort. Spiritually—feeling Indian devotion and unshakable faith instilled in me the power of prayer and sacred rituals. Emotionally—observing a no-armed beggar beaming with happiness motivated my daily gratitude practice. Mentally—noticing my incessant whining inner dialogue compelled me to turn my complaining thoughts into positive self-talk. Doing this took determination, but slowly I felt my sense of entitlement shrivel up and die.

I had lived a predictable life in Australia, which gave me the illusion of control. Enter India, an unpredictable country where nothing, and I mean nothing, goes according to plan. There were no timetables, routines, or structures to support me, so I had no choice but to let go of everything I had ever known, give in to India's rare pace and surrender to her unique flow. I started to appreciate the little things in life, managed to laugh in desperate moments, and became open to surprises. I noticed how much more tolerant people in India are for unpleasant, inconvenient, difficult things compared to us Westerners because their country (in general) is materially deficient compared to ours. India taught me how to put up with more, be content with less, and demand less of life. When I mastered the Indian way of relating to the world, my entire sense of being changed. Soon, I replaced my boring, predictable plans with seamless synchronicity that left me in awe.

Eventually, despite the country's chaos, I floated through my days, marveling at my creation. Traveling solo guarantees invitations from multiple groups all day, "We are having a rave in our room, come and dance with us", "Hey, are you walking up to Savitri Temple to watch the sunset?", "We are planning a full moon party in the desert; wanna help?"

When I left Sydney, Stitty and I agreed we could be with other people. Stitty kissed someone at a dance party, but it did not go anywhere. I, on the other hand, was determined to stay faithful. I wanted to tell our children, "I was never with another man after meeting your Dad."

To the young men who tried to kiss me, I would say, "One of the reasons you're attracted to me is because I am loved by a man back in Australia. So if you kiss me, that will take away my shine. So please respect my happiness and enjoy me as I am." Somehow this tactic worked!

I loved getting to know the world through the backpackers I met, but I knew there was more to India than the party scene. I could not deny my deep desire to give back to my host country. I wanted to share my privileges with those less fortunate. I had been blessed with a university education and wanted to offer my skills to create a ripple effect. I also dreamed of having access to the 'real India.' I fantasized about going without comforts, the convenience of a common language (Indians in tourist towns speak English), the security of the Internet (to read the news and send/receive emails) and public telephones (pre-mobiles), the ease of Western food options, the luxury of touristy hotels, and the reliance on the ever present Lonely Planet safety net. I longed to free fall for a while and challenge myself. I wanted to get behind the scenes where I would feel uncomfortable and out of my comfort zone. My Pandora's box had slightly opened, but I was ready and willing to blow it's lid off.

Sunday, April 20th

POKHARA, *Nepal*

My ache to make a difference was matched vibrationally by a chance meeting in a restaurant. I met a beautiful couple from Melbourne, Victoria, Australia, called Jason (Jay) and Yvette (my close friends to this day). They had incredible energy. They reminded me of Stitty and me because they had previously spent nine months apart. Jay had a gentle, calm nature, a long ponytail, and an 'Aussie surfer' vibe. Yvette had eyes like saucers that sparkled when she began to talk about their volunteer work as nurses with Douglas Maclagan, who founded Child Welfare Scheme Nepal (CWSN). A not-for-profit organization that built pre-schools and health care centers in the foothills of the Annapurna Himalayan mountain ranges.

I almost fell off my chair *Could it be true? Am I about to manifest my dream to be of service, often out of reach for backpackers?*

I discovered they were practicing Buddhists who had attended a month-long Lam Rim (spiritual path) retreat in Kopan Monastery in Kathmandu. We were kindred spirits, immediately bonded by the feeling we had traveled many lifetimes together. We talked all night, going backward and forward with existential questions, hanging on each other's words with breathless passion. This is my first memory of my body physically showing me that I am resonating with the truth. I became light-headed. got butterflies in my tummy and shivered, but the feeling was different to being cold. I know now it is my nervous system signaling that I am thinking, saying, or doing something on track. I am remembering a parallel timeline where I am aligned to my true SELF. To this day, whenever I talk about existentialism my body reacts in the same ecstatic way.

When Jay and Yvette shared the Buddha's teachings, I had an instant affiliation with them. The teachings felt like memories I had heard directly from the Buddha himself! His techniques to train the mind and cultivate inner peace seemed practical and achievable. I was hungry to learn more. When the sun rose, we were still talking. They encouraged me to meet Douglas at the nearby Nature's Grace Lodge, Pokhara (a guest house run by Douglas to raise money and awareness of his pre-school and health care centers in remote villages).

As I sat opposite Douglas, a wiry half-Scottish/half-Dutch former teacher, my heart burst with enthusiasm, "I have been traveling for three and a half months and dreaming of an opportunity to volunteer. Then last night, I met Jay and Yvette, who told me they are training nurses, so I thought I could train early childhood teachers," I explained at lightning speed.

"You can start tomorrow!" Douglas answered excitedly. "I have Nadia from Belgium teaching women in Saimarang but no one teaching in Warchok. So I would love you to join our small team." Douglas explained that he started the pre-schools because the infant mortality rate for under-fives was 34%. He considered this statistic unacceptable. His research found they were vulnerable because Nepalese children could not begin school until they were six years old. In addition, children left unsupervised at home suffered accidents such as falls (no fences), and children taken into the rice paddies were susceptible to snake bites. Douglas was alarmed that one-third of Nepalese children did not live until their fifth birthday. So he set out to make a difference by establishing pre-schools and health care centers (focusing on pregnancy care). He wanted to prove to the Nepalese government that this model would successfully reduce infant mortality rates. He hoped the government would eventually establish a national pre-school model in all government schools. The pre-schools also allowed parents to be economically productive in the paddies knowing their children were safe between 9:00 am and 4:00 pm.

When I got back to our guest house I asked Milly if she would mind if I came back to Pokhara after we met her brother Walter in Varanasi. This would be a 42 hour round trip (we needed to go via Kathmandu to renew our India visas) but I was willing to do it so Milly would not have to travel there alone. However, in synchronistic timing, our guest house neighbors from Perth in Western Australia told us they were going to Kathmandu the next day, and Milly could travel with them. Problem solved. This divine timing was a SELF-realization catalyst: SELF takes care of everything when I align with the good of all.

The following morning Milly and the Perth boys boarded a 6:30 am bus, and at 7:00 am, I met Dassu, the Nepalese CWSN coordinator. He guided me on a nine-and-a-half-hour trek to Warchok, which was 1,328 meters (4,357 feet) above sea level! Dassu dropped me off at Paru's house (the local teacher), who lived with her parents and niece, and that was that! As I waved him *goodbye,* I felt sick in my stomach. *I must be crazy! What have I gotten myself into? Me and my big overconfident mouth. How will I live in a village where no one speaks English? How will I teach these women and children—using sign language?*

Using sign language and a massive amount of enthusiasm, I did teach the children and the teachers how to teach. I played games and did relays to learn the names of colors. I danced and sang, showing them that teaching could be fun. Education in rural Nepal consisted of students in rows copying down information. I wanted to challenge this and demonstrate active and engaging learning. I modeled loving all the children equally, which was challenging for the other teacher Shanti, who was Brahmin. She usually avoided touching some of her students.

My days were busy in Warchok, so my mind was occupied, but at other times I worried about things. A lot of things. I felt overwhelmed and helpless as there was no communication with the outside world whatsoever! It felt surreal knowing nothing except my direct experience. It was weird to know nothing about my loved ones and for them to know nothing about me. It made me realize how attached to them I was. For the first time in my life, I felt alone. I grew up in big cities like Rome, Paris, Indianapolis, and Sydney, so I had never experienced isolation. Without access to news, letters, or the Internet, I knew something could happen, and I would be oblivious. My worst nightmares played over and over *What if someone gets sick and I can't get home in time? What if I have a terrible accident and I need medical attention? We are a day's walk from Pokhara on foot. There are no roads, let alone ambulances. There are no telephones up here, so that means no helicopters. What if I die?*

I devoured the book Love Story by Erich Segal and cried uncontrollably for hours when Segal's female protagonist, Jennifer, died from Leukemia. With no one to turn to for support, I had to face my extreme fear of death head-on. What followed were the darkest days imaginable. I got sick with diarrhea. Illness and homesickness pushed me to my limit, and I considered giving up and leaving. But something, perhaps my evolved self, whispered *Yes, death is part of life and can happen at any time, but if something happens to you, Stitty, or a family member, it will not be the end of your world. You will be able to go on. You are strong enough.* I suppose I decided to listen to this seemingly impossible notion. Somehow found the courage to stay and face my fears.

To emerge from my depths of despair, I had to learn to stop clinging to things beyond my control. Every time I felt my body paralyzed by future *what ifs*, I forced myself to become present in the now. I had to do something; it was 'do or die'—*either I let go of the clinging or I go crazy.* Looking back, I know I was catapulted head first into an experience to practice the Buddha's teachings, just days after Jay and Yvette sparked an innate yearning to live as the Buddha lived. It still blows my mind that this yearning created an immediate and direct lesson forcing me to turn esoteric concepts into lived experiences.

Life without modern amenities or Western luxuries tested my resilience daily. I had to develop the malleability to adapt over and over again. Living this way allowed me to experience how so many people worldwide live. It made me grateful for everything I had taken for granted. It surprised me how quickly I adjusted to the locals' routines. We did not have a vacuum cleaner but have you ever seen a village woman use a homemade broom? They are sweeping machines! We did not have a dishwasher, but we used our hands to eat and used fewer plates and utensils. The Āmā (Paru's mother) made one meal a day, on the indoor fire, called dal bhat in three pots consisting of rice, vegetables (beans, potatoes, cabbage), and lentil soup. There was no shop; they grew all their food.

There was no running water, but the trip to the well was a social outing. There were no showers, but I learned to bathe modestly in public. I felt more connected to Mother Earth because there was no furniture, so we lived closer to the ground, surrounded by natural materials like mud, bricks, and wood instead of glass and plastic. There was no electricity, so we spent time talking after dinner instead of watching television or listening to the radio. We went to bed early. Our body clocks were perfectly synced to sunset and sunrise without artificial lights. I slept on the ground, in my sleeping bag, on the verandah. One night a chicken furiously flapped over my face. The next night, a gargantuan tarantula dangled before my eyes. I screamed so loudly that I woke the entire house. This story was big news and traveled fast! Before I knew it, grandfathers were lovingly teasing me by actioning the spider, squealing, and jumping around! They had no idea that Australia has some of the most venomous spiders in the world, unlike Nepal! This experience made me wonder if the fear of spiders is learned, not innate.

Since I spoke a different language from everyone else in the village, I could not ask clarifying questions, so I started to make assumptions about everything. This was an excruciatingly annoying pastime! I assumed things because I could not understand them, fathom their culture, or comprehend their foreign existence. My brain could not cope with this, so it tried to construct opinions about people, places, and things in the village. Based on my limited observations, I made judgments and attempted to decipher small unrelated details to piece together a narrative about them. Unfortunately, my obsession with connecting make-believe dots resulted in misconceptions, prejudices, and stereotypes. I found this phenomenon fascinating. *Why do I categorize, speculate, and analyze people's values, behaviors, and motivations? Why am I preoccupied with identifying our differences and similarities?* Internal guessing, imagining, and storytelling wasted my time and energy because the language barrier made clarification impossible. This hardwired human habit was me desperately trying to understand my community to form a relationship with them.

I examined why my brain did this and decided it was an evolutionary protective strategy. For early Homo sapiens to survive, around two million years ago, they had to cooperate in social groups. Therefore, our brain evolved to judge another effectively as a friend or foe. Predicting how others would behave to 'know' in advance how to respond was highly beneficial. However, millions of years later, this protective strategy got in the way because I often got things wrong. For example, one time, I imagined Paru, who lived at home with her parents because she had a deformed arm and could not have an arranged marriage, was having an affair with a woman! The things my mind made up!

Eventually, my delusions became so ludicrous that I decided to give up the habit. This was not easy; it took committed awareness to watch where my thoughts traveled and reel them back. I had to keep refuting my brain's ingrained identifiers, such as political biases, economic status, and education level. It took dedication to change the thoughts that followed my sense perceptions. Without my old habit, I felt vulnerable and exposed to 'getting it all wrong.' But I soon realized it was liberating to meet each moment as new and raw. Everything that had happened (or I thought had happened) dissolved, allowing me to experience people with no expectations or agendas. This shift in perception created mutual respect, equality, and harmony.

My Warchok experience showed me humanity's potential. Our brain's built-in identifiers are natural obstacles to unity consciousness. I learned to disregard labels, stories, and discriminatory thoughts that came into my mind. The more I practiced, the more I quietened my judging mind.

The villagers felt my authenticity. They loved how I greeted them with a big smile, my hands in prayer, my head bowed, and said the only word I knew, "Namaste" (languages are not my forte). Locals invited me into their houses on the way home from school. I loved everyone equally, even the men who drank chang (a homemade alcoholic fermented drink), while the women planted, weeded, and harvested in the hot sun, then cooked dinner and cleaned.

After about three weeks in Warchok, Douglas came to visit me. It was the weekend, so we walked along the stone pathway past the two pre-school classrooms and the colorful Vishnu temple. We peered over the little walls enclosing stone houses, haystacks on stilts, thatched-roof structures covering cows and water buffalo, and neat rows of firewood. Looking the other way, we saw rice paddies at eye level because the village nestles into the hillside. A few children sang out, "Namaste, Miss Junu. Junu, Junu, Junu!"

"Miss Moon, how beautiful. Why do they call you Miss Moon?" Douglas inquired.

"Douglas, I have no idea what anyone is saying. They laughed at me being Miss Katie and began calling me Miss Junu instead!" I laughed.

"Oh, maybe because Miss Katie sounds like Miss keti, which translates to Miss girl. Junu is a lovely name because the moon is sacred to the Nepalese. I would be happy with that name if I were you," he assured me.

We reached the top of the hill and turned our heads simultaneously. Awe-inspiring, magnificent Mount Machhapuchhre, situated at an elevation of 6,997 meters (22,943 feet), took our breath away. Known as 'fish's tail' in Nepali, this majestic snow-covered mountain immediately humbled us. Growing up in the United Kingdom and Australia made us unaccustomed to such sky-stabbing wonders. However, the mountain commanded us to sit and admire it. No one has ever climbed to its peak, making it one of the most untouched places on Earth. Hindu legend states Mount Machhapuchhre is home to Shiva, the Indian god of destruction.

I reached into my bag and passed Douglas the 40-page manual I had written.

"Here you go, Douglas; I have included all the teaching games I have taught the local women. I thought another facilitator could use it to train more early childhood teachers."

He smiled, angled his face into the sunshine, and closed his eyes, shaking his head in disbelief. Then, I witnessed a man having a revelation, "I feel profound gratitude. Time and time again, I am shown how supported I am. It is truly unbelievable how angels like you just turn up without me having to do anything. It makes me feel like there's something larger than me running this whole initiative. I know, without any doubt, that my work is meaningful," he shared.

Afterward, we visited my favorite person in the village, Old Buddhi Āmā (grandmother). I adored her. When she was sick and moaning in pain, I stroked her hair, sang *Amazing Grace*, and laid my hands on her stomach to perform the Reiki healing I had recently learned in Rishikesh. She was the oldest-looking person I had ever met. She was stuck in a 90-degree position from being bent over her whole life working in the rice fields (their livelihood) and cooking over the fire in her low-ceiling hut. When she walked, she looked down at the ground and had to sit down to talk to you. She kept my picture in her waistband. Her milky eyes could hardly focus, but she would point at me with my family (who I admit looked like movie stars) and weep with happiness. She cherished that photograph. I do not think she had ever seen one before.

Douglas translated, "She says you are always smiling and that with you, everything is beautiful and OK."

One morning on my regular 50-minute round-trip walk to the temple-like statue at the top of the village, an ominous, eerie scene struck me. A thick wall of white clouds crawled up the valley towards me. In an instant, there was a complete white-out. I lay down on my back and intended to practice remote Reiki on Stitty. I gazed at Mount Machhapuchhre above the fog and thought about Shiva's intense love for Parvati. I imagined Stitty as Shiva, the god of untamed passion making love to me as Parvati, the mother of creation. Parvati creates universes when the divine masculine and divine feminine unite. I tapped into their unrivaled power. This energetic consummation aroused me, and remote healing turned into remote lovemaking. I felt goosebumps cover my skin as Stittys essence entered my body. My whole body tingled. I closed my eyes and experienced love going from my body to his and back into mine. How curious that energy travels instantaneously across 9,875 kilometers (6,136 miles). I connected with him in a way that felt as real as flesh to flesh. This experience was a SELF-realization catalyst: SELF is everywhere; it is not a separate self. My consciousness can travel, via the love frequency to connect and merge with consciousness anywhere in the universe.

I began sobbing and sobbing, alone on the hilltop. Crying out, "Why, why am I here without you, Stitty? Why are you sick? I don't want you to be sick. It must be so horrible. I feel so guilty. I should never have left you. I should be with you, looking after you." Never before had I experienced this level of compassion. I realized that before that moment, my empathy for Stitty had been superficial. For the first time, I was physically and emotionally feeling Stitty's pain. It felt so unbearable that it activated a deep desire to relieve his suffering. I vowed, "I would give anything to have you here looking at this view with me. I love you so much. I would trade my health for yours if I could. Please get well; I want to bring you back here one day. I want you to meet my beautiful village family and witness the Himalayas." When I sat up, the fog sucked up the valley past me to reveal a tree full of white monkeys!

On my last day in Warchok, every villager came out of their 30 houses to say farewell to me as I set off for Pokhara. They had made leis of flowers, leaves, and folded paper fans. I do not know where they found these flowers; I had not seen one! They placed them around my neck until they were piled so high I could barely move my head. I smiled so hard that my eyes became slits (made worse by bushy eyebrows after a month with no mirror and eyes puffy from too much rice and too few fruits and vegetables). Locals rubbed my face and head with red dye for good luck and prosperity. This memory is one of the proudest and most unexpected of my life. Their gratitude overwhelmed me. They waved, cried, hugged me, and thanked me. I realized I had brought them so much joy by just being me.

When I arrived at the next village, Saimarang, to pick up Nadia, who had been living there for a similar amount of time, she told a very different story. She had slept alone in the schoolhouse, and no one came to farewell her. My experience in Warchok taught me that the world is what I make it. I had created my experience with my thoughts. It was my attitude, my energy, and my effort that made it the way it was. I had created my reality.

When I returned to Pokhara, I posted a 38-page letter to Stitty and excitedly opened the love letters he posted to the Nature's Grace Lodge. I missed him incredibly, more than ever. His words were beautifully poetic in perfect penmanship. Stitty was honest and admitted his colitis was causing him pain and stress, and his new drugs made him feel terrible. He wrote that one time he had been so busy at work that he convinced his doctor to give him his colonoscopy without a general anesthetic so that he could return to the office faster. *He sure is tough!* Another day he was forced to ring Mum for a lift because he was too sick to drive. *If fiercely independent Stitty involved Mum, he must be in a bad way.* Even though he shared a few details in his letters, I could never fully ascertain his health status because Internet access and public phones were sporadic, and there were long delays between letters. However, I suspected he was sparing me from the gruesome details, and his illness was worse than when I left four and a half months prior.

From Pokhara, I got an eight-hour bus to Gorakhpur, Uttar Pradesh, India, a 16-hour train to Delhi, then a 14-hour bus to Manali, Himachal Pradesh, to meet Milly and Walter for my 26th birthday on May 29th.

Monday, June 9th

I FLEW from Delhi to my half-sister Janet's apartment in London for Dad's surprise 70th birthday party. Mum and Dad were traveling to the USA and Canada after their European holiday, but Mum had this omen that we needed to be with Dad on his birthday. So she used her powers of persuasion to organize her step-daughter Judy to surprise Dad from Toronto, Canada, and her step-son Bill to surprise Dad from Seattle, USA. Dad's only missing child was Patrick, who had just started his first job in Sydney as an investment manager.

After the party on the 13th, I got to the bottom of Stitty's illness, which was, as I suspected, serious. He was coming to London in late July, and he and I planned to travel through Spain, Portugal, and Morocco.

I started to worry about him backpacking. I felt he was not well enough to be traveling. So I decided I should go home instead.

Before I mentioned anything to Stitty, I talked it over with Dad.

Dad replied, "This is a crucial question, Katie, and I want to answer it carefully, but I am exhausted tonight. Can I think about it and let you know in the morning."

In the morning, as soon as Dad awoke, he came to me and said, "Katie Pops, I have thought about your concerns. I know Peter very well, and I think canceling his trip at this late stage will do more harm than good. While you were away, he often came for dinner, stayed the night, and went to work the next day. He filled us in on all your news and shared how much he was looking forward to seeing you and traveling together. He admitted that this trip was keeping him going and making life bearable. Let him come and decide what to do about his illness when he arrives." I agreed with my wise Dad and told him I would stay in London and wait for Stitty to arrive. In the meantime I would go to the Glastonbury Festival on June 27th and meet up with all the backpackers I met in India - Green Field on Day 3.

Later that day, Dad had a stroke and went to the London Chelsea Westminster Hospital. Mum canceled their trip to Frankfurt, Budapest, Krakow, Warsaw, Canada, and the USA. After three days, the doctors discharged Dad, and he decided to fly home to Sydney to be with Patrick and Stitty, who lived at my parent's house. He insisted Mum and I make their planned trip to Prague and Moscow and then onto the *Waterways of Tsars Cruise,* which went from Moscow to St Petersburg before Mum returned to Australia. It was all paid for, and the insurance company would not reimburse us because Dad had been taking Warfarin. So, Dad insisted Mum, and I go rather than waste it. He would not take *no* for an answer.

6

HAVING TELEPATHIC PERCEPTION SELF

26 years old

Wednesday, July 2nd

Moscow, Russia

I stared at the helmet of Prince Yaroslav Vsevolodovich, the earliest example of Russian armor and jewelry work from the beginning of the 13th century. It was deadly quiet in the Armoury Chamber in the Moscow Kremlin. This beautiful two-story building houses nine spacious halls with over 3,000 rare and precious valuables of the Russian Empire. Artifacts such as weapons, jewels, gemstone-encrusted Fabergé eggs, crowns, ornate fabrics and tapestries, vessels of gold, ambassadorial gifts from Western Europe and the Orient, and imperial carriages. Also within the Kremlin walls are palaces, cathedrals, and the residence of the first freely-elected President of the Russian Federation, in its 1,000-year history, Boris Yeltsin. I pressed my nose against the glass and examined the rusted iron medieval helmet; the silver lining shined in contrast. I tried to think about the silver lining in my situation, but my breath just fogged up the glass. *Why are we here? Mum and I should be with Dad in Sydney, not casually meandering through a foreign museum. I wish Dad were looking through the glass instead of me.*

I struggled to come up with the silver lining and glimpsed it again, shining through the condensation. I admired Jesus Christ, beautifully etched in the metal near the helmet's pointed top. Below Jesus was Archangel Michael, the angelic leader of God's unseen army against the forces of evil and the Guardian of the Orthodox Faith. According to legend, Archangel Michael had done his job to protect Prince Yaroslav in the 1216 battle. His army was defeated, but he survived and fled the battleground, tossing his helmet where it lay buried for 600 years until its discovery in 1808.

Maybe, this is my silver lining, a reminder to call on Archangel Michael, the Angel Of Protection, to assist us. I often sensed angels around me, but at times like these, I felt compelled to ask for specific guidance. I imagined Dad standing before me; I placed the helmet on his thick gray hair. *Archangel Michael, thank you for bringing positivity to this situation and always protecting me, Mum and Dad. May we be together again soon.*

I contemplated the Christianity glorified on this 800-year-old helmet. I thought about the early Russians, who were Slavic pagans connected to Mother Earth and natural law. The rivers surrounding them brought foreigners, such as Vikings (called the Rus). They sailed down these rivers to pioneer trade routes to the riches of the Orient. The simple pagan peasants witnessed greed for material wealth rise before their eyes as the Land Of Rus became a country of warring states. Borders were drawn on maps as pagans watched Mother Earth turn from a unified whole to a dissected jigsaw of parts. Her totality was torn apart by men battling for supremacy and ownership of these pieces of land.

French philosopher Rousseau explained in *The Social Construct* that society is a corrupting influence over human nature, "Man is born free, and everywhere he is in chains." This phenomenon began with the establishment of private property, and exploitation by one person over another began. Social control increased until citizens began to resemble enslaved people. Rousseau believed society distorts human nature, and I understand his viewpoint.

In 988, Prince Vladimir of Kiev sought a single religion to bind his people. He met with Judaists and Muslims but chose the Christian Orthodox faith he had experienced on visits to Constantinople, the splendid capital of the Byzantine Empire (Eastern Roman Empire). His grandmother was baptized Christian Orthodox. However, whether his choice to Christianise the Land of the Rus was a spiritual calling or political pragmatism to strengthen his ties with this prosperous region is unknown. These ties weakened as the rivers that connected people to trade and riches brought invaders. A massive army of Mongol soldiers called The Sons of Genghis Khan attacked from the East like a war machine in 1237. They conquered the Land of Rus.

The Mongol domination that followed moved the country's population away from Mongolia towards Moscow in the far western part of the country. This city, where four rivers meet, became the head of the Eastern Orthodox Church in 1325. It was considered a safe place for spiritual figures to visit due to the city's alliance with the Mongols, who allowed local princes free rule throughout the provinces. Some princes, like Ivan I, Grand Prince of Moscow (Moneybags), were good at skimming money off the top as it traveled to the Mongols.

In the latter half of the 14th century, Ivan III (Ivan the Great) managed the unimaginable by defeating the Mongols and proclaiming a unified Russia. Later, in the 15th century, Ivan IV (Ivan the Terrible) ended princely power, starting the first centralized state controlled by military dominance and totalitarian rule. He called himself Tsar.

In 1485 a stone Treasury was built within the Kremlin walls to house the lavish gifts from abroad to the Russian Imperial family. It was added to by gunsmiths, silversmiths, goldsmiths, and the royal harness and carriage makers employed on site. In 1711 Peter the Great moved these artisans to the new capital St. Petersburg, but all the artistic and historical artifacts remained in the Kremlin museum, built in 1851.

After the October Revolution in 1917, the museum expanded to include items from the palaces of the nobility, Russian Orthodox Churches and monasteries, and private collections. For example, exquisite hand-woven tapestries from Byzantium, Iran, Turkey, Spain, and France. The royals would parade through the streets in carriages skillfully made of bronze, drawn by horses in fine leather and tassels. Royals wore spectacularly splendid crowns symbolizing the might of the Russian state. Their public display of opulence showed off the Russian Empire's power, control, and domination of the world.

A far cry from the early pagan inhabitants who respected the womb, seasons, planets, animals, waterways, stones, cycles of life and death, feminine rule, and goddesses. Pagans were alchemists living in a matriarchal society worshiping Mother Earth's abundance and honoring the lessons learned from the stars. Unfortunately, the Pagan lifestyle was disrupted by men chasing riches and trading fur, wax, and enslaved people. These men enslaved tribal pagans because their Pagan beliefs were considered inferior to their patriarchal Christian belief in a single 'God.' Hundreds of years later, under the feudal system, Pagan's ancestors were still being forced to work as serfs, who were bought and sold by the nobility.

I looked down at the plush carpet and then up at the magnificently painted ornate ceiling. I saw luxury everywhere, from the vast halls to the beautiful lighting, to the smell of money on streak-free, crystal-clear cabinets. Splendor sat juxtaposed with the poverty and gray grime outside the fortified Kremlin walls.

Our guide, Alexander and Mum, approached me, and I asked

him about the obvious contrast between the lightness of grandeur here and the heaviness of oppression out there. He replied that the average man and woman in Moscow is suffering economic hardship due to corruption, hyperinflation, industrial collapse, depleted resources, and tax avoidance. He told me that Russia has one of the highest incarceration rates in the world, fueled by homicides and violent crimes. Pollution and environmental degradation resulted from the Soviets prioritizing industrialization over environmentalism. Alexander spoke honestly about Yeltsin, who recently chose to break down communism in favor of private enterprise and capitalism. Alexander said while President Yeltsin enjoyed chauffeured limousines, his people were struggling. In a referendum, most people voted to keep the Soviet Union. However, three months later, Yeltsin ignored this result when he announced that the Union of Soviet Socialist Republics (USSR) ceased to exist. Yeltsin dissolved the huge federal socialist state consisting of 15 republics, turned each into an independent country in 1991, and ended Communism. Alexander told us that just last year, his brother Dimitri was killed in Chechnya along with 10s of thousands.

Alexander complained that most Russians had it tough due to the rising cost of living, lawlessness, low life expectancy, and high HIV rates. Alexander said his dad Maxim grew up with communism, so the market economy over the last six years had challenged him. Maxim had enjoyed a simple life but now stood before 30 different types of cereal in fancy boxes with confusing labels. He just wanted to buy a box of cereal. He hated all these choices and the complications that come with competition. Maxim sensed the lies in the new marketing campaigns that made him feel inferior. He used to feel satisfied, but now he felt lacking. Maxim hated the new billboards with their bright colors and "bullshit promises." He said the greedy capitalists were turning his people into unhappy whiners, crying for more and more, striving for the next best thing, hustling to make ends meet and never content in the present moment.

Alexander's voice fell into an inaudible whisper as we walked past museum guards. Despite recent changes to freedom of speech laws, there were rumors of journalists dying of suspicious causes. So Alexander shared his father's opinion with extreme caution. Alexander refused to speak of the Stalin days; it seemed a stage in history he longed to forget. Stalin had promised collective leadership but became a dictator with autocratic control who abolished religion and killed millions. Again I was filled with empathy for the Russians and gratitude for Australia, my democratic homeland.

Mum and I left the Armory Chamber and the Kremlin and embarked on the *Sergei Kirov*, a Swiss-owned first-class riverboat with 100 other guests on an *Art Lovers Cruise*. Our home for the next 12 days as we traveled along the famous Volga-Baltic Waterways (used for trade, transporting goods, and tourism). It consisted of artificial canals, lakes, and rivers, namely the famous Volga River (the longest in Europe). Each day we docked to tour historic towns and islands.

A couple Mum knew from her golf club in Sydney, Graham, and Barbara, were seated at our table at the Captain's Welcome Dinner. We discussed previous cruises (Mum and I had traveled to Australia on the Sea Princess when I was ten), and we shared our anticipated cruise highlights.

Mum invited me to go first, "I think my highlight will be the daily talks by Russian professors in art, history, and politics. Dad recently attended an eight-week University of Sydney (USYD) Adult Education Course, but I haven't studied Russian history since school. I want to learn as much as possible to tell Dad everything he missed. I want to be Dad's eyes and ears on this trip, soak it all up and make it worthwhile. He dreamed of coming to Russia his whole life. He's been to nearly every country on the planet except this one, so I want to make him proud of me by remembering every sight and every word." I choked up and fought back the tears.

Graham went next, "Barbara and I are really looking forward to visiting the Hermitage Museum in St. Petersburg because it is more than just a museum; everywhere you look is a work of art."

Mum shared last, "I know I'm going to love seeing Tchaikovsky's *Swan Lake* in St. Petersburg. I adore ballet, and seeing *Swan Lake* in the country where it was written in the 1800s has always been a dream of mine. I think the Russians have the best ballet dancers in the world!"

When we returned to our cabin, there was a message. In that instant, Mum's dream to see the ballet in Russia was to remain a dream.

"It's bad news," Mum sounded matter of fact. "Your dad has had another stroke. I am flying home. There is no need for you to come at this stage. You finish the trip for Dad and me, he would want you to do the cruise for us. Then go back to London and wait for Stitty. Go ahead and do your trip together. I'm sure Dad will be fine. You remember everything you learn on board, and you can talk about it with him when you get home for Christmas. Tomorrow we need to arrange my flight."

Organizing flights took all day. While the rest of our group visited the Pushkin Museum, Red Square, St Basil's Cathedral, and Novodevichy Convent, we went from travel agent to travel agent. No one spoke English. They could barely understand where Sydney was, let alone work out how to change tickets. Mum had tickets from St. Petersburg to Sydney in 12 days, but she needed to fly home from Moscow (via London) today. By late afternoon we staggered back on board, shattered and frustrated but triumphant. Mum had flights home that night. So, before I knew it: she had packed, asked Graham and Barbara to look out for me, and hopped off the boat. Thus, leaving me alone in a strange country, setting off down the Moscow canal in a boat full of strangers three times my age.

I felt dizzy, blurry-minded, and foggy. I slumped in my cabin's desk chair. *What am I doing here? I don't want to be here, but I love*

Dad, and I'll do this trip for him because he is too sick to do it himself. I'll do it out of respect for him.

I looked down at the cruise itinerary and noticed a quote under the title *Russian Literature Lecture: 11:00 am.*

But if you are alive—live: tomorrow you'll die as I might have died an hour ago. And is it worth tormenting oneself, when one has only a moment of life in comparison with eternity?

— Leo Tolstoy, *War and Peace*

It remained on my lips for minutes until it finally sunk in. *I'm alive, I'm in Russia, and I have this moment to live. Who knows when I'll die but when I do, I'll have eternity, so why not fully live in the present moment where everything exists? The past is just a thought, and the future is just a thought, so I'll choose to live right now as if it's my last before eternity. I won't mope around worrying about Dad, I'll seize the day; I owe this to myself and my devoted Dad.*

Sleeping in was not an option; I attended every activity, especially the daily lectures. Pen-poised, I wrote meticulous notes and endeavored to understand Russia, the Russia that perplexed the greatest minds in history, "It is a riddle, wrapped in a mystery, inside an enigma." Winston Churchill.

I enjoyed every tour, from a local farmhouse in Yaroslavl to the 18-domed wooden Church of the Transfiguration on the island of Kizhi to the Chapel of Dimitry in Uglich. I marveled at chapels with ice-cream cone-shaped spires painted in vibrant pops of color and the ingenious progression of locks that lowered or raised our boat when canal waterways were uneven. I knew Stitty would have been impressed with each lock's clever engineering.

Thursday, August 7th

St. Petersburg, Russia

It was 10:00 a.m. on a sparkling summer day. I stepped off the tour bus with my group and waited until they rounded the corner to snap a picture. For Dad. St. Nicholas Cathedral was the prettiest Russian Orthodox church I had seen. Majestic Baroque architecture was celebrated with ornate gold gilded spires that pointed to the sky atop glistening golden domes. White columns sat in contrast to baby blue walls. Peaceful bells poised in silent anticipation. Empty balconies guarded curtain-drawn windows concealing centuries of secrets. Tall gold crosses perched on spiraling points and round windows watched. Its impressive double wooden doors waited breathlessly at the end of a long avenue scattered with cooing pigeons. I paused at the entrance, looked up to admire the Corinthian columns, and thought of the trip Milly and I had made to my birthplace three years prior. The birds sang a busy song, and a faraway horn cried out.

I entered unsuspectingly. The music immediately engulfed me and propelled me into a trance-like state. I could see the choir singing in the distance. The Russian language sounded hauntingly evangelical as the mens' baritone voices led me deeper and deeper into the sacred space. The ethereal singing felt familiar, like coming home. It triggered a remembering of some kind, like I had heard it before, perhaps in my dreams or before I was born. With tunnel vision, I was guided to a painting of St. Nicholas, the patron saint of sea travelers. The notes from the harmonic flute-like organ flooded me with overwhelming emotion. I stared at his haloed face. Known as the 'Wonderworker,' St. Nicholas has miraculously answered Christians' prayers for centuries. As all my attention became focused on the light surrounding his head, I was overcome with the most incredible feeling of bliss and joy. Never before had art created such a visceral response in me. I felt like God looking back at God. This feeling of love poured into my being from the face of St. Nicholas and then seemed to explode out of my heart, igniting every cell in my physical body, then my light body, then my celestial body. My heart expanded to infinity with an indescribable intensity of sensations. Decades later, a teacher of mine, Chris Cheung, described an experience where he had a heart orgasm, and this best describes what I felt in St. Nicholas Cathedral.

As I stared into the eyes of St. Nicholas, I felt a portal open up, which connected me to Dad almost 15,000 kilometers (8,000 miles) away. Looking back, I believe Dad and I entered our true SELF where the distance between us dissolved, and we became one. I felt the most incredibly intense unconditional love pulsing through me and into him immediately, as if we were connected by an umbilical cord. There are no words available to describe the compassion this activated in me. It flowed through my body and into his and then back into mine instantaneously. I had only felt this once before, lying on my back on the Warchok hilltop connecting with Stitty in Sydney. I was reminded: SELF is everywhere all at once. Consciousness does not dwell solely in my physical body because my love frequency is capable of merging with the love frequency of someone across the globe. SELF is not separate because if it was, I could not coalesce with another separate 'self' as I had done twice.

I sobbed and sobbed, the same way I had sobbed for Stitty *Why am I here, Dad? You should be here. I wish you were here. This is your trip, your church, your memory, your dream. Why, why couldn't you be here? I would give anything just to have you standing here instead of me. I would give you all my wellness if I could, Dad. I would give you my life. Please, Dad, tell me, why aren't you here?*

This time I received an answer, *Come home, Katie.* I heard Dad's voice as if he was standing right in front of me. *You don't need to finish the cruise for me anymore. I need you to come home. Right now. I need you, Katie. I love you. Come home*, Dad continued.

Tears streamed down my face *Dad, thank you. That was perfect telepathy.*

I staggered from the painting. I reached into my bag and pulled out all my Russian Rubles. It was about 8,000 Rubles (worth 15 000 Rubles today, 270 Australian dollars, 200 US dollars), but I did not care. I was convinced a miracle had happened, and I wanted to show my gratitude to the cathedral and the choir.

I tried to shove the entire wad into the donation box. The money got jammed in the slot made for coins, and my vision became blurred with tears. I raised my head and locked eyes with a baritone chorister who immediately stopped singing and warmly smiled. No doubt, he sensed my anguish; no rational traveler would stuff that much money into a church donation box. I lifted the corners of my mouth as I forced in the last note, determined to pay it forward.

I approached Graham, "We have to get to a phone, please; something is terribly wrong."

We raced to the nearest hotel, and I called Mum from the reception desk.

Mum sounded shocked to hear my voice, "Oh, Katie Darling, your dad has cancer. I didn't want to contact you on the boat. I've arranged for Milly to meet you with your bags at Heathrow, at the end of the cruise, in five days, to put you on a plane to Sydney. But since you've called, I think you should try and get back earlier. Your dad needs a serious operation. If you leave Russia today, you should make it back before his surgery." Then Mum started crying uncontrollably, which made me cry.

Graham took the phone, "Penny, what's happened? What can I do to help?" He listened and began shaking. I had no idea what was suddenly wrong with him. His speech became stuttered, and he appeared to be going into shock or having a stroke, "Yes, PPPPP... enny," he repeated over and over.

He hung up the phone and said, "Let's go, Katie. I'm getting you on the next flight to London."

"Graham, you can't miss the Hermitage tour; it's your highlight," I insisted.

"Katie, this happened to me with my mother. It would be my pleasure to escort you back to the boat and help you get home."

In the taxi, Graham kindly said, "Tell me about your father Katie."

"He has this huge personality and energy rivaled by none. He tells great stories about his adventures living and working around the world. Dad is a larger-than-life character!"

"Graham, tell me what happened to your mother." I knew Graham had an emotional story to share by the way he struggled to speak to Mum on the phone. I suspected my situation brought up an old, painful memory.

"I had to go to Miami on business. Mother and Barbara took me to the airport. Mother always helped Barbara with the kids while I was away on business. By the time my plane landed in Los Angeles, I found out that Mother had had a heart attack. And by the time I flew home to Sydney, she had died. I didn't get to say goodbye to her," Graham said. "What would you say to your dad if he were here, Katie?"

"I'm sorry that you have cancer. I'm sorry I wasn't there when you found out. I'm sorry that you didn't get to come on this trip. I came on this cruise for you, and I've taken lots of notes and photos so you can experience Russia through me. Please wait for me; I'm on my way home now. I miss you so much, Dad. I love you so much. I don't want to lose you; I'm too young; I'm only 26." I shared.

Back on the boat, Graham took control of the situation and called British Airlines directly. He was unable to get me on the next flight, so he turned his head away from me (hoping I would not hear) and whispered forcefully, "Her father is DYING; you have to get her on that flight from St. Petersburg to London and then onto Sydney

NOW! Someone will need to meet her off the plane at Sydney Airport and escort her through customs to meet her family; she is very upset." He paused, "Yes, thank you, that's perfect. Thanks again." Just like that, I was booked on a flight later that day.

I was meant to be packing, but all I wanted to do was speak to Patrick. Without realizing I was traumatized, I walked in a dazed trance toward the Metro train station. There were no payphones, and nobody spoke English. Unconsciously, I stepped onto the escalator. My eyes were glazed over, and my stomach rose into my throat as I descended. Dirty vertical tiles pulsed slowly in my peripheral vision while ghostly-looking Russians stared at my shocked state. Click, click, click. A psychedelic tunnel of grotesque faces coupled with the distinctive sound of a departing train below followed by a tuba-like horn. *That's a different pitch to trains back home.*

I went deeper and deeper into the unknown and the unfamiliar. Like a zombie, I floated towards the open train doors. Suddenly I noticed a woman whose concerned expression and lowered eyebrows forced me to stop in my tracks and reconsider. I halted on the platform; people flooded past me *Katie, pull yourself together. You can't get on this train. You have no idea where you are, you have barely any money, no I.D., and you don't speak Russian. Getting lost is not going to get you on that plane. You just have to give up on calling Patrick. Turn around now, Katie.*

As the train pulled away from the station, I turned on my heels and got back on the escalator. *I'm so relieved I didn't board that train. What was I thinking? I wasn't thinking.*

There was a flower stall near the entrance where I bought Graham and Barbara flowers. I wrote them a beautiful note thanking them for their support and left the surprise by their door.

Back in my parents' cabin, number 359, I rummaged through their cream manila folder, full of Dad's lecture notes, itineraries, and travel brochures. I was searching for a taxi voucher to the St. Petersburg Pulkovo Airport.

I noticed a scribbled travel tip on a doctor's note paper.

Below the doctor's letterhead was a hand-drawn map of St. Petersburg, including the river, labeled *Neva River*; next to the river was a building with a cross on it. Underneath, written in doctor's scrawl *St. Nicholas Cathedral, St. Petersburg, 10:00 am service, beautiful village choir. A must-see!*

I couldn't believe my eyes. I squeezed them together tightly *Am I imagining things?* I expected to open them and see different words, but the words remained the same *St. Nicholas Cathedral, St. Petersburg, 10:00 am service, beautiful village choir. A must-see!*

Time stopped as the enormity of the situation sunk in. What were the odds of me receiving a telepathic message from Dad at the exact place and time his Sydney doctor had told him to be there? It felt surreal, like I was an actress in a movie. I seemed to be viewing the scene from outside it. It felt like parallel timelines converged. For me to be there at the exact moment Dad sent the telepathic message required perfect orchestration. *I can't believe this.*

I imagined the Doctor, advised by his evolved self, scratching the message on his notepad and tearing it out with a *snap*. Dad packing, hesitating *Do I really need this piece of paper?* Dad hearing his evolved self *Yes, it is very important*. Dad questioning this voice *I wonder why sometimes I get told to do random things with such certainty.*

We know why!

Operation *Get Katie Home* commenced.

Two months later (in linear time), I hopped off the St. Petersburg bus at 10:00 a.m., the exact time the choir started singing. I entered the Cathedral and was guided by angels to a golden icon of St Nicholl's at the exact moment Dad sent the telepathic message, trusting that everything had been executed with precision.

And it had. Everything had gone according to plan, and I received the message loud and clear. As a result, I was able to get home in time, aided by a living angel named Graham.

When I touched down in Sydney, I was escorted, as directed by Graham, from the plane, past customs, and into Stitty's open arms. We had not seen each other for eight months. We went straight to his place and made love.

Afterward, we went to the hospital. I said, "Dad, you have to fight this cancer. Don't you want to see Stitty's and my children?" I encouraged him.

"They will be beautiful children, Katie," he replied in a defeated voice.

After his operation, Dad was never the same. If I had not got the telepathic message, I would not have arrived in time to see him communicating coherently. We would never have shared those precious days talking about everything we needed to talk about. He died three weeks later, on August 28th (Janet, Judy, and Bill made it in time to say goodbye, and we stayed by his side around the clock). Cause of death–advanced carcinoma of the colon, which had adhered to the liver, pancreas, and spleen. He was 70 years old and had only retired the year before after 50 years in the pharmaceutical industry (first with Eli Lilly and then as a business consultant in Sydney). His dream to visit the Russian Federation was left too late, but I believe he experienced it through me. He was with me every step of my journey through Russia, and he continues to be with me on my journey through life.

You will not grasp her with your mind
Or cover with a common label,
For Russia is one of a kind –
Believe in her, if you are able...
Fyodor Tyutchev, 1866

7

MANIFESTING A MIRACLE SELF

26 year old

Saturday, October 11th

Not long after Dad died, Stitty decided enough was enough. We were out to dinner at a North Sydney restaurant when he announced he was taking his health into his own hands. He instigated the whole thing, "I have decided to go off all my medications. I am tired of this merry-go-round. Nothing works, and every appointment is just, "Take more of this, take less of that." So I have decided to heal myself. I'll still leave my job because it is out-of-control busy, but instead of backpacking through Spain, Portugal, and Morocco, I reckon we drive around Australia at the end of the year. If I am going to get better, I have to change my lifestyle completely. I have to escape the stressful construction industry and the party scene. What do you reckon?"

My first thought was excitement. *Wow, Stitty sounds serious!* My second thought was fear regarding my responsibilities. *I am expected back at school in January. Perhaps my principal will grant me another year's leave without pay under the circumstances.*

I replied, "Of course Babe, whatever it takes."

Stitty shared that he had written to his Dad's brother, Dr. Frank Stitt, who advised him not to go cold turkey off the drugs. He warned that abruptly stopping drugs would be hazardous to his health. However, when Stitty told his regular gastroenterologist, Dr. Borody, he replied, "I know how determined you are, Pete, and if you have made up your mind, then there is nothing I can say. But will you do me a favor before you and Katie leave on your trip? I think your ulcerative colitis could be caused by unhealthy microorganisms in your intestines. I have heard that a fecal transplant could fix the problem. In this procedure, a healthy donor defecates, and the stool is put into your intestines using an enema. The healthy human cells plus bacterial, viral, and fungal organisms create microbial changes that may reduce inflammation and symptoms."

Stitty told me that he had decided to do the fecal transplant. I was relieved to hear that his brother Bill had agreed to be the donor so I could keep the dream alive! At dinner, we made plans: in December, after my school friend Lucy's wedding (I was a bridesmaid), Stitty would travel back to his hometown Forbes in Central West, NSW, to do the experimental procedure at *Mungarra*, his parents' cattle station. Then, we would drive around Australia.

The next day Stitty went off all the pharmaceutical drugs and never retook a single one, not even a painkiller.

Stitty encouraged me to leave my job and treat the trip as an 'adventure,' but I was still too fearful and attached to my life. When I explained to my principal that I needed another year's leave without pay to help cure Stitty, she replied, "I lost my husband, so I know how important this is to you and Peter. You do what you must, and we will see you back here at the end of the year." I could not believe my ears.

While we prepared for our trip, Stitty and I lived with Mum in

Randwick. She was grieving Dad, so she appreciated the support. Over the next few months, we bought a second-hand white Toyota Troop Carrier four-wheel drive, a tent, sleeping bags, cooking utensils, a gas cooker, tarps, and all the supplies we needed to live off the grid.

December arrived, and Stitty returned to Forbes to begin Dr. Borody's experiment. The transplant involved Bill defecating and placing the stool into a blender. Then Patti, Stitty's mum, would add wheat germ and saline, blend it, and pour it into an enema bag. Stitty would lie on his side on a towel, and once he inserted the enema bag tip into his rectum, Patti would turn a tap to release small amounts of feces. His bowel was very sensitive, and the discomfort would cause his body to reject the transplant, but they persevered.

The first time Patti cried. Stitty told her, "Mum, you can't be my mum right now. You have to be tough like a nurse."

I still feel terrible contributing to one of the lowest moments of his life. I went with our friends to see Carl Cox on New Year's Eve at *The Metro* in Sydney. Carl Cox is one of Stitty's favorite DJs. When I told him about my night, he was lying on the hard shower floor with an enema in his rectum; it did not go down well (my news, not the feces). Stitty said nothing, but I could tell he felt rock bottom (no pun intended). Even though Dr. Borody recommended six home procedures, Stitty only did three because he was keen to take off around Australia. I arrived the day after his last transplant. A few days later, we departed on our year-long adventure around Australia. He was still very skinny.

Driving around Australia, along one of the most beautiful coastlines in the world, in a four-wheel drive and sleeping in a tent brought Stitty into constant contact with nature. He was outside in the elements most of the day. Long walks through forests, secluded beaches, rivers, mountains, and national parks in Mallacoota, Wilson's Promontory, Arthur River, Bruny Island, Cape Ottway, and the Grampians. Soon, his body began to unwind from the hectic pace of three and a half years in the construction industry. He went from being surrounded by macho men, steel, and jackhammers to running water, chirping birds, and still lakes. His adrenal glands slowly started to recover. They were used to constantly producing hormones for the fight or flight response. Meetings, deadlines, and pressure was replaced by living moment to moment with nowhere to go and nothing to do. His body seemed to remember this chilled lifestyle from backpacking through South America.

We turned off the Eyre Highway in South Australia and picked up a hitchhiker, Jeremy, who showed us a remote spot to camp on Point Bell. He was camping with mates at Point Sinclair, and we met many long-termers and overseas backpackers through him. Every day for three weeks, Stitty listened to his body. He would sleep if he were tired, even if it was 11:00 am. He did full-body stretching, swam, and attempted to surf on the local surf breaks: Cunns, Cactus, and Castles. He did daily guided chakra balancing and 'heal your cells' meditations on his Sony Walkman Cassette player. We spent our nights camped on a deserted beach, gazing at the most beautiful Southern Hemisphere stars imaginable.

We continued anticlockwise around Australia. Along the way we ate freshly caught fish and local, seasonal food sourced from farmers' markets and roadside vegetable stalls throughout our trip. We shopped at delicatessens, bakeries, health food emporiums, co-ops, and visited crystal shops. Whatever shop owners recommended, Stitty tried. He allowed himself to be guided organically to healing practitioners whom he embraced with an open mind and heart. He was willing to try anything, no matter how 'out there' it appeared. He believed that if he brought the cause of his colitis to the surface, he could heal it.

An acupuncturist did Electro Meridian Mapping (EMI) to determine which meridians needed unblocking. Next, she stuck lentils on pressure points to show him where to massage daily to target specific organs and stimulate life flow, or *Ki* in Chinese. Next, a naturopath put him on Ultraclear Maintain powder for gastrointestinal support and detoxification. The program required him to be a vegetarian and give up drinking for a few months. He also consulted an Ayurvedic doctor who recommended Amalaki herbs to improve his immune system. Once, Stitty was given a kinesiology session that involved muscle testing to access his innate healing wisdom by a fellow traveler staying at Cradle Mountain camping ground in Tasmania.

Friends Tristan and Bee recommended a Chiron Healer in Warrnambool, a coastal town in Victoria. Maxine had been trained by Jan Thomas, who originally channeled Chira, then the Master Chiron from ancient Greece. Jan formalized his teachings into a healing modality known as the *International Association of Chiron Healers Inc.* Jan trained Maxine to balance the body's subtle energy systems. Using her hands, Maxine worked on Stitty to repair, clear, and strengthen his etheric energy body to unblock his connection to Source. Maxine saw one of Stitty's "past lives" (which is a parallel life). She saw Stitty as a Native American guide called Blue Feather; he was screaming in pain from a severe stab wound to the stomach. She asked if Stitty had any health issues in that area (we had been careful not to tell her anything about his illness before his treatment). Stitty replied, "Yes, I have ulcerative colitis and I saw a Native American elder while you were working on me!"

Maxine stated, "Seeing your past life stabbing trauma and knowing about your current disease, I think you are in a cycle which can be stopped. Trauma causes blockages in your body's energy centers/chakras, which causes dis-ease. You can clear these blockages and heal your trauma which will end the illness/suffering loop that has plagued you for lifetimes. I did a lot today and you can continue after you leave. I also saw a past life where you were Katie's father. She was killed in an accident when she was very young, and you vowed in that lifetime to find her in this lifetime and never let her go."

After this healing session with Maxine, Stitty used this

past/parallel life knowledge to heal himself. He would meditate and imagine the stab-wound inflammation in his intestines subsiding. He would visualize the old injury closing up and no longer affecting him. He also used self-talk throughout the day to remind himself that the stabbing was not part of this lifetime and no longer served him.

We left Sydney in January to cure Stitty; by May, Stitty's ulcerative colitis symptoms had vanished. It was a miracle. Eight months after he decided to go off the pharmaceutical prescription medicines he had trusted for seven years, he cured himself and achieved his vision (our vision).

Stitty wrote a long letter to Dr. Borody, thanking him for being a dedicated and caring doctor. In the letter, Stitty outlined everything we tried on the road to recovery. He wanted Dr. Borody to know that his healing process combined physical, emotional, psychological, and spiritual factors. Yes, the fecal transplant was instrumental, but not the only factor.

Then Stitty wrote to me.

> Dear Babe, When I wrote my letter to Dr. Borody explaining all the things I did to cure myself, it reinforced again to me just what an amazing support you have been to me over the years. To be so willing to change your life with me in order to make me better is so touching. You were always the main thrust behind me, keeping my sanity. To know that there was always someone I could come back to and lean on for a while. Someone with whom I had no secrets and could just spill it all out to. I really appreciate this, Babe! The best part of all is through our teamwork and determination (in often different ways), we achieved our aim – I

am better, and we are even closer.

Patti often cried with joy when she talked about Stitty's health miracle. She would hug me and say, "Your love cured Pete, Katie. I am forever grateful to you for saving my son."

Stitty would say, "Yeah, Babe, I'd be dead if it weren't for you."

People sometimes say, "I feel disheartened because I can't seem to cure myself as Stitty did."

I answer, "Perhaps your time to heal has not come yet. There is no right or wrong way to cure an illness, there is only your way, and your way is perfect, no matter how it looks, how long it takes, or whether or not it is successful. Perhaps your condition is a vehicle for your life's purpose. Living with a diagnosis and finding ways to thrive despite it could be your unique gift. Maybe telling people what you have learned encourages them to see their ailments as stepping stones to freedom instead of burdens. You do not have to be disease-free to inspire people; just start sharing. Sometimes, speaking up confidently, stepping into your power, and coming out from behind your illness transforms you by lifting your vibration. There is no shame in being where you are; where you are is perfect. You are not sick; you are healing. Your body may have symptoms of dis-ease, but hold the vision of health-ease, and one day your body might match your vision; in the meantime, your confidence motivates others to reach for their potential."

In Stitty's case, we will never know exactly why and how he was cured. In hindsight, I think from a metaphysical perspective Stitty aligned with his evolved self on his highest timeline until his reality matched that higher timeline. If everything exists in the now, including parallel timelines, then we have access to every possible timeline in the now. Therefore, we choose which one we identify with and subsequently which one we create. Stitty chose to identify with his perfect body technology. He ignored his flawed body and got out of his own way, allowing infinite universal wisdom to restore perfect health, proving that wellness is our natural state. Some would say, Stitty's free will overrode his soul contracts.

I think from a Buddhist perspective, in this lifetime or a past life Stitty planted the seeds for ill-health. However, in this lifetime he refused to accept his diagnosis, lie down and die. Instead, he did everything in his power to sow the seeds of health by going off the drugs and trusting his body. By being committed to thinking, saying, and doing thoughts and actions that made healing possible he cultivated seeds for change. Perhaps he paid off his karmic debts or his healthy karmic seeds ripened. Regardless, health became his reality. It was his time to be well.

I think from a teamwork perspective we were the ultimate healing team. The way we navigated those early years fostered a rare intimate bond. We built our relationship on trust, respect, and mutual understanding. He trusted me because I never tried to change him, and I trusted him because of his emotional intelligence, expressiveness, and dependability. We had turned a diseased life into an abundant life, so we felt profound gratitude for everything healthy people took for granted. This expanded perspective created an unspoken vision confirmed by action. Our shared life experience created a telepathic communication style; we intuitively knew what our team needed to do and just got on with it. We epitomize *having and holding from this day forward, for better, for worse, for richer, for poorer, in sickness and in health, loving and cherishing, till death do us part.*

We could give one hundred percent to every aspect of our relationship because we were equally evolved individuals who never harbored resentment. This quality is uncommon. How did we achieve it? Stitty did not rely on me for his happiness, and I did not depend on him for mine. We did not need anything from anything because each of us were sovereign. Therefore, we never took things personally because my 'person' could never be affected by his 'person' because we had evolved from separate selves to a unified whole. It wasn't about 'me' it was always about 'us.' We put in equal effort, so in a way, I became him and his efforts, and he became me and my efforts. Both were faithful to our common cause. We were both optimistic, positive, and content. If something was wrong, we fixed it before it became an issue. Yes, we drove each other crazy, as any couple would after years together. But we were able to love each other despite our maddening habits. A healthy sex life helped move us from annoying flatmates to an energetic team. We were both perceptive and thoughtful. Especially Stitty, who continued being committed to making happy memories with me. We could share honestly without offending each other through the use of jokes to lighten the blow. Communication and humor were our strengths.

8

REBIRTHING IN THE DESERT SELF

27 - 29.5 years old

CHANGE OF PLANS

Friday, May 29th

We arrived in Kalgoorlie (Kal), Western Australia (WA), on my 27th birthday. Back in Adelaide, South Australia, we were hit with unexpected mechanical costs that forced us to borrow AUS$ 1,140 from Stitty's parents. By the time we reached Kal, we had been on the road for five months and achieved our goal of curing Stitty, so we decided to stop and work to pay Stitty's parents back. I had heard the town was the perfect place to make money. I could work as a substitute teacher and Stitty as an engineer in the open-cut mines. Kal was a remote gold mining town (population 28,000), in the middle of the Great Victoria Desert, on the western fringe of the Nullarbor Plain (one of the longest straight stretches of road in the world). Houses were notoriously expensive to rent, so we lived in our tent in a caravan park.

On weekdays, local school staff would call the caravan park owner, Bruce. Like a personal assistant, he would reply, "She'll be right there!" before hurrying to my tent and shouting, "Katie, teaching job at South Kal, job at South Kal!"

Mum was not so enthusiastic, "What do you mean you are living in a tent? You can't waste the best years of your life in the middle of nowhere! What if Peter never proposes and you have given up your whole life for him?"

My brother Patrick was also concerned, "Why don't you just keep driving around Australia? Why would you want to live in Kalgoorlie?"

I took all this on board and started doubting our decision to stop and work.

A week later, Stitty was offered a serious job as a site engineer in a gold mine. "Let's stay awhile; I am loving this adventure," his excitement was palpable. This was his dream come true. But, unfortunately, his definition of 'adventure' was my definition of hell. My future life, tainted by recent conservations, flashed before me, and it was not pretty (put it this way, I was drinking beer).

I became cringe-worthily clingy, hideously negative, needy, and highly unattractive. Yes, me! As a result, we started fighting for the first time in our relationship. At the same time, I began questioning Stitty about marriage, even though I knew I was becoming the last person he would want to marry. The *M word* did not go down well. Stitty brushed it off, "Let's just enjoy each other where we are right now."

The problem was he was where he wanted to be, and I categorically was not!

We had been together for two and a half years, and I had always felt relaxed. However, now I felt stressed, anxious, and miserable. I knew deep down that my true SELF was peaceful, but I did not know how to return to that natural state because my mind was plagued with fear. I whined for five and half weeks until a conversation with an old school friend, Georgi, changed everything. She shared that she was traveling alone to Bali, Indonesia. I badly needed a change of scene, and Dad had left me money, so I asked to meet her in Bali.

During the holiday, Georgi recommended, "Kitty J, this is so unlike you. You need to get back to Kalgoorlie and throw yourself into it. Your Mum and Patrick are scared for you, but you know Stitty loves you. So just go and have fun."

THE NEW ME

Saturday, July 18th

I arrived back in Kal on Stitty's 28th birthday with a new attitude. Before I went to Bali, I was trying to control Stitty because I was desperately clinging to a false *you should be engaged by now* SELF that my family created. I was unhappy because I was trying to change Stitty to make him match my family's expectations, and Stitty refused to change (surprise, surprise)! So while I grasped for certainty in my relationship, I missed the present moment and all its potential magic. In Bali, I realized I had to ignore society's narrative that said *Being in a mining town in the Australian desert without a proposal at 27 is problematic.* Instead, I had to practice what I learned in the remote Nepalese village *The world is what I make it. Stop being attached to things I can't change. Just be here now.*

I vowed to make a life I would never regret and decided to stay in Kal for me; not for Stitty. Suddenly, click, click, click as thousands of invisible doors opened into the future. The ripple effect of this decision propelled me onto a parallel timeline. Like the analogy of the sliding door, the decision I made to create my world, my way, changed the course of my life.

As soon as I shifted energetically, everything I encountered shifted. It felt like I was living in an entirely new Kal, showing me that things change when I perceive them differently. *It is all a matter of perspective.* After I made that intentional decision, everything I attracted matched that elevated vibe and I began living evolved.

A brand new friend

I WAS OFFERED A PERSONAL DEVELOPMENT, Health and Physical Education (PDHPE) teacher job at North Kalgoorlie, the best elementary school in town, which came with subsidized housing! We could finally move out of the guy we met in the pub's house! On my first day at North Kal, a female colleague, Chris, told me, "You have to meet Nikki. She's a Perth girl working as a school counselor at the high school. You two will love each other. So come to the pub Friday night, and I'll introduce you!"

Paddy's Bar was packed. The first Friday of term four. School staff shared holiday stories. Across the crowded room, Nikki and I locked eyes *That's gotta be her*. We knew we were soul sisters the first time we talked because our language was encoded with common interests and shared experiences. Our flowing conversation created a thrilling sense of familiarity.

"I'm looking for a mediation group," I inquired.

"I go to one every Wednesday night; Macey's incredible...we practice psychic readings!" she replied excitedly.

"I'm looking for a yoga teacher," I added.

"I have one. I go on Monday nights!" She exclaimed. "Do you want to go back to my house so we can chat in peace?"

I could not get out of there fast enough.

We opened a bottle of wine at her place and said in unison, "Here's cheers to new friends." It was pretty obvious we liked to drink and talk. We were a match made in heaven, I was a teacher with a psychology major, and she was a school psychologist. We even backpacked through the same countries! So I asked to see her photos.

"No one ever looks through my travel albums," she reported enthusiastically.

"I can't believe it! We both have a photo of ourselves with the same woman in Pushkar, Rajasthan. This is incredible; what are the odds? The only difference is, mine was taken two years later, so in my photo, the woman's baby is a toddler!" I shrieked *This is pure serendipity!*

"I can't believe we both loved India so much!" She responded.

She whipped up a beautiful salad, and I offered to set the table. I opened her cutlery drawer and gasped, "Where did you get these salad servers? I bought these exact ones last week in Bali?"

"I bought them last week in Bali!" Nikki answered, eyes wide.

"So, you were in Bali for the full moon? I probed.

"I sure was," she offered.

"I met this fun Melbourne girl called Jo who was staying in our hotel. She and I partied with this awesome Perth couple who lived in Bali. They invited us to a full moon party in a stunning hilltop house." I explained.

"The night of the full moon, I was involved in a terrible accident. Waz, the friend I was traveling with, hit a Balinese boy. It was very intense but the boy was fine." She replied.

Party people

FROM THEN ON, Nikki and I were inseparable. After school, she would come over, and we would drink vodka, lime, and sodas all afternoon and plan parties. We would run off invitations and give them to PLUs (people like us) on the dance floor. PLUs were the friendly types wearing smiles!

It was not long before we formed a crew that included five DJs. On the weekends, the DJs (including Stitty) would play at the local nightclub, Club 181, or back-to-back sets at our house on Stitty's turntables. The music could go on all night because our neighbors worked mining shifts. We had strobe and smoke machines and crazy dress-up themes. Life was the epitome of fun. We were living my adored dance floor life just as we had in Sydney, creating Kal dance floor moments to last a lifetime. Connecting through music and community meant my body buzzed with ecstatic energy and vibrancy. Killer Kitty (*first time I've called myself this, but I love it!*) was back, ripping up the dance floor, whipping everyone into a frenzy with anticipation for the approaching climax, and spreading love and positive vibes. Again, I used my imagination to pretend I was a powerful angel able to spray love and healing energy onto everyone in the crowd and beyond into the world.

Living in a mining town with young, carefree expats from around the world meant our crew became our family. Some weekends we would do progressive dinner parties. These parties consisted of walking with a wheelbarrow full of alcohol from house to house. Each house hosted a different course (hors d'oeuvres, entrée, main, cheese platter, dessert). Sometimes these dinner parties included themed cuisine and dress-ups, such as Mexican, American, French, and Italian. We were all very creative and by the end of the night, very wild.

Soul sisters

I remember the first time Nikki and I went on a long boozy lunch, just the two of us. Afterward, like old friends, we lay under her jacaranda tree and talked for hours—love, life, death, destiny, and spirits. Inside the house, Nikki's boyfriend Mark (one of the dance-floor PLUs we gave an invitation to) jammed with his band members. I exhaled loudly as my heartbeat synched with each jazz beat *I'm in paradise—a personal concert under the tree from my favorite movie, 'What Dreams May Come' and a new friend who totally gets me.*

A few weeks later, she and I watched the movie *Meet Joe Black*, in which Susan, the main female character, loses her father but gains her soul mate. I explained, "I lost Dad and gained you as a soul mate Nikki! Stitty and I had planned to go to Europe, but instead, dad got sick, and I came back to Australia. Had he not died I never would have met you in the middle of the Australian desert." When a tear rolled down my cheek, Nikki grabbed and cradled me, like a baby, in her strong, capable arms. Her emotional intelligence was impressive and explained why every man in town wanted to be in her presence and fell head over heels for her. She made whoever she was talking to feel like they were the only ones in the room. I will admit, I wondered if Stitty would fall in love with her.

The intensity of our relationship was intimate but not in a sexual way. Through Nikki, I discovered new adult friends can feel as close to me as Stitty. She allowed me to be authentic, joyful, and vulnerable. The mutual trust between us let me discover my true SELF and the false selves just disappeared. Her natural ability to articulately define my strengths and talents (in minute Virgo detail) allowed me to know myself from a female perspective. My female school friend Alex could do this too, but we had been best friends since we were 11, whereas Nikki only knew me as an adult. Personal qualities I viewed as common, Nikki described as unique. I was so surprised to hear that I was extraordinary. I realized how naive I was to think I was ordinary. I had taken my privilege for granted because it was a common denominator among my school and university friends. Nikki also showed me that my relationship with Stitty was rare.

Time to cut the umbilical cord

AFTER A FEW MONTHS IN KAL, I contacted the principal at my Sydney school to let her know I was not coming back after my second year's leave without pay. Resigning was a big deal for me as it meant I did not have a job to return to after our trip around Australia. I told her how grateful I was and acknowledged that to be given a year's leave without pay was incredible; to be given two years was unheard of. She gave me her blessings, "I'm sorry that you can't come back to teach the new year 11/12 PDHPE two-unit course, but I am happy Peter is cured. Whoever you work for, Katie is lucky to have you, and the door here is always open when you return to Sydney."

At that moment, I let go of the shore and floated into an uncharted chapter in my evolution. Stitty and I became unshackled from our Sydney ties and responsibilities for the first time. We could reinvent ourselves, do what we wanted, and live spontaneously. We could be plain old 'Stitty and Kitty' instead of Stitty: third-generation The Kings School and Kitty: third-generation Ascham School. We no longer had to conform to family, employment, and community roles. Without people's expectations looming, we could be whatever we imagined. No more Sunday family lunches meant we could party all night and recover with friends the next day, something we had never been able to do. Slowly, I began to embrace the adventure.

Stitty and I had never lived together before, so setting up house was new and exciting. Our place was always full of people, so I cooked a lot of food every night, just in case. Kal was where I began to cook. Mum had studied Cordon Bleu when we lived in Paris, so I was raised around beautiful food and fine dining, but I was on my own now and needed to learn the basics. So I bought a Donna Hay cookbook and taught myself by following recipes every night. By the time I left, I no longer needed cookbooks because I knew every technique in the book, what went with what, and how to combine flavors.

Psychic development

NIKKI and I consistently attended Macey's Wednesday night meditation circle at *The Crystal Den*. It was there that I learned that supernatural skills improve with practice. We did toning, which uses sounds to release chakra blockages, Native American greetings ("I saw you coming, I recognized you, our hearts are one, and you are truly truly beautiful"), and meditations. Each week we practiced psychometry by doing flower readings. On arrival, we would place a flower or a piece of jewelry on a tray. Macey would walk around the circle with the tray inviting each of us to select an item. We would then give that anonymous person a psychic reading by quieting the mind and doing automatic writing. The task consisted of freely writing whatever messages came through (mediumship). This skill was challenging because I, like many, often dismissed spirit communication as my imagination. As a result, I would second guess and doubt what I heard. However, when we read our readings out, time and time again, they were accurate. Sometimes mid-message, someone in the group would burst into tears or say it was precisely the answer they sought. I, too, noticed how many 'without a doubt' readings the group produced after two years of consistently practicing. My favorite story from this time was when I witnessed one of Nikki's messages. Nikki reported three things, "I saw a motorbike, a long, straight road, and the name Carl."

Macey said, "The flower belongs to me, Nikki, and that was my son Carl who was killed in a motorcycle accident on the road between Kalgoorlie and Esperance."

MY FIRST REBIRTH

Wednesday, March 1st

At midday I lay on a treatment bed in *The Crystal Den* to have my first rebirth. Why had I booked a rebirth? Stitty had one with Macey, so I wanted one too.

What is rebirth? It is a healing modality that utilizes a breathing technique to bring up birth trauma or other trauma to be resolved in the now. These days it's called breathwork.

Paul was Macey's apprentice; this was the first time he had ever facilitated a rebirth without Macey.

The hour-long session involved Paul verbally guiding me to breathe in and out of my nose without pauses. To evoke a rebirth experience, the breathing needed to be circular and uninterrupted by thoughts.

Paul could tell when I was thinking because my continuous breathing pattern would stop. So at these times, he would say, "What are you thinking about?"

I replied with random work-related things like, "The teachers are manipulating the students. The children are not communicating with their parents, I want to help people, but I've misplaced the papers I need."

Each time Paul replied, "Back to the breath now, Kitty."

About half an hour into the process, I asked the strangest question, "How do people feel when they are about to be contacted by E.T.s?" It was as if I sensed their presence.

Paul asked, "The spirit or the person?"

I started to laugh uncontrollably. I had never involuntarily laughed like this. Every time I stopped and tried to breathe, I would start to laugh loudly and hysterically again. My right leg flew up in the air, my back bridged off the bed, and my head arched right back. My eyes remained closed with my face contorted by an enormous open mouth encircled by smiling upturned lips.

I said between the bursts, "I don't know what's so funny!"

Maybe this is Dad making me laugh.

With this thought, I felt as if I was falling backward. Through the treatment bed, floor, and Earth, falling, falling. Like Alice, I was slipping away in slow motion. When I stopped falling, I found myself in a place I can only describe as pure bliss.

I said, "It's pure light; it's beautiful."

It felt divine like I had always imagined heaven. A soft, peaceful stillness. There were other spirits there with beautiful souls. I was filled with unconditional love. I sensed that we all came from this place and that we all returned to this place. I sensed I was just a head on the bed. Air moved around me but I had no body. I felt everywhere all at once - right, left, up, down, East, South, West, and North. Looking back, I think perhaps I was experiencing unity consciousness.

I sensed Dad was with me.

Then a bizarre sensation occurred. Even though my body remained lying on the bed, it felt as though my body was lifted at the hips. In my mind's eye I could see I was suspended with my head and feet remaining down near the bed. I became aware of numerous little other-dimensional beings to my left. They scurried around me and began examining me with larger heads and characteristic black eyes.

Dad, Should I be scared right now?

I heard *It's OK. They just want to have a look.*

So I relaxed and allowed them to examine me.

I felt my body being pressed through technology that I can only describe as an old mangle or meat-flattening machine. As the beings turned the handle, my body became paper-thin. The beings ran to the end of the bed and my body emerged as fine as delicate glass. They seemed to be busily scanning and analyzing my compressed cells.

They disappeared, and I disintegrated into the pure light I now call love frequency.

Dad mouthed *I love you,* but he had no voice. Then he disappeared too.

I spoke to Paul, "Paul, I'm having a complete out-of-body experience right now. Can you please leave me for a little while? I'd like to be alone."

I heard him leave and close the door behind him.

I decided to try shallow breathing because Stitty said when he breathed this way during his rebirth, it brought up his unresolved issues in the form of physical pain. Immediately, my left ear hurt, and my neck felt stiff.

Are these pains birth or childhood trauma?

I heard *You don't have to do this. I love you.*

I did not know who said it, but I smiled as soon as I comprehended these words, and my body became pure light again. I returned to a blissful state, to heaven, where I had been before. It was confirmation that I did not need a rebirth. I just needed to remember that I am loved unconditionally always and that nothing else matters. In hindsight, I think it was SELF who said *You don't have to do this. I love you* to remind me that when I am aligned to SELF (mySELF Expressing Love Frequency), pain does not exist. I am pure love. Since that day, I have heard *You don't have to do this. I love you* at times when I have felt triggered to identify with a false self. As soon as I hear these words, I return to my true SELF with an expanded perspective. These words shift my vibration and lift my frequency. This SELF-realization catalyst showed me that health ease is my birthright and I do not need to suffer.

Paul returned to the treatment room and started to bring me back to my body.

I sighed, "Paul, I don't think I can return from this place. It's so beautiful. I want to stay here longer."

Slowly I returned and wiggled my fingers and toes. My rebirth was a catalyst for my SELF-realization because I witnessed other dimensional beings. I chose not to focus on their intentions. Instead, be grateful that I could empathize with others who have had similar experiences. After this encounter, I imagined I had space babies somewhere in the galaxy. I thought, *OK, space babies, I know you are out there; please contact me. I am open to my multidimensionality and eager to learn whatever you want to teach me.*

Then I waited.

Group telepathy

AT MACEY'S last Wednesday night meditation circle before she left town, I experienced telepathy again. We were sitting in a large circle as Macey expressed how much she valued our friendship, how far we had all come, and how powerful the energy was in the Great Victoria Desert. When she finished speaking, we all sat in silence. Suddenly, I had this overwhelming urge to speak. I felt shy, and my heart began racing in my chest. Eventually, I could not contain myself, and I just spoke up. The words felt incredibly insightful, inspiring, and on point. I had no idea who was talking, but I knew it was not me. My gratitude for Macey and the group tumbled out, directed by a higher force. I finished with, "Macey, thank you for teaching us that whatever happens is the perfect happening."

When I finished, a meditator spoke up, "Wow, Kitty, you just said what I was thinking but couldn't put into words."

Nikki added, "Shit, Kits, you just read my bloody mind; how did you do that?"

Macey was glowing with mother-type love. She smiled and looked each of us in the eyes, "Kitty didn't do that; the group did. You have been working together for so long that you communicate telepathically. You are all psychic. Kitty trusted herself enough to enter the flow state and let the words come through without filtering them. Don't dismiss these occurrences—own them—you did this together. People tell us that we can't do these things so we don't believe we can. So much so that when they occur we either don't notice them or we write them off as coincidences. The only reason these supernatural skills remain dormant in most people is that no one is encouraging them. By owning and celebrating these experiences, we bring them into mainstream consciousness, normalize them, and shift into a new paradigm."

Creating community

I DEVOTED myself to my PDHPE teaching job at North Kal and used my research from my USYD Honors Thesis on HIV/AIDS and drug education to develop the ultimate Health Promoting School. I teamed up with the WA School Drug Education Team and Local Area Health. At the end of the following year, our HEAPS (Health Education and Physical Skills) program won numerous state-wide awards, including runners-up in the WA Premier's Award for Customer Focus after the WA Health Department! We also won first place in two categories of the WA Australian Council of Health, Physical Education and Recreation (ACHPER) awards. The following year, I worked part-time at Centercare, Kalgoorlie as a Drug Education Consultant. My counselor colleague Pat had recently lost her husband, and the veil between them was so thin that they could still communicate and even make love. I could listen to Pat's stories for hours because I knew Stitty and I could do the same if anything ever happened to one of us. Later that year, Nikki and I had an opportunity to join forces professionally through the WA School Drug Education Team. We attended a five-day train-the-trainer course in Perth and then ran the first teacher/counselor-run drug education course of its kind in regional WA. We had always dreamed of giving back to our community. We were on fire; the impact we created over those few days felt like a testament to our vision, creativity, and passion. The gifts we unlocked were the ones I activated when I decided to stay in Kal as a creator instead of a victim. I consciously chose to step onto my highest timeline and begin living purposefully instead of waiting around for Stitty to propose. I shifted from focusing on little me with little petty problems to contributing to the welfare of an entire community, creating a chain reaction, a metaphorical rolling snowball of experiences in alignment with the good of all.

As one chapter closed

WE LIVED in Kal for two and half years until our crew decided to move on, and everyone went in different directions. Stitty and I had saved significant money, so we decided to travel. The Kal days were some of the best days of my life because I made lifelong friends who loved me just the way I am.

Another chapter began

Saturday, January 27th
We flew out of Sydney on a 12-month trip around the world.

Our first stop was Mumbai, India. After that, we set off for seven months backpacking through the states (from south to north): Karnataka, Goa, Maharashtra, Madhya Pradesh, Rajasthan, Delhi, Himachal Pradesh, Ladakh Union Territory, then we traveled through Nepal and returned to India to explore Uttar Pradesh.

9

LEARNING HOW THE BUDDHA MEDITATED SELF

29 years old

The Buddha's teaching of liberation entails a highly empirical study of the mind to become intimate with all arising thoughts, so intimate that we wake up over and over.

Sunday, May 6th

IN NORTHERN INDIA, Mcleod Ganj, Dharamsala, Kangra district of Himachal Pradesh, we discovered His Holiness, Tenzin Gyatso, the Fourteenth Dalai Lama, was doing a public greeting outside his home in exile. So we joined the line with hundreds of people from around the world beaming from ear to ear with joyful excitement, knowing they were about to meet a provocative, gifted man, international head of state, philosopher, freedom fighter, Buddhist monk, and Nobel Peace Prize winner. When he shook my hand, I said to him, "I will not waste this precious human rebirth." He beamed, nodded, and chuckled as unconditional love and support poured from his eyes.

I had just completed an eight-day silent *Introduction to Buddhism* retreat at the Tushita Tibetan Mahayana Buddhist Meditation Centre in Dharamkot, up the hill from Mcleod Ganj, followed by a ten-day silent insight meditation retreat called *Teachings of Wisdom and Loving Kindness* with Bryan Tucker in the local *Tse Chok Ling* Monastery, down the hill from Mcleod Ganj.

Bryan, from the US, had practiced insight meditation since the late 1970s. His first teacher was Ram Dass. After that, he practiced under the tutelage of well-known Western teachers such as Joseph Goldstein, Sharon Salzberg, Jack Kornfield, and Christopher Titmuss at the US Insight Meditation Society (IMS) in Massachusetts. In 1979, Bryan traveled to Burma to attend a three-month intensive retreat under the supervision of the Ven. Mahasi Sayadaw, who was a highly-respected Theravada Buddhist monk. Theravada Buddhism is the form of the Buddha's teachings that took root in Burma, Laos, Cambodia, and Thailand, which differs from Mahayana Buddhism, most notably practiced in Tibet. Theravada Buddhist texts, preserved in the Pali language, were considered the oldest and most faithful to the Buddha's original words. Bryan also attended long retreats at Gaia House meditation center in England and retreats with Christopher in Bodh Gaya, India, the place of the Buddha's enlightenment. Christopher co-founded Gaia House and authorized Bryan to teach three years before I met Bryan in Northern India.

Thursday, May 3rd

ON DAY nine of Bryan's insight meditation retreat, I first experienced a different reality. I was a regular woman, new to meditation, with no unique qualities. I was no different from you. There was no reason for its occurrence. Reflecting now, I think it happened because of my calling to share this other reality with others.

A few weeks earlier, I had read Vicki Mackenzie's *Cave in the Snow,* a story about Tenzin Palmo (now Jetsunma), a western woman ordained as a nun in the Drukpa Lineage of the Kagyu school of Tibetan Buddhism who spent 12 years in a cave. She referred to a deeper level of consciousness, but I had no idea what that meant. I could never have imagined a different reality, so experiencing it surprised me.

I was meditating, as I had for the past nine days (17 days, if I include the first retreat) on a meditation cushion with my teacher Bryan and the other retreat participants. A thought came to me that I had never thought before *You don't need to think to breathe, so don't think.* At that point, I seemed to move into another reality where I existed in an unknown state. It differed from the feeling of bliss I experienced during my Kalgoorlie rebirth. I did not know where I was; it felt surreal, difficult to verbalize, and impossible to comprehend. It felt empty but full, infinitely expansive, peaceful, and void of thoughts: nothing but everything simultaneously, a weird paradox. For the first time in my life, I had arrived at a place where I was supremely content. I was not doing anything; I was just there. I wondered how I would ever exist in my world again after this experience. I saw true reality sitting juxtaposed with the life I had known to be true. I felt more at home here than where I had dwelled for 29 years. I was pure existence without concepts, labels, or preferences. There were no words in my repertoire to describe this foreign phenomenon. When I tried, the ones I chose did not go together. This was because linear time did not exist there. Everything was NOW. So, I was before time, beyond time, before space, before everything but also knowing everything was about to happen. It felt like I slipped in between Creation's breaths. As if my perception had somehow turned from the doer to the perceiver. It was bizarre; even my breaths were perceived by this strange feeling that came before everything, confirming I come before my breaths. I am before awareness. *How was this possible?* This point of view was so new to me that I felt breathless in anticipation. I was convinced I was witnessing something extraordinarily rare which made me feel somehow unworthy.

I wondered *What am I? Where am I? How did I not know this sense of self? Is this true SELF? Could I live in my world as SELF?*

I noticed I was thinking and returned to the emptiness. This emptiness felt familiar as if I had been there before. Perhaps I was there, before creation, at the moment before anything happened; maybe we all were. I sensed the potential of everything about to be birthed. It felt as if everything that had ever existed had either not happened yet or was about to happen again and I was resting in the space between. I felt bizarrely like the awareness that witnessed creation, like an impulse, poised to act or not act and comfortable either way. Nothing to judge, nothing to do, nothing to think about. It was as if I was the only one there and everything that had ever been created came from my original thought. In hindsight I think I was in a strange space before the first thought. Perhaps this is everything's true SELF. Maybe we can all identify with this formlessness, and when we do all previous senses of self disintegrate and we realize SELF is not a separate self, only a feeling of unity, an infinite essence that is the source of everything. SELF has nothing to do and nowhere to go. SELF is awareness, it is one consciousness, and each of us is an aspect of SELF in human form with an individuated consciousness expressing it'sSELF/herSELF/himSELF. Each possesses the same potential to return to their original consciousness. Here, the separate selves merge into one again. I had just directly experienced a self-realization catalyst: SELF is the oneness before anything takes form.

I had learned *We are all one,* but for the first time, I was experiencing it. The idea moved from an intellectual belief to personal truth.

Participants vow to be silent during the retreat but can speak to the teacher. I went straight to Bryan and told him what I had perceived. He simply said, "Do not cling to this experience. Deep insights occur during a retreat but are not the retreat's goal. Try to find joy in all aspects of the practice, not just in the good bits. If you become attached to recreating that experience, you will miss the point of the practice. The practice is to not grasp at anything."

When I went back to my room, I flipped through my travel diary, where I wrote book quotes that inspired me. An excerpt from Tenzin Palmo jumped out, *It's not what you gain it's what you lose. It's like unpeeling the layers of an onion, that's what you have to do. My quest was to understand what perfection meant. Now, I realize that on one level, we have never moved away from it. It is only our deluded perception which prevents our seeing what we already have. The more you realize, the more you realize there is nothing to realize. The idea that there's somewhere we have got to get to, and something we have to attain, is our basic delusion. Who is there to attain it anyway...There is the thought, and there is the knowing of the thought. And the difference between being aware of the thought and just thinking is immense...Normally we are so identified with our thoughts and emotions, that we are them. We are the happiness...anger...fear. We have to learn to step back and know our thoughts and emotions are just thoughts and emotions. They are just mental states. They are not solid, they're transparent. One has to know that and then not identify with the knower. One has to know that the knower is not somebody...that was the Buddha's great insight...You think you've got it when you understand that you are not the thought or the feeling...that brings you to the question: 'Who am I?'...to realize that the further back we go the more open and empty the quality of our consciousness becomes. Instead of finding some solid little eternal entity which is 'I,' we get back to this vast spacious mind which is interconnected with all living beings. In this space you have to ask, where is the 'I,' and where is the 'other.'*

I let her words sink in. *Did I just experience the interconnectedness of all things that Tenzin Palmo referred to? Is enlightenment realizing that everything is interconnected?*

The Mahayana monks taught me during the eight-day Tushita *Introduction to Buddhism* retreat that consciousness is a dependent arising. They said the Buddha referred to the continuity of consciousness that existed before conception. I believe I witnessed this original consciousness on the meditation cushion.

———

THE BUDDHA'S name in Sanskrit means fully awakened. The Buddha was born Prince Siddhartha Gautama to a wealthy family two-and-a-half thousand years ago. Prince Siddhartha's mother died soon after his birth, and his aunt raised him. King Śuddhodana, the Buddha's father, tried to shield him from suffering due to a prophecy from Siddhartha's birth. A highly regarded sage predicted that Siddhartha would either become a great king or a great renunciate - a Buddha. King Śuddhodana hoped that his son would never realize his remarkable Buddha potential, instead remain in the palace and eventually rule the kingdom. To distract his son, the king provided endless worldly pleasures. When Siddhartha was 29 years old, he finally ventured outside the palace, encountered suffering (old age, sickness, deformity, and death), and saw the futility of the fleeting pleasures he had become accustomed to. This realization awakened Prince Siddhartha's interest in something more reliable and meaningful. As a result, he left his home to meditate in the forest. After many years of dedicated practice and overcoming many mental obstacles, he freed himself and attained enlightenment, thus becoming Gautama Buddha. By this time, he was 35 years old. He vowed to assist others in liberating themselves. In his first sermon after enlightenment, referred to in the original Pali texts as the *Dhammacakkappavattana Sutta*, or the *Turning of the Wheel of the Dharma* discourse (*sutta*), he encouraged his first five disciples to avoid the extremes of worldly pleasure on the one hand and asceticism (extreme mortification of the body) on the other. Instead, he counseled them to take the middle way between these two extremes, leading them to attain enlightenment.

In this discourse, the Buddha taught the four truths of the noble ones, those beings who live freely and are committed to the non-harming of others. The first Noble Truth states: there is suffering (Duḥkha) in life. However, Bryan explained that this does not mean all life is only suffering. If the causes are there for suffering, there will be suffering, but if the causes are not there, there will not be suffering. Therefore, the first truth involves acknowledging that there is suffering in life, and it is to be understood.

What is suffering, exactly? A straightforward definition is that which is hard to bear. The Buddha examined what it is in our minds that makes things hard to bear. We have all experienced times when it is easier and harder to bear difficulties in our lives. What governs that ability? If we try answering that question, we can say we understand suffering, perhaps in a new way. We have learned from it instead of merely trying to get rid of it, which is our usual, unthinking reaction. What can suffering teach us? What might we learn from it? Asking these kinds of questions is the First Noble Truth.

The second Noble Truth looks at the cause of suffering. This cause is rooted in our minds rather than in the outside world. In the Buddha's analysis, suffering arises from relating to our experiences in unskillful ways. These experiences arise from physical sensations experienced through our body and thoughts about what we perceive. Bryan explained that craving (desire for pleasure) and aversion (desire to avoid displeasure) cause suffering, "We live our lives constantly trying to gain pleasure and push away whatever is unpleasant. It is an exhausting way to live. We constantly struggle to get things we want and avoid things we do not want. We project our happiness into the future by thinking *I will be happy when I have this and that*—in the meantime, manipulating, stressing, and striving for something here and now that is often beyond our grasp. This craving and aversion are in themselves suffering. These two forces are what make something hard to bear. We are rarely in peace, other than when we are fast asleep because we go from happy when we get what we want to sad when we do not. Despite our wanting it to be otherwise, we can not make pleasant things last because it is not in their nature to do so, and we can't always get rid of or avoid unpleasant things because they will always be a part of life. But the habits of mind to grasp for the pleasant and push away the unpleasant run deep. This constant pulling and pushing for and against our experience is the cause of our mental suffering. The tragedy of our lives is that we do not realize there is an alternative to living in thrall to these forces of greed and hate within our minds."

The alternative is the third Noble Truth, which involves the cessation of suffering by abandoning craving and aversion and resting with what is. The Buddha recommended we live by universal truths (*Dharma*) by discovering our natural state of being instead of being caught up and identified with deluded constructs. I had experienced my natural state of being on the meditation cushion; now, I had to stop identifying with the false mental states I had been identified with since childhood such as unworthiness. Bryan said we could be free from the bondage of our minds by being aware of these tendencies and then relating to them in a new way. Bryan described a powerful image of holding a lump of burning hot coal. The hot coal is like our deluded thoughts that cause suffering. When we wake up and realize we are holding a hot coal, we do not think twice about what to do. We let go of it instantly.

The First Noble Truth describes when we become aware we are holding something that is harming us (we feel it directly). The Second Noble Truth is realizing we are suffering because we are holding onto something we did not previously realize was causing us to suffer. The Third Noble Truth is like knowing we can instantly let go of this painful thing and experience the freedom that comes from that release. The more we do this, the less robotic and conditioned we become. We begin to experience life as it is as soon as we practice the Buddha's suggestion, not to identify with anything whatsoever, anywhere (this goal can take lifetimes to achieve). The goal as a metaphor could be keeping the hand open—not picking up a hot coal, not pushing away a hot coal, just being aware of it. Bryan explained that the seeing of the suffering is the letting go.

The last Noble Truth is the Noble Eightfold Path, which leads to awakening through the cessation of suffering. This involves freeing oneself from the habit of cravings and aversions. This path can be divided into three sections. The first section consists of morality–purity of vocal and physical actions (right speech, right actions, and right livelihood). The second section consists of meditation practice and mental training to see through and be free from habitual tendencies of one's mind (right effort, right awareness (mindfulness), and right concentration). The third section consists of liberating wisdom and insight, purifying the mind of ways of thinking that cause suffering (right view and right intention). This path is like gardening. If we do not pay attention and take action, the weeds (delusional thoughts) will overtake our minds. So we stop doing unwholesome acts such as killing, stealing, sexual misconduct, lying, harsh speech, or taking drugs or intoxicants to the point of being a danger to ourselves or others. Then we plant virtuous seeds instead of those that cause us to suffer. So we think and cultivate wholesome thoughts such as love. As we gain more and more wisdom (through meditating and weeding out delusional thoughts), we develop deep compassion, which turns the inner work into outer action that assists others in reducing their suffering.

According to the Buddha, a certain kind of consciousness continues briefly at our physical death and gets reborn into another body in one of the six realms of existence (we are in the human realm). This birth, aging, death, and rebirth pattern is called *samsara*, a Sanskrit word that means cycling through one existence after another. According to this doctrine, rebirth is conditioned by the results of our past actions, called *karma*. Our thoughts, words, and deeds have karmic consequences that pass into the next birth, like seeds sown in this lifetime bearing fruit in the next one.

The Buddha's teaching invites us to consider viewing the ultimate aim of life as escaping this karmic loop by becoming enlightened: seeing the true nature of existence and learning how to end the suffering of *samsara's* endless wandering. But if our *karma* dictates rebirth, we should hope to return to the human realm, where we can develop the greatest motivation to live freely and benefit others. In this realm, we can actively purify the *samsaric* mind from deluded states (attachment, greed, jealousy, pride, anger, judgment, laziness, hatred, and ignorance), which leave us disturbed, confused, and unhappy. Purifying delusions can lead to great peace even within *samsara*. Another word to describe this peace is *nirvana*, the mind at rest: unagitated, free from greed toward pleasant experiences, hatred toward unpleasant ones, and delusion, so we can become capable of understanding the causes and cure for suffering. Realizing *nirvana* is possible at any moment despite the suffering present in *samsara* (birth, aging, sickness, death, separation, encountering what we do not like, not getting what we want, and dealing with a mind that is programmed to suffer). Once we realize *nirvana* deeply and integrate that understanding more and more into our daily lives, we attain the freedom of the Buddha, we realize our own Buddha nature or gain Buddhahood. We can then choose to enlighten others, as the Buddha did throughout his life. Such a person is known as a *Bodhisattva*, who has developed compassion for all beings caught in samsaric existence and spontaneously acts to relieve their suffering. A Bodhisattva selflessly returns to samsara at physical death to continue leading all living beings into an enlightened, liberated life.

Bryan did not dwell upon any teachings about rebirth; instead, he emphasized paying attention to our current lives by saying, "What seems to get reborn here and now is the sense of self. It seems permanent and continuous but isn't." Bryan told us, "I regard this present moment as a re-birth and an opportunity to let go of past unwholesome karma. For most of us, our rebirth here and now can be problematic. Still, there is a way to transform our suffering right now by realizing freedom from *samsara* in this very life, as the Buddha put it, by gaining insight into the true nature of our experiences. Freedom can arise at any moment when our minds are at rest, not reacting out of habit to whatever we experience."

The Buddha's teachings emphasize that things are uncertain, and constantly changing. This fact of impermanence is inherent in existence. Thus, there is no way to make pleasant things last or keep unpleasant things from arising. But suffering can be understood as something extra laid onto our ever-changing experiences because of habitually reacting with greed or hatred toward what is pleasant or unpleasant.

Most of us need a certain degree of *samadhi* (concentration or calmness of mind) to realize that transformative insights into impermanence have the power to break the habits of the mind that causes suffering. A silent retreat can provide the most conducive conditions for the mind to calm down enough so that insights into impermanence can arise by themselves.

To develop *samadhi* that leads to such insight, Bryan taught traditional techniques based on one of the Buddha's most famous and influential discourses: the *Satipatthana Sutta*, or *The Four Foundations of Mindfulness*. In this discourse, the Buddha identifies four areas of our experiences to which he invites us to bring more awareness (or mindfulness). Why? To develop two essential mental capacities: *samadhi* (calmness) and *vipassana* (insight, or seeing clearly). We can liken the mind with *samadhi* to a pond of clean water that is relatively still. Restless thoughts can be thought of like waves on the water's surface, not allowing us to see through it. But with enough calmness of mind, when those thoughts are not present or have been significantly reduced, the pond's surface is still, and we can see things in the pond more clearly, perhaps to the bottom. This kind of clear seeing can occur when *samadhi* is strong enough.

The four areas or foundations for awareness given in this *sutta* are the body, feelings, mind states, and mind objects. Concerning the first of these areas, the body, the Buddha advised bringing awareness to the basic four postures our bodies usually adopt: sitting, standing, walking, and reclining. In the sitting posture, the Buddha considered the breath the most beneficial object of attention. The most common practice people associate with meditation is following the breath. Regarding feelings, the Buddha did not mean emotions but rather the sense that all our experiences are either pleasant, unpleasant, or neutral. The breath, for example, is considered to be a neutral experience. The third area concerns bringing more attention to states of mind such as sleepiness, calmness, or restlessness. The fourth area, mind objects, reflects upon a list of topics fundamental to the Buddha's teachings, such as the Four Noble Truths.

All meditative exercises are techniques that focus attention on one particular thing to the exclusion of others to develop the ability to be undistracted and see more clearly.

Many different practice styles have arisen over the centuries based on the *Satipatthana Sutta*, such as the one promoted by the well-known Indian meditation teacher S.N. Goenka, who emphasized the sitting posture alone. Others, such as the one developed by the Ven. Mahasi Sayadaw of Burma includes walking as a formal practice in its own right and bringing awareness to all other daily activities such as eating, washing dishes, or brushing one's teeth. Bryan was trained in this latter style and not in the Goenka tradition, though he had taken a Goenka-style retreat in Nepal before teaching independently. Goenka was an Indian businessman who learned a particular *vipassana* meditation technique in Burma and then traveled from Burma to India in 1969 when he began teaching his method. Goenka-style retreats became well known around India and the West, so much so that meditators often recognized the word Vipassana (with a capital V) as his retreat style.

On Bryan's retreat, after a day or two of alternating periods of sitting and walking practice, all done in silence (other than his instructions), my mind began to calm down from the usual rush of thoughts and images that typically consumed my waking consciousness. At that point, *samadhi* got strong enough to allow my attention to penetrate more deeply into the various sensations associated with my breath while sitting and the movement and touch of my legs and feet while walking. I began to experience these sensations as impermanent, this is what insight means. From the moment I woke up until I fell asleep, the entire day was an opportunity to practice living with this insight of waking up out of the normal dream-like state I usually found myself in. Then, when I woke up, I could see what was really happening—I could see that everything comes and goes. What made insight practice different from other practices was that the objects of attention for insight practice are all changing themselves. In other forms of meditation that aim only to develop *samadhi*, the objects stay the same. Those latter kinds of meditation are called *samatha* practices. They include techniques such as looking at a candle flame, visualizing an image, or silently repeating a mantra (usually a Sanskrit phrase) to oneself. By contrast, insight practice focuses on constantly changing objects, such as the sensations from the abdomen rising and falling or the air going in and out of the nostrils while breathing. The *samadhi* developed on these changing objects may not be as intense as an unchanging one such as a mantra. But that was the point: I did not have to have overpowering concentration to develop penetrating insights. The Buddha said it would suffice to establish *samadhi* "to the extent necessary" for insight to arise. I was to discover this liberating truth for myself on day nine.

Another difference between Bryan's insight meditation retreat and Goenka's Vipassana retreat was that Bryan offered evening *Dharma* talks. He began his series of talks by encouraging us to follow the Buddha's example and recognize that the point of life is to wake up. Bryan explained that meditation activates our innate ability to wake up even–or especially–during problems and hardships. Bryan said that meditation would enable us to observe the transparent nature of everything that arises, allowing us to see through these passing occurrences and get a sense, however vague at first, of something much vaster than our small selves. He referred to something– unmoving, unconstructed, limitless, and unchanging. He said this something held everything else, was not different from everything but was instead intimately connected with everything, something we might call our true nature/true SELF.

To witness the transparent nature of things, Bryan taught me how to use a noting technique during meditation that he learned from one of his most influential teachers, Ven. Mahasi Sayadaw of Burma. As previously stated, Mahasi's method emphasized developing continuity of awareness (or mindfulness) throughout the entire day, not just during meditation. Thus, every activity became a practice. During formal sitting sessions, Mahasi's method was to make a soft mental note of whatever was happening in the present moment without getting caught up in analyzing. I noticed what happened to the objects of attention when they were noted; they did not stick around; instead, they tended to disappear, regardless of whether they were unpleasant or pleasant. Bryan taught me to note things this way: *Seeing is happening* (instead of *I am seeing*) or *Thinking is happening* (instead of *I am thinking*). Bryan explained, "Noting things in this way leaves aside the often troublesome notion of the 'I' who is supposed to be behind all experiences, the thinker of the thoughts, the one who hears the sounds, and so on. So seeing, hearing, tasting, smelling, touching, thinking are happening without the extra sense they are happening to me."

This noting technique, when done diligently, quickly reveals the essentially self-less nature of experiences, the way they arise and pass of their own accord, not subject to my control. When Bryan was practicing in Burma under Mahasi's leadership, Bryan was encouraged to note all activities with utmost precision and clarity. So, for example, while eating, meditators noted in the following way.

"When you look at the food, note *looking, seeing*.
When you arrange the food, *arranging*.
When you bring the food to the mouth, *bringing*.
When you bend the neck forward, *bending*.
When the food touches the mouth, *touching*.
When placing the food in the mouth, *placing*.
When the mouth closes, *closing*.
When withdrawing the hand, *withdrawing*.
Should the hand touch the plate, *touching*.
When straightening the neck, *straightening*.
When in the act of chewing, *chewing*.
When you are aware of the taste, *tasting*.
When swallowing the food, *swallowing*.
Should the food be felt touching the throat, *touching*."

(From one of Mahasi Sayadaw's instruction pamphlets, *Practical Insight Meditation*)

IT TOOK enormous discipline and patience to apply the noting technique, but Bryan said it was important to try our best. After a few days of silence and stillness, I began seeing benefits. My mind and body started settling into the routine, and the discipline did not feel so harsh.

Bryan explained the Buddha's teachings regarding the true nature of things. All objects (including our sense of self) are dependent arisings, made up of parts that, when put together, become identifiable but, in essence, do not exist in and of themselves, apart from everything else. In truth, things are interconnected, and separation occurs only in one's way of looking. Separation occurs in the mind. This explanation helped with my deep-rooted habit of clinging to things that gave me pleasure, like my body, loved ones, and belongings. My ego's sense of 'I' as permanent and its tendency to refer to things as *mine* was shattered when I directly experienced my deconstructed sense of self on the meditation cushion on day nine. I realized that nothing exists independent of all other phenomena, which confirmed the Buddha's teaching that ignorance of the true nature of reality is our principal delusion. Soon I realized that I am not my physical sensations, thoughts, past actions, regrets, or stories. This was another SELF-realization catalyst: I had interpreted myself and everything in my world incorrectly.

Bryan confirmed my realization when he said, "If I see that the self or 'I' isn't so solid after all, I can see that it is not something to take too seriously. Instead, it is something to be taken lightly. Maybe enlightenment means lightening up! Maybe it means moving lightly through life because I've seen that things are essentially light, in and of themselves. They are fleeting and insubstantial, nothing to grasp hold of too tightly. When I see the world in this new way, I can never see it the old way again. The landscape of life hasn't changed. But I'm seeing everything differently now. I see things I didn't notice before. Everything is different, yet nothing is different. There are still the same sights, sounds, sensations, and thoughts arising. But my relationship with them is vastly different. I no longer see a center to which all experience is supposed to refer. There are just sights, sounds, and so on. They no longer belong to anyone. They don't refer back to anyone. They aren't me or mine. And this includes the very real felt sense of self! A great Thai meditation master and teacher of anattā (the word for 'not self' in the original Buddhist texts), Achaan Buddhadasa, said, "The 'I' is not I." I tend to say it this way–there is no I within 'I.' The I itself is self-less."

The techniques I learned on Bryan's insight meditation retreat taught me to be keenly aware of sensations in my body as they arose, paying close attention to all of them, even the painful ones. When one became unbearable, I was encouraged to focus my awareness on my respiration until the pain subsided or concentrate on the part of the body that was not in pain. I used a mantra *This too shall pass* that helped me stay with my practice, proving that sensations come and go when I remain present with my breath. The breath became a refuge for me, my constant companion, to which I could return again and again (if I only remembered). Eventually, I realized the breath was always available, even though I often forgot about it and got lost instead in memories, plans, images, thoughts, and emotions. Behind these distractions, the breath kept going, by itself, throughout my meditation sessions. I began to see why the Buddha spoke about the breath as the best object of meditation he had ever discovered. Soon, I was able to apply the skill of returning to the breath even when the most potent emotions or the most compelling forgotten memories surfaced. Practice gave me the confidence necessary to stay with my breath longer and longer. At first, I was incapable of staying with the breath for more than a single breath! Without my mind racing off, I could not even take two breaths in a row! However, I improved as I followed Bryan's advice, "Do not invest your energy in things that come and go."

Meditation showed me that I have a choice: *let my thoughts wander unconsciously or wake up and return to the awareness of the breath.* As a result, I noticed my experiences started to change. For example, I surprised myself when I resisted scratching an itch and felt it fade away instead. Soon I began to extend my meditation practice throughout the day and transfer this skill to daily activities. I realized I had the same choice: *let my thoughts unravel and think, speak and act unconsciously, or wake up and return to the awareness of the breath.* I realized Bryan's words, "True happiness is found in the mind's relationship to things rather than things themselves." For example, I went without the second plate of food and noticed that the urge to eat more passed away, and I got up in the early morning without giving in to the momentary desire to remain sleeping. My daily meditation practice seemed to create an inner space that cultivated the mindfulness necessary to be non-reactive. Each time I surrendered and opened up to the moment as it was, I expanded my boundaries which showed me I could tolerate more than I expected.

Bryan described this mindfulness as a form of renunciation, which he considered a cornerstone of the practice. Why? Because although it has a negative connotation, renunciation is something quite beneficial. It is the mind free of addictions. It realizes the peace that comes when I no longer chase after every thought, image, or impulse that pops into my head. Can I relate to things differently without wanting or needing anything? Can I practice being more accepting of things that come and go? Perhaps with the thought *It is not good; it is not bad; it just is*. When I practice relating to things without judgment, there is no longer the usual reaction. There is no clinging with greed to pleasant thoughts or avoiding with hate unpleasant thoughts, just a state of ease. There is a sense that whatever is happening now is enough.

Retreat conditions forced me to accept my environment the way it was because my usual distractions were prohibited (talking, devices, writing, comfort eating, drugs). Unable to escape my mind by searching for happiness in things outside of me, I had to ask myself *Where can I find joy in the absence of distractions?* I realized that I did not have to be a victim of my mind's usual tendencies. I could say *No* to these tendencies and wake up repeatedly. This renunciation freed my mind from thinking or doing things that cause me suffering. After a while, I discovered joy in the moment as it was, without grasping or pushing away. Bryan quoted Achaan Chaa (a Theravada Buddhist monk of the Thailand Forest tradition), who said, "What joy to discover that there is no happiness in this world." I found this quote to be accurate because if I honestly looked back on my life, I could not say happiness was out there in some object in the world; instead, it lay inside me, in my responses to life's changing experiences. Ultimate happiness, it seemed to me, would be realizing a sense of peace that does not depend on any conditions for its existence. Could I take this unconditional happiness into my daily life so that the retreat experience would have relevance under any circumstances?

During the retreat, Bryan taught us some of the Buddha's meditations designed specifically as antidotes to the three poisons of the mind: greed, hate, and delusion. These are known as the *Brahma Vihara* (or Divine Abiding) meditations and contain four essential Buddhist practices: loving-kindness (*Mettā*), appreciative joy (*Mudita*), compassion (*Karuna*), and equanimity (*Upekkha*). These meditations emphasized that every living being wants to be happy and avoid suffering, just as I do, which means all beings are equal. They deserve equal treatment. This meditation trained my brain to view everyone, even people I have difficulty with, as I view my loved ones, allowing me to love people who challenge me as much as I love my family members. So, even if someone wronged me, I would respond with a wish for that person to attain enlightenment through our interaction. I would put their potential growth before my immediate discomfort. The more I view others as equal, the more motivated I will be to act altruistically with a genuine, authentic desire to help others.

Bryan also taught us antidotes to the Five Hindrances often occurring during meditation. These negative mind states are sense desire, anger, sloth, restlessness, and doubt, which can overtake my mind and lead me toward unwholesome action. He used that famous image of the still forest pool, described so well by Achaan Chaa, in which I am trying to see everything clearly, right through to the bottom. Sense desire-like water is water clouded by colored dyes, anger-like water is water boiling, sloth-like water is water loaded with seaweed, restless-like water is water whipped by the wind, and doubt-like water is water packed with mud. All these hindrances make it impossible to see clearly to the bottom of the pool. But, in one sense, the water is not affected by any of these temporary states of mind. Throughout, the still forest pool itself remains pure. Therefore, during mediation, I do not have to get caught up with (or identify with) negative states; instead, I can apply an antidote. For example, if I felt anger, I would think *Watch this emotion pass like a dark cloud.* If I felt restless, I would challenge myself to sit for two minutes without moving a single muscle. If I felt doubt, I would think *That is doubt arising.* If I felt sleepy, I would do a walking meditation instead of succumbing to the temptation to lie down. If I felt agitated, I would distract myself by utilizing my sense of hearing to focus on distant sounds.

In hindsight, I realize that this teaching was a SELF-realization catalyst: SELF is pure and perfect. Illusory negative and positive mind states temporarily pass in front of SELF's radiance as storm clouds and rainbows pass before the sun. They do not affect SELF; they do not make it better and they do not make it worse.

Bryan also invited me to see where I placed my attention on retreat. Was I mainly focusing on the suffering, or did I notice moments of joy? I experimented with this question and noticed that the more I focused on joy, the more it appeared. Alternatively, the more I focused on suffering, the more suffering appeared. I discovered that I naturally focused on gratitude, abundance, and bliss most of the time. Sometimes I suffered from boredom, but overall I walked around feeling joyful with a massive smile. I loved not talking and being mindful. It made me realize I have very little negative karma. I felt a tremendous amount of compassion for other participants. Some of them occasionally started uncontrollably crying since retreats can release pent-up emotions from memories of past hurts. I would send them love energetically or physically (I made a bowl of flowers with a floating candle in the center for my upset roommate).

Saturday, May 5th

WHEN I LEFT the retreat (the morning after day 10), I thought about Bryan's story from *A Journey in Ladakh* by Andrew Harvey. It was about a starving man. There was fruit in the next room, but the starving man had to walk there. No one could walk there for him, bring the food, or make him walk there. First, he had to believe the fruit was there. Then he had to take steps toward it, powered by blind faith. After 18 days of retreat, this metaphorical story profoundly impacted me the most. I did not need blind faith because I witnessed SELF and true reality directly. Therefore, I had confidence born from experience. This confidence fueled my conviction to realize enlightenment for myself. To achieve this, I would have to trust the Buddha's teachings and follow his path without being distracted by people with less conviction. I would have to engage in rigorous self-inquiry and endure the discomfort of breaking old thought habits. Enlightenment would take undying determination but having experienced freedom on the meditation cushion, I knew the sacrifice would be worth it.

I reflected on Tenzin Palmo's quote from *Cave in the Snow*, scribbled in my travel diary, *The thing is, we say we want to be Enlightened, but we don't really. Only bits of us want to be Enlightened. The ego which thinks how nice, comfortable, pleasant it would be. But to really drop everything and go for it. We could do it in a moment but we don't do it. And the reason is we are too lazy. We are stopped by fear and lethargy...we have no one to blame but ourselves. This is why we stay in Samsara because we always find excuses. Instead, we should wake ourselves up. The whole Buddhist Path is about waking up. Yet the desire to keep sleeping is so strong*, as I looked at the Himalayan Mountain Range. I imagined her, at age 33, in a cave at 13 000 feet. I realized that enlightenment is available to us all, right now—at every moment because we are already free, should we choose to see it that way.

We are enlightened every time we decide to wake up instead of staying unaware and asleep. So all we have to do is wake up over and over.

I understood why Bryan quoted Dogen-Zengi, *To be enlightened is to be intimate with all things.* I can be intimate with everything when I know they are not separate from me; we are all interconnected. Maybe that is what emptiness of self really means. It does not mean no self. It means interconnection. Emptiness means fullness. It means no separation. Emptiness confirms fullness. They are one. This is what is meant by non-dual reality. How could it be otherwise?

10

REALIZING, WHATEVER HAPPENS, IS THE PERFECT HAPPENING SELF

29 years old

What is changeless and immortal is not individual body-mind but rather that Mind which is shared with all of existence, that stillness, that incipience which never ceases because it never becomes but simply IS…Time, the illusion of the ego, the stuff of individual existence, the dream that separates us from a true perception of the whole. It is often likened to a glass vessel that separates air within from the clear and unrefined air all around, or water from the all-encompassing sea. Yet the vessel is not separate from the sea, and to shatter or dissolve it brings about the reunion with all universal life that mystics seek, the homecoming, the return to the lost paradise of our 'true nature. The Snow Leopard, Peter Matthiessen.

To me, Matthiessen's words were not just words on a page. They were mini awakenings.

Sunday, May 13th

A WEEK after meeting His Holiness, Tenzin Gyatso, the Fourteenth Dalai Lama, we traveled from McLeod Ganj to Manali in the Kullu Valley, Himachal Pradesh (northern India).

Before we left Sydney in January, we had a farewell party at Bondi Beach; my friend Nicola gave me *The Snow Leopard* by Peter Matthiessen. This deeply spiritual book combines mysticism with ecological, geographical, and historical facts. Nicola highly recommended that I do what she had done–begin the book in Manali and finish it in Leh, the capital of Ladakh in the Himalayas, near *The Snow Leopard's* setting.

When we arrived in Manali, I took Nicola's advice and started reading *The Snow Leopard* diligently. I felt like I was walking beside Matthiessen on his 1973 two-month, 402-kilometer (250-mile) trek from the Nepalese Himalayas to Crystal Mountain on the Tibetan Plateau. He had teamed up with biologist and conservationist George Schaller to study the Himalayan blue sheep and hopefully encounter the endangered snow leopard.

To follow the rest of Nicola's advice, I had to get to Leh, a town nestled in the Indian Himalayan Mountain Range. Due to its high altitude, it is only accessible by road for four and half months each year. The Manali-Leh Highway was usually open by now, but it had been a particularly long winter, so it was closed to cars, motorbikes, and government buses as snow still blocked Rohtang Pass. The obvious option was to fly there, but as we were five months into a 12-month trip around the world, this was not in our budget. However, I was completely immersed in *The Snow Leopard* and Matthiessen's search for the *elusive white ghost*, so nothing was going to stop me from making this seemingly impossible trip. Stitty traveled fearlessly and courageously, so I knew

LIVING EVOLVED

together we would reach Leh, fueled by our belief *Where there is a will, there is a way.*

The question remained—if I could get to Leh, would I achieve my quest to see a snow leopard in the wild? Would I succeed where Matthiessen failed? He had come close at Crystal Mountain, *...the leopard prints are as fresh as petals on the trail but not close enough...* Matthiessen and I were looking for snow leopards before the 2002 reserve expansion, so our goal was ambitious. The snow leopard, both rare and well-camouflaged, was so seldom seen as to be considered almost mythical and magical.

Stitty and I purchased the necessary permits, rose early, and walked down to the gas station to wait for the first truck to arrive, a 72-ton truck full of tea on its way to Leh from Delhi. We asked the two men to pay them 1000 Indian Rupees (18 Australian dollars, 13 US dollars) to hitchhike to Leh. Minutes later, we were on board for the adventure of a lifetime.

The journey to Leh took three days, driving 12 hours each day on one of the most dangerous roads in the world. Can you imagine sitting for 12 hours, three days in a row? It sounds like a long way, but time flies with a preoccupied mind absorbing breathtaking beauty, dealing with unrivaled fear, and processing an exhilarating experience unmatched by anything else on the planet.

The Himalayas change, chameleon style, to suit their height. The freezing Chandra River carving through huge valleys; natural sand bridges and formations like temples; green fields of snow peas tucked into steep hillsides. Small trees standing tall on grassy plains, contrasting desert terrain spotted with alpine shrubs, contrasting impressive peaks. Colors range from red to brown to icy blue.

The highway led us to remote villages consisting of basic stone huts and tents, cut off from civilization for seven and half months of the year. So, the villagers were happy to see us and welcomed us with steaming hot noodles and warm *chai* (Indian tea). We stayed in Darcha in the Lahaul region the first night at 3,360 meters (11,020 feet) elevation. It is the northernmost permanent settlement in Himachal Pradesh along the Manali-Leh Highway and is situated on the Bhaga River.

The following day's trip was mind-blowing.

Precarious rocks scattered along brown, rubbled, winter-savaged roads. Just plowed, their dull color sat juxtaposed against bright-white snow hedges that towered above us. Road conditions were so horrendous that the four of us had to rebuild the badly damaged road. Landslides forced us to clear huge fallen rocks capable of crushing a car. The newly dug-out path seemed carelessly cut into snow-packed cliff faces. At times the passageways between rocks were so confined that our over-loaded truck almost got stuck. Our companion would hop out and skillfully whistle, guiding the driver through tight spaces. After the town of Zing-zing Bar, I held my breath as we slowly crossed a mighty river of rapidly running, melted glacier water.

At Sarchu, hairpin turn after hairpin turn, 22 in total, zigzagged like a finger running through icing sugar, etching this once-in-a-lifetime memory into my psyche forever.

Our top-heavy truck inched along treacherously narrow roads. Maneuvering past oncoming trucks was horrifying—there were no guard rails, just sheer hundred-meter drops. If we were the truck on the outside, I would look down and see our wheels sending loose rocks plummeting towards car, bus, and jeep carcasses lying eerily below. Ghostly whispers warned *You don't belong here*. At this delicate and uncompromising point in time, I would think about the 13-meter truck tipping, and my heart would race. Every bend in the road felt like it could be my last. I have never experienced that kind of danger nor the adrenaline rush that accompanied it. Coming from a developed country like Australia, with some of the best roads globally, made me unfamiliar with this feeling of vulnerability. I had been scared on Indian roads before, but this was my first time on a notoriously deadly highway.

In the moments when death was close and I was free-falling into anxiety, I would try to approach my fear with curiosity. First, I would question *What would happen if I faced my greatest fear of dying and accepted it?* Then, when the acceptance coping mechanism stopped working, I would pose more questions.

- *What if I turn my back on the real possibility of dying by becoming fully present in each moment, without labeling it as good or bad?*
- *Is it possible simply to witness each turn in the road from a place of non-judgment?*
- *Can I glimpse beauty without the 'what ifs' blinding my view?*
- *Can I pretend to look through innocent, naive, and child-like eyes?*
- *What will I choose over these minutes, hours, and days?*
- *Will I select trepidation or surrender?*
- *Can I put faith and trust in my experienced driver?*
- *What if the way I perceive is my choice?*

I would turn my focus inward and become fully present in my body, looking for early warning signs. If I felt the stress response (gasping, clenched jaw, gripping the seat, sick stomach, fidgeting), I would tell myself *My tension doesn't change the outcome one single bit, so let go.* With this thought, I would consciously slacken every muscle in my body while repeating my mantra *This too shall pass.* Soon I realized *If my time's up, it's up, and there is nothing I can do about it. I may as well enjoy the ride.*

When I was not nearly dying, I could enjoy the spellbinding scenery. The magnificent Indian Himalayas displayed awe-inspiring panoramas moment after moment, day after day, uninterrupted by cars, motorbikes, buses, and tourists.

At times I would laugh because what would be considered absurd in Australia seemed normal here: a herd of wooly sheep, cashmere goats, cows, or yaks trotting across the highway in a sea of horns and loud bleats, flanked by fierce wolf-like dogs and jogging shepherds looking dapper in angular woolen hats and pashmina coats with delicate rugs stylishly draped over their shoulders. These wiry nomads traveled by foot across huge distances and were intimately aware of each animal they tended.

We stayed in Pang Village the second night, in the Spiti District, 4,657 meters (15,280 feet) above sea level. Snow bucketed down and caved in our tent with its weight. In the morning, thick snow blanketed our truck.

Slowly we edged our way up to the second-highest pass in the world, Tanglang La Pass, 5,328 meters (17,528 feet) above sea level. The roadside drop-offs became more and more precipitous, and the air went cold. Here, we heard the frantic flapping of colored Buddhist prayer flags adorning stupas swept up in a festival of howling wind, celebrating pops of color amidst the arid, lunar-looking land.

Arriving in Leh was a culture shock. It was like nowhere else in India because it borders Kashmir, China, Pakistan, and Tibet. Its fascinating political history, ancestral mix, distinct language, and characteristic landscape make this area extraordinarily noteworthy. The mountain lifestyle was such a contrast to the rest of India. The Buddhist influence was evident in the family we stayed with at the Oriental Guest House (recommended by Nicola and her partner James).

Locals with an ethnic mix of Mons, Dards, and Mongols of Tibetan origin were relaxed, friendly, and never badgered us to buy things like in big Indian cities. There were no beggars, and the pace of life was slow. People went about their business without staring or crowding around me. The region had only been open to international tourists for three decades, making it unique to India.

The altitude sickness hit me hard, we were 3,520 meters (11,550 feet) above sea level, so it took me days to acclimatize. However, as breathless as I was, I still managed to climb the mountain to visit the Japanese Buddhist monastery Shanti Stupa. There, my icy-cold cheeks were struck by high-altitude air as I admired a distinctive Ladakh view—brown, rugged, and textured hills blended into splendid shining snowy peaks. Imagine: mahogany moonscape meets glistening mountains, meets cloudless blue sky. I eagerly scanned the horizon, fantasizing, as usual, about spotting a snow leopard.

I was conscientiously reading Matthiessen's story *The Snow Leopard* in the region it was written, absorbing page after page of intimate details of the ecosystem, elements, plants, insects, birds, wildlife, and geological wonders. Every vivid description had immediate relevance as I would turn my head and see what Matthiessen was describing. I could visit a 350-year-old Buddhist gompa, smell what Matthiessen smelt, and taste what he was tasting. I could talk to sherpas, hear the running water that flows through Leh, and watch a large spinning prayer wheel clicking invisible wishes into the wind. Two of those wishes belonged to Matthiessen and me, the wish to see a snow leopard in the wild.

Something about the Himalayas propelled me, Matthiessen, and so many who choose to witness them into an indescribable state. We reached a heightened sense of peace by being super aware and focused on and in nature for a prolonged period. We enjoyed the quiet, as Matthiessen described, *...the sound of Earth and heaven in the silence*. I was immersed in one of the most spiritual towns in the world, surrounded by stone fortress monasteries and humble monks chanting prayers. So, my pace perfectly matched Matthiessen's pace. Every interaction seemed to be an opportunity to explore Matthiessen's ideas. Life's tempo was so languid that I could contemplate every lingering thought. Words seemed to be suspended in the air like floating speech bubbles with ample time to re-read, change or take back if necessary. For this reason, I never wasted words. To be honest, I could barely breathe up there, let alone waste words!

The sheer size of the mountains beckoned the question *What is the meaning of life?* I had the time to pour over Mathiessen's philosophical perspectives and dive deep into his cited research to draw my conclusions about life's meaning. The mountainous landscape somehow put enlightenment on the table to achieve in this lifetime. My desire to connect with the natural awe around me motivated me to seek a spiritual path so pure that I could achieve a union with eternity. It felt like *The Snow Leopard* was pointing me to my calling. I knew deep within me that enlightenment was my birthright, and I was eager to discover how to achieve this vision like so many before me. Matthiessen put it this way, *Snow mountains, more than sea or sky, serve as a mirror to one's own true being, utterly still, utterly clear, a void, an Emptiness without life or sound that carries in Itself all life, all sound.*

Sunday, May 20th

WHEN WE LEFT LEH, we got a lift with a jeep driver headed to Manali to begin the tourist season. The roads were about to open, and he needed to be there to pick up a carload to bring in some much-needed income after the quiet winter. We met him at 2:30 a.m. Pitch blackness enshrouded us in a mystical veil of the unknown. Traveling in India means you are cloaked in this veil most of the time, and this morning was true to form. English was broken and cryptic, relying primarily on gestures to clarify where we were going and how much we wanted to pay.

"Yes, Ok, we go." he pointed in some random direction and grabbed our backpacks.

"You sit in the front, Stitty," I said as we hopped in the jeep. "By the way." I continued, "I want to look at the scenery today, so don't let me fall asleep like I usually do."

I didn't consider that at 2:30 a.m., there was nothing to see except the road in the headlights because everywhere else was unilluminated.

Around two hours into the journey on hypnotic roads, I put my head down on the back seat and peacefully drifted off.

"Babe, you wanted to stay awake!" Stitty yelled back at me.

"I'm up," I said. Then, as I sat straight up and looked through the windscreen, a massive snow leopard came bounding across our headlights.

"Snow leopard!" the driver shouted.

Time stood still as if we were watching a scene zoomed in and in slow motion. We were three meters from an endangered cat with thick fur and giant paws. It was majestic, strong, and characteristically spotted with a bushy gray tail. I could not believe its size and prowess as it effortlessly jumped up the steep hill. We rounded the bend to see a big black cow with a tattered dangling rope around its neck, innocently munching, unaware of its imminent death. An image crossed my mind, the noble nomadic herdsmen realizing one of his valued livestock had broken loose. Certain of its demise, devoured by a cunning and opportunistic cat.

The moment was palpable. We saw this phenomenal animal in the wild on an 18-hour, 480 kilometers (300 miles) trip. It was a silent crescendo, a love song's high note. I felt jubilation, believing that the stars had aligned just for me and that somehow I had orchestrated the whole thing. A cow rarely breaks free, and what are the chances of it being beside the highway at that exact time. If Stitty had not woken me, I would have missed it. And had the snow leopard not jumped directly into our headlights, it would have remained a dream of mine.

How could it not be my dream after finishing *The Snow Leopard*, as advised, in Leh? I found Matthiessen's book highly relatable on so many levels, but I empathized most with his unabated desire to spot a snow leopard in the wild. Matthiessen wrote, *Even those who know the mountains rarely take them [snow leopards] by surprise: most sightings have been made by hunters lying still near a wild herd when a snow leopard happened to be stalking.*

There were many parallels between Matthiessen's expedition and my solo stay in Warchok, Nepal, four years prior. Namely, our relationships with the locals, isolation, and facing our mortality.

Putting words to the remarkable Himalayan experience challenged Matthiessen as much as it challenged me. We both chose to study mysticism as a means to fathom its vastness. I thoroughly enjoyed his exploration of Buddhist traditions such as Mahayana, Zen, Hinayana of Ceylon, Theravada of Sri Lanka, and Tantric Buddhism of the Himalayas, Tibet, Central Asia, China, Korea, Japan, and the West. I was fascinated by his references to Sufi Muslims, Ancient Greeks, Australian Aboriginals, Africans, Egyptians, and Christians. I was engrossed in Matthiessen's descriptions of Lao-Tzu, author of Tao Te Ching and founder of Taoism, Gandhi, Jesus, Hindu Vedas, Eskimo Shamans, Siberian Chukchis, Gautama Buddha (Sakyamuni), the Hopi, Pueblo, and Navajo Native American Indian shamanistic practices, Aztec priests and Tibetan oracle-priests. After investigating these philosophies, Matthiessen surmised, *Everything is Right Here Now...all is present in this moment.*

Matthiessen introduced me to Milarepa, Tibet's 10th-century poet lama who went from murderer to enlightened being in a single lifetime *If he could do it, so can I!* Matthiessen quoted Milarepa from W.Y. Evans-Wentz's book *Tibet's Great Yogi: Milarepa*, *All worldly pursuits have but one unavoidable and inevitable end, which is sorrow: acquisitions end in desperation; buildings in destruction; meetings in separation; births in deaths. Knowing this, one should from the very first renounce acquisition and heaping-up, and building and meeting, and...set about realizing the Truth...life is short, and the time of death uncertain; so apply yourself to meditation...*

Matthiessen shared concepts that explained the altered state of consciousness I experienced a few weeks earlier on the meditation cushion on day nine of Bryan's insight meditation retreat in Mcleod Ganj. The answers I yearned for felt like divine timing. For example, Matthiessen wrote, *Meditation...(is) intuiting the true nature of existence, which is why it has appeared in one form or another in almost every culture known to man...Today, science is telling us what the Vedas have taught for three thousand years, that we do not see the universe as it is. What we see is Maya (which is Time, the illusion of the ego, the stuff of individual existence, the dream that separates us from a true perception of the whole), or Illusion, the 'magic show' of nature, a collective hallucination of that part of consciousness which is shared with all our kind and which gives a common ground, a continuity to the life experience. According to Buddhists, this world is perceived by the senses. This relative but not absolute reality, this dream also exists, also having meaning; but it is only one perspective of truth...the transparent radiance of stilled mind opens out to prajna, or transcendent knowing, that higher consciousness or 'mind' which is inherent in all sentient beings...experience of prajna corresponds to liberation — not change, but transformation.*

Matthiessen quotes Carl Sagan in *Intelligent Life in the Universe, Man is the matter of the cosmos, contemplating itself.* Sagan suggested that the brilliant 'white light' that accompanies mystical experiences might be a primordial memory of creation. This concept blew my mind, but at the same time, it felt plausible. Even though I did not see a 'white light,' I experienced the feeling of being poised at the moment before creation. I wondered if the 'white light' referred to by Sagan was what near-death reporters sometimes witness.

Matthiessen explored how physicists seek to understand reality, whereas mystics are trained to experience it directly. I loved that my journey had incorporated both these techniques, the intellectual and the experiential. However, without a doubt, my real knowing came from first-hand experiences. I not only related to Matthiessen's words, I also understood them deeply. For example, when he wrote, *Nothing exists but atoms and the void— so wrote Democritus. And it is 'void' that underlies the Eastern teachings— not emptiness or absence, but the Uncreated that preceded all creation, the beginningless potential of all things.* And when Matthiessen quoted Lawrence LeShan in The Medium, the Mystic and the Physicist, *When body and mind are one, then the whole thing, scoured clean of intellect, emotions and the senses, may be laid open to the experience. The individual existence, ego, the 'reality' of matter and phenomena are no more than fleeting and illusory arrangements of molecules. The weary self of masks and screens, defenses, preconceptions and opinions that, propped up by ideas and words, imagines itself to be some sort of entity (in a society of like entities) may suddenly fall away, where concepts of 'death,' 'life,' 'time,' 'space,' 'past,' 'future' have no meaning, there is only a pearly radiance of emptiness, the uncreated, without beginning...without end.* And lastly, Matthiessen's perspective, *...meditation represents the foundation of the universe to which all returns, as in the stillness of the dead of night, the stillness between tides and winds, the stillness before creation. In this 'void,' this dynamic state of rest, without impediments, lies ultimate reality, and here one's true nature is reborn, in a return from what Buddhists speak of as 'great death.'* Matthiessen's book described in detail the void I experienced on retreat in Mcleod Ganj.

I felt myself, once again, falling into this void the moment the snow leopard bounded across our path. In an instant, my world and the snow leopard's world collided, and I glimpsed the fragility of my existence. I realized that the human species could be nearing extinction, and I could be as rare and threatened as this snow leopard one day.

I sat back and closed my eyes. I felt guilty. *How did I get to see this beautiful animal when Matthiessen didn't? How did I deserve this dream more than he did? I wish he could have seen what I saw. Matthiessen taught me so much and led me to deep insights, and now I've realized our dream just days after finishing his book. How was this possible?*

Then a wash of visceral gratitude poured over me, dissolving the guilt. It covered my body like sweet nectar, causing me to shiver. I was filled with tingling effervescent light that seemed to peel away a veil revealing a new perspective. Suddenly, I knew, on a cellular level, everything I had read in *The Snow Leopard*. Matthiessen's words coalesced into profound understanding. It all made sense, and for a moment, I felt enlightened. My old clunky reality fell away, leaving me suspended in everything and nothing simultaneously. Past, present, and future were all there in the now. I could sense infinite possibilities, all aspects of SELF, and every expression of the one consciousness.

Later, when I considered why I saw a snow leopard and Matthiesen did not, I saw its perfection. Our experiences were complementary and inseparable like Yin and Yang. Two parts of a whole can not exist independently because they are both true, like two sides of the same coin. Although they seem opposite or dualistic, they balance each other out. To evolve, we must welcome and intimately know both types of experiences. Matthiessen learned the lesson of coping with failure and being OK with not attaining his goal. When asked, "Have you seen the snow leopard?" He cultivated an evolved perspective and replied, "No! Isn't that wonderful?" He was able to surrender to the moment without grasping. *It is not good; it is not bad; it just is.*

On the other hand, I learned the lesson of coping with success and being OK with attaining my goal. When asked, "Have you seen the snow leopard?" I also cultivated an evolved perspective and replied, "Yes! Isn't that wonderful?" I, too, surrendered to the moment without grasping. *It is not good; it is not bad; it just is.*

You see, it is wonderful both ways; whatever happens, is the perfect happening.

11

SURRENDERING SELF

30 years old

Thursday, July 5th

Like nowhere else on Earth

By the time we arrived in Varanasi (Benares), Uttar Pradesh, India, the oldest continuously inhabited city in the world, situated on the holy *Ganges* River, where outdoor funeral pyres guarantee Hindus salvation from the birth-death-rebirth cycle, we had been traveling through India/Nepal for five months. So, we were hardly green gringos (travelers straight off the plane). Still, no amount of backpacking experience softened Varanasi's blow. Despite being my 307th day in the region (counting my first trip) I was not prepared for this city. Why not? It is like nowhere else on Earth.

We must have suspected we would stay in Varanasi for a month because we spent the whole day searching for the perfect place to stay. We turned down guest house after guest house because they overlooked the street or were caged in to save off troublesome monkeys. Finally, our intentions and perseverance paid off; we landed the best room with the best view in Varanasi. *Ganpati Guest House* in Meer Ghat. We occupied the top floor with a green stone and slats balcony that wrapped around the building, giving us a complete view of the *Ganges* River. When I looked over the railing, I saw a dead boy floating in the water, staring straight up, with one arm up like he was waving to me.

I gasped, "Stitto, look! It's a dead child lodged in the railing." We had no idea why it was there. The only people not cremated at the two local burning ghats (series of steps leading to the river) were people with incomplete deaths. These included suicides, pregnant women, holy men, babies under two years of age, snakebite victims, people who died from smallpox, and lepers. These people were pushed out into the *Ganges*. This child looked about seven years old. I felt sad for his family. The river had not been kind to this boy, leaving him exposed like this.

Welcome to Varanasi.

We enthusiastically took off to the main Dasaswamedh Ghat. We knew it was an auspicious day as it was one of three lunar eclipses that year. A lunar eclipse occurs when the sun, Earth, and moon align, and the moon crosses the shadow projected by Earth which lies between the moon and the sun. It was only a partial eclipse, but it brought hundreds of thousands of Hindu worshipers to Varanasi, India's holiest city. When we emerged from the guest house, our senses were violently assaulted. Imagine a crowd so thick and fast-moving that your bodily control becomes obsolete when you enter it. We were jogging shoulder to shoulder in a tight pack pushing its way down to the Mother *Ganga*'s Varanasi ghats.

I squeezed Stitty's hand tightly to prevent a trip and a trample.

The noise was deafening, the sound of joyful chaos—music, bells, drums, and celebrating people happily singing. The smell was severe: sandalwood, incense, and festive breaths. The variety of colors shocked my brain. Everywhere my eyes viewed was another pop of exquisiteness. Sadhus (Hindu holy men) clad in vibrant orange, with smeared white faces and tall, towering headpieces tightly coiled like snakes atop thick dreadlocks dangling downwards, concealing beaded brown necklaces stacked high on their chests. Silk saris in lilac, hot pink, and crimson red. Bangles in gold, glass, and plastic. Bindis adorn foreheads using bright red powder, jewels, and dots. Eyes flash at me: crystal green, piercing black, and chocolate brown. My eyes darted from ring to ring: gilded earrings, titanium nose rings, and silver toe rings. Flower garlands everywhere, I had never seen so many flowers: fragrant marigold; rose; and hibiscus. Dainty jasmine flowers wrapped around Sikh (Indian religion) buns perched high on heads. Mustaches, chiseled jaws, sharp cheekbones, black skin, cocoa skin, betel-stained teeth, no teeth, one tooth, perfect teeth. Foreheads painted in secret codes, like a white 'U' shape with a red stripe in the middle, yellow horizontal lines, and black dots on babies. Everyone seemed to be carrying random things like snake baskets, plastic bags, and tall tridents!

"Don't go down there." A haunting Indian face burst forth and warned.

Ok, but there is no way we are going back.

Thud, my elbow disappeared into cow skin. I dodged a painted horn while admiring its flower garlands fit for a king.

Varanasi reeked of history, the road smoothed by billions of faithful footsteps, many returning as ghosts, walls dripped in drama, scandals seethed from sidewalks, stories slithered, antics in attics, legend layered laneways, countless centuries curdled in cracks, paint peeling poetry, grime in crevices, hole in the wall shops packed with treasures, frothy flowers fermented in gutters, ancient architecture angled awkwardly, electricity dizzily noncompliant, scaffold succumbing to the pressure, and dust as dependable as the cyclicality of life.

"Turn back. It's too dangerous." Another wide-eyed Indian cautioned.

I hoped to the side, almost falling over a beggar. To my astonishment, it was not one, but over 200, sitting back-to-back down the center of the road all the way to the main ghat, holding up silver plates. I noticed the pilgrims walking back up the street, dropping handfuls of rice into beggars' silver cups or straight onto their mats. Some beggars were blind, sick, old, with children, or laying legless in three-wheeled makeshift trolleys. This scene was very confronting.

When we got to the end of the road, we could see the river up ahead, lit with floodlights, but we could not get down there. I do not know what came over me, but I just walked straight up to this big friendly-looking Indian man buying something from a shop.

"Excuse me, do you speak English?" I inquired.

"A little," he smiled warmly.

"Do you know where we can watch this safely?" I continued.

He turned and beckoned for Stitty and me to follow.

He led us to unassuming wooden doors, painted bright blue, the same color as the ghat railings.

As the double doors flew open, we walked into the most incredible month of our lives.

I still can not believe how fortunate we were to be taken in by this family. There were over three million people in the city that night, and I just happened to ask the son of the main priest of the main Dasaswamedh Ghat. The next thing I knew, we were standing upstairs in the private ghat temple looking over the balcony straight at the *Ganges*, the source of life, lapping against the wall below. In front of the wall, standing in waist-high water, bathed pilgrims from all over India. They displayed ecstasy as they received the *Ganga* Goddesses' healing. They drank her up and celebrated as her pure water washed away their sins. They superstitiously prayed to the eclipse's gravitational power. They rejoiced as they imagined their future prosperity. They were floating, chanting bhajans (devotee songs), playfully splashing each other, gazing out to the horizon while symbolically pouring river water from brass vessels, holding their noses and dunking under, hands in prayer, mumbling requests to the *Ganga*, arms waving in the air, cheering loudly, dancing in circles holding hands, or gripping plastic bags of belongings above their heads. They carried statues, burning lanterns, or pitchers to collect holy water. Pilgrims took this priceless liquid home to relatives, too weak to make the journey. Politicians with bodyguards and royal families stood side-by-side with drain cleaners and waste pickers. There was so much joy. I had never seen worship like this before. I had so many questions *What's that white piece of string men wear over their left shoulder and diagonally across their chest? Why do some sadhus have shaved heads and some don't?*

We stayed most of the night intrigued by these ancient customs sanctified by tradition.

The following day we went back to the main Dasaswamedh Ghat and sat with the holy man I had noticed the night before. We had been together on the temple balcony, and I could not take my eyes off him; he looked regal, with the kindest Indian face I had ever seen. He was dressed in impeccably clean, cardinal red robes and said his name was Arimdum. He took us from the ghat back into the family's temple to meet the head priest Babu Maharaj, his wife, and his son Dinesh whom I had approached in the street the night before. Dinesh told us (in broken English) Arimdum's story.

"Arimdum is a sadhu. He visited our ghat every day. One day a German man was abusive towards his female companion. Out of nowhere, Arimdum spoke perfect German to the man, telling him to stop. My father, Babu Maharaj, recognized this as a miracle and invited Arimdum to live with us. Now he lives in our temple and shares our food," Dinesh explained.

What a story, an incredible miracle! India has the largest group of organized monks, called sadhus, in the world. Sadhus traditionally give up their possessions and dedicate their lives to sustaining the

Vedic spiritual heritage. They are committed to the Hindu gods and rely on donations to eat. For Arimdum to manifest this opportunity was astoundingly inspiring.

Hinduism, Buddhism, Sikhism, and Jainism originated in the Indian subcontinent. Lives here center around religion. The Hindus believe they are born into a caste (family group/occupation) due to their past deeds (karma). From birth, they know to be dutiful through devoted thoughts, words, and actions to reincarnate into a higher caste or, better yet, to achieve *Moksha* (escape) from *samsara* (world of rebirth).

Water is a fundamental part of the Hindu religion, and the 2,500 kilometer (1,553 miles) long *Ganga* is the ultimate goddess. It is one of the world's great rivers and a lifeline to millions of Indians who rely on her for their livelihood and daily needs. She begins high in the Himalayas. Her sources converge and fall from the mountains at Rishikesh, Uttarakhand. She then snakes her way through the Indian plains, eventually spilling out in the Bay of Bengal. The city of Varanasi is unique because it lies on the bend in the *Ganges*, where it runs north back towards its birthplace.

That night we saw Babu Maharaj in his element. He performed a *Ganga Aarti*, which is an evening puja or devotional ceremony for the *Ganga* Goddess. On a small wooden bright blue platform that balanced precariously on stacks of stones, Babu Maharaj mesmerized the crowd. In orange cotton as vivid as yoke, trimmed in red and gold, face and limbs adorned in lines resembling dancers in an Aboriginal corroboree. He shared the stage with a silver-faced Annapurna goddess statue, dressed up and propped up on an elegantly decorated swing with flower-wrapped ropes beside bowls of deity offerings, such as bananas, guava, cucumber, rock sugar, and milk cakes. Each is lovingly and intentionally placed like works of art. In the water were floating baskets full of red petals and burning candles paying tributes to the *Ganga's* preciousness. *Aarti* had been offered to the *Ganga* for over 4,500 years, but since the early 1990s, Babu Maharaj used his charismatic flair to turn this daily ritual into a spectacular 7:00 pm solo show adored by locals and travelers alike. The nightly event began with Babu Maharaj inhaling, puckering, and playing a conch shell. The eerie horn commanded the attention of the holy waters. He flamboyantly waved a large red fan with one hand while ringing a bronze bell with the other. Incense dhoop sticks sent pungent aromas to honor the *Ganga*'s power. He prayed and sang while the crowd clapped, clanged percussion instruments, and held their hands in prayer. Babu Maharaj's faithfulness to the sacred river put him into a hypnotic trance. Holding a five-tiered flaming lantern, he skillfully lent over the edge of the platform to skim the surface of the water. The crowd clapped louder. The Dasaswamedh Ghat is considered the main Varanasi ghat because Lord *Brahma* (supreme creator god) sacrificed ten horses here to return Lord Shiva (Hindu Deity/God) from banishment. Varanasi was a thriving trade center centuries ago when it was called Kashi. Rulers built temples and ghats for pilgrims to show off their wealth, and social and political importance. Varanasi reminded me of St. Petersburg, Russia. The difference was that most of the Varanasi temples were rebuilt 200 years ago after the original ones were destroyed during Muslim rule.

The following day when we revisited Dasaswamedh Ghat, we saw Babu Maharaj sitting with his Bihar pilgrims. Dressed in orange, the pilgrims had walked 55 hours, 350 kilometers (217 miles) for a personal blessing with him. Babu Maharaj was the guru to Bihar's 70 million Hindus. He saw us and immediately signaled for us to approach, "Radha (referring to me) Krishna (referring to Stitty), you come, my house tonight, dinner with my family." We felt uncomfortable interrupting the important ceremony, expecting outrage, but in typical Indian fashion, these non-violent and benevolent Indians did not care. As a race, they are inspiringly tolerant because they understand the interconnectedness of all things. Any impatience today could have severe ramifications for hundreds of future lifetimes. Anything goes in India, which is why we love it. Indians have seen it all, and nothing surprises them. Everything is accepted and assimilated, but a robust moral compass always punctuates the undertones. As a result, freedom of respectful expression is unparalleled in other countries.

When we agreed to join Babu Maharaj for dinner, he turned his attention back to his devotees and continued reciting *shlokas* (verses from Hindu scriptures).

We loved how Babu Maharaj called us Rada Krishna because of all the Hindu gods; they represent an everlasting union. They are perfectly balanced because Krishna symbolizes the external energies, and Rada symbolizes the internal energies. They are like one person and can therefore never be separated. Their profound love surpasses duty and obligation and flows spontaneously to break everything that comes in its path. Stitty and I commended Babu Maharaj for being so perspective. We, like Rada Krishna, feel equal in our relationship and acknowledge that we have divine love capable of smashing any obstacle in our way.

Well at least that was how I thought I perceived our love. Until one weird day when I sat down in our Varanasi room to write Stitty a letter. I allowed my pen to flow automatically and journeyed down a dark road of anger, fear and doubt. My words ripped into Stitty: *I am sick and tired of being your girlfriend, I should be your wife. I've done my bit and not mentioned the M word since Kalgoorlie you haven't done your bit. You are still taking me for granted by not honoring me enough to completely commit to me. Have some respect, we have been together for five and a half years and not a single sign of a proposal on the horizon. You're not doing this, you're not doing that, you're not doing bloody anything except* forcing me to sit around while my 30-year-old eggs shrivel up in my ovaries while you decide if marriage is for you! I cried tears into that letter. I did not hold back; instead, I went for Stitty's jugular; words like *betrayal, selfish, rude, disrespectful,* and *arsehole* came tumbling onto the writing paper. I was fed up, impatient, and well and truly over the torturous waiting game. After I ranted and raved for half an hour, I heard a voice inside me *You should send this to Nikki instead*. Without hesitation, I sealed the envelope with one lick, addressed it to Nikki in Western Australia, walked to the post office, posted it, and vowed to take a terrifying risk. Let go and surrender to the unknown

How did I do this? I threw myself into Varanasi, the city of light.

The real Varanasi

BABU MAHARAJ WAS UNDOUBTEDLY the most revered man in Varanasi, and he fell in love with Stitty and me. He and his son Dinesh, showed us the real Varanasi. They introduced us to silk merchants whose ancestors perhaps wove silk for a young Prince Siddartha (the Buddha). Their weaver's looms spun delicate strands that hung like spider webs. We met carpet artisans making handmade *dhurries* (rugs), whose antique looms came from Persia in the 1880s. We met a Hindustani classical tabla player whose fingers and palms combined to produce the most spellbinding dum beats I have ever heard; his family had played this instrument for 200 years. During our month in Varanasi, we immersed ourselves in Indian art, literature, history, and music, not to mention the Hindu religion and culture.

Babu Maharaj involved us in every aspect of his spiritual life. He showed us that the celebration of the family is the cornerstone of the Hindu religion. We celebrated the *Rakshabandhan* (brother-sister bond) Festival in his home in the temple. I placed a red tie of protection thread around his right wrist, put a red paste *tilak* on his third eye, and he bought me a sky blue silk saree and promised to protect me. We ate delicious festive food and played cricket with his 15 young relatives on the temple balcony, where our adventure began.

One day Babu Maharaj took us on a two-hour drive to visit family at Vindhyachal, another Hindu pilgrimage site on the holy *Ganga*. We went deep into the *Vindhyachal Sita Temple*, where I felt strange, out of place, and incredibly privileged. I felt the same humbled way when he showed us the inner sanctum or womb-house of the private *Dasaswamedh Ghat Temple*, an area usually out of bounds to travelers.

There are 88 ghats along the six-kilometer (3.7 miles) Varanasi stretch. Two of them are burning ghats, Manikarnika and Harishchandra. We never spoke to Bahu Mararaj about these ghats. He was a *Brahmin* (the highest caste) and we knew *Brahmins* do not do death. In India, status is equated with purity, and in the upper caste's opinion, dealing with dead bodies is the antithesis of purity. Corpse caretaking is the sole responsibility of the lowest caste, called *Dalits* or *Doms*. Bahu Mararaj was a priest dedicated to the Goddess Ganga. His ghat welcomed Shiva, whereas Shiva cursed Manikarnika Ghat. We did not visit a burning ghat for weeks and once we did, we never returned.

Full Moon at the burning ghat

ALTHOUGH THE BURNING ghat Manikarnika was only four ghats north of Meer Ghat, we took the narrow alleyways because the water was up. Before we knew it, an Indian man had taken us up some steps and we were standing next to a raging fire, spitting amber embers at us. The heat gave my face a hard blow; my exposed skin felt instantly hot. A body burner smashed a bamboo stick forcefully into something next to me, sending sparks, like fireflies, into the night sky. After a few seconds, I registered. He was cracking open a human skull. He danced dynamically between corpses, tending to two simultaneously, wearing sandals, rolled-up cotton pants, a white singlet, and a yellow scarf around his head. The other body was fresher; the smell of burning hair and flesh scorched my nostrils. We had inadvertently stepped onto an open cremation platform. I rapidly scanned the area; black plumes of smoke bellowed from pyres topped with bodies. Ash flakes danced in timeless breezes before settling in their final resting place, the *Ganga Mataji* (Mother River of India), beyond the soot-stained steps. Next to me, male relatives chanted, "Ram Namm Satya Hai."

Our guide yelled over the inferno noise, "No women are allowed here. They are too emotional, and their crying holds the person's soul back."

They worship female deities while they exclude women from funeral rites. Just another Hindu hypocrisy.

He showed us the *Doms* sifting through corpse ash by the river's silvery edge, looking for gold fillings or jewelry before unceremoniously tossing the ashes into the water. He pointed out bodies wrapped in different colored cloths, tinsel and flowers were men, vermilion red were women, and white were widows. I watched as caretakers dipped these wrapped bodies in the Ganga before carrying them towards the burning platform. We followed our guide into a building that felt like an apartment block, but there were no walls and open sides. We ascertained through limited English that this was a hotel where Hindus check in to die. There were weak, rasping people everywhere.

Bells in the distance celebrating life mocked us.

We could cope no longer; we lifted our *let's get out of here* eyebrows, gave the guide a donation, and ran as fast as we could through the hectic hustle and bustle lanes to the safety of our room which was our sanctuary, a place to retreat from the chaos. We slumped in our balcony seats overlooking the holy river and exhaled. We had not uttered a single word to each other since we had left the room. Swept up in one of those incommunicable Indian moments where you wonder *What did I just witness? Will I ever be able to process it? How can I ever describe it?* In a speechless state of shock, we stared out, motionless. Minutes passed to reveal a splendid full moon rising over the River *Ganges*. I walked inside and when I turned around, The view took my breath away. The door frame around the full moon encapsulated the most stunning image I had ever seen. The moonshine reflecting on the glistening, sparkling surface created a bright white, perfectly centered, wavey moonbeam that shone directly through the door into my body. I was utterly in love with life, with Varanasi, and with Stitty. I noticed my birthday card from Stitty sitting on the table.

> Happy 30th birthday... I have the utmost respect and admiration for you. In many ways, you are my mentor and teacher. You help me with patience and giving, you show me selflessness and caring, and I love you for that. You do not judge me. You just support me in the areas I need to change. Not only me but most people who get to experience your personality and warmth come away with a feeling of happiness and power. You are great at setting an example and being a leader at positive thought. I love being with you at home and overseas and feel a sense of purpose and achievement in our lives despite having no idea about where we will live or work in the future. It is scary at times but mostly very exciting. The one thing I really know is that I love you and want to share those future exciting times with you (and, of course, the present ones). We are quite unique in our ability to be apart but be

together. We know we both (me especially) occasionally need space, but instead of making a big deal about it, we just do it and return with rejuvenated love and support. All that I am, Babe, I am! I love you to death and always will. I am committed to you and have the utmost faith in you and us. I don't think anything could change that. The team forever, Stitto.

I WONDERED how I had ever doubted his steadfast love for me. *Why do I feel scared and vulnerable at times? I get overcome with this fear that it won't work out for me. Like I'm not worthy of the happily ever after story. That somehow if I believe it's my story I will jinx it and something bad will happen because I don't really deserve it. Why do I do that? What causes old I am not enough programmed thoughts to resurface sometimes? Is this triggered residual fear from my ex's infidelity? Sitty is not my ex, I am safe.*

When I walked back onto the balcony, I looked left towards the burning ghat (North), and noticed three barn owls on the power lines all facing towards us. With big blinking eyes gazing straight at me. *Freakie. This is definitely an auspicious sign from Dad.* Three wise, intuitive animals capable of seeing through darkness by looking at situations from all angles.

Dad's telling me to take a leap of faith amidst the uncertainty, hey if I can surrender in chaotic Varanasi, surely I can surrender in my relationship. It's the same principle.

I sat down to tell Stitty about the owls, but he got in first, and the night got even more bizarre.

"Babe, you won't believe it. You know how the river level went down a bit, and the boy's body is now lying on the ghat. Well, the feral street dogs are coming for it," Stitty explained.

The hours that followed were a Broadway play. We had exclusive front row seats overlooking *West Side Story* on the west bank of the

Ganga. Dogs and their gangs battled for control of the corpse. We were thoroughly captivated and enthralled. We named all the characters. There was Top Dog, Spot, Mangy, New Kid, Shaggy, Tuff Mumma, Prize Fighter, Gypsy, Timmy, Mr. Cool, Pointy Nose, The Hunter, The Greyhound, and Sores Galore. Each had a distinct personality, a backstory, and a motive for wanting that meat. They were mean and hungry, cunning and tactical. Top Dog would fight off Timmy, then as soon as Top Dog ambled away, Timmy would return with a cavalry. Top Dog would attack and single-handedly gain control again. With barely time to scratch his balls, Top Dog faced Tough Mumma with gnarly teeth and dripping teats. She fought hard but retreated into the darkness. Later in the night, Top Dog relented, allowing Tough Mumma access to the cadaver. We wondered if she would pay for the sustenance with her body. That is the beauty of non-verbal forms of theater; our imaginations could heighten the drama, provide timely wit and impress each other with plot twists. The stage was so close and intimate that the barrier between the audience and the actors disappeared, allowing our worlds to merge. The set changed depending on the night shadows as the moon rose high in the sky. The rhythmic sounds of the city provided the music for brilliantly choreographed dances. However, some ghat fights looked more like playful, improvised tango dances. Meer Ghat's ominous mood contributed to each scene's atmosphere, but the dogs were the stars of the show. The constant realization that the boy's remains were not a prop, but someone's child acted as a shocking reminder that our West Side Story was far from creative fabrication. It was more demanding than it was entertaining. Viewing it as a play allowed us to be one step removed from the harsh reality unfolding before our eyes. We witnessed a part of Varanasi we did not know existed. We knew stray dogs scavenged for food but never imagined we would be privy to their unique underworld existence.

Meeting the *Doms*

ONE FORTUITOUS DAY, we were sitting in Meer Ghat and began talking to a local man. He told us he was Dom Raja whose family, the Chaudharys, had always owned Manikarnika Burning Ghat. We asked him all the questions we could never ask Babu Maharaj. Dom Raja told us that 3,500 years ago, Lord Shiva gifted his family with the eternal flame that guarantees *Moksha* (breaking the karmic cycle). All funeral pyres must be lit from his family's flame to ensure *Moksha*. He dealt with the relatives of the deceased to negotiate payment, and he hired other *Doms* to do the wood chopping, burning and fossicking. Families paid however they could: a watch, gold jewelry, a cow. Poor families who could not afford the wood required to burn the body to ash (five hours worth) would see their partially burned loved ones thrown to feral dogs, vultures, and kites (large birds). He said the rich and the royals request sandalwood and insisted their family members be burned separately to lower caste bodies.

Dom Raja believed his family was the most important in the Hindu religion because, without their flame and their cremation skills, Hindus did not experience *Moksha,* liberation. However, he lamented that most Hindus did not respect him and his people. Although India abolished the caste system in 1950, they were still looked down upon and called 'untouchables.' Higher caste Hindus feared that *Doms*, who handled the dead, would contaminate them, so they would not touch them. *Doms* were still discriminated against; for example, *Doms* were not permitted to enter the main *Kashi Vishwanath Temple*. It was hard for Raja Dom to do basic things like socializing or having a bank account. If he wanted to get another job, he could not because no one would give a *Dom* an apprenticeship or support their shops or restaurants. Therefore, the cremation business was his only option. He said it was hard seeing so many dead bodies in so many forms.

We asked him why we heard male relatives at the burning ghat saying, "Ram Namm Satya Hai." He explained that it meant *truth is the name of Lord Rama* and is chanted to aid enlightenment, redeem evil deeds, and give the person over to God, who is the ultimate truth. We inquired why his workers cracked open the human skulls. He said to release the *atman* (soul) from *samsara*. He added that if the skulls were not smashed up, they would be used by Aghori Sadhus as bowls. We thought we would leave that subject right there; sometimes, India's religious practices are too gross to even comprehend.

Raja Dom invited us back to his house. We accepted excitedly. *How is it that Stitty and I attract these extraordinary opportunities?* We entered his big blue waterfront palace. As we stood on their large balcony overlooking the *Ganga* I contemplated the irony of the grand-looking tigers that symbolized the king's power. Raja Dom said Raja meant king; he laughed, "There are two kings of Banaras." In a way, he was right. In other parts of India, *Doms* were banished to the outskirts of shanty towns, but not in Varanasi, where they occupy prime real estate. *Just another Indian contradiction.*

He showed us his gym. Again, I pondered the paradox: they *are rich enough to have a private gym in their home but can not access town water elsewhere.* His family was training local men in traditional wrestling called *Akhada*. Some were whirling around huge concrete baseball bat-shaped apparatus called *jodis*; others used ancient-looking exercise props or weights that looked like stone boulders on one-ended barbells. These men were strong, agile, and combative. Raja Dom invited us to attend a *Kashti Akhada* tournament. *Akhada* was the one sport in Varanasi where all castes and Muslims competed against each other. We looked forward to seeing this event and were not disappointed. Hundreds of people gathered in the middle of Varanasi to watch the archaic spectacle.

. . .

The story behind the myths

ON STITTY'S 31ST BIRTHDAY, we traveled ten kilometers by cycle rickshaw to Sarnath, where the Buddha gave his first sermon. Babu Maharaj contacted Sriram, a Benares Hindu University academic who asked me to proofread his handwritten thesis on Rama's Hero Journey. Sitting on the floor, surrounded by floor-to-ceiling books, musty with century-old, scholarly philosophers' pages, I squinted in the dim light for seven hours until my job was done. I wondered *Had one of Sriram's relatives attended the Buddha's famous sermon? Did the Buddha personally inspire the words scribbled within these moldy manuscripts?*

Translating Sriram's thesis gave me a penetrative insight into Indian archetypes. This fantastic Ramayana story follows the dutiful, strong, and handsome prince protagonist Rama on his hero's journey. First, he leaves his palace to enter a dark, unknown world. Secondly, he must resist evil temptations by fending off the demon king's sister's advances and passing specific tests to prove his worth. Thirdly, he enlists celestial help from Hanuman, the monkey god, to rescue Sita, his beautiful bride. Fourthly, Sita must prove her fidelity by passing through fire unscathed. Lastly, they return to their old life more evolved than when they left.

Before proofreading Sriram's dissertation I thought Hindus who believed in these far-fetched stories were naive but after talking with Sriram, I understood the hero myths place in society. They establish archetype characters that allow one billion Hindu's worldwide to learn values, morals, and ethics. Rama, the main character, explored his personality and his place in the world just as those listening to the story establish their identity. This self-exploration contributes to collective identity. I finally got it. Knowledge of mythology is central to Hindu life; children grow up cradled in the tradition of oral storytelling, thus, actively engaging in conversations about human behavior. Regardless of their literacy levels and socio-economic status, Hindus can explore what it means to be human, our natural tendencies and how folklore has shaped us for centuries.

The Ramayana story, for example, highlights what it takes to achieve your goals. Rama had to believe in something greater than himself, which symbolizes humans' quest to identify and connect with something greater than themselves to help navigate life's challenges. Rama's tale also normalizes individuals' strengths and weaknesses and shows how gods support humans to achieve their desires. For example, Rama's faith and devotion to Hanuman provided the superhuman aid necessary to save his beloved Sita. As Rama matures and evolves, he personifies each stage of human development. He gains the resiliency skills and virtues necessary to deal with life's ups and downs. Rama empowers Hindus to be humble and never jealous of the gods.

Rama's story was similar to my hero's journey. When I first traveled to India/Nepal, I left my comfortable Sydney Eastern Suburbs existence and ventured into a mysterious country. I was scared and wanted to turn back, but I went anyway. I encountered many evil temptations in the form of men who tried to kiss me, but I resisted them all and stayed faithful to Stitty. I had answered the call to go traveling, but I ignored a deeper calling to give back to my host nation. Finally, I answered this ultimate call to be of service and went alone into the Nepalese village. Here I encountered my dark night of the soul and questioned everything I had ever known. The silence and the mountains mentored me. Next, I crossed a symbolic threshold by journeying alone through Russia, entering a metaphorical innermost cave. Like all the heroes, I called on divine intervention, in the form of angels at St Nicholl's Cathedral and the living angel Graham to get home in time to see my father before he died. I came back to Australia, not like Rama, on a flying chariot, rich with floral ornamentation but on a 747 Qantas jet. Meanwhile, Stitty had been through his ulcerative colitis dark night of the soul and was ready to answer the call to heal himself. With my newly developed qualities, I was able to accompany and support Stitty on his hero's journey to wholeness.

My birthday letter to Stitty contained none of the anger, fear and doubt present in the first letter I had written just three weeks earlier. No, this was a true love letter.

Dear Stitto,

I'm sitting here overlooking the Ganges feeling supremely happy and content. Babe, I am totally happy - there is nothing I need or want. Nothing except enjoying each day with you, something so easy, so comfortable. Here's to enjoying many more days together. Happy 31st birthday, Stitty - we sure had a magical day in Sarnath - we sure have a magical life! I love you and trust you completely.

Love,
Your Babe

Once upon a time in a row boat

FRIDAY, **July 27th**

Stitty told me he had booked a row boat and boatman for a sunset trip along the *Ganges*. He encouraged me to wear a sari as he was dressed in his white Indian kurta pajama (white tunic top over white drawstring pants). So, I put on my hot pink sari, a locally beaded necklace, a red teardrop bindi, a toe ring, and red powder on my part (which symbolizes marriage—*we told Indians we were married*). I noticed he was repeatedly cross-checking the contents of his bag before we left our room, but civil engineers do this kind of thing.

We walked downstairs to Meer Ghat. "Hello," Stitty said to the boatman, "I booked you yesterday."

"No boats today, Kolkata man drown, no boats on the *Ganga* allowed now," replied the boatman.

Stitty pulled the man to the side and somehow convinced him to break the law and take us out. Of course, two of his friends would be accompanying us or "no deal." The four of us hopped into a small, bright green rowboat and set off—the only boat on the *Ganges*! This was unheard of!

To be gliding solo through the water felt surreal. We had studied this river for weeks, and there were usually hundreds of boats out at this time, but not today; we were in the only boat. The whooshing of the oars juxtaposed silent ripples. I peered into the mirror-like *Ganga*, half expecting the dead to peer back. Instead, I saw my face reflecting a twinkling *Ganga* goddess vibe. I smiled to myself. *Even mundane acts become divine here.*

When we reached the other side, during the last moments of the sunset, Stitty leaned over and took my left hand. "Babe, I love Varanasi, and I love you (he took a ring out of his pocket and placed it on my ring finger). I couldn't think of a better place to ask you to marry me. Will you marry me?" He nervously asked.

"Are you joking? Of course, I will!" I squealed.

"I don't know what else to say, Babe. I guess I don't need to say anything else. I've always known it would be you if I got married. I just wanted to be sure that marriage was for me. I want to have kids with you, Babe. I want us to share the rest of our lives together. I was waiting until everything was perfect and now it is. I was going to propose on the top of the Eiffel Tower, but then I thought why am I waiting? Right now is the right time. So I just did it!"

When we pulled into the main Dasaswamedh Ghat, it was evening *aarti* time. Suddenly, the whole city went into darkness. A blackout caused a momentary hush to fall over Varanasi allowing the instruments precedence as *aarti* candles luminously shone against a blackened backdrop. As boats were banned that day, we were the only ones watching the *aarti* from the water, like a private performance. The show was made more special by the locals who warmly waved to us from the steps. When I locked eyes with Babu Maharaj on his bright blue stage, I had a smile from ear to ear. *How had Stitty managed to orchestrate this outrageously romantic proposal? Complete with a Varanasi blackout! I am the luckiest woman alive!*

I was listening to the same noises I had heard on our first night in Varanasi, but the pandemonium of notes now harmonized. Every sound had meaning, turning the deafening noise into melodious music. I understood the clamor of symbols, the purpose of the chants, the reasoning behind the prayers, the significance of the offerings, where the goddess statue lived in the temple, why Babu Mararaj's grandson wore a black dot on his forehead, the importance of the early Vedic texts, the caste system, and the Varanasi cooking style. I felt at home in Varanasi; I knew where to get the best *chai*, who made the best *thali* (a plate of Indian food), how to make *peda* the famous local sweets, and the contents of *Banarasi paan* which is constantly chewed.

Gently undulating, I savored the magical moment. Stitty and I were the only two people in the world who knew of our sacred union. We had attracted so many generous, kind people by being the love that we are. However, I had almost blown it all. Had I given Stitty that first letter, he would have been put off by my pressure to propose. Knowing him and his stubbornness, I suspect he would have postponed the whole thing until he felt trusted again, if ever! Luckily, I used Nikki to vent my feelings. By the time I wrote to Stitty for his birthday, I had shifted my perspective from lack to abundance, which allowed me to focus on gratitude. My vision to get married came true when I stopped identifying with a false *I need to be engaged by 30* self. As soon as I let go of that expectation, I became something greater than *little me having little doubts*. I realized I was projecting my happiness into the future by thinking *I will be happy when Stitty asks me to be his wife*—in the meantime, this craving was preventing me from experiencing joy. Once I applied my mantra *It is not good; it is not bad; it just is* to me being 30 and not engaged, the desire for the moment to be different disappeared. I no longer needed to try and control Stitty. Instead, I surrendered, focused on being happy in the now and soon my new thoughts created the reality of my dreams. Looking back I notice when I was mySELF Expressing Love Frequency everything just fell into place.

We sought out our sadhu friend Arimdum to tell him the truth: we were unmarried but now we were getting married. He gave us his blessings and gave us a tiny symbolic print on a little frame and a miniature stone Shiva lingam, a representation of creation and masculine and feminine unity.

On the way back to our room Stitty told me he rang Mum the day before and said, "In the absence of Mr. Joyce, I have something to ask you. I want to ask if it's ok to ask Katie to marry me?" Apparently she started crying and replied, "Finally! Oh, she will be so thrilled!" He then added, "I only hope she says yes." Mum insisted, "Of course she will."

Back in our room, I flipped through my travel diary, where I wrote book quotes that inspired me. And there in one of Bryan's insight meditation handouts, was a quote that perfectly summed up my desperate clinging.

Free and Easy: A Spontaneous Vajra Song' by Ven. Lama Gendun Rinpoche

Happiness cannot be found through great effort and willpower,
But is already present, in open relaxation and letting go.
Don't strain yourself:

There is nothing to do or undo.
Whatever momentarily arises in the body-mind
Has no real importance at all,
Has little reality whatsoever.
Why identify with, and become attached to it,
Passing judgment upon it and ourselves.
Far better to simply
Let the entire game happen on its own,
Springing up and falling back like waves,
Without changing or manipulating anything,
And notice how everything vanishes and
reappears magically, again and again,
Time without end.
Only our searching for happiness
Prevents us from seeing it.
It's like a vivid rainbow which you pursue
Without ever catching
Or a dog chasing its own tail.
Although peace and happiness do not exist
As an actual thing or place,
It is always available
And accompanies you every instant.
Don't believe in the reality
Of good and bad experiences:
They are like today's ephemeral weather,
like rainbows in the sky.
Wanting to grasp the ungraspable,
you exhaust yourself in vain.
As soon as you open and relax this tight fist of grasping,
Infinite space is there, open, inviting and comfortable.
Make use of this spaciousness, this freedom
and natural ease.
Don't search any further.

*Don't go into the tangled jungle
Looking for the great awakened elephant
Who is already resting quietly at home
In front of your own hearth.
Nothing to do or undo
nothing to force,
nothing to want
and nothing missing,
Emaho! Marvelous!
Everything happens by itself.*

I SAT in awe as this profound life lesson sunk deep into my psyche. Then a wave of gratitude washed over me like holy water *Thank you to whoever told me not to give that letter to Stitty. Thank you, thank you, thank you.* In hindsight I believe it was the voice of my future self on a parallel timeline.

I peered at Mother *Ganga* through the green balcony that wrapped around the Ganpati Guest House, I was already pining for her. The eternal bond we developed with this city was as indescribable as the city itself. The most visceral place on the planet can not be confined to English words. Our glowing adoration for Varanasi will linger in our consciousness until our very last breath and beyond.

On the day we left, Sitty waded into the *Ganga* polluted with dangerous bacteria. I laughed and sang out to him, "If Dr. Barody could see you now, he would be horrified but proud at the same time." I smiled widely as I marveled at Stitty's unwavering belief in his invincible SELF's health.

Babu Maharaj is right, we are Rada Krishna, with a divine love capable of smashing any obstacle in our way.

12

MAKING BABIES SELF

30 - 37 years old

Trigger warning: Story contains potentially triggering content for trauma survivors relating to pregnancy, miscarriages and childbirth.

AFTER VARANASI, we visited the beautiful Taj Mahal and flew from Delhi to London. We had two weeks in London and two weeks in Paris and spent more money that month than the seven months in India/Nepal! We lived it up! After that, we traveled for four months through Brazil. When our twelve-month trip was over, we considered forgoing our return plane ticket to live in São Paulo. We dreamed of Stitty being the resident DJ at *Love Night Club* and me being the door bitch, since I am so proficient at languages (not)! After careful deliberation, we decided to come home to Sydney.

We rented an apartment on Bondi Road in Bondi until we bought our house in Newtown in Sydney's inner west.

Before we knew we had traded in our backpacks for a mortgage, a car, two jobs, and an upcoming wedding with 160 family and friends. We instantly transformed from young and carefree to mature and responsible. Commitments, obligations, and schedules created opportunities to stay connected to our traveling mindset. But it was not easy, it was a balancing act. We had left Sydney embarking on a one year trip around Australia and returned after four years! So we needed to adjust to the pressures of family, friends, and employment expectations.

Stitty got a job as a project engineer building a challenging Sydney tunnel for electricity cables. Despite the immense stress of his career, his health never faltered.

I worked part-time as an Education Consultant in the Drug Education Unit at the University of Sydney (USYD). The unit was coordinated by Meg, an old university lecturer of mine. Yes, I was working back at the university where I did my four-year degree! Meg had even given me feedback on my Health Promoting Schools honors thesis! The unit consisted of a drug education resources library and provided expert personnel to run community workshops and assist with policy writing and educational resource development. For example, I wrote a school resource on values education for Father Chris Riley's Youth Off The Streets.

I walked to work along King Street, Newtown and on my days off, Mum helped me organize our wedding which was scheduled for September 20th.

The chosen ones

IN JANUARY, I went off the contraceptive pill to prepare my body for a honeymoon conception nine months later. Instead, we accidentally conceived our first child in April (just before my 31st birthday). Two weeks before the conception, I was overwhelmed with the urge to be pregnant. I had never felt this way throughout the six years we had dated. I told Pammie, Patti's friend, "There is no way I can wait five months to get pregnant. I am so dying for a baby; it's unbelievable! I have never felt clucky before; it is the strangest feeling."

The next time Stitty and I made love, at the moment before he ejaculated, he asked me, "Is this a safe time?"

I replied, "Well, it wouldn't matter." I could not believe what I was saying! Subconsciously, I must have sensed our baby busting in and I intuitively let it in.

He questioned, "Wouldn't matter because it's safe, or wouldn't matter if you got pregnant?"

That was it. That was all the window our baby needed; bang, it was in! After that day, I no longer felt clucky and never thought about a baby again until I found out I was seven weeks pregnant!

How did I find out? A dolphin told me. Yes, you read correctly; a dolphin gave me the news. My friend Holly and I went swimming with wild dolphins at Bunbury in WA on the morning of Katrina's wedding. We stood in the ocean in chest-deep water and patiently waited for the wild dolphins to approach. One dolphin swam straight to me and rubbed its snout back and forth on my belly. I could feel its vibration and heard a sound. This extraordinary occurrence caused me to jump back in surprise.

The ranger said, "Oh, you're pregnant."

I replied, "Oh no, I'm not; my wedding isn't until September."

He smiled and said, "I think you'll find you are. These dolphins use sonar to detect fetuses, then rub against them. They never get it wrong."

Two days later, I went straight to work after getting off the red-eye flight from Perth. I fell asleep at my desk at USYD. This fatigue was unheard of. I was only 30 years old, so a Saturday all-night wedding followed by a midnight flight arriving at 6:00 am would ordinarily be easy for me. Not this time. I wondered what was wrong.

When I showed Stitty the positive home pregnancy test stick, he was shocked and said it was impossible. He was convinced it was a false positive, adding, "I'm not ready for a baby yet Babe." A second pregnancy test at the doctors confirmed my pregnancy. Then an ultrasound showed our baby's gestational age. Seven weeks (taken from day one of my cycle, meaning I conceived five weeks prior). In typical Stitty fashion, he sucked up his surprise and disbelief, "Well, this is unexpected but ok."

Being 30, I had partied hard, not knowing I was pregnant. In fact, I had had four all-nighters since the baby was conceived. I panicked and rang a doctor who told me to relax, it was early days, and my alcohol consumption would have no effect on the baby because plasma transference through the umbilical cord did not fully kick in until six to eight weeks gestational age. I felt relieved but still guilty, so I immediately gave up drinking.

My uncharacteristic desire for a baby coupled with my apathetic response during intercourse proved to me that bardo beings exist. I learned about bardo beings at the eight-day silent *Introduction to Buddhism* retreat at *Tushita* in McLeod Ganj in northern India. Bardo beings are the intermittent state or vehicle for consciousness. They leave a body at the time of death and search for a karmically matched rebirth. At the point of conception, when the sperm enters the egg, the bardo being/consciousness enters the new physical body. On this occasion, I directly experienced these teachings. I felt the bardo being hanging around, waiting to be conceived. I witnessed its power and ability to give me an undeniable yearning for a baby, a yearning never before felt. I watched it create an opportunity to become our baby against all odds. Mum had already paid the deposit on my slinky silk Nelson Leong wedding dress, but somehow, this bardo being managed to orchestrate the whole thing! Incredible.

Pregnancy and birth

I WILL BE HONEST; I have no idea where I got the confidence to choose a drug-free pregnancy and birth. I did not even have a doctor. I can assure you this confidence did not come from my father. Donn Joyce worshiped drugs and doctors. He left Michigan State University and became a sales rep. at one of the biggest pharmaceutical companies in the world, he needed doctors to prescribe his drugs. Fast forward 27 years he was one of the Senior Vice Presidents of the whole company! Growing up, if I had a sore throat, Dad would fling open a cupboard door and pass me antibiotics. Medication ruled his world. But I wanted to do it differently. I longed to stand in my power as a woman able to bring forth life naturally. I had deep empathy for newborns. I appreciated how different life was on the outside compared to life on the inside, in the placenta. I wanted their first experience in the world to be as trauma-free as possible. I did not want doctors hooking me up to machines, forcing me onto my back. I did not want anesthetics to block my body's signals and interrupt our baby's communication. I did not want staff poking, prodding, and probing. I planned on intuitively bonding with my unborn child during the birthing process instead of being constantly distracted by medical practitioners.

For these reasons, I chose a birth center and a team of midwives over an obstetrician. No one else in my friend group made this decision. Fortunately, there was a birth center at the Royal Hospital for Women in Randwick (where I grew up) near Mum's new house in Queens Park (Mum moved while we were living in Kalgoorlie). The birth center was about 35 minutes from our Newtown place. Their birthing rooms look like bedrooms with dimmed lights, a double bed, a bean bag, and an adjoining room with a bath, basin, toilet, and shower. Experienced midwives ran the center without a doctor in sight. I only had ten appointments throughout the pregnancy and saw a different midwife each time. They would put the doppler on to listen for the fetal heartbeat, assess fetal growth and development by measuring the fundal height, measure my blood pressure, and order necessary antenatal blood tests or required scans. I surprised myself; I had complete confidence in my ability to communicate with my unborn baby telepathically. I believed that if something were wrong, I would know. I also trusted the birth center staff, who were highly professional, relaxed, and non-invasive.

As a sports teacher, I hoped our baby would wait until January to come so they would be the oldest in their age group at sporting carnivals! So I told the baby, "Wait until the new year, little one." On New Year's Eve, we went to the Taylor's in Vaucluse to watch the Sydney fireworks from their balcony. Afterward, with thousands of other revelers, our car crept down the iconic 'S' bends in bumper-to-bumper traffic. We did not arrive home until 2:00 am. I spent the next day honoring the silence, burning labor-inducing essential oil blends, massaging my feet, and telling the baby the new year had arrived, and it could come out now. I sang, meditated, and chanted until bedtime.

Thursday, January 2nd (31 years old)

I COULD FEEL our baby's spine against my belly button as soon as I opened my eyes. While I was sleeping, it had turned a quarter turn and was facing backward; experiencing this unique position was surreal. I knew it would be born that day, but I never imagined it would be out by lunchtime! It was 7:00 a.m; I rang the birth center and said I felt constipated; the midwife suggested I dissolve psyllium husks in water and drink it to clear me out., Stitty and I went for a long walk around

Sydney Park. My waters broke and my contractions started. They were so strong that I had to stop and moan audibly. When we left the park, I urgently needed to empty my psyllium-inspired bowel, and there were no toilets. I was not going to make it home, so we approached a woman getting into her car. Stitty said, "You hop in, and I'll run home." The woman gasped and demanded he get in too; there was no way she wanted to be alone with a birthing woman!

We should have left for the hospital when we got home, but I wanted to stay home for as long as possible, famous last words! We had completed a 10-week birthing course with the best in the business, Maree Burrows, at *Birthing Rites* in Bondi Junction. As instructed, I put my hands on the wall during every contraction and circled my hips, groaning, "Wha, Wha, Wha" low and deep. Throughout the birth process, I only deviated from this once. On this occasion, my breathing went shallow, and I made a high-pitched squeal.

Immediately, Stitty stepped in, "Babe, keep it low." He was right; as soon as I went low and deep again, I felt fear subside and a reconnection with our baby and my base chakra.

Stitty repeatedly told my cervix what to do, "Open for our baby, open for our baby."

Birth felt like a mother and unborn child tango using synchronistic telepathy. I followed its instructions, and it followed mine, guided by our primal knowing. The teamwork was impeccable because we had an evolutionary memory that felt innate and instinctive.

The contractions were getting intense and close. I was hot and then cold, which was the transition stage. The contractions were one minute long and two minutes apart. So when Mum called, I had to put the phone down twice mid-sentence, "Wha, Wha, Wha."

Mum shrieked, "Where's Peter? Go to the hospital now; you are about to have that baby. I will meet you there with the birth snacks."

I suddenly realized we were 35 minutes from the hospital, and I could feel the head moving further and further down the birth canal. In an instant, I went from bringing our baby out to trying to keep it in.

On the way, Stitty calmly queried, "Babe, where do we go at the roundabout?"

"Round-about, what round-about. You've missed the turn." I shouted from the back seat, he was driving away from the hospital while I was bracing myself on the baby capsule, trying not to give birth! "Babe, get an ambulance to meet us at the car. It's coming out! I can't hold on any longer," I pleaded.

"Sorry, Babe, there's no time for an ambulance; you will have to take the lift," Stitty replied.

Yes, I was that woman we all dream of seeing in a hospital, wearing a long black dress, sunglasses balancing on the end of the nose, groaning excruciatingly loudly. Everyone in the elevator stared with wide-open mouths, wondering if I would drop the baby onto the floor.

As the elevator doors rolled open, I burst into the birth center and called out to Kristy, the midwife, "I need to push!"

She ushered me into a room.

I was delirious and wished I had just stayed home to give birth. Holding it in felt counterintuitive. I ripped off my clothes and leaned on the beanbag letting out an almighty sigh of relief.

I've made it.

"Um, Babe you might need to take your underpants off," Stitty teased.

Even in my deranged state, I managed to laugh. The thought of me trying to give birth in my underpants was too funny to deny.

Kristy examined me, "OK, wow! You're right; you are ready! You are 10 centimeters dilated," she confirmed. "I'll gather my things," she assured me.

When she returned, she passed Stitty a bag of food and clanging drinks, "Katie, your Mum's here. What should I tell her?"

"Tell her to wait please; this baby's about to come out!" I replied between contractions.

I squatted, and Stitty sat behind me on a chair, supporting me under my arms. He spoke calmly into my right ear, telling our baby what to do, "Mum's fine; all this noise is normal. We are so excited to meet you. You can come now. We are ready for you." Stitty was incredibly present, he had not learned what to say in birth classes, but he intuitively knew how to support us. I was impressed.

After half an hour of pushing, a baby girl was born. I cried and cried when I held this eight-pound healthy baby.

Stitty held us in his arms, then looked me deeply in the eyes, "Babe, I am so proud of you. You were amazing."

I let her find her way to the breast and begin feeding. Later, Stitty cut the white cord and took off his top to hold her, skin on skin. After I birthed the placenta (which I buried under the tree at home), Kristy examined her to determine her APGAR score. In Australia, newborns are given a Vitamin K shot and a Hepatitis B vaccine. I said no to both. I refused to believe our baby would be low on Vitamin K and unable to clot her blood. She was perfect as she was and did not need invasive injections. Concerning the Hepatitis B vaccine, I knew I did not have Hepatitis, so there was no chance of me passing it on to her. I was not anti-vaccine, but I did not understand the rush. I felt confident I could arrange an oral Hepatitis B vaccine when she was older. Others are free to do what they think is right for them. There are so many factors to consider.

During birth classes, I must not have listened when Maree taught us to pant and let the perineum skin stretch to avoid tearing. Instead, I pushed her straight out and gave myself a second-degree tear. Luckily, Kristy supported early bonding and agreed to stitch me up on the double bed rather than going into the operating theater. We named our daughter Ruby after a Ruby (short for Reuben) we met in Kalgoorlie. He was a 150-kilogram (330-pound), Māori legend with the most beautiful heart on the planet. That was good enough for us!

Peter was allowed to stay until we left the hospital a few days later. Ruby slept in the middle of us, and we continued this attachment-style parenting after we left the hospital. She stayed by my side the whole time. During the day, she slept on my chest or in an African sling which consisted of a long piece of fabric that I tied behind my back. She slept between Stitty and me during the night, curled up in the space between my chin and hips. Close to the heartbeat she had always known, near my breast's nourishment and the love that created her. She was exclusively breastfed, even while I battled with recurring mastitis.

The first week was bliss but after that was tough. No one told me how hard the first few months can be. I had absolutely no idea what I was doing. I thought motherhood would come naturally to me but I it did not. Ruby cried all the time and never slept. Stitty and I spent the whole time asking each other random things like, is she hungry/tired/thirsty/too hot/too cold/sick/windy? I had postnatal depression because I was expecting to be the perfect mother with the perfect baby. Mum was away in Antarctica, and I was tempted to do controlled crying with my six-week-old, but my friend Franca came over and taught me how to rock Ruby to sleep in the stroller. I am so grateful to her for encouraging me to persevere with attachment parenting.

Six months after Ruby was born, I approached a Faculty of Education lecturer at USYD and offered guest lectures on the award-winning Health Promoting School program I developed in Kalgoorlie. After a few presentations, I was offered a part-time lecturing job in the Faculty of Education, opposite the famous main quadrangle containing the iconic Great Hall.

Click, click, click parallel timelines converged. The decision I made in Kalgoorlie to stay for me and not for Stitty was opening a door at one of the most prestigious universities in the world. I was lecturing, writing my PDHPE teaching courses for undergraduate and postgraduate Bachelor of Education USYD students, running tutorials, and marking assessments. It was a dream job because Mum picked Ruby and me up, dropped me to work, took Ruby back to her house with bottles of expressed milk, and then in the afternoon she picked me up again and dropped us home. It was only 2 days a week too. It was so easy. It felt like my calling to empower individuals to inspire future Australians. I encouraged my students to resolve their trauma before they began teaching personal development topics such as grief, sexual assault, relationships, and suicide. I received emails from students thanking me for helping them realize they needed to deal with some personal issues before teaching. I was way before my time: no one was talking about the psychological effects of trauma back then. As a result, I was nominated, by my students, for a Teaching Excellence Award.

When Ruby was thirteen months, my post-natal depression, coupled with exhaustion from multiple night feeds (I was a human dummy), wore me down. I felt I was attachment parenting without a village and wondered when I would get my life back. We reluctantly went to a Tresillian residential stay to teach Ruby how to fall asleep independently using the controlled crying technique (heart wrenching). It did not really work, and I wish I had known then just how quickly it all goes and not to rush the process.

I weaned Ruby at fourteen months, ovulated two weeks later, and conceived our second baby before my first menstruation post-baby. I had not menstruated in two years while pregnant and breastfeeding Ruby, so I was shocked to discover I was pregnant again. I sensed I was pregnant because I get a distinctive feeling in my eyes. They only feel this way when I am pregnant. Again I gave up drinking completely during pregnancy and returned to the midwives at the birth center.

My first two children were born 22 months apart.

Monday, November 3rd (33 years old)

THIS BABY WAS eight days late. I was doing every wife's tale imaginable to bring on the birth: sex, drinking castor oil, burning clary sage essential oil, meditating, acupuncture, nipple massage, and the local playground seesaw/teeter-totter! On the morning of my second birth, I went to our regular Centennial Park (Sydney's Eastern Suburbs) 'rocket park' catch-up. I decided that if I held the newborns, it would bring on my birth. So I cuddled them all, especially the crying ones!

It worked!

That afternoon I went walking with my bridesmaid Georgi. By the end of the walk, I was reporting contractions, so Georgi convinced me to go to the birth center. We left Ruby with Mum, and Stitty drove me peacefully to the Royal Hospital for Women. Like Ruby, this baby arrived quickly, within five hours.

We were the only ones in the birth center that night, just us and Tess, the midwife on duty. When my contractions got close together, Tess joined us but watched quietly from a chair. Her unobtrusive manner made me feel empowered and capable of following my body's cues. I also felt uninhibited, knowing we were the only people in the birth center, so I did what worked during Ruby's labor. With every contraction, I made the same low and deep groans while standing with my hands on the wall, rotating my hips clockwise, and visualizing the head moving down like a corkscrew. I kept active between contractions by circling my hips on a medicine ball.

At one point, I stood up to pace and was overwhelmed by an unexpected wave of euphoria that washed over my entire body—a gush of endorphins throbbed through me. My body had naturally produced the oxytocin hormone causing a surge of energy to help me cope with the pain. As a result, I felt as high as a kite. Tingling sensations ran from the top of my head to the tips of my toes, igniting extreme pleasure.

I felt weightless, as though floating; I tipped my head back, opened my mouth, and powerfully moaned while sensually rolling my head from side to side. Slowly I articulated what I was feeling. Each word was uncontrollably drawn out, "Oh my God, this feels so beautiful. I feel ecstatic. I am off my face."

I dropped to my knees and put my hands on the wall. I unconsciously dropped my head back and opened my throat chakra. I connected with the voice of my unborn child and spontaneously started singing these beautiful toning sounds. It started so incredibly low that I felt like a male humpback whale. Then the next sound was slightly higher, and each one went up, up, up in octaves until I sang the highest note I could physically sing. This final note seemed to raise the roof. My toning was hauntingly harmonic and reminded me of Ariel singing in *The Little Mermaid*. After I hit the top note, I bent over my swollen belly, convulsing with an intense orgasm that came out of nowhere. It was so unexpected that it took my breath away and replaced it with a sobbing sound as air escaped with each strong shudder.

"I need to push," I announced.

"Then push," Tess replied.

Stitty scooped his arms under my armpits from behind and shifted me from kneeling to squatting as I pushed our baby out in one push. Like an Olympian goalie, Tess dove to catch the slippery newborn as it flew out of me!

"It's a baby girl!" Tess exclaimed as she passed her to me.

Again, I had forgotten to pant and stretch, so needed stitches for my second-degree tear. But I could not feel anything. I was still blissed out and shocked by the orgasm. *How did that happen? I've never ever heard of a woman orgasming during the final stage of labor. I guess the song I sang heightened the effects of oxytocin and caused an orgasm—wow, the power of sound and the hormones.*

We named our second daughter Georgina, Gigi for short, after her adored 86-year-old great-grandmother Sally Sutherland (Mum's mum), known as GG, short for Great Granny. Granny loved having a granddaughter named after her but did not love being referred to as 'Old GG' from that moment on. She was still an incorrigible flirt, wearing Ferragamo shoes, beautiful pencil skirts, colorful shirts, and pink lipstick.

Mothering a newborn second time around was easier because we knew what we were doing and we knew how fast it went. By the time Gigi was a year old she was falling asleep with Ruby so we never had to do controlled crying with Gigi.

I chose to wait a few years before conceiving again. I wanted to get my body and my mojo back. I wanted to feel sexy again. I had been pregnant or breastfeeding for four years straight without a single menstrual cycle. Like Ruby, Gigi shared our bed and had 24/7 access to the breast for 14 months. So, you can imagine Stitty's desires were not my priority. As a result, those times were not peppered with passion.

There was a lot of passion for the next two and a half years. When we decided to have a third baby I went to the doctor to have my copper IUD removed. I asked her if it was ok for me to conceive straight away. I probably should have mentioned that we only have to be naked in the same room, and I get pregnant!

She told me, "You might as well have a go."

We already had two girls, so I bought *How To Have A Boy: A Step-By-Step Guide to Scientifically Maximize Your Chance of Conceiving a Son* by J Martin Young. The author advised us to abstain from sex until I ovulated. I did not ovulate until day 17 of my cycle. *No wonder we have never had a boy! We have never gone 17 days without sex the whole time we have been together.* According to the book, the female sperm can last longer than the male sperm, so in our case, every time we made love, a female sperm would hang around until I ovulated and would get in before a male sperm got the chance.

On the morning of my third conception (17 days after the doctor removed my IUD), I rang Stitty, "Come home from work. I've tested the hormone levels in my wee, and today is the day to conceive a boy." During intercourse, I imagined Stitty's male sperm entering my healthy fertile egg. I kept my legs up for 15 minutes afterward.

Sure enough, a few weeks later, I had that distinctive feeling in my eyes, and a pregnancy and ultrasound confirmed the pregnancy. I had conceived our son Donn Wrixon Stitt (Donn after my Dad, who changed his name from Donald to Don with two 'n's when he tired of being called Daffy Duck in America in the 1940s, and Wrixon was Stitty's Dad's middle name and great-grandfather's first name).

Then about five weeks later, I miscarried Donn Junior after eating liver in a Newtown restaurant.

All my children are my teachers, even Donn Junior. He taught me STOP TRYING TO CONTROL EVERYTHING INCLUDING THE GENDER OF YOUR BABY. Losing a son was a massive wake-up call. I had micromanaged the conception to try and get my needs met when I did not need to—we did not have fertility issues. Grasping for a boy and pushing away a girl implied that I would only be happy if our baby were a boy, I could not accept the baby the way it was and that I was incapable of practicing unconditional love.

Donn reminded me that I lose sight of the bigger picture when I want something too much. We had always created our babies impulsively during acts of passion, lust, and love. The spark that made them was magic. When I studied the *How To Have A Boy book*, I became rigid, clinical, and structured. The instant I lost Donn Junior, I knew my inability to trust cost me a son.

Looking back I realize my choice to identify with the false *mother-of-a-son* self caused me to vibrate at a lower frequency. Surely my evolved self whispered *Remember Varanasi. Don't grasp too tightly, Kitty. Release your hold, let infinite intelligence do its thing. Let go, have faith, and everything will work out as it is meant to work out. There is no need to pull or push; surrender.* Why did I choose to ignore this inner voice?

For my fourth conception, I was determined to be spontaneous again. I vowed to leave it up to the universe and return to making babies the old-fashioned way. Based on the amount of sex Stitty and I had, I suspected we would have another girl, but I was ok with that. I promised Donn Junior that I would welcome whatever was perfect for our family with my mantra *It is not good; it is not bad; it just is.*

Wednesday, September 24th (37 years old)

ON THE MORNING of my third birth, I was at our regular 'rocket park' catch-up with my girlfriends, when my waters broke. Everyone started fussing over me and offering to take Gigi (Ruby was at school). Suddenly, one of my friends started laughing at my soaked maternity jeans, and we all got hysterical.

I went to the birth center and Stitty met me there.

When I found out the midwife's name was Donna, I knew Dad (Donn with 2 'n's) was watching over me. When I found out Donna had five girls, I knew I was having another girl! Donna was a substitute midwife because all the Royal Hospital for Women midwives were at a meeting, so, like my second birth, we were the only people in the birth center.

I expressed my concern, "Donna, I'm really worried that I will tear again."

"Look, Katie, while ever you are using the word tear you are telling your body you want it to tear. Do you want your body to tear?" She questioned.

"No, I definitely don't!" I declared.

"Well then, start telling your body what you want it to do. Start saying words like stretch, expand, and elastic," Donna reassured me.

My third birth was another quick one, around five hours. Again, I did what I knew worked. Stayed present to connect with our baby and followed their lead. I consistently made low and deep groans during each contraction while circling my hips. Between contractions, I did a lot of dynamic movement on an exercise ball. Birth felt like meditation, an opportunity to use my mantra *This too will pass*.

After I asked Stitty and Donna to run me a bath, I had this bizarre past/parallel life abandonment flashback. The second they left the room, an intense fear of being alone, triggered cortisol hormones that flooded my body with fight/flight/freeze feelings. Terror coursed through me like electric shocks having the opposite effect of oxytocin.

I can't give birth to this baby. I can't do it. I whipped my legs together tightly and began running on the spot in a panic as if I was on hot coals. Sensing what panic does to the body during childbirth must have jolted me to pull myself together.

I slapped myself across the face *Kitty, stop. You are the only one who can turn this around. There is nothing to dread. You are fine. You are not alone. You can do this. Stretch for our baby. Stretch for our baby. Surrender to our baby.* I went onto all fours and began panting.

"Stretch for our baby; you can do it. Stretch, stretch, stretch." I said as I imagined my elastic skin expanding.

When Donna and Stitty returned, they could see our baby's head crowning. Stitty sat cross-legged in front of me, held my shoulders, and looked straight into my eyes, "Ok little baby, you can come now, we can't wait to meet you. We love you."

I skillfully let the perineum skin stretch by listening to Donna, who told me when to pant and when to start pushing. The skin miraculously expanded! So no lacerations requiring stitches. The experience showed me that the brain does what it is told to do. By shifting my language and intention, I created my vision.

What did we have? You guessed it, a third girl–she is incredible, and we love her. We named her Matilda. Our friend Nicola suggested this iconic Australian name (*Waltzing Matilda* is an 1895 Banjo Patterson bush ballad) because Stitty is the quintessential Aussie bloke–legendary, laid-back, and tough.

To this day, Stitty and I make love like we are making a baby. Just today, the energy created during our coordinated orgasm could have easily conceived a baby if the timing was right.

Over the years, I have realized that it does not matter how parents make a baby or how it is delivered into this world–it is perfect for all involved. Babies choose us for the lessons we will teach them, and we choose them for the lessons they will teach us. So there are no accidents, only perfect orchestrations.

13

HEARING THE EARTH MOTHER'S CALL SELF

38 years old

WE LIVED in Newtown in Sydney's inner-west (4.7 kilometers/3 miles from Sydney's CBD) for seven years and we still have the house there. There was so much I loved about urban living. I loved walking to University of Sydney (USYD), where I lectured. I enjoyed the neighborhood culture, the charismatic locals, the diverse community, the tight support network, the cafes, the op-shops, the vibrant restaurants from around the world, the late-night street vibe, live music, and Sunday sessions at the local pub (kids and all). I loved living reasonably close to Mum, Old GG, brother, nieces, nephews, and cousins. I loved the way Stitty's old USYD college friends had a dinner club every month. We would meet at different people's houses to catch up on each other's lives. I loved my old school/university girlfriends; we met weekly for a kids' dinner. I loved my new Newtown girlfriends; we did daily playdates in the park accompanied by a glass (or three) of wine. I loved having access to services like community playgroups, kindy gym, and music classes. I loved going to the theaters, museums, art galleries, and stand-up comedy. I loved taking the girls on adventures to Circular Quay and onto a Manly ferry. I loved that our Newtown house was only two and half hours north of Stitty's family's Mollymook beach house, on the south coast of NSW, and we popped down there every other weekend.

I especially loved being near the Sydney Foundation for the Preservation of the Mahayana (Buddhism) Tradition (FPMT) center in Ashfield, called the *Vajrayana Institute.* Founded by Lama Thubten Yeshe and Lama Zopa Rinpoche, FPMT has over 150 meditation centers worldwide (including the Tushita Meditation Centre in McLeod Ganj, northern India where I did my eight-day introduction course). I occasionally attended retreats, workshops, meditation sessions, and their annual *Happiness and It's Causes* conferences. I heard His Holiness the Fourteenth Dalai Lama speak at the Institute and also at numerous conferences. I learned from inspirational teachers such as Venerable Robina Courtin (when I was 30 years old, Robina welcomed me into the Sangha (the community that follows the teachings of the Buddha) and gave me my Buddhist refuge name which is Thubten Péma, meaning lotus flower), Venerable Tenzin Palmo, Matthieu Ricard, Renate Ogilvie, and many other monks and teachers at the center. Living close to a Buddhist institute of this caliber for seven years consolidated what I had learned through Jay and Yvette and on my retreats in India.

But there was also so much I did not love about living in Newtown.

Monday, June 1st

MY NINE-MONTH-OLD MATILDA and I spent five days and four nights in the Royal Prince Alfred Hospital in Camperdown, Sydney.

Unfortunately, Matilda had a bad case of influenza right in the middle of the Sydney SARS (Severe Acute Respiratory Syndrome) outbreak. Doctors were concerned she had SARS because we had spent time with a family who had stopped in Singapore. They advised us to give her Tamiflu, a SARS medication not approved for babies, and we reluctantly agreed. Nurses wore personal protective equipment in the hospital, which made me feel incredibly isolated.

On the day of our discharge, Mum was driving to pick us up when a Thunderclap headache struck her. She pulled over and called emergency services. They took her straight to Prince of Wales Hospital in Randwick because her uncommon type of headache warranted investigation as it could indicate a brain bleed. Poor Mum and poor me. I was already feeling emotional and this news tipped me over the edge. I felt guilty for giving Matilda such substantial doses of medicines (Erythromycin, Tamiflu, Salbutamol, and Augmentin Duo). I was missing Stitty and Ruby, and Gigi (aged four and six). I was fragile from so many days of seeing my baby poked and prodded, needled, and x-rayed. They checked her temperature, her blood, her oxygen levels, her feces, her urine, and her microorganisms. They were extremely thorough, but I just wanted to take her home. I was purely breastfeeding her, so I was desperate to nourish myself with some good old-fashioned, home-made bone broth.

Wednesday, June 3rd

STITTY WAS AWAY in Queensland for business, and I was at home, howling on my bed. I had not cried like that since Dad died 12 years earlier. I felt defeated: my children and Mum were sick, I only had one tree, I lived in concrete, Stitty worked long hours, and I spent my days behind a steering wheel.

I did not know what was wrong with me. All I knew was something big had bubbled to the surface and erupted like an active volcano. I realized I was crying for nature. Why did I have this sudden indescribable yearning to get out of the city and into nature? When I started dating Stitty at the age of 24, I told my friend Lysa that I did not think I could stay with him. If there were any chance he might one day choose to return to his roots and move back to the country, I could not bear to go with him. The mere thought of it filled me with horror as it resembled torture by boredom. Fast forward 13 years, and I was sobbing, face down, spread eagle and desperately screaming to escape my city life.

I lamented *Something is seriously missing. There must be more to life. I need nature, space, big skies, and more trees. Ruby and Gigi, have had colds and coughs all winter; there's mold on the wall in their bedroom; we're a five-person family living in a tiny two-bedroom semi-detached cottage. It constantly feels messy because everything has to be in its place. Mum's got an aneurysm. Stitty goes to work at 4:00 a.m. to write policies for his new startup company within the company he works for, then works late and takes calls into the night.*

Neighbors' houses utterly box in my horizon. The walk to the girl's Australia Street Infants School is along one of Sydney's busiest, most polluted roads: King Street, Newtown. On school mornings, we walk faster than the bumper-to-bumper traffic emitting toxic fumes containing chemicals such as carbon monoxide, nitrogen dioxide, sulfur dioxide, benzene, formaldehyde, particulate matter, and polycyclic hydrocarbons! I just read Toxic Childhood: How the modern world is damaging our children and what we can do about it by Sue Palmer and she's right: my children can't play outside unsupervised because there are fewer eyes on the street now that more people are working. So while I'm doing housework and cooking, they are confined to a tiny paved courtyard. Even though we have Sydney Park on our doorstep, I choose to commute, in traffic, to the Eastern Suburbs (45 minutes there and 45 minutes back) to see my family and school friends. I could live locally, walk everywhere, and embrace inner-city living but instead, I haul us across the city every single day. Stitty's lucky; his officer is in the next suburb.

My craving to connect to Mother Earth was visceral. I felt it in every cell of my body, and I could not deny it. It was like she was calling me home to a home I had never known in this lifetime. I had lived in cities my whole life (Rome, Paris, Indianapolis, and Sydney), and I knew nothing else, except Stitty's property. I did not know the seasons, moon cycles, sunrises, or sunsets.

Mother Earth's call surprised me, I thought I was doing fine without her. These intense feelings of desire were out of character, foreign and surreal. Yet, I was incapable of stopping this uncharacteristic display of emotions. I was in an altered state. Longing for the touch of Mother Earth, grieving our separation, pleading for freedom, crying for my children's health, worrying about Stitty's stress levels, fearful his Colitis would return, yearning for well-being, desperate for wholeness, and dreaming of living free from mold and chemicals.

I had a strange foreboding feeling, like a premonition warning me to get out of the city.

It was one of the most powerful messages I have ever received.

I raised my arms to the sky and begged for change, "Please, please, universe help me."

Click, click, click as thousands of invisible doors open into the future. Letting myself be raw, honest, and vulnerable signaled to the universe *Enough is enough!* Before that moment I think the universe probably thought *She's fine, she's happy enough.* Why? Because I had been raised to focus on the positives, so I avoided complaining because I did not want to appear ungrateful. I feared that I would jinx myself if I admitted there was something lacking considering I was surrounded by so much abundance. To even suggest my life had downfalls seemed weak. So I ignored any whispers from my evolved self. Tonight, my evolved self stopped whispering and starting yelling.

As soon as I expressed my painful innermost fears rather than stuffing them down I allowed them to pass through me to be acknowledged and alchemised. For the first time, I gave myself permission to grieve my lack. I lacked a connection with nature which I had no idea was part of my identity, an aspect of SELF. An aspect I had never known but was me nonetheless. Perhaps, more me than the city me. Maybe we all have an innate burning desire to intimately know Mother Earth.

Stitty returned from his business trip in Queensland two days later and said, "Babe, our parent company, the company I work for, might be going under. How would you feel about moving to the country?"

"Well, that was fast," I replied. The image of me with my arms raised to the sky popped into my head and the words *The universe provides!* You see I did not need to know how things would change, I just needed to know I wanted change. Once I made myself clear, the next most important step revealed itself and all I had to do was take that step.

Eight weeks later, we had rented out our Newtown house, had four farewell parties, and moved to a beautiful lake house in Forbes (population 8,000) a rural town in Central West NSW, where Stitty grew up (before he went to boarding school at age 12, followed by USYD).

How did we do this so effortlessly? We shifted our attention from our problems to our new chapter. We could have moped, sulked, despaired, and put all our energy into worrying about the parent company going under. We could have been 'Mr. and Mrs. Doom and Gloom' and talked about the drama to everyone we met. We could have played into a 'poor me' narrative, but instead, we created a new life for ourselves. We knew that being grateful for the catalyst would make the move more positive, so we looked for things to be grateful for. While 'Mr. and Mrs. Doom and Gloom' would have made the whole story about the negativity of the parent company, we made the entire story about transitioning into an exciting new adventure—a tree-change!

Thursday, July 30th

AS WE DROVE into Forbes behind our removal van, we were singing at the top of our lungs *Waltzing Matilda* as it blared through the car speakers. I remember seeing a big seed-sowing machine in a plume of dust. Sunset rays were shining through the brown cloud. I thought it was one of the most iconic sights I had seen in ages. I felt excited to be moving to the country with my little family.

When we arrived at *Mungarra*, Stitty's parents' cattle station, a car pulled up behind us. It was an old family friend, Nordo. He exclaimed, "Oh, I felt so sorry for you when I saw that tractor in the dust. We are in such a serious drought!"

It's all a matter of perspective. I saw precisely the same scene, but to me, it signaled a fresh start, country life, and a wide-open sky. Not for a second did I feel sorry for myself. I was too busy singing my way into prosperity and good fortune.

Unfortunately, my body was not so convinced. I developed a stiff neck. A few weeks later, Mum came to help me unpack boxes. The next day I woke up in more pain from something called wry neck (acute torticollis). Clearly, my body was incapable of seeing the move from my expanded perspective, which triggered old fears and programs. My body was stressed about everything, which manifested a debilitating physical symptom. Mum and I went into town to the physiotherapist, but it was closed. Then, she noticed a sign in front of a house, *Natural Rhythms Massage*.

Mum said, "What about this place, Darling?"

I walked down the side path to the backyard. Out of the house stepped a woman who looked my age. She was holding a wooden spoon. "Hello," she said in a distinctive Aussie accent.

"Hello," I replied in my international intonation. "I was wondering if you are available for a neck massage?"

Without hesitation, she put down her spoon and cheerfully replied, "Sure." As her smiling eyes signaled me into her studio.

As the door creaked open, I walked into a new chapter in my evolution.

As soon as her warm, strong, healing hands touched my tight neck, I felt my shoulders soften.

"I'm Two Crows," she stated. Her voice was powerful. It seemed to emanate from deep in her belly.

"I'm Kitty, " I mimicked her confident candor.

While she massaged, I inquired, "I'm looking for a mediation group."

"I run a regular Wednesday night meditation/drumming circle here. Tonight we are doing sound healing to release physical blockages!" she replied excitedly.

I could not believe my ears, but then again, I could! I felt the same way I felt when I met Yvette in Nepal and Nikki in the Australian desert. I sensed that Two Crows and I spoke exactly the same language, fluent in Spirituality!

How do I meet soul sisters in the middle of nowhere?

A few hours later, I was toning (free sound expression) with a group of like-minded women. I was wearing my hippie India pants which I bought in Pushkar, Rajasthan. I never imagined I would wear them in this small country town! The first thing Two Crow's best friend Roey said to me was, "Cool pants!"

At one stage, during the sound healing, I hit a high note and then made this weird releasing sound that resembled an orgasm followed by a whimper. I was surprisingly open. Being with them made me feel relaxed, seen, and heard. I knew I had met members of my soul family because we shared the same frequency. I found out that Two

Crows was a Native American/Hawaiian shaman, psychic medium, energy healer, and KaHuna and Lomi Lomi Massage therapist. She was born in Canberra, Australia two weeks before I was born in Rome, Italy.

While she led us through a guided meditation, she played her Native American Medicine Drum, rattles, an uplifting Native American flute, and an Aboriginal rain stick. This shamanic journey took me to a place I had never been in this lifetime. First, I went into the spirit world and met my guides, ancestors, angels, and animal totems. Next, a massive eagle lifted me in its talons and carried me into outer space, where I witnessed a tranquil stillness. Her repetitive drumming then took me back to a time when I was Native American. I was drumming in a teepee. Then I went back into the womb where I felt a rainbow pulsing from Mum's body through me, back into her, and back into me again. This journeywork was incredibly transformative. I was hooked.

After the meditation, I learned that Two Crows did not have Native American blood but had trained, for the past six years, with a Native American Shaman called Medicine Crow whom she met in her hometown Canberra. Medicine Crow is the Chief of the New Jersey Sand Hill Band of Lenape and Cherokee Indians. He lives on Sydney's Central Coast. Medicine Crow is a Doctor of Metaphysics, an ordained minister, has a Ph.D. in Religious Philosophy, and Master Status in the esoteric disciplines of Huna (taught by Dr. Serge Kahili King), Usui Shiki Ryoho Reiki, and Isis Seichim, is a Certified Clinical Hypnotherapist, and a Certified Neuro-Linguistic Programming (NLP) Life Coach and Mentor. I could not wait to meet him!

In no time I moved from Two Crow's client to her friend. We teamed up with Roey to study a book called *The Artist's Way* by Julia Cameron. It is a step-by-step guide to breaking down personal blocks to unleash dormant creativity to birth art. Each week, we would read a chapter, do the exercises, and discuss the process. The activities challenged us to identify obstacles to our painting/writing which exposed our deepest fears and vulnerabilities. As a result, Two Crows and Roey got to know me very quickly. I was the new girl in town, sharing confidential details that I would not be comfortable telling the whole community. However, I felt safe authentically sharing with them because they felt more like soul sisters than strangers. Thus, unshakable trust built the foundations of our relationship and we are still close.

My family and I were living in a stunning heritage-listed lakeside house. Before we left Sydney I searched for a place to rent and could only find ugly houses with shag carpet. Patti, my mother-in-law said, "Leave it with me, you've done your time on shag carpet in Kalgoorlie, you deserve something better now." A few hours later she called back to say her friend had a house on Forbes Lake but was not ready to move into town yet. Her friend said we could rent there until we found a farm to buy (this took two years).

A couple of weeks into *The Artist's Way* course, I invited Two Crows and Roey to the lakehouse to talk about that chapter. I made a special lunch, set the table on the verandah, bought out the linen napkins, and served white wine in Waterford crystal.

Roey spoke up, "You know we manifested you, Kitty?"

"What!" I was shocked, "I thought I manifested you!"

Roey and Two Crows explained that the lakehouse had been empty for months. So they would sneak onto the veranda and practice their Hawaiian KaHuna massage moves (this looks like calisthenics or Tai Chi, but each movement is a massage technique). Two Crows had done the master level at *Mette's Institute at High Spirits Retreat* in Queensland, Australia. KaHuna massage is an ancient Hawaiian practice. 'Hu' means male energy, and 'na' means female energy, and the technique aims to balance the two. Often when they were practicing they would say to one another, "Imagine eating cucumber sandwiches and sipping champagne here."

Then a few months later, they were doing just that.

The truth was we manifested each other. It was because of Roey that Two Crows ended up in Forbes. Two years after Two Crows left her alcoholic husband with her two children, she met Roey through mutual friends of Medicine Crow. Three years later Two Crows was under the shower when she asked for guidance, "Ok Spirit, where am I going? A huge flashing neon-lit sign popped up with F, O, R, B, E, S. She followed the sign, excuse the pun, which led her to her soul mate, Adam. Together they had two children and are happily married. This neon sign also led Two Crows to me. I am in constant awe of invisible hands working behind the scenes to create magic.

While we were studying *The Artist's Way*, I started having a repetitive dream in which I was dying. So I went to Two Crows and asked her, "Am I going to die in real life?"

She assured me that it was the opposite. The dreams represented new beginnings and the death of an identity that no longer served me. She offered a guided shaman's death and rebirth journey using her medicine drum, rattle, and flute. I accepted immediately. She referred to shedding an old snakeskin; I felt it peeling off to reveal a new version of myself. This analogy felt relevant and profoundly transformational. I had a choice: I could grieve the *city me* or birth the *country me*. I had no idea what the *country me* looked, sounded, or felt like; I just knew she could not appear until I let go of my attachments to my old self. I had to view my country experiences neutrally; to do this, I had to resist comparing everything to the city. Instead, I would think *It is not good; it is not bad; it just is*.

After my drum journey healing, Two Crows urged me to focus on the positives. When I did this, surprise, surprise, the stiff neck miraculously went away.

To help me focus on the positives, Two Crows taught me the ancient Hawaiian principles she learned from Medicine Crow, who was trained by Dr. Serge Kahili King Ph.D. (author of *Urban Shaman*) visiting Byron Bay from Hawaii. As soon as Two Crows explained the principles to me I was excited to study this Polynesian Huna wisdom. So, being the diligent student I am, I bought the *Urban Shaman* and began studying the principles. Here is a summary: Principle number one *Ike*: The world is what you think it is (be aware). Principle number two *Kala*: There are no limits (be free). Principle number three *Makia*: Energy flows where attention goes (be focussed). Principle number four *Manawa*: Now is the moment of power (be here). Principle number five *Aloha*: Love is to be happy with (be happy). Principle number six *Mana*: All power comes from within (be confident). Principle number seven *Pono*: Effectiveness is the measure of truth (be positive).

Once I understood these principles, I endeavored to live by them to form new habits. Why? I realized that I could use Dr. Serge Kahili King's principles in every situation in life; I just needed to practice them until they became second nature. When a problem arose, I noticed that one principle jumped out at me. Sometimes a combination of principles could be applied. Once I viewed the problem from this new perspective, a solution appeared. When I researched, I discovered these ancient principles existed in numerous Indigenous cultures throughout the world. They had worked for centuries and continue to work in modern times. I enjoyed Dr. Serge Kahili King's exercises to increase personal and global creative energy, such as bodywork, crystal and symbol usage, shapeshifting, dream interpretation, and performing ceremonies and rituals such as blessings and drum journeys.

I liked the way Dr. Serge Kahili King did not teach the principles as dogma or truth but rather as a set of hypotheses that allowed me to practice sharmancraft in day-to-day life effectively. Dr. Serge Kahili King taught me that if the principles work, then use them; if they do not, use something else. I found they worked for me and combined well with everything in my bag of tricks.

By the time I visited my friends back in Sydney, I had been through a shamanic death and rebirth, I was doing weekly meditation sessions, practicing a Hawaiian modality, and in the middle of an intensive *The Artist's Way* creativity journey.

My friends were shocked.

One friend Katrina, shook her head in disbelief and exclaimed, "I can't believe this, Kitty! You just moved to a conservative farming town in but-fuck nowhere, and you have already met cool people and experienced spiritual shifts. Only you, Kits, could turn potential disaster into happily ever after!"

Later I reflected on Katrina's comment and wrote down my *'potential disaster into happily ever after'* process using my newly acquired Hawaiian principles (Dr. Serge Kahili King taught Medicine Crow who taught Two Crows who taught me). I wrote *Principle number one Ike: The world is what you think it is (be aware). I never thought about the parent company going under as a 'disaster'; I just thought about its potential. Principle number two Kala: There are no limits (be free). Anything is possible if you figure out how to do it. Principle number three Makia: Energy flows where attention goes (be focussed). I paid attention to what I had, not on what I didn't have, which meant I noticed and created abundance. Principle number four Manawa: Now is the moment of power (be here). I made the change by staying in the present moment. The past was over, and the future was uncertain, so my power to change existed in the now, where I could create the new and leave behind the old. This empowered viewpoint shifted everything vibrationally. Principle number five Aloha: Love is to be happy with (be happy). Our family's ability to be content with the moment as it was without wanting anything to make the moment better helped us create change seamlessly. Principle number six Mana: All power comes from within (be confident). That night in Newtown when I raised my arms to the universe, I had an epiphany that energetically created change. I had to make that change happen, no one could do it for me. Principle number seven Pono: Effectiveness is the measure of truth (be positive). As soon as I was out of alignment with my truth and life was no longer working for me, I had to be flexible and change it. Knowing there are alternative ways to do things allowed me to walk through doors as they opened. The cool thing is I did all this before I even knew about the principles. Perhaps I was guided to the principles because my life choices matched their frequency. I know something greater than me led me to Two Crows, I have lessons to learn that can't be learned living in a city.*

Tuesday, February 9th

SIX MONTHS after meeting Two Crows and finishing *A New Earth* by Eckhart Tolle, I received a download with the ending to this book. The plot included a woman in rural Australia (me) with a dream to change the world. The book ends with the moment that changes the world–human consciousness evolves. As I lay there next to my sleeping baby processing this monumental download, I thought *This conclusion isn't fiction. Art can and does create reality. I vowed I won't just write about the evolution of human consciousness; I will make it happen–starting with my evolution.* I sat down and typed up the ending to this book.

I did not know it then but the book was my purpose for being. I believe I was led to Forbes to heal so I could write the book I came to write.

Perhaps during those intimate times with my single lemon-scented gum tree, she whispered, "Kitty, you answered a call from Mother Earth to assist with the evolution of human consciousness. To do this you must first get to know the Earth Mother by learning respect and humility. Once you feel the way she loves you as a mother loves her child, you will love her back and the book will be birthed."

It was scary leaving my family, friends, and University of Sydney job. Everyone I met marveled at the big transition, but I knew the country was where I needed to be. I could not articulate this, but I knew it was part of a bigger picture on some level. Uprooting my life came with challenges that were opportunities to practice what I preached. If I was going to write a book about being happy (my aim at the time), I would have to learn to be happy in the midst of events society perceived as misfortunes (the parent company going under, stiff neck, isolation, dust storms, droughts, floods, and mouse plagues).

It turns out adversity is my most outstanding teacher.

SELF knew it was out of alignment and took care of everything, all I had to do was go with the flow until SELF was back in synch with the vibration of love. The whole catalyst was created by SELF, for SELF to come home to SELF.

14

ADDING TOOLS TO THE TOOLBOX SELF

39 years onwards

I BEGAN a shaman apprenticeship with Two Crows. Her first teaching was, "You are already a shaman, you just need to acknowledge the power within and claim it." She taught me countless tools that I placed in my toolbox of healing modalities. Now when a challenge arises, I reach for the most relevant tool for the job at hand. Knowing which tool to choose gets easier with practice, intuition, and trial and error. The more I expanded my repertoire the more adept I became.

Thinking tools

TWO CROWS INTRODUCED me to Dr. Masaru Emoto's findings. He is a Japanese scientist who discovered that thoughts impact physical reality. He proved this phenomenon using high-speed photography and Magnetic Resonance Analysis to examine water after being exposed to loving words versus water exposed to negative, angry words. He found that the thoughts' intentions impacted the water's physical molecular formations. I was fascinated to learn that scientific research showed that humans' sounds, words, and thoughts affect things physically. Two Crows showed me a picture of water exposed to "thank you" and a picture of water exposed to "I will kill you." I could not believe the difference. "Thank you" looked like a beautiful crystal, whereas "I want to kill you" looked like diarrhea. I was interested to learn more from Dr. Emoto through his book *The Hidden Messages in Water*. His studies were SELF-realization catalysts motivating me to pay close attention to my thoughts and Principle number one *Ike*: The world is what you think it is (be aware).

Soul retrieval tools

WEDNESDAY, **December 15th**

I was at Two Crow's regular Wednesday night meditation/drumming circle when Two Crows taught us how to do a soul retrieval/release. I had never done this before. That day there had been a boat accident. An Indonesian fishing boat carrying 89 Iraq and Iranian asylum seekers and three crew members was swept up in a massive wave and crashed into the rocks at Christmas Island (an Australian territory). Fifty people drowned, including 15 children. Two Crows explained that her friend came to her in spirit the night after he was suddenly killed in a car crash. He reported feeling very disoriented and confused. So during a guided meditation, Two Crows invited us to travel (using imagination, intention and focus) to the Christmas Island accident scene and assist souls in transition. The idea freaked me out, but I gave it a go. When I first allowed myself to imagine the number of bodies, I felt overwhelmed by grief. However, I focussed on connecting with individual souls, especially the children. When I explained to them what happened, I felt deep empathy for what they would feel hearing this news. I paused and waited until it felt appropriate to escort them up through the water where we were met by their loved ones in spirit, who led them into their new vibration. I sensed relief and freedom. Then I went back down to assist the next soul. Over and over until I heard Two Crow's drum and her words, "It's time to come back now."

Communicating with nature tools

TWO CROWS also taught me how to detect the energy field of trees and the energy portals inside groups of trees. She often took me into nature and gave me exercises relating to energy, such as sustained focussed attention. She told me to spend time outside communicating with Mother Earth by listening to the different ways trees (dead and alive), rocks, plants, and foliage vibrate. This subtle detection took a lot of practice because, at first, I could sense nothing. Two Crows also asked me to study *Animal Speak* by Ted Andrews to discover the meaning of animal messages. Andrew's wisdom coupled with learning how animals relate to their environment allowed me to decipher their significance when they crossed my path. For example, if a crow showed up - I would interpret that sign as an encouragement to form a team to tackle my problem (crows never defend themselves against owls alone). Animal messages can turn up in different forms: seen, heard, on a screen, in a song, or in a dream. *Animal Speak* taught me how to work with animals as totems and spirit guides by interpreting their signs until I no longer needed the book.

I loved Two Crows' down-to-Earth Aussie nature. She did not take herself too seriously. She would say, "Not everything is a sign, Kitty; sometimes you just stub your toe."

Spirit communication tools

I WAS FASCINATED by Two Crows because she constantly communicated with the spirit world (sometimes mid-sentence)! The stories she told me could fill my next book. I could not comprehend them with my logical mind, so time and time again, she left me speechless. Each story expanded my knowledge of what was possible. For example, a spirit asked Two Crows if he could use her body to talk to his wife.

When Two Crows answered, "You've got two minutes," the movie *Ghost* went from a Hollywood fantasy to a full-blown reality.

How did she say she felt when he 'stepped in'? She felt utterly freezing - like she was nude in the snow. She shivered until he stepped out and had no knowledge of what happened while he was in there. I found this story fascinating because it proved to me that only one consciousness can inhabit a body at one time.

Dreaming tools

TWO CROWS' is a black belt in karate. She applied the same discipline to developing her dream travels, other realm communication, and dream recall. As a talented artist, she could draw the beings that communicated with her during her dreamtime. Often these beings' appearances were not of this world and their messages were always timely, relevant, and profound. Two Crow's advanced dreaming skills intrigued me and motivated me to diligently practice dream techniques.

During my first lucid dream, I had a nightmare. Ruby (who was on her restricted learner's license at the time of the dream) was driving my car on her learner's permit but instead of supervising her, I was relaxing in the back seat reading a magazine. She plowed our car into a local shop front causing considerable damage. She and I were standing next to the car and shattered glass, surveying the carnage of property and perhaps people. My body and mind ached with guilt and sorrow. It was a vivid moment of harrowing fear laced with excruciating guilt. We were discussing how to tell Stitty which caused me more anxiety. Suddenly out of nowhere, in desperation, I decided to investigate my surroundings to see if there was another option (telling Stitty was too terrifying to even consider because I did not want to disappoint him). Somehow I worked out I was dreaming and excitedly grabbed Ruby's elbows to look into her eyes. "We don't have to do this Ruby, we can just wake up instead," I exclaimed. And with that thought, I woke up and knew I had lucid dreamt.

The first time I astral traveled I was still living in Sydney, I was told (in my dream) that I was going to astral travel, and my friend Sandra would support me. So I sat cross-legged, with others, in a large circle, and Sandra stood behind me with her hands on my shoulders. I immediately shot up like a rocket ship into outer space. The second time I astral traveled I was with Two Crows and we went through a tunnel that seemed to go for ages. Together we went on an intense psychedelic trip exploring a galaxy. I could see energy as colors, I traveled through time, into the past and the future. I visited planets and experienced places unfamiliar to me. We were communicating but it was not English—we were singing like angels. When I returned, I was taken to the local school playground where a student telepathically spoke to me. She translated the light language messages I had received while astral traveling. When I woke I messaged Two Crows who told me she had been meditating at the same time. I think she entered my dream space to support me.

When I explained my dream to our local friend Georgie, a quantum astrologer, she told me that there is a Starseed marker on my chart and on Two Crows' chart that shows we traveled into this galaxy through a wormhole from the Andromeda Galaxy. Perhaps I accessed that past/parallel timeline during the dream. Who knows? This experience showed me that our consciousness goes on adventures when we meditate and when we sleep. Imagine if we could access all these adventures. I believe we can because dreaming is accessing parallel timelines which are all held as memories. This explains the feeling of *déjà* vu, that feeling you have when you are convinced you have experienced something before. A bit like my memory of the moment before creation and my memory of the evolution of human consciousness–I have already experienced these events on a parallel timeline. This was a SELF-realization catalyst. Every moment contains limitless possibilities, it is up to us to use our free will to pick the timeline we choose to exist on. Our choices write our future.

Massage tools

TO BE friends with a KaHuna and Lomi Lomi massage therapist and healing practitioner of Two Crows' caliber felt like a blessing. Knowing health-ease is my birthright, I vowed to make the most of this opportunity by booking monthly massages. I was comfortable enough to use my voice/throat chakra to produce spontaneous sounds (toning) to release physical blockages as she massaged them. We did significant trauma-releasing bodywork during these healing sessions. During one massage, Two Crows told me Mother Teressa, Mother Mary, and Jesus came into the room. Firstly, Mother Teressa told Two Crows, "Use tough love." Then, Mother Mary said, "Use unconditional love." Finally, Jesus said, "Just hand them over to me."

Dying tools

I EXPERIENCED profound realizations during these monthly massages. During one treatment, I slipped into a deep meditative state. My breathing slowed, and I felt like I went through the stages of dying I learned at the Tushita Meditation Centre in northern India during my eight-day silent *Introduction to Buddhism from the Tibetan Mahayana Tradition* retreat. I felt as though I entered the death space. I became acutely aware of my subtle nervous system. I could sense thousands of hollow tubes running through my body around my seven chakras. I visualized them crossing over at my heart and radiating out. As the dying process progressed, I felt myself withdrawing towards the center of my body, sinking into the Earth. As the Earth element lost its power and dissolved, I felt like I had lost my sense of sight. The water element went next, and I felt my bodily fluids dry up. I felt as though I could not smell, hear or touch. With a cold chill, the fire element went next. I sensed the next element to go would be the wind element. I knew I needed to keep this element, so I consciously breathed in and out. I imagined the visions the monks reported seeing in this dying state, like fireflies, an orange sunset, blackness, and then the clear light of death. My heart rate slowed right down. I observed my subtle mind at this final stage. I endeavored to tap into my karmic imprints, which felt like codes running a computer program. I decided to explore the bardo states. I had felt Ruby as a bardo being before she was conceived. Now I wanted to experience myself as a bardo being. According to Tibetan masters bardos are intermediate beings that exist between death and rebirth. I imagined myself entering the first bardo stage. I sensed myself becoming an astral body consisting of my mind. I could see, hear and feel, but I had no physical body. I was pure consciousness. I was floating, propelled by karma, searching for karmically suitable parents with just the right conditions to be re-born.

I noticed how this state of consciousness felt similar to dreaming. It occurred to me that my pursuits in exploring altered states through meditation, multidimensional work, lucid dreaming, and astral traveling would assist me when I was really dying. If I can recognize this final stage, then I have the potential to wake up within it. Having the skills to navigate this usually unconscious realm consciously has many implications. According to the Buddha, at the moment of death a restless mind full of fear, regret, and helplessness generates different karma than a peaceful mind full of loving compassion. If I explore this death space often enough, could I skillfully choose the direction I take when I die? Perhaps I could avoid death altogether if I felt I needed more time on Earth. Or maybe I could choose to escape *samsara* (birth-death-rebirth cycle) by entering *nirvana* as an enlightened being. Or lastly, I could become a Bodhisattva who forgoes *nirvana* to liberate the suffering of others through a targeted rebirth. This all felt very exciting.

The work I do in this lifetime to resolve personal and collective trauma, eliminate limiting beliefs and misaligned emotions directly influences my inevitable death and subsequent rebirth. I believe all humans can completely and permanently erase their karmic loops before the time of death, thus preventing babies from being born with unresolved trauma to deal with. This is the way of the future.

Entering the death space was a SELF-realization catalyst confirming consciousness exists after our death and before our birth, so perhaps past, future, and in-between lives exist and SELF is eternal. If everything is happening in this now moment then I have access to these parallel timelines. They are no different from my awake and dream states, they just require a conscious shift in perspective to experience.

I heard Two Crows drum beats in the distance.

"It's time to come back now, Kitty," Two Crows encouraged.

When I brought my attention back to my body, lying on the massage table I still felt dead, as though nothing was functioning except my very faint breath. Yet, strangely, I had no fear, just awe. Slowly I returned to my normal state of consciousness and opened my eyes.

I sighed, "Sis, I just went about as deep as you can go." She replied, "So did I." She explained that she had been hovering over my body with an ear to my stomach for what seemed like eternity.

Reiki tools

ANOTHER VALUABLE TOOL I learned from Two Crows was Level 1 and 2 Usui Shiki Ryoho Reiki. Reiki utilizes symbols to transmit healing, and universal life energy through the hands. The practice originated in Tibet. Dr. Mikao Usui rediscovered and revived Reiki in Japan in the middle of the 19th Century. Usui taught Grand Master Hawayo. Hawayo trained Dr. Chijiro Hayashi. Hayashi led Medicine Crow. Medicine Crow instructed Two Crows. Two Crows guided me. So I was confident the lineage was authentic. I found Two Crow's training very empowering, and I still use Reiki symbols daily. I even embedded them into this book to heal humanity.

On my first trip to India, my friend Lysa and I learned Reiki from an old Indian man in Rishikesh in Northern India, on the banks of the River Ganges. Unfortunately, the Reiki master's English was poor, so we could not ask clarifying questions. I knew Reiki was a modality I wanted to study from that moment. I had done it intuitively before going to India, so it felt natural. Perhaps I sowed the seeds to meet Two Crows thirteen years prior at the birthplace of the Holy *Ganga*.

Native American astrology and animal totem tools

FORTY YEARS

When I met Medicine Crow at his *Medicine Wheel/Zodiac* workshop in Two Crow's studio, he said, "Well, you and your Dad are both Geminis, which makes you guys *Mental as Anything* (Aussie band name)."

I replied, "Dad's in Spirit."

Medicine Crow replied, "I know; he was the one who told me you were both Geminis." I was shocked.

During the workshop, he taught me that Native Americans do not focus solely on people's sun sign (the zodiac sign relating to your birth date). He taught me that we are 33% our sun sign, 33% our ascendant sign, 33% our moon sign, and 1% our midheaven. So for me, that translates to Sun in Gemini (born May 29th, 1971, 1:00 pm in Rome, Italy), Virgo (ascendant), Leo (moon), and Gemini (midheaven). He also taught me that each part of the Native American Medicine Wheel has corresponding sun signs, each with a specific premise, and together they make up a clan group with a major life lesson. Each of us travels around every spoke of the Medicine Wheel during our Earth walk, but our overarching life lesson will be the one we were born into (our sun sign).

The sun signs born in the East direction (yellow) are Taurus, whose premise is 'I have,' Aries 'I am,' and Gemini 'I think.' They make up the Eagle Clan, and their major life lessons involve illumination and enlightenment (this is me, surprise, surprise). The sun signs born in the South direction (red) are Cancer 'I feel,' Leo 'I will,' and Virgo 'I analyze.' They make up the Mouse Clan, and their major life lessons involve innocence and trust. The sun signs born in the West direction (black) are Libra 'I balance,' Scorpio 'I desire', and Sagittarius 'I see.' They make up the Bear Clan, and their major life lessons involve introspection and going within for the answers. Finally, the sun signs born in the North direction (white) are Capricorn 'I use,' Aquarius 'I know' and Pisces 'I believe.' They make up the Buffalo Clan, and their major life lessons involve understanding abundance, wisdom, and prayer.

Medicine Crow taught me about each Zodiac's animal totems in three parts of the world: Europe, North America, and Australia. Taurus - Bull, Beaver, Wombat, Aries - Ram, Hawk, Red Kangaroo, Gemini - Twins, Deer, Sugar Glider, Cancer - Crab, Woodpecker, Kaola, Leo - Lion, Salmon, Frill Neck Lizard, Virgo - Virgin, Brown Bear, Echidna, Libra - Scales, Crow/Raven, Cockatoo, Scorpion - Scorpion, Snake, Spider, Sagittarius - Centaur, Owl, Kookaburra, Capricorn - Goat, Snow Goose, Goanna, Aquarius - Water Bearer, Otter, Emu, and Pisces - Fish, Wolf, Platypus.

Medicine wheel tools

I COULD NOT BELIEVE that Two Crows and Medicine Crow were teaching me about the Native American Medicine Wheel because I had begun exploring Native Americans' connection to the Great Spirit and Mother Earth when I was living in the Australian desert at the age of 27. My soul sister Nikki had walked into the Kalgoorlie *Book and Crystal Den* (where we did weekly meditation classes and my rebirth) and asked our teacher Macey, "What's your favorite book?" Macey recommended *Dancing The Dream* by Jamie Sams. After Nikki read the book, she bought me a copy. Sams explained that each direction on the Medicine Wheel has corresponding initiations or rites of passage. She called these directions sacred paths to transformation, including East (illumination), South (trust), West (introspection), and North (wisdom) as well as Above (spiritual, unseen, unknown), Below (connection to Earth and Spirit in all things), and Within/Now (bringing infinity/void knowledge into our physical beings in the present moment). Each direction's lessons are revisited throughout our lives to a deeper extent with each new level of initiation. Some lessons might be put off and addressed later on another path, but we can never avoid them. It is not hierarchical; we dip in and out of initiations as we journey around the Medicine Wheel. We also never graduate because consciousness is constantly expanding. So we continue to evolve throughout our lives until our last breath and beyond in another dimension. For this reason, every time I read *Dancing The Dream,* I understand a little more of it because my perspective has expanded since I last read it. Sams described her book as a safe road map through consciousness. By exploring unknown paths, we realize our potential as dream weavers. If we want to change the dream, then we have to learn how to dream differently. When I first read *Dancing the Dream,* it resonated with me immediately. I knew it contained the ancient tools I needed to attain spiritual enlightenment, however, I did not get it all straight away because I had not had the life experience yet.

Incredibly, eleven years after Nikki gave me *Dancing the Dream,* I again found myself living in a rural and remote Australian town where I met two shamans happy to take me further into the Native

American teachings. And it all happened so easily–I did not even have to travel for the lessons because Two Cows lived in Forbes and Medicine Crow came to Forbes to teach. For me to effortlessly manifest a shaman apprenticeship, I must have subconsciously yearned for it. Perhaps my devotion to *Dancing the Dream* catapulted my desire into the Dream Weave, which Sams describes as *...a web of our combined human creative energy.*

Shaman tools

MY SHAMAN APPRENTICESHIP involved making a rattle, a smudge kit for Grandfather sage burning, sourcing a flute, and making a drum under Two Crows' guidance. The first Native American Medicine Drum I made was deerskin. It took eight hours to birth (longer than my children's births). Like childbirth, birthing a Native American Medicine drum involves intentional focus. The resulting drum reflects my mindset throughout the process. The whole drum-making journey was a meditation because I had to stay focused on the present moment. If my mind wandered into an old story, lack or limiting belief, the drum became those thoughts. I created what I was thinking.

With each snip, stitch, pull, and tie of the sinew, I metaphorically traveled clockwise around the Medicine Wheel (East, South, West, North, above, below, within). I was open to every lesson I encountered and soon realized that practicing acceptance, compassion, and forgiveness for myself and others brought me back to the NOW, where I had access to infinite intelligence and flow. To achieve my goal, I had to be slow and steady. The way I reacted to drum-making challenges mirrored the way I dealt with obstacles on a daily basis. During the workshop, I instantly saw the results of my mind chatter.

The journey, like life, required meticulous mindfulness and present awareness.

Once I birthed my Native American Medicine Drum, I had to wait a week to play it, and each day I did a smudge ceremony. It felt deeply spiritual when I finally played my drum because I had worked hard and gained many personal epiphanies through its medicine. Native Americans believe everything is part of the Great Spirit, so everything is medicine. Medicine is their way of saying self-realization tools.

Manifesting tools

I ATTENDED Medicine Crow's *Manifesting Your Dreams* workshop in Two Crow's studio. Medicine Crow taught me to use imagination, focus, and intention during the workshop to manifest my dreams.

Step 1: State your dream in the present tense like a prayer.

Step 2: State how you will give back if you achieve your goal.

Step 3: Set a date.

Step 4: Celebrate it NOW as if it has already happened.

After the workshop, our dream farm came onto the market which had been owned by one family since 1880, so I applied Medicine Crow's shaman teachings to manifest it.

STEP 1: I stated *Thank you—we won the July auction for the advertised secluded, run-down block on Wiradjuri Country in the bend of the Galari (Lachlan River), 5 kilometers (3 miles) from town at the end of a dead-end road.*

. . .

STEP 2: I stated *We won the auction, now I can give back*

Medicine Crow taught us Hawaiian shamanism - *Ku* (Higher Self/God) likes pleasure, harmony, and being in flow. So, it's my job to convince *Ku* that it will have peace if it manifests my wish. Therefore, it is a trade-off; I get what I want by pledging to give back. How? By being in service to others, helping the planet, and supporting future generations and species. These things give *Ku* fulfillment. *Ku* never delivers when the request is selfish or when intentions are not for the good of all.

I promised *Ku* I would give back in the following ways:

- **Emotional well-being** – *I am so grateful to live on the river and have a beautiful sandy 'beach' to connect with Mother Nature. The girls are so blessed to be growing up near flowing water. Stitty is content having land to do what he was born to do. Working outside makes him thrive and keeps him stress and disease-free. I am using my increased emotional well-being to write a book for humanity.*
- **Physical well-being** – *I love the big, open skies, being in nature, and having space. I am using this opportunity to get to know the land and my animal totems to show me how to make a difference in the world. The children love to run and play, jump off the rope swing, and float around the bend. Stitty loves being active, doing cattle work, fencing, and improving the garden.*
- **Social well-being** – *Friends from Sydney love coming and camping here. Their trips enhance their mental health and allow them to return to the city revitalized and capable of contributing positively. The workshops I run on this land heal the land and the people.*
- **Spiritual well-being** – *Thank you for giving me this land to write a personal development book to contribute*

positively to the planet's spirituality. It has created a positive ripple effect, benefiting the whole world.
- **Ecological well-being** - *I am improving Earth by cultivating native plants, supporting grasses, enhancing soil conditions, avoiding generating polluting waste, and rejuvenating the land. These practices sustain our ecology and have long-lasting positive effects on animals and humans.*

STEP 3: I set a date.

Medicine Crow instructed that once I convinced *Ku* that creating my dream is the perfect scenario for everyone and everything in every way, I needed to set a date for it to happen.

"This step is the most important step," Medicine Crow explained. "Principle number two applies. *Kala*: There are no limits (be free). Therefore, we must set a limit in the form of a time frame. Without a specific date, how will *Ku* know when to manifest the requested dream?" In my case, Step 3 was easy because there was an auction date. I wrote all the steps on a poster with photos of the farm from the real estate advertising brochures. I also included the predicted amount it would cost (next time I would write *Bought at the perfect price* instead).

STEP 4: I celebrated it in the present tense.

Medicine Crow taught us that the more we feel, with every cell of our bodies, that the dream has already happened, the more likely *Ku* is to create it. Why? Because *Ku* gets to experience firsthand how good it feels to achieve it.

A week before the auction, I was alone on a one-hour drive when Katy Perry's song *Firework* came on. I pretended that we were the final bidders *Going once, going twice, going three times. Sold to the Stitt family!* I turned the radio up loudly and screamed with ecstatic joy, "YES! YES! We got it. Thank you, I'm so happy! Thank you, thank you, thank you!" I began sobbing uncontrollably with feelings of intense happiness. The extreme pleasure aligned me vibrationally with my dream. I energetically celebrated the fact that the farm was ours, and it already was on some parallel timeline. So all I had to do was convince *Ku* to make it my reality. Every day, in the lead-up to the auction, I drummed my drum and thanked *Ku* for the farm. I imagined locals congratulating us after our victory.

I also applied principle number three: *Makia*: Energy flows where attention goes (be focussed) by keeping quiet about the farm. I only told Two Crows, Medicine Crow, and my family that we were interested in buying it. I knew that telling everyone in my community would create interest and subsequent competition, pushing the price up. People would hear, "The Stitts are keen," which could make them keen too. So I wanted to draw as little attention to it as possible. I didn't even tell my friend Nik who had the girls on the day of the auction.

At the auction, another bidder won but afterward explained that they could not pay the total amount. The Auctioneers asked the children of the owners if the winning bidders could pay some now and some later. They said they would sleep on it. That afternoon I drummed and connected with their mum in spirit letting her know we were an honest, kind, old Forbes family who would have known this family back in 1880. I promised we would take good care of her beloved land. In the morning her children decided to accept our lower offer because it was guaranteed. I believe their mum in spirit whispered this recommendation to them. Well done, *Ku*!

WRITE HERE WRITE NOW

Sacred ceremony tools

FORTY-ONE YEARS

Medicine Crow and Two Crows taught me how to conduct sacred circles and rituals. Indigenous cultures celebrate, appreciate and honor all life. Like the Australian First Nation people, they sing century-old songs to give thanks, call in, protect or preserve. They grow up aware of their symbiotic relationship with the elements, sharing resources, witnessing the unseen, sensing the unknown, purifying the toxic, and cultivating connectedness. Through these teachings, I entered a world I never knew existed, and there I noticed blessings in simple places. I began to appreciate the life-giving things I hardly saw before. I was experiencing what the Russian pagans rightly worshiped.

I learned how to do chakra balances, energy clearing, and drum/journey circles. The circles were my favorite. They involved leading a guided meditation using the drum, rattle, and flute. At the beginning and at the end of the ceremony we burn Grandfather's sage to cleanse and purify. We tell meditators that a drum journey requires the same three elements used in dream manifestation: imagination, focus, and intention. The journey starts with the ceremonial drum beat (1, 2, 3, 4). Then we invite participants (using Crow's hypnotic tone) to take deep cleansing breaths, in through the nose and out through the mouth. The exhalation should resemble the popping sound air makes when it comes out of a dolphin's blowhole. We call these releasing breaths 'dolphin breathes.'

Next, we say, "In your mind's eye, imagine a staircase, stepping down now 7, 6, 5, 4, 3, 2, 1. Before you is a door, open the door, go through it, then close the door behind you. You are walking into the Spirit World towards your sacred circle. Look down at your feet on the path. Welcome your guides, ancestors, angels, and totems." From there, we take them on a drum journey where the drumbeat gets faster and louder, we play rattles and an Aboriginal rain stick to shift energy, followed by the beautiful flute to send their prayers into the wind. At the end of the ceremony, we instruct them to drop into gratitude for their guides, ancestors, angels, and animal totems before encouraging them to make their way back along the path to the door. They open the door, go through it, then close the door behind them, back up the stairs 1, 2, 3, 4, 5, 6, 7.

Mentoring tools

OVER THE YEARS, Medicine Crow has become a father figure, partly because his voice and accent reminded me of Dad. Like Dad, Medicine Crow is an epic storyteller with quick wit and impeccable style. Medicine Crow's humor is always perfectly placed. Communication is all about timing, and Medicine Crow knows when to lighten the mood with a good laugh or stir things up with a brutally honest comment. He is a gentle, cuddly bear most of the time, but occasionally the crow comes forward to peck my eyes out! Nothing makes him happier than drumming hard with Two Crows and me and hearing me rev up the group by unashamedly using my voice. I have assisted Medicine Crow and Two Crows in running local retreats. He constantly praises us, his sisters, for carrying on his work. He believes the future lies in empowering the sisterhood. Medicine Crow gave me my spirit name, Sunshine Kitty Hawk during one retreat. Like the crow, the hawk carries bird medicine which symbolizes flying up to achieve an expanded perspective. Having a hawk as my animal totem makes me a messenger with powerful focussing skills and clear vision. Medicine Crow added, "Kitty is a ray of sunshine, so her spirit name has to have the word sunshine in it."

Medicine Crow and I have spent hours around the campfire on retreat discussing everything we have in common. For example, I studied linguistics at University of Sydney (USYD) and then taught neuro-linguistic programming (NLP) when I lectured there. Medicine Crow is an NLP Life Coach, so we love discussing the power of words, their origin, and how they have taken on meaning over the centuries. I also did a psychology major (three years at USYD) and philosophy (independently), and I am fascinated by religion and metaphysics. I had grown up in America's Midwest or the Bible Belt. Everyone attended church, so our local Episcopalian church was a social event for my parents. I attended Sunday school, studied Bible stories, and prayed (a lot). Medicine Crow also grew up in America, so we talked about our childhood experiences for hours. He had become a minister before embracing his medicine man roots, so he would patiently answer my existential questions long into the night.

I also drilled Medicine Crow about Hawaiian shamanism and the seven ancient principles he learned from Dr. Serge Kahili King. He told me he added two more. Principle number 8: Your future is a road, don't block it. Then he made up Principle number 9 in Canberra; when he asked a group about the last principle, a little old lady called from the back of the room in a little old lady voice, "Make it sacred." He loved it, and it still uses it today.

Meeting and working with Two Crows and Medicine Crow shows that dreams can come true without following conscious steps. How? The vision I birthed a decade earlier in Kalgoorlie to explore Native American dreaming societies was in alignment with my calling to write this book which contributes to the good of all. So *Ku* made the teachers and the insights appear without even asking.

Why? SELF takes care of everything.

To that I say, "Wanishi (thank you) for spontaneous creation!"

15

INVITING SPIRITS TO GIVE ME INFORMATION SELF

41 years old

Trigger warning: Story contains potentially triggering content for trauma survivors around the topics rape, child abuse, violence and death.

Wednesday, December 5th

AT TWO CROW'S regular Forbes Wednesday Night Drum Circle in the shed behind her house.

"Some serious shit's been going down since I last seen you, Kitty." Two Crows looked serious.

I carefully placed my drum bag on her studio floor and sat down on the carpet next to her.

My eyes were alert and inquisitive.

"Years ago in Canberra, I did a clearing at a nightclub that everybody said was haunted. I was shown a murder scene and uncovered some dark, dark information. The one who'd been murdered recently contacted me in spirit and wanted to give me names and details. I said no. I have a family to protect, and me knowing this stuff puts my kids at risk. So I'm putting up boundaries and stopping the contact."

"How were they murdered?" I inquired.

Knock, knock, knock.

"Hi girls," Pippy called out.

The conversation changed.

When it was time for the guided meditation, Two Crows started the usual way, "Take three deep breaths in and out before you is a staircase. Going down those stairs, now, 7, 6, 5, 4, 3, 2, 1. In front of you is a door, open the door and close the door behind you."

Then, Two Crows guided us into a past life regression. I have been doing drum journeys with her for 12 years, and this was the only time she ever led us into a past/parallel life regression.

"You are safe and comfortable. Allow yourself to drift into another time and space significant to something you are experiencing in your present life. Allow yourself to float into that body calmly. Remember yourself as them. Now look around and tell yourself what you can see."

It's an enormous grand manor like the one I imagined in Rebecca *or* The Secret Garden. *It feels like England because I can see the North York Moors. It feels like winter. I sense the light rain pattering on the roof could turn to snow at any moment.*

"What are you wearing?" Two Crows asked, still slowly drumming to a steady ceremonial four-beat.

I am in a black long sleeve dress covered by a frilly apron, tied in a bow at the back. I'm wearing a stiff domestic servants cap. My collar is crisp and laced, and I'm wearing black stockings.

"Look down at your feet; what do they look like?" Two Crows asks.

I am wearing shiny black shoes that lace up like school shoes.

"Look at your hands; are they your hands?" Two Crows probed.

No. My hands look small, like a teenager's hands.

"Are you male or female?" She questioned.

I'm a girl.

"How old are you?"

I'm 15.

"What year is it?"

It is the Edwardian Era around 1910.

"What are you doing? Who is around you?"

I am performing my duties at an elegant dining table. Even though I've grown up here, I'm invisible to the family. My fingertips know bone china. I expertly pour decanted red wine into crystal glasses. I glide between tall mahogany chairs serving food with pristine precision. I feel ghost-like, afraid to make the slightest mistake, fearful of being punished or demoted to a scullery maid. The food smells so good. I am so hungry.

"Ask yourself, why have I been brought here? What is it about this life that's relevant to your life now?" Two Crows instructed.

I'm walking down a bitterly cold, narrow hallway. Returning from somewhere that feels wrong. I feel deep shame for what I've done, but I had no choice; I'm powerless. It's just the way it is. It's just what girls like me are made to do. I feel dirty and abused. Sir is old and smelly. He wheezes his stale breath into the back of my neck, and he's heavy on my young body. I am the child he's vandalized and spoiled for my future husband. I was innocent, but now I'm degraded to a piece of meat he forces himself into every night. I enter our room, and as usual, my mother is waiting for me on our bed. She has a tear in her eye. At my age, she was an orphaned, homeless prostitute. At least I am safer than she ever was. I lay down with my head in her lap; she smells like roses. She brushes my hair with long loving strokes. I hear Tchaikovsky - Symphony No. 6, fourth movement 'Pathetique.' A longing for freedom pulses through my veins to the beat of the slow tempo as each mournfully composed note drifts up the stairs from the gramophone's flower-shaped hole.

Two Crow's voice startled me, "Now going to the time of your death. What is happening? How are you feeling."

I am back in that bitterly cold, narrow hallway. *"Sir, I'm not coming into that dingy room. I don't care what you do to me. It can't be any worse." He raises his fist and punches me across my left cheek, sending me down the steep servant's stairs. My world circled me. Limbs tumbled and rolled over one another, twisting and hitting the walls and the slippery steps with a thud and a bang. I instinctively covered my face, but my head violently smashes against the bottom door frame. I'm knocked out dead. Sir runs down the stairs and calls out to someone.*

I viewed the scene from above.

Sir and another man look down at me. Sir laughs, "Well, she's a fallen woman now," as he kicks my limp, lifeless body.

The other man responds, "Worthless piece of shit. We'll take her out the back and bury her. You can easily get another girlie like this one." I watched myself being dragged away by my hair. Blood dripped from the corner of my young mouth.

"Bringing your attention back to your body in this lifetime. Make your way back along your path to the door. Open the door, go through it, close it behind you, back up the stairs 1, 2, 3, 4, 5, 6, 7. Breathe in life, breathe out life. Feel something, see something, hear something."

After I shared my past/parallel life regression, Two Crows said, "Kitty, that is exactly how the girl was murdered. She was pushed down the nightclub stairs when she threatened to expose the pedophile ring."

I was shocked, I had asked, "How were they murdered?" so the girl's spirit guided me to one of my past/parallel lives when I died the same way she did.

This experience confirmed that SELF is eternal and that past/parallel lives exist in the now, and we can access them at any time. This catalyst showed me, without a doubt, that spirits can communicate information to me when invited to do so.

Not long after this past/parallel life regression, I began a psychic development course run by Two Crow's over nine Saturdays. During the establishing energetic boundaries session, I learned that spirits recognize us as sovereign sentient beings and respect the universal law of free will. They are always right here in another dimension, but they wait for us to instruct them. We tell spirits when we want to converse with them, when we need them to assist us, or when we want them to stop communicating with us. I decided in the future if a spirit approaches me without an invitation, I will immediately ask them to go away because they are trespassing and may have ulterior motives. The multidimensional beings that examined me in Kalgoorlie, during my rebirth, used Dad to make me comfortable enough to give them my consent. In hindsight, I wonder if Dad was there at all. Perhaps the multidimensional beings produced a holograph of him to trick me. These days I am less naive.

Spirits have been part of my life since I was four years old, living in Paris, and in all those years, only one has tried to harm me. A spirit pinned me down on a bed at my friend's Alexandria house when I was 32 years old. I do not know why it happened, and I can only hope it never happens again because it was terrifying. That spirit did not respect the universal law of free will.

Other topics covered during the psychic development course included: card reading, using crystals, aura reading, mediumship, freewriting, mind-reading, crystal pendulums, astrology and numerology, face reading, flower and bush essences, and utilizing the senses.

16

FINDING THE LIGHTWORKERS' PATH SELF

41 years old

Friday, January 4th

STITTY, me, and our three daughters were a few days into a one-month holiday at the Stitt family's beach house in Mollymook, on the south coast of NSW, Australia. After a yoga class at the beach in Ulladulla Harbour, I said to Kerri Wild, my south coast teacher, "I would like to get a massage. Do you know anyone who does massage?"

She replied, "Yes, I do massage."

We arranged a time and a price which she wrote in her diary. Then out of the blue, she said, "If you want someone who sings and does that kind of thing, then I'm probably not the one for you. Sadhana might be better."

I exclaimed, "I want to sing. I use sound healing with my friend Two Crows in Forbes, who does KaHuna massage."

"I think Sadhana does KaHuna also; I will give you her number," Kerri explained.

When I walked away, I thought *Wow, that was strange. Who would mention another massage therapist when an appointment is already in the diary? Perhaps there's a reason I need to meet Sadhana.*

That afternoon, at my appointment, I learned that Sadhana had trained at the same institute as Two Crows, Mette's High Spirits (Sunshine Coast, Queensland, Australia). Sadhana was buzzing with excitement because she had just returned from working with orangutans in Borneo.

Sadhana's KaHuna massage was a beautiful experience. She has the voice of an angel, and we sang together as she massaged me. The spontaneous notes seemed to clear my body's blockages. Sadhana was above my face at one stage, and we were toning; I felt like a Tibetan singing bowl. After the massage, we talked about our interests, and she invited me to a retreat on the weekend run by locals Lilaea and Vanessa. I said I would bring my friend Nicola, who was visiting from Kenya. When I told Sadhana, that I was writing a book on the evolution of human consciousness. She reached for a book in her bookcase. "You might like this book *Truth Creates Heaven on Earth*," Sadhana advised. "It was written by a local woman Karen Wade."

As soon as I read the back cover, I knew I was going to love it *Dormant seeds of knowledge held within each human soul will blossom into life, genetic codes within their DNA will open, allowing the truth of each human soul's Divine heritage to awaken within them.* Sadhana gave me a few books that day, but I did not even open the others; I only had eyes for Karen. I could not put it down. I felt like it spoke directly to me. I devoured each chapter feeling as though my dormant DNA was lighting up and becoming activated and electrified by truth.

To write *Truth Creates Heaven on Earth*, Karen acknowledged, like me, that it was a gift that wanted to be expressed through her and that on some level she had agreed to it. She referred to the book as a free-flowing expression of truth that is not owned by anyone. She allowed her field to open up and then utilized her innate ability to 'hear' the collective of lightworkers with messages for humanity. All she had to do was get out of her own way and scribe what she heard. The lightworkers in spirit included her dear friend and mentor, Barbara Joy Poschinger, Barbara's husband Dr. Paul Poschinger, Krishnamurti, Ezekiel, Archangel Gabriel, Saint Germaine, Saint Francis of Assisi, Archangel Michael, Lord Melchizedek, and the Lord. I was fascinated by Karen's first chapter which explained the process of writing her book. Like me, she was a mother, a wife, and a teacher. She knew her book needed to be birthed; she just needed to find a way to make it happen. She used her long service leave to take a paid break from teaching in Loftus in the Sutherland Shire in Sydney's South. She got access to a Pigeon House Mountain cabin near Mollymook and then went there for nine weeks to write the book. She had been with her husband since she was fourteen and a half, and this was her first time away from him and the children. First, she had to face her fears of being alone. Once she got over this hurdle, spirits started speaking to her. She would go into a meditative state and ask, "Who wants to come through today?" Then she transcribed what she heard. Sometimes she had doubts, but she had to trust that she was hearing the spirits and not herself.

The contributors confirmed information about the spirit world that I had always known but had never been taught or told. I had been born with this knowledge (we all were). Growing up, I had spirits in my room all the time, but I was the only one in my family who saw them. My friends at school never talked about them, so I thought it was just me. I did not have access to books about spirit communication, and these were the days before the internet. My parents were mainstream, affluent, and conservative and did not seem to know people who shared my abilities.

Chapter after chapter, I said to Stitty, "This book is enlightening me. It is telling me what I have always instinctively known."

I loved hearing about Karen's teacher Barbara. They met while learning a healing modality called 'Living Light Energy.' Lightworkers use the light, available to us all, to bring about healing by first connecting to their inner light. Then they empower others to heal themselves through their pure light. Karen quoted Barbara in *Truth Creates Heaven on Earth The greatest gift you can bring to this life is your true self fully expressed. Humanity's collective consciousness will make a huge shift, lifting those who are awake into a new dimension, with a new way of being. Earth's ascension...will be wonderful for those who ascend, each person expressing the truth of who they truly are, a world based on love...no sense of lack, masks, war, pollution, disease. The body will heal itself... People will nourish themselves with natural food and fresh water.* This vision felt real; because it was part of the vision I received when I was 38 years old. Barbara continued *Some awakened souls on Earth are already starting to create this (ascended) reality. They can bring into existence that which they focus upon by their trust in the law of attraction because they are in alignment with their true self. Their outer world is reflecting this and their experiences support this truth.* Barbara's words profoundly resonated with me. When Barbara was alive she advised Karen to question everything, so while Karen retreated in the cabin, she questioned her family, culture, school, university, workplace, and community.

Karen introduced me to new words and concepts. For example, she explained that we live in a 3rd dimensional (3-D) reality and are ascending into a 5th dimensional (5-D) reality. I had heard the word 3D before but I had never inquired what it meant. Never before had I read words that confirmed my innate knowing. It was surreal because I had a deep, unexplained memory of being in higher dimensions, living in a Golden Age with advanced powers to heal my body organically, existing in a light body without the concept of time, and being able to manifest things instantly. Knowing that the places I traveled to in my dreams and meditations were real and not imagined felt comforting. *I am not insane after all!* As I read *Truth Creates Heaven on Earth* I knew why I came into this body. I understood my vision and I knew what I had to do–create the new aligned to what Karen called Source (we can call it God or any other name, I call it SELF).

Barbara explained that we realize our truth by making it real. We do this by expressing it through our being which integrates it into our consciousness. This integration raises our harmonic resonance, which vibrates at a specific frequency. *The more expanded the consciousness, the higher the frequency and the closer to Source you become.* I finally understood what the word Source meant. Barbara, in spirit, explained that we are Source having a human experience capable of experiencing a range of archetypes, the shadow side of life, and possessing the potential to know ourselves as Source. Now that Barbara was in spirit form she explained that she was in an expanded dimension without a physical body. She experienced everything in the now. Barbara observed many awakened souls living like this in our 3-D human dimension. Barbara said all who ascend would experience life this way. She explained, *To live your life fully present, expressing your truth, radiating light and love into the world is a blessing beyond measure...Now is the time on Earth to step into your Divine heritage, claim your freedom, know your truth and express the bliss and love this creates.*

Karen wrote Barbara's husband Paul in spirit's perspective *The expanded dimension is your true reality, and by expanding in consciousness, you can begin to experience this while still in physical form and thus create the experience of... Heaven on Earth.* Paul confirmed that the true reality I witnessed on the insight meditation cushion in northern India was the same as the death space. So the spirits who visited me were existing in an expanded form that matched human's potential.

Paul went on to explain, ...*once incarnated, the veil of separation is fully down by the age five to seven. Prior to this time of forgetting who they really are, the soul is still very much aware of the expanded dimension. Most children have imaginary friends, as the grownups label them, but they are very real* (I always knew my Paris 'friends' were real). *The children can sense, see or hear them... The unaware, desensitized adult can do none of this, therefore assuming they are not real.* Paul continued, [*Spirits like Paul*] *are helping Earth and mankind to ascend to the New World. When enough shining lights are present, expanding consciousness to a critical mass, the transition will occur, and those awakened souls will effortlessly find themselves in a new dimension free of chaos and fear.*

I found it fascinating that I wrote the ending to my book three years before I read *Truth Creates Heaven on Earth*. I had the vision to evolve human consciousness, and now I had Karen and her collective of lightworkers in spirit to explain consciousness further. The fact that I got Karen's book unexpectedly confirms Paul Clethero's quote in The Alchemist *When you want something, all the universe conspires in helping you achieve it.* The universe, Source, higher self, Ku, Divine timing, God, whatever we call it made Kerri recommend Sadhana, then made Sadhana recommend Karen. I never take synchronicities like these for granted because they show me I am on the right track and in alignment. I like to acknowledge when unseen forces look after me. Eckhart Tolle, *A New Earth,* explains it this way *By consciously participating in higher purpose unfolding, you can witness universal intelligence which emanates from the formless realm of consciousness.* Karen quoted Krishnamurti *Trust that with your decision to shine your light, all manner of unseen help is waiting to shine their light and love into your life, enabling you to realise your truth.*

Karen wrote that Archangel Gabriel shared *There are many angels incarnating on Earth at this time to help raise the consciousness of the planet...Angels can be anywhere, anytime, to help with every-*

thing. Nothing is either too grand or too menial. However, your soul's growth is paramount, and any request that does not serve your soul's growth, or interferes with that of another, will not be responded to...An archangel is expanded energy that is closer to Source in frequency than angels...Ask your angels to help you, and your inner light will respond to their radiant presence, expanding it, revealing more truth. Karen wrote that Saint Germaine explained *A soul is also multidimensional and can choose to exist in dimensions other than Earth at the same time. So while one aspect of the soul is having a linear Earth experience in form, other aspects can be experiencing different dimensions in another form or without form.* This explains how I have witnessed the evolution of human consciousness even though it has not happened yet on Earth. My memory of it implies that I have already experienced it on a parallel timeline (we all have).

Karen wrote that Saint Francis of Assisi shared *You are here on Earth in a physical form to learn through experience that you are an individual expression of the Divine, of Source, with all the same qualities and unlimited potential. Knowing this truth...then expressing it through your physical form brings its realisation into consciousness, thus expanding it...Every human soul yearns for this awakening that takes them from the pain of perceived separation, into the unconditional love of oneness, their truth.* This last sentence hit me hard, I yearned to intimately know this oneness, the same interconnectedness I experienced on the meditation cushion.

Archangel Michael highlighted that there is no one way or right way to connect with Source *There are many paths that will lead you home to your Divine nature and they are all lit by the inner light of the traveller...The purpose of life on Earth is to know your true self and express the light and love of your Divine nature through your physical form.*

Lord Melchizedek explained that we can change mass consciousness by changing ourselves first, which was the whole premise of my book! He explained (through Karen) *Some people blame mass consciousness for their fear and chaos when they should see if their fear and chaos are causing the mass consciousness.* I liked this perspective because it encouraged me to take responsibility for being the way I am instead of blaming family/society/government. Lord Melchizedek encouraged me to shine a light on unconscious beliefs and patterns that no longer served me to expand my consciousness. His advice felt relevant as seven weeks prior on the 12/12, I decided to stop drinking alcohol (I never had another sip). Melchizedek also advised *Every single soul incarnated on Earth at this point in time chose to be present for the transition into the fifth dimension.*

Finally, Karen allowed the Lord to express himself *All life is energy and thoughts are energy forms. As you think, you send out energy forms that attract their likeness and this is then what you bring into your experience...Mankind will know the truth, as illusion crumbles around him. Many will feel lost and fearful not knowing what to trust and who to believe. This is why knowing your true self is so vitally important, as it is in this knowing that you find your internal guidance, your only true authority...trust [this] not your logical mind with all its human fears, doubts, beliefs, concepts, opinions, limitations, and illusions...My eternal light is the same for all, it shines its radiance on all life...As you awaken to this truth, your inner radiance is illuminated and shines brightly through you into the world. Your expression then becomes an expression of love and light...You realise that you are a creator as am I, you realise your Divinity.*

Since reading *Truth Creates Heaven on Earth*, I have realized and Karen has too that angels, archangels, and ascended masters are all just aspects of SELF because we are all one consciousness. This means each of us has access to ourselves in this higher dimension anytime we choose. All that is required is a subtle shift in frequency.

We were still on the south coast when I read Karen's last words *May your inward journey to your true self be one of beauty unfolding, illuminated by the love and light of the Divine.* Immediately I contacted Karen. I had picked up her card at a local bookshop and noticed she had moved to the south coast. When she answered the phone, I told her the words in *Truth Creates Heaven on Earth* felt like an awakening. She replied, "You know you're a living angel, don't you? This book resonates with angels." *Well if I am an angel, then you're an archangel.*

I booked in for a clarity session later that day. The door to her Lake Conjola house blew open with a sea breeze, I followed her in and entered a new chapter in my evolution. The first thing I noticed was how much she looked like me, just a slightly older version. She possessed the same lightness of being. Her reading was spot on. She told me my angelic name is Hallelujah which was interesting as I had always loved KD Lang's song by the same name. At the end of my session, I gave her more than she requested because I was grateful to have her teachings in my life.

Following that meeting, I began attending her Tuesday night meditation group whenever I was on the south coast. Eventually, she began running these on Zoom, which meant I could join in remotely, and I still do, to this day.

When my daughters were young, I took them to meet Karen. The first thing she taught us was how to use our internal guidance system. Our internal guidance system shows us, through our bodies, when we are out of alignment with our true selves. When we detect misalignment, we can decide how to think, speak, and act to align ourselves. We are one hundred percent responsible for our inner state of being. It is our number one priority. Listening to our internal guidance system gives us the confidence to act instead of react, which empowers us.

Karen explained that we could use our internal guidance system to make decisions. We can ask ourselves *Should I think/say/do this?* When we can read our body's signals, we know how our body feels when it is a yes and how it feels when it is a no. Karen shared her indicators, "When it is a yes my body moves forward slightly and when it is a no my body moves back slightly (this is a kinesiology technique). Karen explained that sometimes we think, say, and do things because we believe it is what people we love expect. Sometimes we believe something just because our parents or friends feel that way. Sometimes we follow society or the media and get influenced to believe things that are not our authentic truth.

Karen taught us a technique she made up for working out what types of thoughts dominate our thinking. *Catch Your Thoughts* involved putting post-it notes all over the house and in the car with CYT written on them. Whenever we saw those letters, we would notice our thoughts. She invited us to consider *Is this really what I think, is this something I know to be true or have I just heard it, is it relevant, is it in the past, is it in the future, is it negative, is it judgemental, is it a limiting belief, is it a bias, is it fear-based?* She pointed out that many of our thoughts are habitual and the result of years of conditioning and programming. Once we caught a misaligned thought, she recommended we apply the STOP technique. S stands for stop. T stands for take belly breaths. O stands for observe the feelings until they pass. P stands for practice doing what Love would do. She taught us how to belly breathe. We lay on our backs, placed a hand on our belly and felt it rise as we inhaled and fall as we exhaled. We observed the belly remaining flat when our breaths were shallow.

Thank you Kerri and Sadhana for guiding me to Karen who ultimately guided me home to SELF.

17

FORGIVING SELF

41 years old

Trigger warning: Story contains potentially triggering content for trauma survivors relating to sexual assault.

Friday, April 12th

MY LOCAL FORBES DOCTOR SAID, "You have Hashimoto's Disease, an auto-immune disorder that causes your immune system to attack your thyroid."

Friday, April 26th

TWO WEEKS LATER, I went to Dr. Anthony Chan, a general practitioner and accredited medical acupuncturist combining conventional medicine with a wide range of alternative treatments. Dr. Chan said Hashimoto's Disease originated at a time when I felt helpless. First, he asked me to place my hand on a bioresonance technology machine (NES Health) designed to measure my electromagnetic waves to detect illness. Then, during a guided visualization, he asked me to notice the first thing that came to my mind when he said, "Now, think of a time in your life when you've felt helpless."

My eighteen year old friend's massive, hard body is pressing down on my small sixteen year old self. I can feel his breath too close to me. His fingers are fumbling at my underpants, groping for access to have intercourse with me. Another guy friend is keeping watch at the cabin door. I feel powerless. Terror turns to strength. I struggle, kick, and scream, "I'm a virgin; what are you doing?"

He replies, "Oh, I didn't think you were a virgin."

I wiggle my way out from underneath him, run past our friend, and out the door.

After the visualization, Dr. Chan told me that I could not resolve my Hashimoto's until I cancel this moment of helplessness. He put me on the O blood group diet to cleanse my system and reduce my blood histamine level to make me clairvoyant enough to investigate the impact of this event. When I left his office, I was curious *How can thinking about a past event help me with my disease?* I could not come up with a single answer; it seemed too weird and unmedical. But I was willing to give it a try. It occurred to me that I had never dealt with this incident. I never told my parents because I felt responsible. I thought I deserved the violation because I was a flirt. I had pushed the whole thing down deep in my guts for twenty-five years. I started the detox immediately

---

Wednesday, May 1st

The following week, Two Crows, my Native American shaman teacher, provided a tool to do exactly what Dr. Chan recommended. At our regular meditation/drumming circle, Two Crows talked about a Hawaiian ancient spiritual healing practice called *Ho'oponopono*, which is Hawaiian for 'to make right' or 'bring into balance using forgiveness'. It utilizes a prayer, translated as *I'm sorry, Please forgive me, I love you, Thank you* (the order of these phrases is not important).

This practice was made popular by Joe Vitale, who wrote a book called *Zero Limits* about a psychologist named Dr. Ihaleakala Hew Len. Dr. Hew Len had been trained by Morrnah Nalamaku Simeona, founder of Self I-Dentity through Ho'oponopono. Dr. Hew Len later worked in a Hawaii State Psychiatric Hospital. Dr. Hew Len's patients had killed and raped people and often acted out against him. In an interview with Rita Montgomery and Dr. Rick Moss, Dr. Hew Len explained that when he arrived at the hospital, he did not focus on what was wrong with the patients; he instead inquired, "What is going on in me that I'm creating these experiences such as people being violent and hostile in my presence." He chose to take full responsibility for the outbursts he was witnessing. He began to view the patients and their behavior as reflections of himself. He began to see that they showed him shared memories that he needed to release. Through them, he could be free. Dr. Hew Len discovered that we only experience people based on the subconscious data/memories we hold regarding them. For example, if we believe someone is crazy, then we only focus on the elements of that person that confirm this belief system. This pre-conceived data then affects our perceptions. In other words, if we view them as violent, deranged, sick, or angry, that is precisely how they will act when we observe them. He hypothesized that changing how we subconsciously view them will ultimately change how they present themselves to us. He views the mind as a computer program and proposes that changing the programming enables us to see things in a new way.

Dr. Hew Len said the first step is to know what the mind is without the programs running. Dr. Hew Len refers to this as the zero point, the point we reach where there is nothing but God, and explains this part of the process using a quote from Mathew 6:33 in the Bible *Seek ye first the kingdom of God*. This line means we should know the mind's potential, which Dr. Hew Len calls our infinitely zero essence. Dr. Hew Len also quoted Shakespeare's Hamlet character Polonius, *To thine own self be true*. He stressed how important it is for us to know ourselves. The goal is to let go repeatedly, which erases data, creates clarity, and allows us to become God. Buddha called this space void, Shakespeare called it blank, and quantum physicists call it the force of nothingness. From there, we are moved by flawless information rather than stuck in the old conditioning. Dr. Hew Len suggested that we, and everyone we meet, are faultless and that it is only our programs that are flawed and imperfect. By recognizing the God in self, we naturally see the God in all and realize that everyone is ultimately pure.

Dr. Hew Len beautifully explains that when a thought comes up that is not from that God space, we can be sure that it is data running. It is simply false programming based on memories/conditions/limiting beliefs. Therefore, we do not need to attach negativity to it, judge ourselves harshly, or even question why the thought is there. All we have to do is clean ourselves, the thing, the thought, the person, or the situation by applying the *Ho'oponopono* prayer *I'm sorry, Please forgive me, I love you, Thank you*. This cleaning realigns us with our divine self, allowing us to be an enlightened soul at that moment.

Incredibly Dr. Hew Len's patients began to recover after he arrived at the hospital and started using the prayer. He said in the interview that he did not intend to heal the patients; it just happened. He acknowledged that all he did was clean himself, and the staff created various programs that benefited the patients. Dr. Hew Len displayed no ego regarding the patients' improvement. It was as if Dr. Hew Len tapped into their shared highest potential timeline until reality matched the vision. He did not need to work out how to cure them; he just needed to clean his programmed thoughts, and infinite intelligence, flow, and magic unfolded spontaneously.

The story reminded me of one of my favorite Wayne Dyer quotes *When you change the way you look at things, the things you look at change.*

After Two Crows explained the *Ho'oponopono* prayer, she led us on a guided drum journey. I decided to use the prayer on the boy who violated me. Whenever I thought *I'm sorry,* I acknowledged that I had created the experience. According to the Buddha, I violated someone in this life or in a past/parallel life. First, I apologized to those I had wronged. I deeply connected to the wounded child in; me, those I wronged, and the boy who wronged me. I acknowledged that we all felt unheard, alone, and scared. Immense empathy rose when I saw us all as innocent children doing our best despite our trauma. I also apologized to the boy's future self, knowing that he sowed negative seeds and would someday experience suffering similar to the cause (as I had). Then, I apologized to myself for becoming sexually promiscuous two years after this event (probably because I believed I was not enough). I realized the promiscuity was just data running; it was not the true me.

Whenever I thought *Please forgive me,* I accepted full responsibility for creating the experience. I apologized to the boy for having to be part of my creation, knowing that it would have been uncomfortable for him too. To cultivate forgiveness I utilized a Buddhist technique where I imagined the boy's mother and how much she loved her son. Then I imagined the boy as my mother in a past/parallel lives. This love motivated me to do another Buddhist practice *Tonglen* (Tibetan for 'sending and taking'). I imagined the boy's struggles, mistakes, and guilt appearing as a cloud of thick black smoke. I visualized this emanating from his forehead. As I breathed in, I took in that cloud of negativity and brought it into my heart chakra, where I transmuted this pain into pure love. This act of loving compassion turned the black smoke into pure light. As I breathed out, I imagined sending that light directly into the boy's heart, soothing him and giving him comfort and peace. I continued with each breath. My imagination was vivid. I could see the black cloud leaving his third eye, entering my mouth, traveling to my heart to be purified, and then returning to his heart as a radiant light. It felt like I was exchanging suffering for joy.

Whenever I thought *I love you,* I felt incredible love for everyone involved. Using a third Buddhist exercise called Metta Loving-Kindness Meditation I elicited the feeling of equanimity. To do this I viewed the boy the same way I viewed my love ones. I thought *May he be happy, may he be free from suffering.* I then chanted *Om Mani Padme Hung*, a Sanskrit Buddhist mantra cultivating compassion by combining altruism and wisdom to purify impure thoughts. When I sang these six syllables in my mind, I felt the painful memory dissolve into unconditional love.

Whenever I thought *Thank you,* I felt gratitude for an event I had always viewed negatively. I thanked the boy for showing me I could be enlightened at this moment regardless of what happened to me. I thanked the boy for the selfless love he showed by agreeing to this soul contract; he took on a human form to give me the insight I needed to grow. This realization showed me SELF creates all obstacles for SELF to know SELF. Realizing this took me from the helpless victim to the empowered creator.

After the meditation, I was appreciative of my Hashimoto's diagnosis. Before this awakening, I had never accepted and unpacked what happened to me as a 16-year-old. The diagnosis revealed that when I internalize traumatic events by pushing them down into my body, they manifest as dis-ease. When I researched Hashimoto's, I discovered the thyroid gland is in my throat chakra, directly below my Adam's Apple. And thyroid problems signal communication blockages caused by not speaking authentically. I realized that I had been creating experiences on multiple timelines to confirm the belief that I did not deserve a voice and that no one would be interested in my truth. For example, I witnessed my past/parallel life during a regression when my employer did not respect me. He had raped and murdered me. I suspected I was in a karmic loop. I made a vow there, and then *It's time to stop* writing a defenseless sufferer story. *No more! I refuse to die with this unresolved trauma. I know past, present, and future timelines exist in the now, so clearing one clears them all. I can be free from my trauma because I have free will. SELF is beyond all narratives. Resolving my trauma in this life means when I die, there is no trauma returning to the land to be picked up by future babies. This clearing is my gift to humanity.*

I had chosen to keep a secret lodged in my throat for two and half decades; no wonder I developed inflammation. So why did I block out that memory and repress the associated emotions? I was terrified to relive the event, fearful of the feelings, worried I would drown in them with no support or strategies to cope, frightened I could not forgive myself or him, and scared to be vulnerable and exposed.

When I was diagnosed with Hashimoto's, I had a choice. I could simply do what the mainstream doctors recommended and take medicine (a manufactured version of the thyroid hormone thyroxine), or I could explore the underlying causes of my dis-ease using alternative practitioners. I chose the latter. When I met Dr. Chan, I stepped onto my healing path and into a new chapter of my evolution. Dr. Chan empowered me to deal with my feelings of helplessness and put me on a detox to support clear-sightedness. Then in divine timing, five days later, I learned the *Ho'oponopono* prayer to be an antidote to the trauma I experienced all those years ago. The *Ho'oponopono* tool gave me the strength to revisit the distressing memory. I finally had the tools to lift the vibration of that story in the now. As soon as I took responsibility for my dis-ease, everything I needed showed up.

I decided to resist medication for as long as possible and instead investigate my known/unknown unresolved trauma, limiting beliefs, habits, lifestyle, and diet (I stopped eating gluten, dairy, and processed sugar).

YEARS LATER, when my eldest daughter Ruby turned 18, I shared my story with her and explained how I used the *Ho'oponopono* prayer. She asked if using the prayer meant I would have let the boy off scot-free had he raped me.

I replied, "Applying the prayer does not excuse people's actions–if he had raped me, he would have been held accountable and faced his consequences. The prayer can not change my past; it can only change how I interpret it. Our trauma does not have to define us. Practicing *Ho'oponopono* gave me a broader perspective which helped me deal with the event more skillfully. It turned a negative experience, heavy with guilt, shame, and anger, into something more manageable. I was able to access peace by letting go. By telling the story differently, I shifted the trauma associated with it. The Buddha said we are our own masters; our future depends entirely on ourselves. *Ho'oponopono* is a gentle and accepting technique that replaces bitterness and resentment with love and understanding."

Ruby said, "That makes sense because people have to find a way to live with their trauma. It sounds like forgiveness is the first step, forgiveness of themselves and others, regardless of what they did to them."

DO you sometimes feel misaligned emotions, dis-ease, or triggered? Could it be unresolved trauma or limiting beliefs? Could Dr. Chan's suggestion to resolve the cause of the dis-ease work in your case. Or perhaps the *Ho'oponopono* prayer could help you heal your wounds, rewrite old stories and write your evolved future?

Remember, we write the new in the now. So what story will we write; write here, write now? To help align to the frequency of love you could try my strategy, every time I come across a person/event that challenges me I think *Thank for this opportunity to be an enlightened being in this now moment.*

18

JOURNEYING WITH THE NATIVE AMERICAN CLAN MOTHERS SELF

42- 49 years old

Wednesday, January 8th

AT A REGULAR WEDNESDAY NIGHT MEDITATION/DRUM circle, Two Crows announced we were beginning a journey with the 13 Original Clan Mothers the following week (full moon). I could not believe my eyes when she held up a book by the same name by Jamie Sams (who wrote Dancing the Dream, the book Nikki gave me in Kalgoorlie). I picked it up with disbelief. Reading the cover *Your sacred path to discovering the gifts, talents, and abilities of the feminine through the ancient teachings of the sisterhood.* I flipped it open to check the copyright date and was surprised to see it was published before *Dancing the Dream,* and yet I had never come across it.

Two Crows explained that the book celebrates women coming together during their moon time (menstruation), to honor their sacred life-giving cycle which mirrors Mother Earth's cycle. To be initiated into this ancient knowledge we would meet every full moon to explore each Clan Mother's rite of passage. Together they represent the thirteen ways we can honor the truth. The 13 Clan Mothers and their respective Cycles of Truth are: Talks With Relations - Learn the Truth; Wisdom Keeper - Honor the Truth; Weighs The Truth - Accept the Truth; Looks Far Woman - See the Truth; Listening Woman - Hear the Truth; Storyteller - Speak the Truth; Loves All Things - Love the Truth; She Who Heals - Serve the Truth; Setting Sun Woman - Live the Truth; Weaves The Web - Work with Truth; Walks Tall Woman - Walk the Truth; Gives Praise - Grateful for the Truth and Becomes Her Vision - Be the Truth. Together these aspects of truth make up the Earth Mother's unconditional love for humanity.

According to Native American teachings, Jamie Sams writes that our spirits travel like a shooting star from the Spirit World with the Eternal Flame of Love (Earth Mother's love) in our hearts. Our destiny is to fulfill our dreams by mastering our unique skills and contributing to humanity's wholeness to fuel the creative energy necessary to return humankind to its indigenous ways. Each of us is Spirit emerging into form. When we finish our Earth Walk, our fiery essence (Eternal Flame of Love) returns to the night sky and the Starry Medicine Bowl.

Clan Mothers are in Spirit, but they lived as Two-leggeds for as long as it took them to experience and learn the lessons they needed to be of service to Mother Earth (some lived for hundreds of years). Through their Earth Walks, each of them learned *...the art of changing their perspectives to restore beauty to any difficult situation.* As humans, the Clan Mothers accepted each lesson with gratitude, knowing their first-hand experience would allow them to authentically guide the sisterhood from the Spirit World once they returned to the Sky Nation.

Two Crows explained that when we commit to journeying with

the 13 Clan Mothers, each month the corresponding Clan Mother provides tailor-made lessons to elicit personal healing. I intended to give it one hundred percent and expected to get smacked in the face with some tough wake-up calls. I had a lot to learn. My third daughter, Matilda, pushed all my buttons. As a school teacher, I had to be at school early, but Matilda had other ideas. Her socks felt weird in her shoes; her jumper was scratchy, her stomach ached, and she did not want to go to school. She would not succumb to being controlled, which meant I felt uncomfortably out of control all the time. The more I tried to control her, the more she cried. The more she cried, the angrier her sisters became, which made her cry more. Some mornings felt like a horror movie. I became so frustrated one school morning that I lay down on the laundry floor and had a screaming temper tantrum. Yes, this was the teacher running parent workshops at school! I told my co-facilitator this story and we worked it into the workshops by assuring parents that managing children is challenging and even teachers with decades of experience are still learning.

I was ashamed of my inability to stay calm. I studied Buddhism and had a four-year education degree with honors and a psychology major at one of the best universities in Australia, University of Sydney. However, I only knew anger management intellectually. As soon as I became triggered, I could not apply my knowledge. I had read *The Tao of Motherhood* by Vimala McClure hundreds of times, but I could not remain in the Tao when Matilda was fussing, and I needed to get to work. Looking back, I see her as my greatest teacher who came to set me free. We were, and still are, incredibly energetically connected. Everything I feel, she feels. As a result, I saw my misaligned behavior, mirrored by her, over and over until I could stand it no longer. Finally, I realized there was nothing wrong with her; my reaction to her was wrong. If I wanted peaceful mornings, I would have to learn how to be peaceful. I needed to be the change I wanted to see. This epiphany invited unseen helpers to illuminate my path out of the darkness into the light. The 13 Clan Mothers showed up at the perfect time to support me through the stages of change. I honestly think they saved me. I threw myself into their open, loving arms because nothing else was working, and I was desperate.

The Clan Mothers course took 13 months and was very intense because it involved shadow work (looking at aspects of self I kept hidden). In the off years, we retreated within to explore privately, integrating each Clan Mother's lesson.

Full moon Clan Mother ceremonies were sacred. We began by sharing using a talking stick. The premise is *When I have the stick, I am sharing from my heart what feels relevant about this month's journey. When I do not have the stick, I am listening from the heart.* After sharing, we read the next Clan Mother's chapter and welcome her during a drum meditation. While I drummed (badly to start with, it took me years to build confidence), I visualized the clan mother entering my sacred circle. Each month she appeared differently and stayed with me until the next full moon. It was incredible how each spirit guide gave me specific lessons to experience truth the way they do. They are master teachers who have been supporting women for hundreds of years, so each catalyst they delivered was perfect for my growth. Therefore, I surrendered to whatever they had in store for me. I trusted the Clan Mothers implicitly because they had all been human like me and knew what I was going through. For example, Loves All Things, the July Clan Mother, had endured so many deaths that she *...found herself judging all acts of life as never being good enough to fill the growing hole in her heart. She insisted on living in the past and forgot the joy she once found in being alive.* She had expected life to be ultimate happiness and found life with pain unfair making her sorrowful, promiscuous, angry, bitter, jealous, and fearful. She adopted these hurtful emotions to mask her pain. The Thunder Chief warned her, "*...you have learned nothing of the scarcity you bring when you refuse to love. You, too, must weather the storm that you have brought forth, and you must see for yourself the kind of pain* *you have created inside your body and how that pain can harm the natural world."* Eel advised her to reclaim the abundance she once knew by building a rainbow bridge of forgiveness from her shadow side to her heart. To do this, she allowed all her emotions to wash over her while focusing on the joy to be found in simple things, like walking by the seaside. Instead of being reckless, she developed a habit of being grateful for every lesson, and slowly she transmuted her feelings of unworthiness. She learned how to practice unconditional love. Soon she felt capable of walking among humans without inflicting her past pain onto them. She began to feel whole again by understanding both sides of her nature: the shadow side and the light side. She had finally learned the lesson she came to learn *To love all things is to love every reflection of who and what you are.* This Clan Mother helped me deal with the shame I felt for being an impatient psycho in the mornings. I was able to love even this uncomfortably embarrassing part of me.

The Clan Mothers taught me how to balance giving and receiving and showed me how to use my free will to change the habits I had learned growing up. They taught me how to manifest my dream of being a calm mom through compassion, tolerance, honesty, self-love, responsibility, creativity, support, freedom, strength, nurturing, honoring, balancing, nourishment, and stillness. All the qualities I yearned for as a woman. However, I did not magically acquire these skills. I had to work hard for them. They came to me through rigorous medicine administered by the Clan Mothers in their own time, and in their own way. To learn the qualities I needed to be balanced, I had to be patient as initiations can not be rushed. Teachers who are spirits are compelling because there is no fooling them. Once I asked for their help, they continued sending me catalysts, year after year, until they saw a change. Each catalyst forced me to dissolve my ego enough to travel into the darkest corners of my psyche. No matter how hard it was to face my shadows, the Clan Mothers encouraged me to stay. I wanted to run but I wanted peace more, so I kept showing up and being honest with myself. A spiritual bypass would have been the easy option. When the journey became unbearable I could have hidden behind the illusion of love, light, and rainbows. But I knew avoidance meant the coping mechanisms I habitually used to cope with life's traumas would just continue for the rest of my life. It was hard to admit I was addicted to controlling my environment to feel safe, I resorted to anger every time others were non-compliant, and I was obsessed with what people thought of me. But I knew that taking responsibility was the first step toward change.

For this reason, every time I walked the Medicine Wheel with these inspiring clan mothers by my side, I gained more and more confidence in who I was and what I came to do. Each journey was different, no two lessons were the same. A Clan Mother who was easy on me one year was full-on another year. This was because each time I journeyed with her, I was being initiated at a more profound level and from a different starting point. Each month my perspective broadened. However, regardless of how aware, awake and wise I thought I was, the Clan Mothers always had another lesson for me. As Jamie Sams said in *Dancing the Dream It is important to remember that every time we think we have no more to learn in any given area, it is our weaknesses, not our strengths, that will be tested. What an opportunity!*

About six months into my first journey, I realized the Clan Mothers are all aspects of SELF. Therefore, they are all within me and no matter what challenge presents itself, I can look to the Clan Mother with the most appropriate method for restoring balance to the situation.

Each time I journeyed with these mothers I humbly added their tools to my toolbox.

19

GRIEVING LOST CHILDREN SELF

43 years old

Trigger warning: Story contains potentially triggering content for trauma survivors relating to grief, death, miscarriages, suicide and kidnapping.

Wednesday, November 5th

MEDICINE CROW WAS in town to run a *Shamans Full Moon Intensive* with Two Crows, and I was attending. It was a four-day retreat at a property in Eugowra, NSW, 33 kilometers (20 miles) East of Forbes, consisting of a one-day vigil (in nature) designed to prepare us for a more arduous Vision Quest. I was in the 11th month of my first journey with the Clan Mothers so I felt ready to go within and process my learning.

The night before the retreat, Two Crow's organized a public circle at Soul Tree, our local crystal shop in Parkes, owned by Linda, one of the women in our meditation group. Medicine Crow spoke about self-love. Then led us through a shamanic medicine drum journey. He and Two Crows drummed so hard that it felt like the roof blew off. Afterward, Medicine Crow said earnestly, "Now we may have stirred up some stuff here tonight, people. So I want to recommend you use duck medicine." We leaned forward in excited anticipation of wise Native American advice but instead, we got typical Crow wit, "When shit hits the fan, duck."

Well, shit sure hit the fan!

While driving home, I saw a boy who looked like Donn Junior, the son we never had. He was getting out of his car. Tall and athletic with sandy hair, a little disheveled from exercising. He was fit and freckle-nosed with the same pale blue eyes as his father.

"Hi, Donn Junior," I said from my car as I passed.

I allowed my mind to drift into a beautiful imagining of Donn Wrixon Stitt. His handsome, cheeky smile, his energy around the dinner table, him rumbling with Stitty, joking with his sisters, watching him play footy, and hugging him lovingly. Raising an emotionally intelligent man for some lucky partner felt exciting. I noticed an inkling of sadness rising. I allowed it, even welcomed it. The emotion grew into an intense pining for a son. This was not a new feeling, it had been with me for months. I had shared with Stitty, "I have not felt this clucky since Ruby was hanging around before we conceived her. Maybe I am meant to have a son."

His response, "No chance!"

I brought myself back to my body driving the car. I had learned to fully experience uncomfortable feelings rather than stuff them down. So I began witnessing this undeniable longing for a son. This surrender felt perfectly aligned and strangely freeing.

When I got home I was making the bed when I hit my *funny bone*. I shot down in excruciating pain, which activated spontaneous sobbing. Either my miscarriage or a past/parallel life memory thrust me into unimaginable grief. I wasn't just grieving the son I conceived in this lifetime, I was grieving all the sons I had lost in the past, in the future and on behalf of parents/carers across the planet losing a son in that moment. We had all lost a son. He was in utero, an infant, a toddler, an adolescent, an adult. He was adopted out, he was stolen, he was lost, he ran away or he had died by suicide. He was gone and I was left howling for his return. I allowed the tears to stream down my face and run off the tip of my nose into the sheets. Uncontrollably wailing, huddled in a fetal position, and being alone triggered further releasing and processing. I felt profound empathy and compassion for people losing a child today, in the past, or in the future. I allowed myself to drop down into my anguish which reflected the depth of my love for humanity. I allowed my unresolved trauma to express itself through me by embracing whatever feelings presented themselves. I became intimate with them rather than ignoring them, and it felt good. I was no longer afraid to feel distressing emotions because I had the strategies to cope with them. I had the confidence to relive the miscarriage, knowing I could transmute the pain. Instead of thinking *I can't bear this, I don't want this; I can't handle this, make it go away.* I thought *I'm letting the sorrow flow through me. I'm becoming one with it. This heartbreak is part of me and part of the collective. It needs to be acknowledged to be alchemized.*

I'm sorry, Please forgive me, I love you, Thank you. I'm sorry, Please forgive me, I love you, Thank you. I'm sorry, Please forgive me, I love you, Thank you.

It is done. It is done. It is done.

At the time of my miscarriage, I did not mourn a single bit because I had two young daughters relying on me. Recently I had been yearning so badly for a son that I felt mis-aligned. Today, knowing health-ease is SELF's birthright I fully allowed myself to grieve the loss of that baby which cleared the associated trauma on all timelines. By healing my younger/past/parallel self, I inadvertently healed my current self. The desire to get pregnant simply vanished.

From that day on, I was able to see Donn Wrixon Stitt, the son we never had, without feeling any lack.

A few days later on Sunday, November 9th during my one-day vigil (sitting inside my meditation circle on a rock from dawn to dusk) Lou, a colleague, in spirit, came to me. She had died of throat cancer two months before. A few hours after she died (I was unaware she had died) she came to me in a dream. In my dream, I was laughing and partying with the teachers in the staffroom and feeling guilty for being intoxicated with them on school grounds. Lou grabbed my face and looked me in the eyes, "You have to have fun with your students and love them like your own."

Now Lou was visiting me again. This time, I wept tears of compassion because she would not be able to care for her three children. Her youngest son was only four years old and still slept in their bed. She was a dedicated, devoted, and selfless mum who would do anything for her children.

My suffering was agonizing, I became inconsolable. I realized I was now connecting with another way we lose our children, we die before them. Then out of the blue, I made this strange, determined, unwavering promise to her. I cried out, "Lou, I will always look after your children."

I wondered *Where did that come from? Why did I say that with such conviction? How am I going to do that, I don't even know her family? What a weird thing to say.*

THREE YEARS later my 15-year-old daughter Ruby started dating Lou's middle child, Jack, who was 16. For two and half years we loved him like a son. We still love him. The first time Jack walked into our house I said, "Now listen, you don't have a mum and I don't have a son so whenever we see each other we are going to hug." I always knew it was Lou doing the hugging but I did not mind in the slightest.

One time she made me tell him she was proud of him, I felt shy saying it but I had to put aside my fear to pass on the message.

Years later, Jack told Ruby that she was the first person he felt comfortable enough with to grieve and that Stitty and I made him the man he is today. I have no doubt Lou orchestrated the whole thing. How cool that I entered the silence during the one-day vigil and witnessed the parallel timeline where I was looking after Lou's son. The vision felt surreal because my logical mind could not comprehend such a random promise but my evolved self knew that I was going to do for Lou what she could not do for herself–love her son until he finished year 12. I feel honored that she chose me and my beautiful daughter to help her.

Isn't it incredible that as soon as I let myself mourn Donn Junior I replaced a desire for a son with a seed to manifest a son.

———

CAN you think of a time you sowed a seed that seemed completely unrealistic at the time that came to fruition? When did allowing yourself to fully feel something set off a chain reaction of healing or manifesting?

20

ASSISTING A CHILD TRANSITIONING TO THE SPIRIT WORLD SELF

41 - 43 years old

Trigger warning: Story contains potentially triggering content for trauma survivors relating to childhood death.

DEATH DOES NOT INTERRUPT *the inner conversation of two hearts that have met in the Light of Reality. If anything, it makes that conversation even more profound.*
A Journey in Ladakh by Andrew Harvey

43 YEARS

Monday, January 19th

Kellen, my fourteen-year-old nephew, peacefully transitioned into an expanded dimension, we were all by his side in the Seattle

Children's Hospital. He had been diagnosed with cancer two years earlier.

I had transformed that year guided by Jamie Sams and the 13 Clan Mothers and through my five-year apprenticeship with Two Crows and Medicine Crow.

Now, the time had come for me to step up as a shaman.

When people hear I lost my nephew, their fears surface, and they interpret my story through their trepidation lens. They feel triggered and scared that they could lose a child.

I invite you to read this chapter with an open mind. The death of a child is traumatic, but it can also be a gift once we see the bigger picture. The role these children play in metamorphosing lives can be monumental. I believe these children come here to change people.

We mourned Kellen when we could no longer experience him physically, but we continue to communicate with him in spirit. We know Kellen is always around us and available to help whenever asked. Kellen has proved to us, that an aspect of ourSELF lives on after we leave our bodies or perhaps they exist on a parallel timeline where they did not die. Either way we have access to them any time we choose.

Kellen (in spirit) came to me a few weeks after he transitioned into the spirit world and asked me to talk about his joyful life instead of talking about his sad death. I realized I was in the habit of sharing the details of his death which made people feel fear. I thought *Why was I doing this? Was I trying to shock people to get attention? Why was I sharing intimate moments that no one needs to know unless they lose a child? What was I gaining from revealing these details?*

This wake-up call forced me to talk about death from a shaman's perspective instead of making Kellen's story about me and how I suffered. Telling people that Kellen had died in a positive way was not easy. People looked at me and thought *What is wrong with you? A child has just died. How can you say it is a beautiful story?* Regardless of how uncomfortable I felt, I respected Kellen's wishes and always shared his impact on the world rather than the intensity of his death. How did I do this? I simply told people Kellen inspired others to choose love over fear.

It was interesting; as soon as I shared stories about his life instead of the details of his death, I felt him around me.

The backstory

KELLEN WAS BORN three years after his brother Hayden who was born with a genetic disorder called Tuberous Sclerosis. This condition would mean Hayden would be living with his parents, my half-brother Bill and his wife Melissa, for the rest of their lives. I believe Kellen was a living angel whose soul stepped into this life knowing he had a job to do, and he accomplished that in his short time here. What was his job? He needed to prepare his parents for the long road ahead of them. Hayden's genetic disorder causes many medical issues, such as seizures and abnormal growths throughout his body. In addition, Hayden is significantly cognitively delayed and is on the Autism Spectrum which causes repetitive behaviors, difficulty with appropriate social interaction, and challenges with self-regulation and impulse control. These characteristics require Bill and Melissa to cultivate unimaginable amounts of patience. Hayden can not be left alone which requires Bill, Melissa, or a caregiver to be with him at all times. However, the behavioral aspects of Hayden's disorder make it such that his parents provide the bulk of care. When Hayden became an adult, travel in airplanes became too challenging, which meant Bill and Melissa could no longer travel overseas together. Kellen taught them to live in the present, knowing tomorrow is not promised. Through Kellen, they learned it is up to them to find happiness in the moment.

Bill and Melissa met while picking up to-go food from the restaurant inside a random St. Louis, Missouri hotel. Melissa was a flight attendant on a layover, and Bill was a lawyer on a business trip. When Hayden's bardo being was looking for karmically matched parents they needed to be a specific type. Due to his condition, very few couples could help him navigate his Earth experience. He chose well; Bill and Melissa could raise him, but not without the lessons Kellen taught them.

---

41 YEARS

Sunday, February 24th (diagnosis day)

Seattle, Washington, USA

"MELISSA, I heard Kellen's in the hospital. I'm calling to tell you how he was before he hopped on the plane." I said on the phone from Australia.

Melissa moaned, "It's worse Katie, It's so much worse." Sobbing broke up her sentence, "He has an inoperable brain tumor."

Bill and Kellen, aged twelve at the time, had just returned from visiting us in Australia. Kellen did not seem himself during the trip. He vomited multiple times throughout his visit and lacked the energy you would expect of a young boy when we hiked down the Giant Staircase in the Blue Mountains National Park, Katoomba. Kel was too tired to stay up at night watching movies with his cousins. He could only tolerate certain foods. He slept a lot. Near the end of the trip, he was habitually crunching on ice cubes out of Patrick's ice machine in Manly, Sydney. On the last day of their holiday, Patrick noticed that Kellen was strangely holding his arm, but Kellen dismissed all inquiries, assuring us he was fine. So Bill and he continued ahead with their planned flight home.

By the time Bill and Kellen got off the plane after 18 hours of flying, Kellen was dragging his leg on the same side. They took him straight to the Seattle Children's Hospital Emergency Department. Scans confirmed the doctor's suspicions; Kellen was diagnosed with an inoperable grade IV glioblastoma brain tumor.

Patrick hoped straight on a plane to Seattle to support Bill and Melissa as they met with doctors and discussed prognosis and treatment. But, unfortunately, doctors told them that chemotherapy and radiation treatments might extend his life, but there was no cure, and the tumor would most likely take his life.

I flew to Seattle a little later to support Melissa with Kellen's treatments. On the way, in the San Francisco airport book shop, a blue butterfly caught my eye. It was on the cover of a book called *Proof of Heaven* written by Eben Alexander, a neurosurgeon. I read the back cover that told of Eben's near-death experience and journey into the afterlife. I felt guided to buy *Proof of Heaven* for Melissa as I thought it might be helpful.

Melissa read the book; then Bill read the book, then I read the book.

Melissa always had an interest in spirituality, but Kellen's diagnosis and reading about Eben's experience began to open her eyes to other realms of consciousness.

After Melissa read *Proof of Heaven,* she and I continued exploring consciousness together.

As I journeyed (for the first time) with the Clan Mothers the year after Kellen's diagnosis, I went through profound initiations. I taught Melissa everything I was learning. She was hungry for knowledge. She read book after book on spirit communication and devoured books on past lives. She studied soul contracts to understand how she and Bill chose two children requiring intensive daily care. She and I had been sisters-in-law for a long time, but now we were soul sisters. Before Kellen got cancer, I had not shared this information in great detail because it was irrelevant. Now there was an urgency to our sharing. As a result, our relationship grew stronger and stronger. Today, we know each other intimately and talk regularly. We trust each other impeccably and express everything as sisters do, including our vulnerabilities and triumphs. There is nothing we do not share.

Anyone assisting a child to transition to the spirit world could look to Bill and Melissa for guidance. They made his last two years magical by simply carrying on with their lives with positivity. His illness never detracted from their abundance; if anything, it added to it because it made them vigilant about where they placed their attention. They lived every day as if it was their last with him. They never closed Kellen away; he was consistently in the center of all the action. The house was always full of music and visitors, of all ages, from all over the world (neighbors, family, old college friends, the builder, law school buddies, and Bill's band members), which brought vibrancy to Kellen's life. Bill and Melissa epitomized *When you can't go out, bring the world in*. Everyone contributed to Kellen in their unique way and received from Kellen in his unique way. Visitors left the house with an appreciation for life which rippled into their relationships. They took away a bit of his magic. They experienced moments of enlightenment, insights, and awakening. Kellen had the best life. His illness did not extinguish his light; it made it brighter. If we measure a person's life by the amount of magic they create, then Kellen lived an extraordinary life. It was as if creating magic was his purpose for being, his calling. What he taught people to do for themselves was genius. For example, anytime he sensed someone feeling sorry for him because he had cancer, he would tell a joke to make them laugh, lifting their mood. This phenomenal skill required awareness, empathy, and an expanded perspective. Here was Kellen, a teenage boy teaching adults how to live in a state of gratitude. He led by example, showing us how to experience the now instead of being lost in past thoughts or future worries. Everyone he met noticed how his decision to focus on love attracted so much beauty. Bill and Melissa intuitively rode Kellen's wave by following his lead and spontaneously creating his world with him. This co-creation touched the hearts of everyone, everywhere. His body became a vessel of thankfulness, humor, and kindness.

The second time I flew to Seattle, Ruby, who was twelve, came with me. Kellen missed his school friends because he was too weak to attend school, and he and Ruby had a special connection. Ruby and I were in awe; Kellen was a young boy speaking like a wise sage.

"You're so beautiful, Aunt Katie. Thank you for being here." Kellen would say to me.

To Melissa, he would share, "Mom, you really are the best Mom. I appreciate everything you do for me so much."

43 YEARS

The third time I flew to Seattle, I assisted Kellen to transition to the spirit world. Four weeks earlier, Melissa rang to say that she and Bill suspected Kellen's tumor was advancing again because Kellen was sleepy. We talked about not telling Kellen the news. It was Christmas, and the whole family was visiting. Kellen's Aunt Janet (my half-sister) and Grandma Pat (my dad Donn's first wife) lived in Seattle, and Kellen's Calgary, Canada Aunt Judy (my other half-sister) was flying in. Kellen had a memorable Christmas day surrounded by his family.

Monday, December 29th

MUM'S MUM (Old GG) transitioned peacefully in her sleep at the age of 93.

Wednesday, December 31st (22 months after diagnosis)

Janet and Pat joined them for dinner to celebrate New Year's and Pat's 86th birthday. They were all gathered around the Seattle table and Melissa said, "Kel, would you like to share your words of wisdom for the new year?"

Kellen replied, "Not many people have happiness, so when you get that feeling, cherish it because it is one of the best feelings you can have in life. And I want to say I am so grateful that I've had the feeling and that everyone else here has had that feeling too. I just want to say thank you so much for this amazing year. I loved it so much, it couldn't have been better, and I look forward to the future as well."

Monday, January 5th

The following morning, Kellen's scheduled MRI confirmed that his tumor was growing and he likely had months or weeks to live. Melissa and Bill told Kellen that the reason he was feeling unwell was because the tumor had grown back and they asked him if he had any questions. He replied no. He was not feeling well at this point and asked Melissa to help him lay down to sleep.

The same day in Australia

I completed my first 13-month Clan Mother journey around the medicine wheel during a ceremony where we met the 13th clan mother Becomes Her Vision. I honestly believe that Old GG and Kellen waited for me to meet Becomes Her Vision to have the skills necessary to support Mum and Melissa.

Monday, January 12th

The following week, Kel had a seizure caused by the tumor's progression, and Bill and Melissa called 911. He was taken by ambulance to Seattle Children's Hospital where he was given medicine to halt the seizures, which put him into a medically induced coma.

Immediately, Patrick and I made arrangements to go to Seattle. In the air, I told Kellen's higher self (telepathically) that he needed to wake up from his coma so that everyone could say goodbye to him. By the time we touched down in Seattle, he had miraculously woken from a three-day coma. Melissa told me she had also been praying and talking with him to give us a little more time together.

We arrived in the hospital room at the same time as the doctor who said how astonished he was that Kellen had come out of his coma, "We thought we'd lost you, Buddy. You had other plans, I guess. Your regaining consciousness is remarkable. What a fighter!"

The doctor's comment prompted me to ask Kellen, "Do you remember anything from the coma?"

Kellen replied, "Oh, yeah, I met Grandpa Donn. He had gray hair and a leopard print jacket."

"Wow, that is amazing! Did he say anything to you?" I inquired.

Kellen replied, "He said, "It's great to meet you, Kellen" (Dad died before Kellen was born). We were driving in Patrick's car. We were driving and driving, and then we pulled up at the hospital, and

Grandpa Donn said, "It's time for you to get out now, Kel." I got out of the car, and Dad met me there and brought me into the hospital."

"Did you see anything else?" I asked.

"Yes, I saw a lot of lights and a lot of people." He added.

I could not believe my ears. Kellen had had a near-death experience. Dad had met him to escort him into the afterlife but decided Kellen had people to say goodbye to, so he took him back to the hospital to meet Bill.

Every night as I fell asleep, I communicated with Kellen's higher self (this felt easy, I was sleeping in his bed). I assured Kellen that Grandpa Donn would guide him when he transitioned, but I insisted he hang on till Monday because Melissa's Mom (Grandma Beverly) and brother Art were coming from Ohio on Sunday (everyone else was already there).

Melissa and I tag-teamed with Bill and Patrick each day, taking turns at the hospital and doing things to provide respite. Patrick used humor, and I used meditation. We were perfectly suited to each of them. Janet and Judy had other jobs. Janet, an extraordinary chef, prepared meals, and Judy looked after Grandma Pat and eventually Grandma Beverley.

At first, Kellen was articulate and told jokes. As the days progressed, though, Kellen got weaker and weaker. His words remained as sweet as always, but I sensed he already had a foot in the unseen world.

On Sunday night, doctors advised that Kellen was in the last stage of life. So, for the first time since Kellen went into the hospital, Bill and Melissa were together with him. We (the four siblings) were put in charge of Hayden so that they could spend the last night with their son. We prepared a hamper for Bill and Melissa with a beautifully cooked meal, a bottle of red wine, glasses, candles, and a tablecloth, which we delivered to the hospital room.

Monday, January 19th (transitioning to the spirit world day)

THE NEXT DAY I was at Bill and Melissa's house, with Janet, Judy, and Patrick, when I noticed Melissa's 44-card deck, *The Soul's Journey* by James Van Praagh. I shuffled the lesson cards and asked myself *What card relates to Kellen transitioning today?* I did not expect the card I pulled, Happiness. I thought *This is a weird card. How can death be happy?* Then I remembered the video Melissa shared of Kel's New Year's Eve speech. *Maybe happiness is Kellen's word because he taught us how to be happy. Cool!"* I read the message in the book *I am aware that being happy means that I am on the right path. Before incarnating, your soul created a blueprint for you to follow in this physical dimension. The easiest way to chart this path is to follow your bliss...The signposts are always there, but you have to acknowledge them and have the courage to follow them. Others will want to learn from you...you can be their teacher. When you are filled with love and compassion, not only do you bring happiness into your life, but you lead others by example. Be the light.* I reshuffled the deck and returned them with the book to the box.

I spoke telepathically to Kellen and thanked him for holding on until Monday so everyone could say goodbye. I assured him that he could go now (Melissa and I also told him this the day before when he was last coherent). I started feeling pulled to be at the hospital because Melissa had sent me a text message asking me to join her and Bill. She could sense Kel was going, and she wanted me there. Then, one of Hayden's carers turned up in divine timing, allowing us to call a cab. Patrick stopped to buy food for Bill and Melissa and when we got back in a cab he sat in the front seat, and Janet, Judy, and I sat in the backseat. My mobile phone rang.

"He's just taken his last breath," Melissa whispered.

I let out a whimper. "Ok, well, we are on our way," I promised.

The four of us held hands and cried. Nothing prepared me for the moment I knew Kellen was gone. It is an indescribable feeling of finality, where hope drains, revealing an empty hole. Kellen had transitioned in the arms of his parents. It was perfect that they were alone with him. They brought him into this world together, and they watched him leave this world together.

When I entered the hospital room, the memory of Dad's lifeless body assaulted me. The gray color, the chill, the hollow shell. A body void of life force is unrecognizable as a human body, yet very distinctive. It looks nothing like sleep; it looks like undeniable death. The spark that occupied his vehicle, the Eternal Flame of Love, had transitioned to another dimension. A dimension most people do not witness. The light which filled every cell, bringing them to life, had withdrawn, leaving an inanimate thing on the bed. It was confronting because it resembled Kellen, but all the qualities that make us human were missing, so it was not him. Nonetheless, I sensed his presence in the room.

We were all hugging Bill and Melissa when Grandma Beverly and Uncle Art walked in. We continued embracing.

"Let's all make a circle around Kel; I would like to say a few words," my authority and confidence surprised me. I had not planned this. I believe it was Kellen guiding me.

We joined hands. Melissa picked up Kellen's right hand, and Grandma Beverley picked up his left hand.

I was spontaneously creating in a flow state. There was no need to filter the words coming through; I trusted everything would be aligned.

"I would like everyone to take a deep breath. Breath in life and breath out life (a Two Crow's expression). We are gathered here today to support Kellen as he transitions. We can feel you here, Kellen. We want you to know how much we love you and how proud of you we are. Kellen, your name means Mighty Warrior, and you have been just that. The warrior of truth. It took bravery for you to come and teach us how to choose happiness, not fear. This lesson is your gift to us, and we receive it with thanks. Kellen, you were eloquent beyond your years. You summed it all up on New Year's Eve, choose happiness, and when you feel it, cherish it because not everyone gets to experience it. Bill and Melissa live this happiness daily. Through parenting you and Hayden, they have learned love in all its forms. They are selfless, compassionate, and love unconditionally, which is rare. These traits were reflected in you, Kellen. You never complained about your bent arm or your altered gate; you just celebrated being able to walk. You brought smiles to faces with your everlasting appreciation. Even when you were getting a needle, you were grateful. You showed us our potential. Thank you for being our living angel. Would anyone like to say a few words?" I encouraged.

Everyone said goodbye, and I love you.

I took in a long slow breath, marinating in the intense silence. Then continued, "Let's all close our eyes. Feel the love flowing through our hands? This is Kellen. Feel our loved ones in the circle? This is Kellen. Feel our hearts beating inside our chests? This is Kellen. Feel the air in our lungs? This is Kellen. Feel the support for Bill, Melissa, and Hayden from around the world? This is Kellen. Feel our true nature, full of love and light? This is Kellen."

The moment we dropped hands, Patrick rushed to me from the opposite side of the circle. He threw his six-foot-four arms around me and said, "I am so proud of you. That was incredible. Just when I thought it couldn't get any better, it just skyrocketed again."

I was no longer Katie Pops, everyone's 'little' sister. I was a shaman.

Melissa asked me to stay and support her, and Bill asked Patrick to stay and support him. What followed were the most harrowing hours of my life. Patrick and I experienced what parents who have lost a child go through. At one point, I nudged Patrick because he did not realize his anguished groans were audible. The experience activated every sense and heightened every emotion. Intermittently, Patrick and I would have to leave the room to hug and recompose ourselves. I felt displaced like I was watching myself from outside my body as if I was the director of a movie. No shaman apprenticeship prepared me for this surreal scene. This was Kellen, my nephew, my big brother's baby. Kellen would never have his first kiss, take someone to his prom, or be a father. The reality sunk in.

Preparing the body was hard enough but leaving the hospital was harder. Bill and Melissa had fought every second for Kellen, and now they were going home without their son. Defeated, exhausted, and shocked.

I traveled in Melissa's car. I held space for her imagining the Clan Mothers cradling her in their loving arms. Three weeks earlier during that final Becomes Her Vision initiation I felt empowered to access truth in all its forms. On this car trip, Listening Woman's way of restoring balance was required—we uttered nothing.

When we arrived back at the house, it was late afternoon. Bill and Melissa took a warm bath; they had not been at home together since Kellen had gone into the hospital one week prior.

They exhaled.

Suddenly, we heard Hayden speaking loudly with his caregiver on the front porch.

Patrick opened the door to the carer who asked for Bill.

"Bill, we have a situation you need to deal with down here, please," Patrick called up the stairs.

As Bill walked past us with a towel around his waist, he gave us the most beautiful smile imaginable and shrugged his shoulders, "This is just how we roll here, guys." Bill's open acceptance demonstrated his attitude to life. He never complained, "Why me?" Instead, he would say, "It is what it is." Bill's optimism, steadfast dedication to his children, and undying support for Melissa are rare and extraordinary qualities. He would often say, "I feel so lucky. I want nothing in life. I am blessed." Together Bill and Melissa make a formidable team.

After Melissa's bath, she picked up the *Soul's Journey* Deck, "Hey, Sis, I am going to pull a card."

I responded, "I pulled one this morning. I shuffled but be sure to shuffle again."

Melissa inquired, "What card did you pull, Sis?"

"The Happiness card," I responded.

"So did I!" she sang out, a little shocked but not really. This was the first of many spirit communications with Kellen.

That night Melissa mourned. She followed her instincts and let every emotion flow through her body. Tears trickled, pain pulsed, grief crippled, sorrow rippled, and bit by bit, she released her trauma. I just held her in my arms as she let it all out imagining I was the She Who Heals Clan Mother. The guardian of serving the truth and the mother of all rites of passage *Catch my babies when they are born, Sing my death song, teach me how to mourn* (Sams, 1993).

Seeing a child die caused a visceral reaction that burned like a deep tattoo into my psyche. The memory is a constant reminder regarding what is important in life. It provides endless motivation to play, live for today, love while I can, and appreciate the small things. I have no idea what is around the corner, so I stay in the now. Kellen's transition taught me to parent as if my children could die tomorrow. I do not think about them dying because principle number three applies: *Makia*: Energy flows where attention goes (be focussed), but I say everything I want to say. I tell them they are heard, seen, and loved.

I now know that I assisted Kellen to transition while he assisted me to live.

The fourth time I went to Seattle, I spoke at Kellen's memorial service. On the day I flew from Sydney to Seattle, Two Crows said to me, "The apprentice has become the shaman."

At the memorial, I invited everyone to stand and hold hands

while we listened to *A hundred thousand angels* by Bliss. Bill and Melissa displayed their usual grace as they celebrated the life and spirit of Kellen Monroe Joyce.

Let's reflect

People often ask me, "How does Melissa do it? How is she joyful when losing her teenage son and caring 24/7 for a high-needs adult son? I couldn't live if I were her."

How do I answer this question? What do I think makes Melissa resilient? How can she endure tragedy and challenges better than others? What is her secret?

Hayden is a 25-year-old man who sometimes behaves like a toddler. Parenting him has taught Melissa how to love unconditionally. Melissa can only view Hayden with pure love and acceptance. Many parents expect their children to meet their needs, desires, and expectations. When their children do not conform, they withdraw their love and approval to coerce them to think, say and act the way they want them to. This conditioning leads to mutual feelings of disappointment. Hayden does not understand other people's needs; he can not be manipulated or controlled. So Melissa has to love him as he is. For example, Hayden will ask questions that can not be answered repeatedly for hours, days, weeks, and years on end. "Mom, is it going to rain, Mom? Is it going to rain, Mom? Mom, is it going to rain? Hayden has limited comprehension but unlimited persistence. Many of us would go clinically insane but not Melissa. When I call her a saint, she replies, "Nice of you to say Sis, but I am human and have my moments of frustration." Regardless, a lot of the time her needs are not being met, but she puts these aside to cater to his needs. We could all benefit from experiencing the moment without filtering it through the lens of our own needs. Without our self-centered minds in the way, we create space to enjoy the exchange as it is rather than how we imagined it would be. Not needing anything from anyone is liberating because it does not matter what they do or say; we love them regardless. When I ask Melissa how she maintains a state of balance between her service-to-Hayden and her service-to-self requirements, she replies, "It's a daily practice–caring for his needs and honoring myself at the same time. I have to make time for myself every day so that I am replenished enough to support him. Bill and I are a great team. We work together to allow each other downtime. I like to go hiking, biking, take nature photographs, and be creative when I am alone. These activities keep my cup full."

Melissa, due to her circumstances, learned to live mindfully. She had to view things neutrally and think *It is not good; it is not bad; it just is*. My insight meditation teacher, Bryan, said that renunciation was the cornerstone of Buddhist practice. Renunciation is relating to something completely without wanting or needing anything. Melissa lives this way. She did not need a 10-day silent retreat in northern India to learn the Buddha's teachings because the experience of being Hayden's mum gradually taught her how to wake up over and over. Also, parenting Kellen in his last couple of years allowed Melissa to take his lead and live anchored in the present moment, which liberated her.

By paying attention to her joy instead of her suffering, Melissa attracts more joy through the law of attraction. The alternative would be to focus on her grief which would attract more suffering. For example, if she spent her day complaining about Hayden's fixated behavior, she would notice more and more of it. So instead, she is thankful for the little things like nature, friends, family, music, technology, and beautiful teachers all over the world. Melissa is a true beacon showing humanity how to dwell in the light.

When Hayden started having seizures as an infant and then developed behavioral problems, life became so unpredictable that Melissa's expectations became malleable. To this day, she has to adapt instantly every time her plans change to accommodate Hayden's needs. For the past 25 years, Melissa and Bill have fitted into Hayden's life. When they spend time with children content to slide into their parents' day, they marvel with fascination. Melissa and Bill have never known an average parent's life. Family dinners with the neighbors, spontaneous outings, and trips away with friends were not options. One of them must always stay home with Hayden. When Hayden has aggressive outbursts, Melissa can not cling to how she wishes the moment could be. Nor can she push away what she does not like about the moment. These reactions (attachment and aversion) would be a pointless waste of time. Instead, she has trained herself to surrender and simply respond to the moment as it is. Melissa says, "Hayden is my freedom teacher. He exists in the now, forcing me to exist there too." Therefore, Melissa lives moment to moment. If she chose to get disheartened every time things went badly, she would never do anything. If she did not treat each moment as a new, fresh start, she would be crippled with fear. She has to be hopeful to bounce back, again and again. Melissa is resilience personified. She has to focus on what she wants to create, even when faced with the opposite. This commitment takes courage. It would be much easier to fall into a desperate heap.

Not long after Kellen transitioned, Melissa said, "I hear mothers on the radio who have lost a child. They can not get out of bed; they can not get over it. Sometimes I wonder if something is wrong with me because I don't feel like they do. Sometimes I feel guilty for being happy. But Kellen taught me how to find the light in the darkest moments by focussing on the light. Living this way honors Kellen's life."

A few months after Kellen's memorial service Melissa began hearing him talking to her. Knowing that she could still communicate with her son in the expanded dimension helped her cope with the loss of his physical presence. Melissa's realization that life is eternal made death less traumatic and contributed to her resiliency. A medium explained Melissa's soul contract, Kellen had cared for Melissa in a past life, and it was her turn to care for Kellen in this life. Knowing this was not her first Earth walk with Kellen assured her it would not be her last. This past/parallel life knowledge helped Melissa put Kel's transitioning into perspective and made her less attached to this version of him. She understood that she had a lesson to learn, and the catalyst would be losing Kellen. This perspective took her from the helpless victim to the empowered creator. Recently, Melissa trained as a psychic medium with Suzanne Gieseman. Melissa was also part of an active mediumship group that focused on welcoming spirits that wished to communicate, creating a safe space to hold, honor and support one another as they practiced their mediumship skills. Melissa is becoming more and more confident at communicating with Kellen and unknown spirits. Bringing through without-a-doubt signs from Kellen gives others hope that they too can stay connected to their loved ones in spirit.

In a way, Melissa was more fortunate than Mums, who suddenly lost their children because she could tell Kellen everything she wanted to say to him. After diagnosis, Melissa referred to his two years of life as a gift. Before Kel transitioned, she asked him, "If I go to heaven first, what will my sign be to you?" and he replied, "A heart." Then she asked him, "If you go to heaven first, what will your sign be for me?" and he replied, "A ladybug."

Kellen sends us ladybug and heart signs, flickers lights, balloons, and rainbows, plays his favorite song when we think about him, makes his number 313 appear, sends us people named Kellen in random places, and gives without a doubt messages to psychics. For example, one medium, Suzanne Giesemann, asked Melissa if they donated Kellen's eyes (no one else knew this except a few family members). He said through Suzanne, "I don't need those eyes Mom, I see you just fine."

Melissa seeks out communication from Kellen and posts these stories on Instagram @lifeinheartuality where she explains this unique name *Heartuality - combining heart and spirituality to define a state of being in the world with my husband, my differently-abled son, and my son in spirit.* Melissa's posts give support to other mums who have lost children. Melissa's stories show ways spirit communicates to support them from the unseen world. She teaches how to detect subtle pointers and messages from their departed loved ones. Melissa's resilience makes her a powerful role model to mums going through challenging situations. She is genuine, relatable, and generous with her time. She openly shares the lessons she has learned, knowing that she can make a difference in people's lives. She has pure compassion for others doing it tough, and her altruistic nature has positively impacted so many people worldwide. Kellen's transition allowed Melissa to activate her creative power and achieve her vision to empower women. This facilitation is her purpose for being. Her kindness and willingness to be of service release endorphins in the brain that further enhance her resiliency.

Lastly, Melissa's resilience is strengthened by our relationship. Melissa often says to me, "I feel so grateful for you, Katie. I am so thankful to Kel for bringing you and me together." Melissa and I acknowledge that our relationship may never have blossomed had Kellen lived. Melissa and I both know our bond is a silver lining. She teaches me as much as I teach her, and together we are an outstanding team. There is nothing we can not get through. Kellen knew life with Hayden would become harder and harder, and he wanted me by his Mum's side.

Through Kellen, Melissa and I know events can not be judged as positive or negative because seemingly adverse events can open doors and create opportunities. It's all a matter of perspective.

21

VISIONING THE VOID SELF

44 years old

Thursday, April 21st

I ARRIVED BACK at the property in Eugowra, where I had done the *Shamans Full Moon Intensive* and one-day vigil 17 months earlier. I was finally doing a Vision Quest. A Vision Quest is a Native American rite of passage traditionally undertaken by boys to enter adulthood. First, they would walk out nude with only a blanket and remain in their sacred circle for four days and four nights, without food, water, or sleep. There, they would ceremoniously tie prayer ties, meditate, contemplate and cry out to the Great Spirit for a vision to guide them into adulthood.

So why was I doing one? I trained as a shaman, so I knew the experience would initiate me as an Elder and give my life direction.

However, I had resisted because I was scared of being alone, murdered, hungry, and, worst of all, bored.

On the eve of the quest, a meditation sister, Jenny, from our clan mothers group came to my bed clutching *The 13 Original Clan Mothers* book by Jamie Sams.

"Let's read about the clan mother coming in with the full moon tomorrow night. She is the one who will guide us on our quest." Jenny exclaimed.

I offered to read because I love reading aloud; it is the teacher in me.

"Looks Far Woman's cycle of truth is see the truth.

Mother teach me how to see

The shining lights of stars

The faces of the Ancestors,

In worlds both near and far

Show me how to welcome

The visions appearing to me,

Seeing the truth in detail, Unraveling each mystery.

Walk me through the Dreamtime

Of altered time and space,

That I may share those visions

With every creed and race.

Doorkeeper of all dimensions,

I seek your Medicine ways

Of how to earth my visions,

Seeing truth, inside me, today.

She is the Doorkeeper of the Crack in the Universe and the Golden Door of Illumination that leads to all other dimensions of awareness. She stands at the Crack in the Universe and safely guides all human spirits taking Dreamtime journeys into the other realms and then, back home, being present and fully conscious of their bodies.

This Clan Mother is a Seer, an Oracle, a Dreamer, and a visionary... She shows us how to see truth in every vision we see in the tangible and intangible worlds... She knows that all Two-leggeds can access the ability to see the truth in all dimensions, if they seek the light of the Eternal Flame of Love and if they are willing to receive the visions that come when the heart is open... In the final development of this Clan Mother's lessons, human beings are able to fully understand any signs, portents, omen, or symbols presented to their awareness... If they are willing to give away their illusions, they pass through the Golden Door into their next level of understanding. If they fear their own potential, they will return to the place within themselves that gives comfort, until they are ready to grow."

IN THE STORY, Looks Far Woman heals a young girl named Star Fire. The trauma of Star Fire's rape sent fragments of her spirit into the vastness of the void. It took many moons to take her through small healing steps. Looks Far Woman regularly traveled into the void to return shards of Star Fire's spirit. When she was ready, Looks Far Woman took Star Fire to the Crack in the Universe where a Golden Door of Illumination appeared. The Eternal Flame of Love blazed in Star Fire's heart showing that Star Fire had forgiven those who had wounded her. Star Fire realized that her pain had served her by opening her to her gifts. She was now *a healed healer who had passed through the dark night of the soul to reclaim the love.*

I continued, "The worlds within worlds are opened to every Two-legged who chooses to travel beyond the pain that limits our ability to see the truth.

Looks Far Woman will always stand at the Crack in the Universe, holding the Golden Door of Illumination open for those who have the ears to hear, the eyes to see, and the hearts to understand."

I was bursting with excitement. Of all the clan mothers we had journeyed with (17 over two and one-third years), the one who would support us on our Vision Quest was the clan mother of visions, who was responsible for helping us *see the truth*. I thought *I am going to the Crack in the Universe and through the Golden Door of Illumination. I'm not exactly sure what that means but I know I'm doing it!*

"Jenny, are you excited to go through the Crack in the Universe? I can't wait!" I exclaimed, grabbing both her arms and staring into her eyes.

"I'm terrified." She replied. I wondered *Why are you holding back, Sista?"*

The following day a soft drum beat drifted through the darkness. Medicine Crow and Two Crows instructed us to respect the silence. Some people drank fresh juice, but I chose to fast. In my backpack was a small shovel, toilet paper, tarp, a sleeping bag, an airline sleep mask, a yoga mat, water, a small bag of salt, a small bag of cornflower, a blank notebook, a pen, a lead pencil, and *The Trance Workbook: Understanding & Using the Power of Altered States*. I figured if I was going to be starving and tired, I may as well make the most of the delirium and explore consciousness.

We met by the ceremonial fire. Medicine Crow and Two Crows burned Grandfather sage and gave each of us a prayer kit. They explained that they would keep vigil by tending to the fire, drumming, saying prayers, and holding space for us throughout the whole quest. They were available to support us if we needed them, and it was up to us to decide when our quest was complete. I felt the same way I did at the day vigil. *There is no way I am coming down; you will have to drag me off.*

Medicine Crow and Two Crows drummed and chanted prayers. Two Crows bellowed out a powerful Hawaiian prayer; each word was delivered with conviction and felt utterly commanding.

The next few minutes were eerie. We walked single file behind Two Crows like soldiers heading to war. Leaves crunched, stillness shattered, flashlights flickered, anticipation escalated, expectations welled, and fear fluttered. Finally, we stopped at the bottom of the hill while Two Crows tossed some polenta as an offering and asked the ancestors, spirits, stones, trees, and animals to enter. We followed her up. One by one, she dropped us off at our power spots that Medicine Crow and Two Crows had selected.

I loved my spot; it felt like an energetic vortex. It was on a ledge with rocks behind it. I followed the steps I learned during my day vigil. Firstly, I asked permission to enter the space. Secondly, above me, I tied my tarp between the two trees on either side of me and placed my yoga mat underneath. Thirdly, I created my sacred meditation circle, which involved scattering a clockwise circle of salt around the outside of my mat to keep out the insects. Then a circle of polenta as a blessing to the animals who were sharing their space with me. I would stay within the limits of my circle for three full days and two nights.

Suddenly my mood changed. Resentment and anger ran through me like an electric current *I can't believe it. Maralyn has moved her circle to a spot that is visible to me. Doesn't she know that on Vision Quest, you are not meant to see anyone? How am I going to have a vision now with her down there?* Bla, Bla, Bla. I could hear my victim narrative going on and on. I had to nip it in the bud quickly. *She is there for a reason. Let go of how you thought it would be and accept it as it is. I acknowledge that I am disappointed because I had prior expectations. If I had no expectations, then I would be fine now. I chose to use this as an opportunity to practice non-attachment, my first test.*

I shifted my attention and focussed on the task at hand, the prayer ties. To do a prayer, I selected a colored square of fabric (5 centimeters squared) and then faced the direction of that color (yellow - East, red - South, black - West, white - North, blue - Above, green - Below, magenta - Within/Now). I pledged one prayer into each piece, then sprinkled Grandfather Sage, tobacco, and cornflower into the center of the square, twisted the top, and created a slip knot to tie it to the long piece of string which would become my prayer tie necklace. As instructed, all prayers were for others except the final prayer, which could be for me. We were taught to make each prayer a thank you statement in the present tense as if it had already happened. I noticed that the vibration of thankfulness was higher than that of pleading, so it made sense. So instead of saying "I pray for the hungry children" I said, "Thank you for the abundance of food and fresh water that is getting to the children to nourish them." The latter tells *Ku*/the universe precisely what the children need, nourishment. This is an example of positive neuro linguistic programming and of course manifesting step 1!

I had so much time to meditate. I experimented with different methods, such as using a mantra, single-pointed focus, focussing on the air on my top lip, and the labeling technique. Unfortunately, my meditation circle was too small for walking meditations!

I watched my thoughts like a hawk and identified ideas on a loop. I caught myself going over the same old things, recalling boring versions of events, and planning things I would say to people. It surprised me how often my mind dwelled in the future.

I looked with curiosity at my personality. In particular, the way I had attacked my prayer ties. I had sat down and done 28 prayers in a row which took hours. My Virgo ascendant had insisted I do them all in order. So I did one yellow, one red, one black, one white, one blue, one green, and one magenta around the Medicine Wheel four times, without stopping for a single break. My good girl identity ensured I turned and faced each direction, each time, no cheating. I imagined the prayer tie necklace of a more relaxed, spontaneous quester. I pictured spaces between ties, double-ups of colors, a variable amount of each color, and a lot fewer. I pondered my traits and questioned their origins, benefits, and downfalls.

Boredom crept in when I thought about another two days of sitting here. I practiced what Bryan had taught me on my 10-day silent insight meditation retreat in northern India. He encouraged me to work with boredom very directly. I noticed every time I felt aversion to my boredom I empowered it. Instead, I chose to sit with it. By experiencing it fully, rather than pushing it away, I realized nothing is permanent. When I let boredom come and go like a cloud passing in front of the sun, it simply did its own thing and disappeared on its own. I realized that boredom, like all mind states, is dependent on conditions for its arising and continuing, and when those conditions were not present, those states of mind were not either.

On a Vision Quest, there is nowhere to hide. So, I had to look at my way of being in the world. This examination made me uncomfortable. I wished I could push the thoughts away with a distraction; any distraction would do. How I longed to check my Instagram feed, pop the kettle on, have a snack, or call a friend. This was a valuable opportunity to recognize how often I do things purely to avoid an unpleasant state of mind. On Vision Quest, each time I resisted the temptation to distract myself, I realized the power within me to practice renunciation. I discovered that I did not need any of my mindless, avoidance habits. Incredibly, I was left feeling liberated instead of punished. This realization had life-changing repercussions as it showed me that my addictions were insubstantial, fleeting, and unsatisfying. As the Buddha said, "There is no greater happiness than peace."

I recognized how often fear held me back. I laughed at myself for thinking someone would murder me on Vision Quest. I had imagined myself sleeping near a deserted highway. Then, in the dead of night, a man who resembled the predator in the movie *Wolf Creek* stumbled across my vulnerable body cocooned in a sleeping bag. He thanked his lucky stars as he scooped me up and carried me to his car, never to be seen again. Although this fear was ridiculous, I noticed how quickly I replaced it with a new fear. I inherited this worry gene from Mum, who inherited it from her mother, Sally. So I had to rein in these debilitating thoughts continuously.

Another habit I worked on breaking was reporting on everything I was doing as if I was answering an interviewer's question by beginning with *I always...*or *I am one of those people who always...* I had to constantly interrupt myself *You don't always do that, and who are you telling anyway? It's weird. Stop doing it.* I wondered if it was a byproduct of my strategy when I first flew to India. I had pretended I was taking a group of students on an international excursion. It had served me at the time to settle my nerves, but two decades on, it was just an annoying habit. Besides, when I was honest with myself, I realized that it was my ego telling everybody how good I was, showing off to anyone who would listen, even if they were imaginary people. The pathetic ness of this epiphany inspired me even more to break the patterned way of thinking.

I also took a long look at my relationships and how often I put conditions on my love. Giving unconditionally with no strings attached had not been a focus at my school or in my house growing up, so I viewed others from the standpoint of my needs. Stitty's Mum Pattie was a woman who wholeheartedly catered to the needs of others. She always gave her children her full attention, as if she had nowhere she would rather be.

Hunger came and went; somehow, my body adapted to it. This process was made easier because I followed Two Crow's advice to detox (no coffee, meat, sugar) for three weeks prior. So at least I was not dealing with addiction cravings as well as hunger.

I also noticed negative thoughts arising. So every time a negative thought came up, I applied my antidote: *think of five things to be grateful for*. I found this raised my frequency very quickly. Why? Because Principle number three applies *Makia*: Energy flows where attention goes (be focussed).

A beautiful, pink full moon rose that night, followed by an exciting electrical storm. Lightning was crossing the sky for kilometers/miles into the distance. Thunder crashed beside me. Rain poured down as I huddled under my tarp. I could see Maralyn, with no tarp, sitting under her shawl, clutching her bag with a sleeping bag under her legs. At one point, I could not believe my eyes; below the full moon was a long dark cloud with lightning bolts going horizontally across it. I had never seen this before. It felt like a good omen, as though a colossal portal was opening up. Plus lightning had been mentioned in the Looks Far chapter, so now I knew without a shadow of a doubt *I'm going to the Crack in the Universe.*

It was Full Moon Clan Mothers night, so my meditation sisters had driven from Forbes to welcome Looks Far Woman by the ceremonial fire. I imagined Medicine Crow retreating to his room to leave the women to it. I wondered what they were sharing about their month journeying with Weighs The Truth. Then I visualized them reading the chapter by campfire light before we drummed together. I waited for Looks Far Woman to come into my meditation circle. She did not appear as a woman; she appeared as a golden light that felt more like an angel than a clan mother.

I could hear Medicine Crow, Two Crows, and others drumming long into the night. I promised myself that I would stand up and join in every time I heard the group drumming. For hours, I remained in a seated position with my back against the tree. I stayed awake most of the night until my eyes grew weary, and my head began to fall off my shoulders. Then I finally lay down to sleep.

The next day I woke up just before sunrise and did it all over again. As I unwound, I settled into the rhythm of nature. Every blowfly, ant, wallaby, spider, lizard, and bug reflected something to me. So, I talked to them and thanked them for their insights *If my Sydney friends could see me now, talking to animals!*

I was fascinated by the two trees that formed the energy portal around me. They were the opposite. One was being suffocated by vines that wrapped tightly around its trunk. The other was clear and free. I resonated with the free one, but I knew that I was the constricted one. Bound by conditioning, patterning, and programming.

Using my *Trance Workbook,* I danced until I entered an altered state. Then I slapped my entire body and shook like a crazy person to release tension and connect with my tribal ancestors. Afterwards I did a free-drawing activity aimed at accessing my subconscious.

I watched in wonderment as clouds changed colors and shapes while they moved across the sky's arc. Nature came to life, and I saw the spirit in all things for the first time in my life. The plant world opened up to me and shared *As a plant, I have the utmost respect for Australia's First Nation two-leggeds who make up the oldest civilization in the world. Once, the middle of the Australian continent was lush and plentiful—a place where my brothers and sisters produced edible seeds. The whole of Australia was abundant and cared for by intuitive humans who respected our symbiotic relationship. Without us, you could not breathe. Never forget how interconnected we are in this intelligent web of life we find ourselves weaving together. My message to humanity is to unite with Mother Nature to replenish the ravaged ecosystems. You are her, and she is you. What you do to the planet, you do to yourself.*

I sat motionless, processing this intense message. Six years before, I had come to Forbes to connect with Mother Earth, and now I was receiving direct dialogue from her. Humbled, I bowed down to honor her. I was finally connecting with the Talks With Relations Clan Mother who teaches us to learn the truth from the Tree People, Plant People, Little People (Devas and Fairies), Cloud People, Thunder-beings, Creature-beings, Stone People, Clan Chiefs (Air, Earth, Water, Fire), Earth Mother, Grandmother Moon, Grandfather Sun. Finally, I was familiar with the seasons and my moon cycles. I respected the rhythms of all beings, and as a result, I had a reciprocal relationship with my Planetary Family. I had experienced the interconnectedness of all things on the insight meditation cushion but for the first time, I was directly experiencing it with Mother Earth. This was a catalyst: SELF is everything.

Everywhere I looked, I saw nature's perfection. I observed a leaf and saw the divinity in it? Its lines mirrored the meridians in the human body. I observed the tree's strong trunk and felt its textured bark; I heard stories singing through its leaves. I imagined its deep roots connecting with life-giving water and followed them as they turned into tiny tentacles capable of communicating with all the trees in the area. I sensed that trees are like humans; they share, laugh, cry, celebrate and commiserate. I witnessed the tree's energy; it was so playful that I giggled and danced again. My feet stomped into the sacred earth and sent dust into the air.

Large brown kite birds circled above my head. Their distinctive shrill reminded me of the Varanasi burning ghats and my death. I lay down on my back and felt Mother Earth's consciousness merge with mine. Then, my body seemed to spread like water and seeped deep into the ground.

I meditated, I drummed, I toned, I sang, I did more trance exercises, I gave myself Reiki, I did yoga, I practiced breathwork, I stared at the clouds again, I danced again. I tried to guess the time again.

By that afternoon, I was over it. My mood turned dark *This is a bloody waste of time. There are no visions. I have done everything right for two full days and nothing. They just tell you there's a vision to get your money. What's the point? I have tried everything. Should I give up or beg? I'm going to beg. Please, can I have a vision? Please, I'm begging.*

It felt ridiculous, but I was desperate.

Then I waited. But nothing happened *I knew it, bloody waste of time. There are no visions. I'm going to give up.*

That night I felt defeated. I discovered my sleep mask in a backpack pocket. I did not feel motivated to stay awake and drum with the group. I wanted to avoid everything by putting on my mask and sleeping (how symbolic).

When I woke and removed my mask, I was horrified to see the sun high in the sky. I sat bolt upright, and I gasped *Oh, shit, I've slept in; it must be 11:00! Today is my last day, and I have wasted half of it.* Fear's venom pulsed through my blood. I believed I was in trouble because I had lost valuable time. I had cheated and failed, and now guilt coursed through my veins. Disappointment surged, and criticism followed.

I noticed that Maralyn had packed up and returned to the ceremonial fire. I could hear her loud, cackling laugh. I used to love that laugh but not now. Now it activated FOMO (fear of missing out). I stood up quickly and felt sick to my core. I sat back down, buckled over with pain *I think I've twisted my bowel*. My heart raced with *what ifs*. Fear tightened its hold, but now FOMO turned to FODA (fear of dying alone). *What was I thinking, attempting to not eat for three days? I have an auto-immune disease. People with Hashimoto's have to eat. I might die up here, and it will be my fault.* I tried to stretch but sitting upright sent daggers through my stomach; the pain was excruciating; I felt paralyzed. *This is really serious now; I have done something terrible; it's definitely a twisted bowel.*

Then it hit me *What are you going to do, Kitty? Are you honestly going to crawl back to the fire limping in agony and crying out, "Help, I need an ambulance?" No! That is not an option. Snap out of it* (I slapped my cheek hard). *This gut pain is not real; it is the same fear that came up during your third birth. You did not come here to be crippled in pain. You are where you need to be. Pull yourself together. Stand up, pick up your drum and tell Maralyn how happy you are for her.*

Wincing, I picked up my drum and stood up. I wanted to look toward the ceremonial fire without a tree blocking my view so I staggered (buckled over) to the side of my meditation circle and stepped out (one foot in and one foot out). I took deep breaths and started to drum. I called out, "Way to go, Maralyn, way to go!" Surprisingly this was enough to straighten me up. I felt a life force enter my body and was drawn to repeat those words, "Way to go, Maralyn, way to go!" This line took me back to the final scene in the 1982 movie *An Officer and a Gentleman*. My all-time favorite scene as a teenager. Paula (Debra Winger) is swept off her feet by the handsome officer Zack Mayo (Richard Gere) and carried out of the factory to live happily ever after. Her best friend, Lynette, is jealous at first but quickly moves into happiness, clapping and yelling, "Way to go, Paula, way to go!" I was happy for Maralyn like Lynette was happy for Paula. Growing up, Alex, her sister Lucy and I cried, hugged, and cheered watching this scene. So I channeled the exhilaration of that treasured childhood memory and called out again, but this time with an exaggerated American accent, "Way to go, Maralyn, way to go!" The feeling of ecstasy I elicited by tapping into this recollection made me rush with euphoria.

At that point, everyone at the fire (all questers except me) started drumming to let me know they were still there. I began to thank the people in my life who had made the Vision Quest possible. Two Crows, Medicine Crow, the 13 Clan Mothers, my meditation sisters, Stitty, my girls, my siblings, my old friends, Melissa, Mum and Dad. I was alternating between crying and laughing hysterically.

Being out of my meditation circle allowed me to see a rock formation that had previously been out of view. Between the two rocks was a large crack in the shape of a vagina (or an upright eye). The sun was shining through it at that exact moment, causing a shimmering golden mirage that looked like water. *Am I hallucinating?* I squinted my eyes. *Is this the Golden Door of Illumination rising from the Crack in the Universe as prophesied?*

I was witnessing a portal to other dimensions of awareness. It was sparkling so magnificently that I knew in an instant *This is my vision!*

At that moment, the perceived water in the portal dried up to reveal a gaping cavernous hole. I sensed Looks Far Woman standing next to the door, and I called out to her, "Looks Far Woman, what do you look like?"

She held up two infinity mirrors, one going backward with mothers, aunties, and grandmothers and one going forwards with sisters, daughters, and granddaughters.

I inquired, "Can all humans travel through the Golden Door of

Illumination to retrieve pieces of their wounded self to become whole again?'

Yes, Kitty, I wait here to guide Two-leggeds into and out of other realms to explore consciousness safely. You are here, Kitty, because you have the ears to hear, the eyes to see, and the heart to understand.

I felt like I was standing at the entrance to the place I slipped into 15 years earlier, on the insight meditation cushion. I had simply arrived there that time, but now I witnessed a new perspective. What if there is a door: we experience the created on this side and the uncreated on the other side? Or the parts on this side, and the whole on the other side. In this analogy, when we are at the door, we are SELF where nothing has happened yet - no choice has been made. We are poised in a void of limitless possibilities. We can act or not act and feel comfortable either way.

If I exist, moment-to-moment, at this metaphorical door, then as SELF I always have a choice. Do I choose the 3-D world's duality, or do I choose non-duality? Do I choose society's drama, or do I choose peace? Do I identify with a false self or SELF (our true essence)? I imagined myself standing at the Crack in the Universe with one foot in the seen world and one foot in the unseen world, ready to guide fellow humans to their potential. Jamie Sams wrote a road map for me to find Looks Far Woman. Then Looks Far Woman showed me the Crack in the Universe. It is my turn to explicitly teach others how to journey to the worlds within us. I vowed at that moment to write my book for anyone interested in exploring consciousness.

I closed my eyes and allowed myself to go through the Golden Door of Illumination and into the Crack in the Universe. As I passed through the light, I entered the creation void described in Looks Far Woman's chapter. The drumming became muted as the vision's impact rippled through all timelines. I remembered the story of Star Fire. I felt The Eternal Flame of Love blazing in my heart to signal I had forgiven those who had wounded me. I took a big expansive breath in and felt thousands of shards returning to me. Once the fragments returned, I felt whole again, knowing I was a healed healer.

This place feels like heaven. Stop Kitty! I wanted to compare, label, and commentate. *Who are you talking to anyway? There is no one else here. On this side of the door, we are one consciousness. Just be, just be SELF. Remember the ending of 'The 13 Original Clan Mothers', You are - the moment you decide to Be.*

I took my attention back to my breath and returned to the blissful place I went during my Kalgoorlie rebirth when my body dissolved into pure light. Everything fell away as a tear ran from my eye. I longed for everyone to experience this level of peace and joy.

I stepped back into my meditation circle and sat down to journal my experience. An orange and black butterfly landed on my notebook to celebrate my transformation. As I turned the pages, I was astounded to see a sketch I made during the free-drawing activity. It was precisely the same shape (vagina or upright eye) and had 22 hearts exploding out of it. Around it was a fire (Eternal Flame of Love). I was speechless and sat there stunned.

A few minutes later, I felt drawn to write a song. So I allowed the lyrics to be written through me. I should add here that this was very uncharacteristic; I have never written a song before or since that day.

THE SOURCE

Take me to the Crack in the Universe.
Take me so I'll never look back.
I know now I'm going home.
Home to my ancient heart.
I choose love. I choose love.
Met there by Looks Far Woman.
Met there by all my mothers.
I'll go through for daughters
and for future sisters.

Follow me. Follow me.
I went to worlds within worlds
Through a shining golden door.
Now the sights etched in my brain.
Oh, I will fear no more.
Changed forever. Changed forever.
Thank you for my sacred vision.
Thank you for this special day.
Thank you to my soul family.
Who helped me all the way.
I love you. I love you.
Let me stay inside that door
Each and every day and night.
Powerful in every way.
Let my light shine big and bright.
Choose to stay. Choose to stay.
Now my eyes are open.
Like my open heart.
I see my higher self.
Now we're not apart.
We are one. We are one.
I can co-create now.
I can co-create.
I will write my story
full of love not hate.
This is my song. This is my song.
The closer I go to the source
The more love I attract.
The closer I go to the source
The more love I attract.
This is truth. This is truth.

. . .

I FINISHED the last line of my song, put down my pen, and heard a faint rattle sound coming up the hill. It was my sis' Two Crows, "Time to come off now, Sista."

I slipped my prayer tie necklace over my head, packed up my things, and made my way down as the sun was setting in the west. I felt different, lighter in my body *I feared this rite of passage so much, but I did it! I can't believe it! I did it!*

I imagined myself jumping up and tapping my heels together in the air.

When I reached the ceremonial fire, Medicine Crow closed the Vision Quest with a Fire Drum Journey. Afterward, he invited us to throw our prayer ties into the fire. He explained that the nicotine would emit smoke making our prayers visible to *Ku*. We watched our prayers traveling in the wind. Two Crows then performed a water blessing ceremony taught to her by a local Indigenous elder.

By the time we ate the ceremonial cake, I had been fasting (water only) for 72 hours. Afterward, we shared our experiences. I explained, "Maralyn moving her circle seemed negative but ended up being positive. I had unknowingly relied on Marylyn for security and comfort, so when she left, an old abandonment narrative kicked in that triggered a painful physical reaction. I created it so I was the only one who could shift my focus to alleviate my pain. I chose to drum for Marylyn which moved me into a state of gratitude, which I guess brings on visions." I told the questers about the vagina-shaped Crack in the Universe and the Golden Door of Illumination. Then I sang my song as I drummed.

Afterward, the three women who had stayed on after the Full Moon Clan Mothers circle came to me with wide, blown-away eyes. They reminded me that the shape of Crack in the Universe in my vision was the same as the Aboriginal sacred site on the property where we stood. Two Crows had discovered it just after our one-day vigil 17 months earlier. It was a vagina or upright eye-shaped hole that First Australians dug out over thousands of years. Originally it would have been where the fire was, and it got deeper and deeper the more it was scooped out. Now it was mid-thigh deep. When Two Crows took a local Elder up there to see it, it was full of water. He recommended she clean it out once the water dried up. Two Crows took Melissa and me there six months prior (after Kellen transitioned). I sat beside the vagina-shaped hole (still full of water) and wrote down my dream to leave my job and write my book.

While I was on Vision Quest, Two Crows and the three women had left Crow at the fire, driven to the sacred site, and found the hole empty. So they scooped out the dirt, as instructed by the Elder. They cleaned the vagina-shaped hole and covered their bodies in the mud. They agreed it felt like they were digging to the Crack in the Universe after welcoming in Looks Far Woman the night before. They began to feel their past vagina and womb trauma surfacing. Some cried, some danced, and some meditated. They mourned the babies they had lost, the babies their relatives lost, the Stolen Generation, their suppressed feminine power, their silenced voices, and centuries of persecution. Then, one by one, they stood in the hole, took cleansing breaths, and allowed the sacred rock to heal and purify their wounded womb. Two Crows said she could not believe how cleansed her vagina, cervix and womb felt afterward.

I was astonished to hear that my meditation sisters had transmuted personal and collective trauma at the sacred site; perhaps at the same time, I entered an altered state and drew the vagina shape or upright eye, with 22 love hearts and fire coming out of it. Maybe the hearts symbolized timelines of women gaining their sovereignty and taking back their rightful place in society. Then the Crack in the Universe and the Golden Door of Illumination appeared in the same vagina-shape. It could have been any shape, but it was the shape of the portal my sisters had opened up. During my vision, I saw the deep cavernous hole they had lovingly dug. I witnessed something my 3-D physical body had not seen; therefore, I accessed the vision via another dimension or parallel timeline.

On Monday, when everyone left, Two Crows and I drove to the sacred site. I stood inside the vagina-shaped hole created by millions of hand strokes and sang my song, with tears running down my face.

I had intended to go to the Crack in the Universe and through the Golden Door of Illumination during my Vision Quest, and that is what I did. All I had to do was find the key. When I identified with my pain false self, I dwelled in a lower state of consciousness with a fear frequency. When I identified with my joy self, I moved to a higher state of consciousness with an enlightenment frequency. Gratitude unlocked my 'Looks Far Woman vision'. As Jamie Sams wrote *The vision that every human encounters on the other side of the Golden Door, through the Crack in the Universe, are the reflections of joy that exist beyond the illusions of physical sorrows. In that other world, we are shown how to use the energy that we once used to heal ourselves, to experience the joy of human life. The worlds within worlds are opened to every Two-legged who chooses to travel beyond the pain that limits our ability to see truth.*

Medicine Crow taught me that *Ku* delivers dreams to people who give back, and who support future generations, species, and the planet. As soon as I moved my focus from my pain to Maralyn's success, my dream manifested instantly. *Wanishi Ku!*

AFTER THE VISION QUEST, I felt drawn to read through Jamie Sams's *Dancing The Dream*, the book my soul sister Nikki gave me in Kalgoorlie, WA. Eighteen years and countless SELF-realization catalysts later, I understood, for the first time, the final three rites of passage (initiations five, six, and seven, I call these densities 5-D, 6-D, 7-D), which are the journeys into the Above, Below and Within/Now Directions of the Medicine Wheel. These teachings were not relevant to me previously because, until now, I had no personal experience with them. After personally going through the initiations,

I finally understood Jamie Sams's teachings. How? Teachers, in form and spirit, guided me to the Above Direction: I explored the galaxies, stars, the intangible, formless, and spiritual. Next, they showed me the Below Direction: I established a relationship with the Earth Mother by honoring natural law. Here, I learned to integrate the Above expanded consciousness teachings while remaining grounded. Finally, they led me into the Within/Now Direction: I directly experienced infinity in the present moment, and the void. I learned how to bring all the directions of the Medicine Wheel into my physical body to live in the now.

So much of what Jamie Sams wrote made sense to me like never before ...*when we connect to the universe as it exists within us. We are training for the ever unfolding adventure of BEING, which evolves beyond matter and time, beyond duality, and into absolute oneness...On the final lessons of the seventh path we see the infinite state of BEING, and we know that the journey is never over. We learn that we are being exactly what we are being at any given moment, and that we are all reflections of the constantly evolving universe, divine expressions of the Great Mystery's love. The physical realms are equal to the nonphysical realms, and each person's path is one part of divine expression that is no greater or lesser than any other...The completion of the seventh path simply means that we are awake to the unlimited possibilities that we can choose to embrace within our universe and in other universes of sound, light, movement and content. We have gone full circle and arrived within, and we choose to walk the wisdom that we have encountered, using a physical body, dancing the dream of infinite oneness in the here and NOW.*

Hallelujah!

22

EMBRACING DISCOMFORT SELF

46 years old

I TORE *myself away from the safe comfort of certainties through my love for truth—and truth rewarded me.*
   Simone de Beauvoir

THE FIRST TIME Melissa visited me after Kellen transitioned I took her on retreat with Two Crows to the Aboriginal sacred rock. The second time Melissa visited (October two years later) I took her on a retreat with Karen to the South Coast. Karen agreed to consolidate her five-day *Soul Immersion Program* into three days and facilitate us together instead of the usual one-on-one format.
   In the lead-up to the retreat everything seemed to go wrong. Mum was on holidays overseas when she got sick with pneumonia, Cirrhosis of the liver, and a pulmonary embolism which forced her into a Hong Kong hospital; my third daughter broke her arm at her eighth birthday party; I splashed boiling water on my second daugh-

ter's hand while helping her strain pasta; I cut my friend's son's arm on a piece of wire as I passed him the mini-tramp; there was yelling, and fear everywhere. I felt out of control. Even though Melissa was booked to come I wanted to cancel her to deal with the drama. I could have seen these events as signs telling me not to go to Karen's retreat. But something deep inside me knew I absolutely had to attend. It was as if my future self whispered, "The ego is putting up smoke and mirrors to stop you evolving. Don't listen to it. These signs are not signs you shouldn't go on retreat, they are the opposite. They are cries for help. You are out of alignment and need to pay attention. Your outer world is showing you the state of your inner world. It's chaos in all its forms. Your true SELF is pleading for you to stop and heal. It's begging you to leave your comfort zone and go on this retreat." So, despite all odds, I took a risk, organized the family, picked Melissa up from the Sydney airport and made the trip to the South Coast.

Karen taught us that our only job in life is to remain as our true essence. She said, "Cut your head off Kitty and drop into your heart space." This reminded me of Medicine Crow who always laughed, "You're *Mental as Anything* (Aussie band name) Kitty!" Karen's sessions highlighted that the blissful, expansive place I go to when I meditate is my true essence. She called that place *source*. She used her hand (hanging down) as a metaphor for SELF-realization. Above the wrist is the uncreated (where I went on the insight meditation cushion—I call this SELF), the wrist is the first expression which is awareness, knowledge, data, information, and the big knuckles are individuals' higher selves (who always have our back). These higher selves conspire with other higher selves (other knuckles) to help the fingers (individuations) to do what they came to do (like the time Kerri and Sadhana's higher selves conspired with my higher self to lead me to Karen).

Karen said the more I practice connecting with my higher self the more I notice signs pointing me in the right direction. Karen also used the analogy that my higher self is the director and I am the actor in the play called *life*. If I do not like the role I am playing then it is up to me to zoom out, change my perspective and operate instead from the purity of source (which I call SELF).

We can take care of our inner state of being by listening and responding to our internal guidance system. Karen was a living example of this. You could see her pausing to drop into her heart space, be discerning, and choose her words wisely. She told us the conditioned mind will always go into old stories, but we can turn our attention back to source by being aware, mindful, and focused. This choice is worth repeatedly making until it is no longer a choice but our natural state of being. She assured me that eventually, I will be living my truth, and the world I create will reflect my inner peace.

During the Soul Immersion, Karen introduced us to Bentinho Massaro, who's retreat she had recently attended in Sedona, Arizona, USA. Bentinho is a young, dynamic teacher with a vision for an enlightened world. Despite his young age, he had studied worldwide both ancient and modern non-duality work that suggests the existence of one consciousness. His teachings resonated with me because he was direct, eloquent, and passionate. I loved how he spoke of enlightenment as being up for grabs right now, meaning there was no need to spend decades on the spiritual path. We can realize the truth of SELF immediately. From the moment Karen showed us his videos, Bentinho inspired me. His incredible intellect appealed to my *Mental as Anything* mind. Bentinho described the place I went to on the insight meditation cushion in India as the *Absolute* because it contains absolutely everything. He was the first person to put words to what I witnessed. He described the first manifestation from the Absolute as *pure isness* (formless awareness) and he called living aligned to this *isness, Being Love-isness*. He called source the *One Infinite Creator*, and I called it SELF. Bentinho said we are the awareness that everything appears to.

In divine timing, I directly experienced source/SELF while eye-gazing with Karen. We held each other's gaze until we were both laughing hysterically. It was surreal; the more I stared, the more we merged. The more we merged, the more time collapsed, allowing me to experience infinity directly. After a long time, it felt like we were the only ones in the universe. We had coalesced into one consciousness, into a state of interconnectedness. Why was this so funny? It is hard to explain. When reality as I knew it collided with true reality, the two appeared diametrically opposed. The contrast was so confronting that all I could do was laugh. I sensed I had activated an innate knowing, but this just made it even funnier. It was so obvious that I had spent my life viewing the world entirely wrongly. This was a collective misinterpretation, so the joke was on humanity. I felt like I woke up from a dream, the dream being life as I had known it for the last 46 years. When we stopped laughing, I was still in a state of awe. Karen offered a perfectly timed teaching.

She said, "It's the ultimate cosmic joke, each of us exists right now before creation, we exist before God, God appears inside each person's awareness because we are one consciousness expressing itself in infinite ways. This means, Kitty, that you are the creator; we all are. You are the creator of your reality"

This was a new concept to me because the Buddha did not put it that way. This was a SELF-realization catalyst—at any moment I can choose to embody my creator self and access my highest timeline. This massive epiphany freed me, life was not happening to me, I was the creator creating it.

If I am pure existence, then it does not matter what happens to Kitty, the character in the play called life, because it can not affect SELF. Therefore, SELF is indestructible.

———

AFTER THE SOUL IMMERSION RETREAT, I had scheduled a knee operation. I stayed with Mum in Sydney for three weeks to recover together, with the help of aunties, friends, and neighbors. I treated this as a continuation of Karen's *Soul Immersion Retreat* by studying and practicing Bentinho's SELF-realization teachings all day, every day. I watched the recordings from his recent Amsterdam retreat, as well as his Trinity Academy videos. His explanations felt highly relevant. He taught me that each human is an individuated consciousness coming from unity consciousness (which Karen had touched on with her hand analogy). He explained that the only way the One Infinite Creator can know itself is to individuate into infinite expressions of itself, thus creating contrast, duality, light, and dark. He explained the Absolute as coming before we individuate into humans with a blueprint to know ourselves as the One Infinite Creator. Bentinho's descriptions continued to confirm my direct experience in India.

During my three-week online retreat with Bentinho, I was a diligent student and methodically practiced his meditation pointers to access SELF and true reality. Bentinho taught me to say to myself at the beginning of my meditations *I don't want anything from anything*. These words evoked neutrality, acceptance, and surrender. The *neti-neti* meditation technique also helped me remember my true essence by negating over and over what I was not to reveal what I am. *Neti-neti* is a Vedic method found in the oldest Indian text, the *Vedas*. Truth seekers selected this method as a tool to inquire into their sense of self. To practice this style I would repeat internally *I am not this, I am not that*. For example, if I had an itch, *I am not this*. If I heard a sound, *I am not that*. If I thought of myself as a mother, *I am not this*. If I worried, *I am not that*. If I thought of a story, *I am not this*. If I tried to make a plan, *I am not that*. After a while, I arrived at what *I am*.

Another powerful method Bentinho taught me was to shatter all containers during meditations. This destroyed my mind's habit of identifying with mental container after mental container (limiting beliefs).

To do this, I would repeat internally *I am before this*. For example, if I identified with my thoughts, *I am before the thought container*. If I identified with my body, *I am before the body container*. If I identified with my mind, *I am before the mind container*. If I identified with my breath, *I am before the breath container*. If I identified with my humanness, *I am before the human container*. If I identified with space and time, *I am before the space and time container*. Finally, if I identified with anything, *I am before all containers, I simply exist*.

ONE DAY during one of Bentinho's guided meditations, I combined the three pointers above. I wanted nothing, I practiced the *neti-neti* technique, and I shattered all perceived containers. I zoomed further and further back until I was left with no choice but to experience myself as my true essence.

After three-and-a-half weeks of SELF-realization boot camp, my commitment and devotion to Karen and Bentinho's teachings paid off. I left Sydney with a highly sophisticated metaphysical, non-dual view of consciousness. Therefore, I could begin to accurately discern what was real and what was unreal.

23

SEEING THE WORLD IS WHAT I THINK IT IS SELF

48 years old

Sunday, January 26th

AUSTRALIA DAY AT DAWN.

My Forbes meditation sisters and I drummed in a local park. We had chosen to drum despite the stir in the media and the protests against the country's decision to celebrate Australia Day on the day Captain Cook took over this land in the late 18th century. From this time, white men locked up, maimed, raped, degraded, killed, and alienated First Australians from their culture and traditional lands.

We chose to drum to acknowledge the present moment.

We drummed with the throbbing pulse of the Wiradjuri land; the rhythm of the tides; the hammering of waves; the patter of animals' feet; the flapping of birds' wings; the melodic slither of the Rainbow Creation Serpent; the orbiting moons; the heartbeats of the ancestors and the Elders; the twinkling of stars in distant constellations; the blinking of humanities lashes; the lapping of rivers; the disco dance of wind; the sparking of fire; the delicate vibration of the deep, dark ocean and the tapping of the Palm Cockatoo. I felt our innate oneness. I imagined Australia as an evolved nation of humankind living in their hearts, embodying love. This vision merged with the songlines on the land where I drummed.

Afterward, we threw white flowers off the bridge. I imagined a new world *Thank you for a unified planet where opportunities for First Nation Peoples to thrive are embedded in everyone's thoughts, words, actions, workplaces, communities, and homes.* Then I celebrated this vision as if it had already happened.

We could see the town's official Australia Day celebrations from the bridge. Two Crows said, "Hey, let's go down there and get a coffee."

I can't go over there in my hippie India pants; people will judge me. "No thanks," I replied.

A stern voice came to me, loud and clear *Kitty, living in the now is all about being authentic and turning up your light. Hiding and playing small is not an option anymore. Stop caring what people think!*

"Sure, I'll come; why not? I tried to contradict my original fear of being judged. But it was too late; my fear was already energetically out there.

On the way to the counter, we walked past a group of women in their 70s. I recognized two of them. One of them said, "I saw you drumming, or whatever it was you were doing over there."

"Yes, it was relaxing." I smiled. *I hope it ends there.* But, unfortunately, it did not.

"And in front of everyone." *Was she hissing at me, scolding me with her raised eyebrow, and shaming me with the tilt of her head?* Unspoken words tumbled from her mind to mine. *We disapprove. We've been talking about you. Fancy doing that in public!*

My whole body ached. I felt like a schoolgirl in trouble. We turned and continued to the counter. I stared, in shock, at my beautiful friend Roey. "What a bitch," I exclaimed. Immediately, I knew I had reacted habitually; I could feel it in my body. The word *bitch* set my internal guidance system spinning, telling me something I was saying was out of alignment with SELF. The word 'bitch' caused my life force to weaken, my heart to shrink, and my face to contort. I put my hand on my chest and shared, "Roey, my pain-body is suffering. I feel heavy, but I can't let her bitter words dim my light." I was at a choice point; I had instantly caught my thought, which changed me from an unconscious victim to an empowered observer. So now, I needed to zoom out and gain a broader perspective. I remembered the *Ho'Oponopono* prayer and said to Roey, "I'm sorry, please forgive me, I love you, thank you."

Roey was also at a choice point. She could collude with my original limited viewpoint, feed my ego, and add to the negativity by continuing to condemn this woman. But instead, she skillfully reframed things to contribute to my expansion instead of my contraction. "She is a master teacher. Give thanks to her. She is a miracle," Roey assured me. Those words were music to my ears. I felt my heart enlarge, my shoulders relax, and my belly unknot. I sighed *I'm back, feeling good again.* I gave thanks for having like-minded friends and the opportunity to feel how my body feels when triggered. The contrast showed me how feeling judged presents in the body and gave me empathy for others feeling judged. Years ago, I would have remained in my emotional pain-body for hours before arriving at the positive. But today, I managed to lift my vibrational state amidst her harsh words.

A few minutes later, the frequency of my new thoughts attracted a chance encounter with an inspirational man with an exposed metal prosthetic leg. He said to me excitedly, "I lost my leg in a motorbike accident and broke my neck too. So I just live every day being positive about my leg. I could be a paraplegic, but instead, I can do anything!" He was grateful for his artificial leg because he knew it could have been much worse. So instead of *please pity poor me,* he chose a positive state of mind and said, "I can do anything!"

This man was also a master teacher—two master teachers in one day. One master showed me how I wanted to be, and the other master showed me how I did not want to be—one the antidote to the other.

———

WHEN I REFLECTED on the day, I wondered if I got the whole thing wrong. Perhaps I created the scenario based on Dr. Serge Kahili King's principle number one *Ike*: The world is what you think it is (be aware). I thought I was going to be judged, so I was judged. I had judged myself (and my pants) first; what followed reflected the depth of my self-judgment. How I responded depended on what I was thinking. Maybe the woman did not judge me. Perhaps she was connecting and unsure what to call the drumming. Maybe I was searching for things in my environment to confirm my lack belief, or I misinterpreted the woman's intentions because I had a preconceived idea of her? I would like to apologize to that woman. She never had a chance. I viewed her through my distorted lens. I needed to be judged, and I expected her to judge me, so to get my needs met, I interpreted what she said in a way that confirmed my expectations. In psychology, this is called confirmation bias. It did not matter what words she used or how she delivered them; my perception of them made the difference. I would choose to be judged no matter what came out of her mouth.

My reaction to her illustrates negativity bias. I could have ignored what I perceived as negative, but I gave in to my brain's tendency to pay more attention to negative experiences/things/words/events than positive ones. Negative bias is an evolutionary response that kept us safe because we needed to be psychologically impacted by adverse circumstances to ensure survival. However, our evolved brain can override this program.

Suppose I could rewrite the story with a different ending. I would hear the woman say, "I saw you drumming, or whatever it was you were doing over there."

But this time, I would have no thought of being judged. Instead, I would reply, "Thank you. It was our way of celebrating Australia Day."

I would hear her say, "And in front of everyone."

But this time, I would have no thought of being hissed at or chastised. Instead, I would reply, "Yes, the park is a beautiful place to drum; you are welcome to join us next time." I would smile into her eyes, and she would smile back.

In hindsight, I know SELF orchestrated the situation for SELF to go deeper into SELF. The experience showed me my tendency to judge others because I judge myself. It was a SELF-realization catalyst showing how our thoughts create our reality through the law of attraction.

The frequency of every thought creates the frequency of the now. How could it be any different? So the world is what you think it is!

24

CALMING THE COVID-19 CHAOS SELF

48 years old

WHEN THE OLD FEELS BROKEN, we have a choice, we can fix the old or create the new. What should we do? Create the new, of course!

For me, the coronavirus pandemic started in fear, the same way it did for millions of people.

Thursday, March 18th

FORBES, a school day.

I spent the day being hyper vigilant, following department procedures and protocols (social distancing, hand sanitizing, washing sports equipment). In a constant state of flight or fight, I said to a colleague, "I feel like we are living in a war zone." My 3-D emotional pain-body went into survival mode so my internal guidance system was going off *what if, what if, what if*. I was so far removed from SELF that it is painful to recount.

The next day was Friday, my day off.

I read my friend's raw COVID-19 stories on our WhatsApp group (catering companies disabled, financial stresses and home schooling to stop the spread). I wept. Just eleven days earlier, we were together on a girls' weekend feeling expansive, connected and grounded. Now the contrast felt immense. We felt constricted, isolated and like a rug had been pulled from under our feet. I felt profound grief for these sisters I had loved for 25 years.

I needed insight into how to navigate these unprecedented times. I felt like a floundering fish out of water, struggling to breathe and unable to make sense of my new surroundings.

I lay on my bed and contemplated *What's happening?*

I did my favorite meditation to expand my consciousness. Suzanne Gieseman's *Radiant Heart* on YouTube. Suzanne says, "I am far more than the physical body. I am without form, without limit, beyond space, beyond time. I am in everything, and everything is in me. I am the light, I am the light, I am the light. This is alignment. The state of being in the heart. No longer prisoner to the head but in a state of awareness of your true being. A unified whole comprised of the Earth energies and the spirit energies." This beautiful meditation blew my mind into uncreated nothingness powered by gratitude.

I walked down to the *Galari* (Lachlan River) running through our farm to swim and play music.

Cool breezes on bare, wet skin; silky mud oozing between toes; Eucalyptus scents signaling the Aussie bush; the sting of cold water; the silence beneath; watching water striders gliding; falling gum leaves spinning like propellers; a laughing kookaburra; a melodic Magpie; a clicking Willy Wagtail; screeching Galahs, cawing Crows and squawking Cockatoos. Pummeled stones massaged my back as I lay splayed open on the sandbank in the middle of the river soaking up the sun. When I sat up, I was startled by a black-shouldered kite perched on a low branch. The bird's black shoulders sat like a majestic queen's cape over pristine fluffy snow-white feathers. She could turn her rapture head almost right around to show off an aristocratically-hooked, black beak profile. Her talons were enormous and golden yoke yellow. Her face was sharp, neat, regal. Her red, deep-set, piercing eyes penetrated me when our eyes met. Her gaze was intimidating, leaving me breathless—frozen in awe. Her size was impressive. The exalted kite opened her striking wide-spanned wings like oriental fans, revealing contrasting colored tips. She graciously glided to a fallen tree in the river, beckoning me to follow.

I stepped back into the water, looked down, and gasped. My foot was beside a spiraled venomous brown snake. It took me a moment to realize it was dead and perfectly preserved in the shape of the Fibonacci Spiral. I picked up the stiff snake in disbelief. Held it in front of my face and traced the coil with my eyes. As I peered through its activating pattern, sunbeams danced on my cornea, making me dizzy. *Am I falling down the rabbit hole?*

Time stood still. I entered what felt like another dimension. *I've been welcomed into the animal kingdom.* I delicately placed one foot in front of the other in slow motion, trusting I would know when I was close enough to the splendid bird. I felt humbled but at the same time worthy of being privy to this imperceptible world. Its magnificence reflected my true essence in all its magnitude. I stopped, quietly returned the stiff snake to the water, and stood in Tadasana, mountain pose. I felt my feet extend like roots under the silt. My outstretched palms tingled in the sun's nourishing rays. I closed my eyes and patiently waited.

The bird began telepathically speaking to me *Sunshine Kitty Hawk you have been preparing for this time your whole life. The Coronavirus came from the East because its message for humanity is one of illumination. You, my Gemini Two-legged, are a master communicator. We animals will illuminate your path if you choose to listen to us.*

Rest in the present moment where the animals, stone people, Mother Earth, Father Sky, Grandfather Sun, Grandmother Moon, and the Wind, Water, Air, and Fire Spirits can guide you. Your awareness is heightened, intuition sharpened, connection to spirit amplified, perceptions crystallized, synchronicities intensified, and integrity clarified. Feel these messages in your heart as you will never feel them with your head.

Your spirit name is Sunshine Kitty Hawk which represents a messenger in the Native American culture. I warn you not to let your over-analytical Virgo-rising mind run rampant as this blocks clear-sightedness. You have the psychic ability and vision needed at this time to observe the subtle messages around you to discern the truth. You hold the key to higher levels of consciousness, and with this comes the responsibility to share your knowledge. So, practice what you preach, be calm in turmoil, choose love when faced with fear, harvest compassion, and loving-kindness, and trust your instincts. You are a link between the seen and the unseen worlds. We hawks are birds of the heavens capable of stirring humanity from its spiritual amnesia. You have what it takes to lead. You have the courage to apply your wisdom at this time. Humans need to wake up. They need to remember who they are. This is an exciting time in human history. Kitty, for a decade, you have dreamed of the evolution of human consciousness, and now it's happening. If the human collective completely owns their COVID-19 creation they can evolve as a species. If humans across the globe examine themselves and realize their modern lives are destroying Mother Earth they will take responsibility for their thoughts, words, and actions and create harmony.

We advise you to bunker down and write your book, which focuses on manifesting love. Avoid the staffroom stories, news, and mainstream social media which fuel your body's fear response. Hold space for others who are responding the best way they can. Spend time in nature every day. Drum, meditate, and swim. Trust your knowing. Be the Light.

As I listened to the black-shouldered kite's message I thought *There it is again, 'be the light' like in the meditation this morning and in the Happiness card Melissa and I pulled on Kellen's transition day. I think 'be the light' is my mantra.*

When I opened my eyes, I smiled. The bird stared at me for a few more seconds before taking hawk-like flight. I watched her disappear around the bend with my hands crossed over my heart. I noticed each white wing contained a black patch that felt symbolic. Her body personified our potential. White and black, light and dark, yin and yang, and love and fear exist side by side, and it is up to us where we place our attention. Now more than ever.

I climbed back up the riverbank and picked up my Native American reed flute (C key). I gently blew my dreams for humanity into the smooth wood carved by Six Bears. The notes carried my intentions into the gentle wind, releasing my prayers to *Ku*—encouraged by the birds—moved by infinite intelligence. Set in motion by my ancestors and championed by Mother Earth. Understood by all sentient beings and prophesied for eons. Afterward, I stood up and drummed the ceremonial beat for over an hour. Then the intensity increased, sending my vision into the cosmos. Finally, with my ear close to the kangaroo's skin (I had birthed a new bigger drum the previous month), I changed my rhythm to a heartbeat and closed my eyes. Tap, tap. Tap, tap. Tap, tap. Tap, tap. Over and over again. Hypnotic. Everything ceased except the sensation of the drum beats vibrating through my body, sending ripples into the ether. I was poised, embryonic, and alone with the sound of knocking. I imagined it was humanity's potential knocking on Creation's womb.

The difference in my state of being now, compared to that morning, was immeasurable. I felt aligned with my purpose for being. The black-shouldered kite's urgent call to action took me from tunnel vision to visionary. From powerless victim to powerful creator.

Monday, March 22nd

AFTER THE WEEKEND I went back to school revitalized with a whole new COVID-19 outlook. At the emergency staff meeting that afternoon, my principal told me to work from home. And just like that, I manifested a lockdown retreat to go within and be the change I wanted to see in the world.

I realized that the COVID-19 crisis was a global wake-up call with a local solution—me. I thought *To create the new each of us needs to metamorphose into an evolved version of ourSELF, complete with a whole new perspective. If each of us does this in our portion of the planet, we create the global transformation we deeply desire, awakening our universal creative power.*

25

FEELING LOCKED AND LOADED SELF

48 years old

Tuesday, March 24th

TWO CROWS RAN a drum circle via Zoom every morning during my lockdown retreat, which allowed me to connect with like-minded people. We would drum, meditate and discuss what was happening on the Covid world stage. I was not engaging with mainstream news or social media, but I still picked up on what was going on globally. One morning I told Two Crows that I wanted to set up a meditation circle on my farm similar to the ones I made during the one-day vigil and Vision Quest. I wanted a space to do multidimensional healing work. Multidimensional work recognizes that the past, present, and future exist in the now, so energetic healing occurs on all levels, throughout all dimensions, timelines, and realms.

Thursday, April 2nd

I CHOSE my meditation circle spot by walking along the southwestern side of the bend in the river until I found a natural circle of trees that felt like a vortex of energy. I asked permission from the First People and ancestor spirits, plant consciousness, and animals to enter their space. I shared my intention to lovingly heal the trauma held in the land's songlines and indigenous Dreaming tracks. I collected large rocks to make a circle, and as I placed each one down, I noticed a lot of cow dung. As I raked, overwhelming waves of grief flowed through me. *You are full of shit. Look at your space; it is full of bullshit, literally.*

I had never experienced an epiphany that felt like pure disgust. I was howling because I repulsed myself. *I am a fake, a fraud, and a liar. I don't love myself. No one can believe anything I say. I am full of shit. I am revolting bullshit. I don't ever want to talk again. I want to take a vow of silence.* I was bawling profusely and raking while trying to work out how to support my children as a selective mute, especially my seventeen-year-old who was doing her high school finishing exams. Finally, I allowed myself to cry uncontrollably. I had not cried like this since I screamed out to the universe for a way to leave the city (11 years prior). Now I was screaming out for change; I was utterly over myself and everything about me. I was sick of making excuses for not being the best version of myself *I can't; I don't have time; I'm not worthy; being calm isn't physically possible with my genes; I'm scared; I lack motivation; I'm comfortable; I need to fit in; I'm not ready; I'm attached to drama, stress, and lack; renouncing those will be hard work; I don't know what I'll be without my limiting beliefs; I won't fit in; what will I talk about; I'll be boring; I'm happy enough.*

I was done with telling myself these lies, feeling out of alignment, and thinking, saying, and doing things that did not serve me. I was tired of running on the spiritual hamster wheel. I was as desperate for peace as I was for my next breath. It felt like a matter of urgency, like a life-or-death situation.

I felt vulnerable, humbled, and naked with a ferocious hunger for change. The feeling was so visceral that it provided the impetus that had been lacking for three decades. I vowed to use this powerful fire energy as fuel to change my life. I was finally ready to liberate myself. I had suffered long enough.

When I got home after building my meditation circle I called Two Crows and told her how I was feeling. She said, "Do you think maybe the trauma isn't yours? I reckon it's the land's trauma. During morning meditation I have been feeling the pain of our sisters who lost their babies to the stolen generation. I think you might be feeling that collective grief."

I did not know exactly what ignited my immense desire to change, but I finally wanted to evolve badly enough to actually do it. Incredibly (or in divine timing) I had a rare opportunity brought on by the Covid pandemic. Lockdown created the perfect retreat-like conditions. I needed to explore my inner world rather than being distracted by my outer world. I needed to remove myself from people and situations that would trigger me to think, speak and act unconsciously. So, I remained on my farm, and Stitty, who was also working from home, did all the town jobs like shopping and the post office. We have no neighbors so I could exercise without seeing anyone (our house is two kilometers, 1.2 miles, to the main road and back). I was able to get my work done and spend my spare time in meditation because my daughters were old enough and independent enough (17, 15, and 11 years of age) to homeschool themselves (schools had gone online). I had a two-week vacation period coming up which meant I could spend all day focusing on changing my thoughts. I had internet access so I could connect with others doing healing work. I had nature, animals, and the great Galari (Lachlan River) in my backyard. Often we camped out under the stars and cooked on the campfire.

I was in a constant state of gratitude for my lockdown conditions and full of compassion for those doing it tough due to loneliness, abusive partners, toxic relationships, or confined spaces. Knowing they were suffering compelled me to liberate myself to be in a position to lead them to enlightenment. I knew that I could not write the book being called forth by humanity for humanity without this initiation.

I was living in a global crisis so I had to practice selective attention or I would waste the energy I needed to shift my ingrained patterns of behavior. Therefore, I had to be acutely aware of what I was thinking, saying, and doing at all times. I had to be vigilant about who I was listening to, and what I was reading and watching. I needed to turn my back on negative fear-based stories and not invest time in the unraveling, tumultuous Covid chaos. Instead, I had to be in nature, eat clean food and meditate in the stillness.

I was locked and loaded on the precipice of transformation.

26

CLAIMING MY CREATOR SELF

48 years of age

TO TRANSFORM, *I would have to set aside everything I thought I knew to allow myself to receive all that I truly am.*

Tuesday, March 24th

ON DAY one of my lockdown retreat, Karen recorded this meditation during our regular weekly Zoom call (she had just returned from doing healing work in Malta), "As our fields merge, we become one unified field of pure divine essence, pure love, each adding the unique tone, flavor, codes, and gifts they hold. Everyone shares their piece of the puzzle so that all have all pieces. All pieces of the divine plan. All are whole and complete unto self, but each is drawn together with their unique piece of the puzzle for the new world. As we unify, all the pieces come together to create a key. We all have access to this key. And it opens a gateway for each of us. A gateway that is a portal to your future self who lives in the new Earth. You can access this whenever you are drawn to. If you are drawn to, you can go through that portal now, imagine the key opening the doorway, the portal, and there you are in your life in the new Earth after the transition, after everything has settled. You can feel into your new life. You may see, hear, and know, allow whatever comes to come. Take yourself into the energy of it and have fun exploring for a little while and now embodying the vision, the feeling, the knowing of that future timeline. Share that vision in our unified field and feel it expand and heighten the frequency of our unified field. Let this move into every cell of your being, breathe it into your body, and let it permeate every cell. Feel the cells in the body responding and the whole body feeling uplifted. Allow this to penetrate on all levels so that there is no separation between your future self in the new Earth and the physical self that seems to be existing in the old. Then anchor this deep into the heart of Mother Earth as she is shifting too. Knowing that we work in unison with her in perfect harmony. We are no longer anchored in the old Earth but in the new. Feel a deep knowing and a deep allowance that every single soul's choice and every single soul's experience was perfect as it brought the Earth to a still point so that it can shift into the new. Feel gratitude for the beauty of this creation, knowing that the souls that are leaving have already chosen this. Even though it may not appear this way to the 3-D world, our hearts know the truth. We hold great compassion for all who are still in the cycles of suffering. We know this suffering can not be a part of the new. It is of the old vibration and was perfect for all the experiences that it offered. We have all contributed to creating the new by remembering who we are and shining our lights brightly in the world. What a gift to be alive in a body at this moment to witness this incredible unfolding that we have created and continue to create by just being who we are and following the joy of our hearts.

Remember this feeling in the times of adjusting ahead and hold the feeling, the vibration of your future self, in a time when we are all settled. This will help you navigate through the times that appear bumpy or rocky. Your heart is your anchor and ballast; your knowledge of the divine perfection is your gift. We are the lighthouses that offer smooth sailing to those at sea with love and compassion for those who don't make it, knowing all is perfect in the divine plan. Feel our unified field with Mother Earth, holding each other, helping each other, and stabilizing each other. The stability, the stillness, and the excitement for the new world built from love. The new coming into being is what our hearts have yearned for. The time is now. Feel your heart rejoicing with all those beings around the world in form and not in form who have contributed—the universal celebration of the heart. Hold true to this field; hold steady in it. What the eyes see may be the opposite of what you know to be true; hold the vision until it appears. The embodiment of the new and the celebration activates, rejuvenates, and energizes the physical body's cells—it upgrades them to the new frequency. Allow the body to adjust as the old gives way to the new. By being in your heart, you are the calm in the storm, the peace in the chaos, the love in the field. We are all that. Stay in the feeling of all that you are. Take a few deep breaths and open your eyes when you are ready."

This meditation resonated with me so much that I did it every day of my lockdown retreat.

Sunday, April 5th, 12:45 pm

I joined a worldwide meditation to end Covid. I laid down on my beanbag and listened to Karen's recording. I connected to SELF. I had a beautiful vision of Earth from an expanded perspective; as I looked down at our planet, a deep desire to preserve the human species welled up inside me. I imagined humanity's susceptibility beneath that delicate atmosphere separating us from larger galaxies. I intuited that the planet might outlive our species, and I was compelled to do whatever I could to sustain human life on Earth. I saw portals of light shining out one by one, very quickly. As each lit up, I heard *Mother Nature, the Amazon, Uluru, Sedona, Machu Picchu, Lake Titicaca, Glastonbury, the Pyramids, the Ganga, and the Hanging Gardens of Babylon.* Then I witnessed other lights coming on— firstly, the millions doing the worldwide meditation, children, evolved humans, lightworkers, healers, spiritual beings, starseeds, yogis, way-showers, selfless humans of service to humanity, plants, and animals including the water animals which lit up the rivers and oceans and before I knew it the whole globe was completely illuminated. It was an incredible sight.

Tuesday, April 7th

Two days later during Karen's regular Tuesday night Zoom guided meditation, I returned to that glowing image of Earth. Then suddenly, I felt like I popped through some sort of rubbery film.

A hush fell over the expansive space. I became still and weightless, suspended in a weird void. Peace and tranquility filled my body. Linear time, material objects, and thoughts ceased.

Just like that, I returned to the place I witnessed on the insight meditation cushion 19 years earlier. I entered the uncreated, surreal, unknown, and unexplored. I felt an indescribable oneness, like everything was interconnected and poised in this weird space before anything was anything.

I could have stayed there with only the sound of my expanding and contracting lungs, but I wanted to come back to share my experience with my Tuesday night meditation Sisters.

I began with, "Karen, I just went to the Absolute again. I experienced ultimate SELF/true reality as I did years ago on the meditation cushion in India. I realized that everything ever created happened inside my/our awareness, and nothing exists outside this awareness."

After the meditation group zoom call I wrote this *We are all part of one consciousness which contradicts mainstream society's perception of reality. We are not separate consciousnesses when we return to our origin, to our innateness, to our oneness, to our beforeness. The duality I cling to like; male and female, light and dark, right and wrong, me and you, us and them, good and bad, this and that, happy and sad, now and then, were just illusions. These illusions makeup humanity's shared reality, whereas tonight I experienced a different reality. In that reality creation had not happened yet. If I can perceive creation, then I can not be creation; I must come before creation. This means I am the Creator—we all are. When we return to SELF, we are before everything, even before awareness. Therefore, all creation occurs inside SELF's awareness. When I first experienced this reality on the insight meditation cushion, I said I slipped in between Creation's breaths, but now that I know SELF is the Creator, I realize I haven't slipped in between Creation's breaths, I have slipped in between my breaths/SELF's breaths. This blows my mind. Perhaps*

- *SELF's in-breath is unity consciousness/unconditional love.*
- *The pause between breaths is being SELF in a void of SELF's infinite potential.*
- *Then SELF's out-breath is the infinite expressions of unity consciousness/infinite individuations/infinite aspects of SELF.*

USING THIS ANALOGY, *then, the moment of creation occurs right when I exhale–right when oneness bursts into infinite expressions of itSELF. This means, as SELF, I have access to all timelines (past, present, future) of all the individuations/aspects of SELF that have even been expressed because it is all happening in the now!*

It's time to claim my creator self. I create everything in my reality because I am the only one experiencing it. How I interpret everything I perceive dictates the life I have. My creator self can write my story's past, present, and future because present expressions, past expressions, and future expressions all exist in the now. I can live fully anchored in the present, accepting whatever arises as perfect expressions of mySELF. I am the way, and the truth, and the life. Maybe Jesus asked people to repeat "I am the way, and the truth, and the life: no one cometh unto the Father, but by me" about THEMSELVES. In other words, he wanted them to know they could access the way, the truth, and the life through themselves. But due to their limited perspective, dense body, and unevolved consciousness, they could not comprehend Jesus's words. They could not fathom that they were the creators of their reality, so they made God the creator of their reality. They chose to be dependent instead of empowered. Rather than being the creator and creating everything themselves, they looked outside themselves and made God the creator. Maybe Jesus was ahead of his time. Perhaps if he came today, human consciousness would be evolved enough to understand his message. When we embody SELF/unity consciousness, we spontaneously create the way God does. We have the same special abilities as Jesus; we just need to believe in ourselves. Like Jesus, our innate state of being is pure love. Through ourselves, we occupy the kingdom of heaven on Earth (Karen's book title).

Tonight as I witnessed infinity, the same question came to me

Could I live in my world as SELF? This prospect seemed beyond imagination because it is so different from daily life. However, I vowed to close the gap between my world and this world.

Wednesday, April 8th

The following day at 10:00 am I had my first of four one-on-one two-hour Zoom sessions with Karen. I had booked in to do her *Beings Of Magnitude (BOMs) Here To Change The World, Quantum Self-Realization Course* months earlier (way before COVID). The timing felt perfect. Five days earlier, my meltdown catapulted me into a state of mind ripe for transformation. In addition to this catalyst, Karen said experiencing my creator self the night before was divine timing.

I could not believe the perfection of it. I had realized (made real through direct knowing) that we are one consciousness on the eve of a four-week journey into my heart to reach my potential. What are the chances of gaining an evolved perspective at the exact time profound teachings turn up? This was a miracle. I had to claim it as such. I had manifested retreat-like conditions at home, and now I had an enlightened teacher available to enter it (via Zoom). Karen was willing to support me in making the transition from knowing to being. Karen could draw on personal experiences because she had made the transition herself. She would give me tools, pointers, and signposts to embody my truth.

Karen asked me to list which senses of self no longer served me.

I said, "I can think of the following false selves: habitual, triggered, judgemental, bullshitting, playing the role, trauma, enslaved, self-blame, blocked, lack, inauthentic, stressing, caring what people think, not wanting to get into trouble, perfect, and yelling. Just to name a few!"

"You have directly experienced your true self, moving the concept from a thought in your head to an experiential knowing in your heart. Now you know what you are, the invitation is there to operate in a way that is authentically you. As your creator self, you can create whatever you want to create at each moment." Karen continued, "Are you willing to give up your identification with those false selves?"

"Yes, I am desperate to," I replied.

"Kitty, there is no need to judge yourself because those selves served a purpose up until this point. You can see why you adopted those roles, but now you can see how limiting they are. Take perfectionism, for example; that false self will not be relevant once you no longer need validation for your self-worth. I had all that going on too, and it was exhausting. When I let go of that false image, the one that wants to be seen as having it all under control—I felt so relieved. It just took willingness and devotion to develop the muscle of focus until I became the focus."

Karen explained that she would lead me through a chakra clearing guided meditation. She acknowledged that although I had done this numerous times, doing it now from the creator's perspective would be different. Karen invited me to clear programs, patterns, beliefs, and blockages, starting from the base chakra. To do this, I was guided to flood each chakra with my pure loving light. This opened and transmuted every cell, gland, and organ allowing them to function at their optimal level. Clearing these felt effortless and instant because I had witnessed my perfection the night before. Plus I was working at a quantum level so the clearing occurred across all timelines and individuations/aspects of SELF. I visualized known and unknown personal and collective trauma falling away from each energy center, replaced by unconditional love. Next, I cleared my physical, emotional, and mental bodies and became my infinite body which felt soothed, calm, and expansive.

When I came out of the meditation, Karen said, "When you truly know yourself as the creator, everything takes care of itself. Everything you think, say, and do becomes relevant and for the good of all. Just be the love that you are. This is self-Sourcing self-love. True self-love. You self-Source because you know you are Source!" I thought *That would make a cool book title The Self-Sourcing Pudding.*

I was honest, "Karen, I understand what you mean, but I need to break some misaligned habits before I can embody my creator self all the time."

Later in the session, she invited me to dissolve my Merkaba. Many believe humans use their Merkaba to travel into their present incarnation, to travel into other dimensions/realms, and to leave their physical body at their time of death. Karen explained that the Merkaba is old technology (useful in 3-D to 6-D), and is no longer needed because there is a more evolved, quantum, infinite way of being. The Merkaba (a three-dimensional eight-pointed star made from two equally sized interlocked tetrahedra) was a useful tool for becoming self-realized but the plasma (liquid) is a more advanced fluid-like tool to create the new. She said the plasma is an advanced 9-D Divine intelligence technology that knows what I came here to do. It knows my unique codes and will help me release these codes when they are required. The plasma offers freedom, amplification, acceleration, malleability, dimensional travel, and healing. It provides a translucent visceral force field that aligns with my highest timeline as set by my blueprint. *Sweet, bring it on!* She said at any time, I could connect with the consciousness of the plasma. She explained that, at first, the plasma goes around my toroidal field, and in time, it goes down through the center of my toroidal field. Then, the plasma merges with my vibrational field. Eventually, I could dissolve my field altogether and be a conduit to Source and all there is by accessing the unified infinite field. At this point, my chakras would merge into white light, and my body would become less dense and more like a celestial being with access to higher states of consciousness. Once tapped into pure consciousness, I can access limitless creativity. She taught me that everything in the universe has a toroidal field, so my plasma field will give me access to the torus, the universal self-organizing system/pattern found in nature, black holes, and our universe.

To replace my Merkaba with white gold liquid plasma (for 6-D and beyond), Karen would lead me through a guided meditation, but first I was instructed to check in with my body technology to ensure I was ready for it.

Is it in alignment for me to have a plasma field now? I received a resounding *YES!*

At the end of the visualization, she shared how my body received the plasma. She explained, "Whenever I apply the plasma, it is different. Some people need plasma placed a couple of meters away from them to integrate it slowly. But not you; your body just lapped it up (she made a sound like a monster slurping)." I laughed. *My life is honestly a sci-fi movie!*

Karen explained my homework, "Throughout the week, concentrate on where you put your focus. Use your internal guidance system to notice if you are out of alignment then return to your heart space, over and over again. You can also connect with your plasma over the next week."

27

EXPERIENCING A KUNDALINI AWAKENING SELF

48 years old

Sensitive content relating to sexual intercourse.

Friday, April 10th

TWO DAYS after my first Beings of Magnitude (BOM) session with Karen, I had a Kundalini awakening.

Stitty and I were home alone making love.

I felt close to orgasm, but I wanted to wait for him.

I began to sing the song I sang during my second birth which caused a surge of oxytocin hormones and increased arousal. Using imagination, intention and focus, I tapped into the white gold liquid plasma running through my toroidal field. I visualized energy coming from my base chakra and channeled it as it traveled up, out of my head, down, and around my toroidal field, and finally, back up through my base chakra again. I activated each chakra by saying the corresponding color in my mind as the energy moved through *red* (base), *orange* (navel), *yellow* (solar plexus), *green* (heart), *blue* (throat), *indigo* (third eye), *violet* (crown), *white* (SELF). I could feel the energy connecting and then flowing up, out and around, and back in, tracing a toroidal coil. Then I shifted my attention by imagining my physical body dissolving into my toroidal field and becoming the plasma. I smiled *Gee this pussy plasma is powerful stuff* and giggled at the alliteration and marketing potential *powerful pussy plasma pill: orgasm guaranteed*. I returned my focus to the energy and was close to orgasm when I felt drawn to forgo my orgasm to build intensity. I imagined reversing the direction of my toroidal field. So instead of the plasma flowing up, I switched it, so it went the other way. I internally said each color in the reverse order *white, violet, indigo, blue, green, yellow, orange, red*. The energy hammering into my base chakra was extremely intense.

Stitty let me know he was about to climax. I held my breath and rolled my eyes back in my head as if I was looking at my third eye (I had never done this before).

BANG.

Everything went white.

An atomic bomb went off in my base chakra, exploding outwards in infinite love frequency waves. These rippling rings of energy expanded out into the ethers and connected me to every living organism in the universe. I realized *Everything is energy*.

Stitty was orgasming too, mine went for longer, or it was multiple.

We lay in each other's arms, completely spent. Our intimate physical union had created a synchronized orgasm that felt sacred. I thought *I just experienced a Kundalini awakening* even though I had no idea what these two words meant.

"I love you, Babe." I sighed.

"I love you too." He sighed back.

Afterward, I texted this story to Karen. She replied *What this points to for me is a perfect experience of Self as the creator... YOU were the director of the energy, the body experienced the energy, and you were the energy all at the same time. Beautiful.*

I realized that during my Kundalini awakening I experienced true reality. Like everything else in the universe, we are perfect packages of toroidal energy, part of the whole but whole unto ourselves. When my physical body's toroidal field became one with everything ever created I experienced the supreme nature of all things. Sages and Buddhists would say my physical body shattered and returned to its rightful existence. Mystics have taught for centuries; the separate body is an illusion, agreed upon by others and experienced as part of a shared consensus, but it is not an absolute reality. The truth is SELF is one consciousness. It is everything and everywhere. My Kundalini awakening allowed me to feel this hard-to-fathom fact. My physical 3-D experience of the interconnectedness of all things took it from an intellectual concept to a deep knowing on all levels.

Again the question arose *Is enlightenment realizing that everything is interconnected?* When we orgasim we experience interconnectedness which is enlightenment. So, this means we are enlightened every time we orgasm. Each of us can orgasm (alone, with a consenting legally aged partner or partners) so each of us can experience what SELF feels like. To me, orgasms feel like the moment of creation where oneness (SELF) bursts into infinite expressions of SELF. If we could extend this feeling of oneness into our days it would put things into perspective. We could let go of our attachments and aversions to things knowing they are not separate to us. We could live an ecstatic life tapped into the universe's intelligent, creative flow, feeling blissful, charged, and dynamic. Imagine our world if everyone lived this reality, there would be no dysfunction, suffering, or chaos, just unity, cooperation, and peace.

Later that day, I had a Zoom call with Karen's international friends (she was running one meditation group on Tuesday nights with her regular Australian group and one on Fridays with overseas women). Karen told us that one of her teachers, Drunvalo Melchizedek, had taught her that Ancient Egyptians manifested their dreams by stating them at the point of orgasm using the Ankh symbol. Karen explained that the ankh is a hieroglyphic symbol that looks like a cross, but the top vertical bar is replaced with a teardrop shape. Egyptians would imagine their dream/vision leaving their base chakra and traveling up to their heart chakra where it exited the body and traveled in the Ankh symbol, up and over their head, re-entering the body again through their back heart chakra. The symbol symbolizes the word *life* and is a key to unlocking the life we dream of.

After the Zoom call, I looked up the Ankh symbol. I was stunned. It was the same symbol I sketched after a dream a week before (on the eve of setting up my meditation portal). I was being guided to ancient symbols/tools to manifest my vision to write a book and evolve human consciousness. *How cool?*

The next time Stitty and I made love; I birthed my book into what I now call The Kundalini Coil Creation Loop. At the point of orgasm, I repeated my book title, which was *Honey Heart*. I imagined the intention going from my sex organs up to my heart then out of the front of my heart, over my head and back through the back of my heart and then back down to my sex organs again, tracing an Ankh shape each time. Then I envisaged the book taking a journey of its own, energetically traveling to where it needed to go, changing the world on its way by lifting people's frequency. I felt the intensity of stating what I wanted during this incredible full-body, mind, and spirit moment. I thrust what I wanted to attract into the symbol of life (the ankh) and used the energy of the orgasm to shoot it out into the universe.

The following time we made love, I used the Ankh technology on behalf of humanity. I propelled the idea of unity consciousness into the loop and imagined/witnessed humanity having a profound Kundalini awakening. I saw my vagina as the core of Mother Earth and 9-D plasma flowing from me into her. It was symbolic of our highest potential timeline where we exist in perfect harmony with Mother Earth's pure essence.

Every time we orgasm, we awaken universal creative power. What if harnessing our orgasmic sexual energy ignited the evolution of human consciousness? What if feeling that connection to our unified consciousness was all we had to do to evolve? What if it was that simple? Perhaps it is, let's try it.

Together let's birth our new world vision into the Kundalini Coil Creation Loop to manifest it.

Each of us will express ourSELF by embodying SELF, living evolved, and creating our dreams, thereby raising the frequency of the planet and igniting humanity's vision to awaken human consciousness. The collective will hold the idea of a new world in their vibrational fields until it becomes our reality. It is done, it is done, it is done.

28

CHANGING SELF

48 years old

I TOOK advantage of the school holidays and meditated (alone and with online groups) for two to four hours a day. This helped quieten my habitual thoughts. I slowed down and became so mindful that I would notice as soon as I identified with a false self. Ignore, ignore, ignore. I gave those false selves zero attention but some proved to be very loud. So much so that I wondered *Will I ever be able to ignore these noisy false selves?*

Goodbye, *habitual* self

My first job was to prove to myself that my thoughts were conditioned habits that I could change. To do this, I returned to the research I did during my Psychology Major at University of Sydney (USYD). I investigated how the brain functions. Neural pathways are like roads; the more ingrained the habit becomes, the more the brain takes that well-formed, easier to take road. I decided that if I identified what triggered my habitual thoughts then I could retrain my brain by choosing a new thought every time I perceived the trigger.

My research pointed me to Cognitive Behavioural Therapy (CBT). CBT is an effective tool to change conditioned thoughts by choosing a new thought until the brain plasticity rewires itself. CBT is a fancy term for catching your thoughts (remember Karen's CYT method). This would require razor-like focus to stalk myself 24/7 but I was more committed than ever. Motivated by a belief that eventually the mind would perceive exactly the same trigger but go down a new pathway instead. In other words, instead of thinking my old predictable patterned thought, I would think a new positive thought. YES! Bring it on!

Goodbye, false triggered selves

I explored my thinking by asking the following questions.

Question 1

What types of thoughts do I have?

After years of exploring myself as an expression of one consciousness, I know my thoughts are either aligned with SELF or not aligned with SELF. I am either aligned, mySELF Expressing Love Frequency (unity/harmony) or misaligned mySELF Expressing Low Frequency (separation/disharmony).

Question 2

How do I determine which thoughts are misaligned and need to be changed?

I use my internal guidance system to show me when I am out of alignment with SELF. My body shows me my feelings (fear, anger, melancholy) with symptoms such as a clenched jaw, churning stomach, tight shoulders, and increased heart rate.

I observed how quickly and unconsciously I identified with a false self when I had these misaligned thoughts. At these times I felt triggered.

Question 3

Why are some triggered false selves so persistent?

According to brain analysis, changing our thoughts is challenging because humans are cognitive misers. Why? Because cognition (thinking) uses a lot of brain energy. The brain travels along familiar roads in fallback mode by automatically thinking conditioned thoughts to conserve energy. Changing these fallback thoughts would take a lot of effort, but I knew I could do it. Determination is one of my strengths. Also I believe triggers activate trapped trauma in our bodies. So our physical state changes involuntarily (fight or flight response, increased heart rate, tense muscles) because a memory has been accessed. You can see this when someone jumps disproportionately high to a small stimulus—like a hand being lifted, a loud crash or a car suddenly breaking. The deeper the trauma the more spontaneous the reaction that triggers a false *I am not safe* self.

Question 4

Which antidote will curb these deeply ingrained false selves? The ones that cause my thoughts to loop and loop?

Inventing the Standard STORY method

I decided to make up a simple, easy-to-remember and practice technique to apply whenever I caught myself identifying with a triggered false self. I wrote it down on palm cards and left them everywhere. For example, in the bathroom drawer, above the kitchen sink, and behind the bedroom door.

- **S**—Stop you're out of alignment. *Ctrl Alt Delete.*
- **T**—Triggered. Name the false self.
- **O**—Own it. You're the only one who can shift the misalignment.
- **R**—Realign. Take action.
- **Y**—You are here embodying SELF.

See Appendix 2 for examples.

The STORY Method recognizes that I write the new in the now. I choose to write my story, my way, not the old patterned way. This method writes the present which writes the future because I attract the next moment aligned to that elevated iteration. The STORY Method also rewrites the past because thinking about events from an expanded perspective changes their vibration in the now, which attracts thoughts, people, and experiences that match that higher frequency. Thus, moving me, humanity, and Earth onto our highest timeline. I am not a victim of my thoughts and feelings, I am an empowered creator who transmutes triggers to access a love/enlightened/interconnected frequency.

Goodbye, *triggered* self

I discovered that my best realignment tool was going into nature. The joy that flooded my body was heightened because it sprung from a place of contraction. Like taking off a tight pair of shoes, the relief was immeasurable. To realign my internal state of being, all I had to do was calibrate with the natural environment: incredible red river gum trees, wild grasses, tiny finches, dragonflies—vibrant green, yellow, blue, beige, and brown. Busy bees pollinating, whispering plants, weeping willow branches swaying, noisy Aussie crickets. As soon as I synced up with Mother Earth's consciousness I went to Y —You are here embodying SELF. Realignment accomplished.

What is your best realignment tool? Perhaps it's following a recipe, dancing, or running.

Inventing the Advanced STORY Method—The S Method

I noticed that I did not need to use the whole STORY Method for day-to-day slip-ups. I knew what story my programmed brain would write, so I stopped it in its tracks and course-corrected. This required me to sense the possibility of an old pattern popping up while remaining in alignment. Then shut it down before I was triggered.

I invented the S Method which involved just doing the S part of the STORY method.

S— Stop you're out of alignment. *Ctrl Alt Delete.*

Stopping and thinking *Ctrl, Alt, Delete* intercepted a triggering thought and took me straight to *Y* —You are here embodying SELF.

I invented the S Method when I walked down the steps into the garage to grab my shoes off the shoe rack. To my surprise, a long upright ladder was blocking my path. I did not break my stride and confidently thought *Ctrl, Alt, Delete* as I walked (for the first time in my life) under a ladder! I grabbed my shoes, turned around, and again thought *Ctrl, Alt, Delete* before walking back under. I intuitively knew the ladder would trigger my life-long superstition narrative *You can't go that way, Kitty; it's bad luck to walk under a ladder; something terrible will happen to you.*

I found the Advanced STORY Method (S Method) worked when I was about to identify with a false self about 90% of the time and for the other 10%—it was too late and I was already triggered so I would have to use the whole Standard STORY Method. The realignment speed depended on my overall state of being. So, I had to maintain my daily practices such as 10 minutes of yoga, healthy whole foods, hydration, clean living, adequate sleep, and walks in nature.

Goodbye, *judgemental* self

While practicing the STORY methods, I noticed that I viewed my triggers as wrong, separate and imperfect. This lingering judgment sounded like *Boring, I am so over feeling not good enough. Shut up, stop complaining when you have so much to be grateful for. Why is this belief still surfacing after all the work I've done? What's wrong with me, why do I still think I have to be so bloody perfect all the bloody time?* As soon as I became aware of how out of alignment I felt every time I caught myself being triggered, I dreamt the solution. I woke up, and heard the words *There is only love and becoming love.* I grabbed my journal, and wrote: *There is only love and becoming love. Every expression of SELF, even my triggered self, has the potential to be love, so why am I judging my thoughts as either good or bad (a 3-D construct). Can I, instead, maintain the frequency of love regardless of what triggers show up. I have noticed that when I am flowing from a place of love, I can easily think I am love. But as soon as I have a thought that is not love, for example, identifying with a false self, I am hard on myself and think I am not love. Can I, instead, be gentle with myself and think I am becoming love. Just like I would say to a toddler, "You are learning to walk" instead of "You are bad—you can't walk." SELF-realization wobbles are as normal as toddler wobbles. What matters is what I make them mean. So how I talk to myself is vital. If I respond to a trigger with frustration, a story, or disappointment, my vibration is the opposite of love, which creates the opposite of what I am trying to express.*

Once I have mastered using these two affirmations (I am love and I am becoming love) with my thoughts, I can start using them with others. When I witness opinions and behaviors that feel out of alignment, I can be gentle with the person by thinking 'They are becoming love.' This replaces judgment with loving-kindness. It unifies instead of divides. It does not excuse the person/events, it just energetically alchemizes the effect their misalignment has on me. Trusting that everything is happening as it should allows me to remain in alignment when I view these people or situations. This is difficult to do when the person's words and actions are offensive, illegal, murderous, or adulterous. However, this unconditional love acknowledges that they were not love when they made that choice, but they have the potential to be love in this moment. Having unconditional love for them does not condone their wrongdoings, it just stops the negative ripple from affecting our internal state of being.

WRITE HERE WRITE NOW

Wednesday, April 15th

DURING OUR SECOND Beings of Magnitude (BOM) session, I told Karen about my dream and how viewing others in this loving way felt really good. I had learned through *The 13 Original Clan Mothers* by Jamie Sams that everyone is a reflection of me but after recently experiencing ultimate SELF/true reality I knew everyone is me—we are all one consciousness/the creator. Karen explained that everyone is an aspect of the multidimensional SELF. She led me through a meditation to demonstrate this, "Welcome all of SELF to coalesce and flow through this vehicle. Completely accept and fully love every expression of SELF without judgment and with full compassion, knowing that every expression adds to the wonder that is life, that is creation. Every expression is a service to the whole. Every expression is equally valid, whether judged a hero, saint, villain, terrorist, or anywhere in between. Give permission for all of SELF to be here now, knowing that all the gifts you hold, all the lessons you've learned are available to you now. They come online and into conscious awareness as you are ready for their expression and sometimes as the collective calls them forward. You came to help create the new, not perpetuate the old game of duality and separation. Allow all aspects of SELF to merge. All the colors of the rainbow completely unify to become pure light. Anchor that here in this feeling state. Let this flow through and into your physical, mental, and emotional body so it can feel and know and remember the unified state. The state of the original pure light, before it began to create, before it began to individuate, and before any distortion. Holding this state takes care of everything because everything purifies in its resonance. You are this unified being. You have already mastered separation. BOMs are all about embodying unification in this physical body. We are moving away from the old way of duality and contrast and moving into a community of beings who are part of a unified field."

Goodbye, *bullshitting* self

Karen also explained the subtlety between knowing and believing. This was a huge wake-up call. She said, "As masters, the level of discernment is huge because we have so much knowledge." Karen invited me to become acutely discerning by asking myself *Is this coming from my knowing, from my authentic self, or am I just regurgitating something I have read or heard.* This questioning allowed me to feel the subtleties of distortion. I found this tool useful when I was writing. So much so that I rewrote the beginning of my book because it did not feel authentic. I also began to pause before I spoke and check-in *Is this really my truth, is this relevant to share, or should I just keep quiet?* I called this my *Bullshitometer,* and I used it all the time to hone in and select wisely. Slowly, with practice, I began to feel trusted and reliable. As the weeks progressed, my *Bullshitometer* became more and more refined. I began to talk less because I realized that many of my thoughts, words, and actions were fear-based, irrelevant, and not serving me. As a result, most of what I said came from my heart space and was aligned. For example, I would observe my tendency to parent as I was parented instead of inquiring how that style made me feel and did I agree with it? I often concluded that it felt self-righteous and that my children needed love first and foremost, so I dropped that sense of self and tapped into mySELF as unconditional love. This created a more harmonious household and modeled conscious parenting to our children.

Goodbye, *playing the role* self

Wednesday, April 22nd

IN MY THIRD BOM SESSION, Karen encouraged me to clear all vows, contracts, oaths, and obligations across all timelines. During a guided meditation, I transcended all plains to embody SELF instead of being bound to false selves created by karma, society, family, and institutions. I felt like a being of magnitude empowered with free will to express all that is in alignment.

Goodbye, *trauma* self

To stop identifying with my trauma self, I had to do multidimensional healing work because I needed to heal my trauma, generational trauma, parallel/past life trauma, the trauma of the land, collective trauma, and other people's trauma.

Trauma includes parallel/past life trauma

HAVE you ever wondered why you are the way you are and why you react to things the way you do, especially when there is no obvious reason in this lifetime? I have read studies that suggest our RNA molecules are encoded with intergenerational traits established to cope with trauma and these traits are passed on from generation to generation (these claims are controversial, a psychologist might agree but a geneticist probably would not). For example, intergenerational trauma passed down from the Indigenous Stolen Generation in Australia. This theory implies that a person living a good life now can still have traits/triggered thoughts their grandfather established to survive during the Stolen Generation. What if we could change these traits and resolve the trauma once and for all? This would be a generous act of service because it puts an end to karmic loops and prevents the trauma from being passed onto future generations (through the land or through the bloodlines). If we live in a multidimensional universe, then we have access to all timelines and clearing one, clears them all. This is what I refer to as multidimensional healing work.

To explain multidimensional healing work further, we can identify with any timeline we choose because we have access to every timeline there is. How? Every expression of SELF exists simultaneously, therefore I am every one of the infinite expressions—past, present, and future (linear time is an illusion). So, I am a future person, I am an orphan girl in Yemen right now, and I am an African American enslaved person 400 years ago. I am every expression of SELF that expresses at the same time in the now. I know this is hard to comprehend.

To further explain our multidimensionality, imagine everything existing at once, as a universal unmeasurable wave. To measure it, let us pretend, you pinch it up into a steep peak. This immediately changes it from a flowing wave to a sharp point needle. Imagine then each expression of that universal wave is now stacked on top of one another. You could say these are parallel timelines, but when you release the pinch and stop observing, they return to the oneness, the universal wave which is SELF (or whatever you call it). Therefore, in any given moment we can identify with one of these infinite expressions of SELF, or we can rest as the oneness. For example *Do I choose to be an aspect of mySELF that is traumatized or do I choose to be the universal wave of love?*

It is a paradox: *I am every form of trauma that has ever existed but at the same time I am none of it because when I return to the oneness I am pure.* This means that no matter what happens, has happened, or will happen, SELF is eternally untouched. *Write here, write now I am perfect, there is nothing to heal.*

Land holds personal and collective trauma too

TO DO multidimensional healing work on the land, I would go to my meditation circle and ask the animals, flora, fauna, and ancestors for permission to enter the sacred space and sprinkled polenta as an offering. I would sit cross-legged and face East. As I drummed, I paid my respects to the traditional custodians, the First Nation people, the Wiradjuri clan, who sustained the land by honoring the role of each organism upon it for over 45,000 years. I connected with my breath and imagined my consciousness, Mother Earth's consciousness, and the consciousness of all indigenous people worldwide merge. Together we purified whatever felt present—for example, collective trauma. I visualized the victim and perpetrator roles collapsing into the Earth's crystalline grid. No blame or guilt, just love for all involved. I imagined all moments, no matter how horrific, bathed in pink light. I invited compassion into the space to transmute pain to love. I imagined higher frequency light codes resonating through all cosmic dimensions activating the DNA of all living beings. Wounds would instantly resolve on all levels: personal, ancestral, historical, cultural, and spiritual. I could not change what the white men did on this land, but when I tapped into Mother Earth's spiraling unconditional love, we energetically healed the land and its people (past, present, and future). The more I did the multidimensional work, the more I connected with my evolved self on a timeline where the land and the First Nation people are healthy and abundant.

This multidimensional healing work forged a new relationship between Mother Earth and me. We connected at a deep level. I began to feel her elements in my body and love her as my original mother. Indigenous tribes remember this truth, but I grew up in the western world that disrespects Mother Earth by polluting her. I felt more and more motivated to drink clean, fresh water and eat whole, organic fresh fruit, and vegetables, and choose a vegetarian diet (no meat or seafood) to purify my body and the planet (I had not had alcohol for eight and a half years). I invited Mother Earth to show me how to follow natural law to preserve humankind. I was also drawn to explore our First Nation people's interconnectedness with everything and their unique ability to live in the now. I was fascinated by the Dreaming and songlines and was eager to learn more. I sent these intentions out with my drum beats. A few months later I met an indigenous medicine man who gave me an Aboriginal Didgeridoo healing session that felt profound.

After weeks of doing this multidimensional healing, which felt guided by Mother Earth, I realized that humans have an antenna that perfectly communicates with Mother Earth. My internal guidance system intuitively let me know when unresolved trauma was present. When my antenna was in tune, I detected trauma throughout my day, not just in meditation.

Unknown trauma

Often it was difficult to know if the detected trauma was personal or collective. So I treated all trauma the same way. I would think *It does not matter where this trauma came from, I choose to clear it now. I allow it to flow through me. I trust the tool I choose to clear it will be perfectly aligned to the good of all.* Responses took many forms, such as imagining my body as a conduit for the trauma to be absorbed by Mother Earth, crying, dancing, shaking it out, or unquestioning forgiveness (of self and others) using the Ho'oponopono prayer. I knew there is no right or wrong way to clear trauma as long as I was expressing from my heart. This surrendering attitude maintained a high vibration flow state whereas attaching a story to the trauma, labeling it, or pushing it down would have created disharmony, chakra blockages, and eventually dis-ease.

We can all do this form of trauma healing because trauma is part of our human make-up in this 3-D reality. When we resolve trauma:

- We take responsibility for every expression of trauma we experience in our life.
- We become less triggered and more empowered.
- We can untangle ourselves from trauma narratives by actively alchemizing them into the love vibration.
- We can observe our thoughts/words/and behaviors with acceptance, knowing we developed them as armor to protect ourselves from trauma and realize they are no longer relevant.
- We can recognize choice points and skillfully choose a new positive thought instead of an old predictable patterned thought.

When we resolve trauma, celebrate!

I own my breakthroughs. I never give my power to the catalyst, the teacher, the healer, the medicine person, the book, the guru, the artist, the friend, or the quote. Why? Because I created them all—everything everywhere is SELF. Therefore, they did not cause the epiphany, I did. *I was telling myself 99 times and on the 100th time, I listened. I was the one saying the same thing in different ways (relationships, accidents, messages) until I finally got it.* Claiming responsibility for my growth and my healing takes me from the helpless victim who needs others to teach me to an empowered creator who teaches myself.

Goodbye, *self-blame* self

When I woke with a stiff neck, headache, and intense pain at the base of my skull. Stitty responded, "You're over-meditated; you're doing too much."

I replied, "I refuse to believe that I am doing too much. How can meditating 4 hours a day be doing too much?" I knew the neck pain was not a sign I was out of alignment but instead collective trauma passing through me to be alchemized. Sometimes pain just happens. I did not need to make it more painful by beating myself up. I could experience the pain without adding stories such as *I am not evolved enough, I did something wrong, I am in my old patterns, I thought I dealt with this, I ate toxic food, I am weak*. This was the old narrative. In the past, I would have retreated to my bed to discover where I had not been spiritual enough (limiting belief). Instead, I patiently allowed the physical pain to be felt and transmuted without making it mean anything. This tool creates the new when faced with the old.

Goodbye, *lack* self

Stitty had pointed out, constructively, that I had an underlying lack mentality. He said in the past I was in the habit of making him think I was never happy. I would get something, for example, a new kitchen, and then move the goal post and need a new bathroom. Stitty said he felt like he could never please me. When I self-monitored, I noticed he was right! So during my lockdown retreat, I worked with Karen to make that narrative irrelevant. Soon the old destructive lack mentality began dissolving. How did I do this? Well, once I committed to being present and grateful for what I had, I stopped noticing lack. I was too busy celebrating my grateful fors. Once I trained my mind to align to SELF, attachments and caring what people thought about me, lost their attractiveness.

When I stopped putting energy into everything lacking I began to see so much unnoticed beauty. It was bizarre, my world became psychedelic. Did you know that grass glistens like glitter after a rain shower? I think this is what Bryan Tucker (my insight meditation teacher) meant when he said, "Finding the extraordinary in the ordinary." When my mind was resting peacefully, these little moments were moments of enlightenment. Opportunities to wake up over and over again.

Stitty has since said I no longer make him feel inadequate, which is a relief. I rewired my brain to focus on abundance instead of deficit.

Hello, *changed* self

I had experienced *ah-ha* moments before but this time I felt transformed. I think it was a combination of prolonged intensity, isolation, conviction, and access to skilled teachers. My lockdown retreat lasted six weeks, so for 42 straight days, I trained my brain to think new thoughts by taking the roads less traveled to forge new routes. Thus, evolving my thought processes. This gave me the energy I needed to be of service to family and friends, humanity, and Mother Earth.

Maybe, spending around 84 hours meditating developed a muscle allowing my alignment to become stronger and stronger. I became so conscious of my body and its communication with me that my penetrating intuition could feel even the most minute trigger. My newly developed sixth sense would alert me whenever my optimum vibration waned or there was disharmony in my environment. When I detected something was off I would realign as quickly as possible using the STORY Method (Standard or Advanced). I became better and better at these techniques and I no longer needed the palm cards. False selves started to feel ridiculous. I began to laugh if I caught myself playing an old role, buying into an exhausting story, or clinging to an unproductive narrative. I was confident that eventually, these deliberate decisions would be replaced by an evolved way of being.

Embracing my unique expression in my little piece of the world

ALREADY, I felt as though my consciousness had expanded. I could not help but notice that I had more creative energy. This excited me because I knew I was contributing to our new world vision. I was expressing mySELF by embodying SELF, living evolved, and creating my dream of being a calm mom, thereby raising the frequency of the planet and igniting humanity's vision to awaken human consciousness.

29

ANSWERING THE CALL SELF

48 years old

Wednesday, April 29th

IN MY FINAL BOM session with Karen, she led me through this series of questions and guided meditation:

Karen: "Drop into your source space or your heart... Ask yourself this... Is there anything in the way of my full SELF-realization and embodiment of my magnitude?"

Me: "No"

Karen: "Sitting in the perspective of all of SELF. Ask SELF. Did I come here for the cycles of karma and learning?"

Me: "NO I did not"

Karen: "Did I come here to assist?"

Me: "Yes, I came here to assist with creating the new."

Karen: "Ask or feel into. What is it that I have to share? What wants to express through me here?"

Me: "A book."

Karen: "Is this my gift?"

Me: "Yes."

Karen: "Is this book specific to my blueprint?"

Me: "Yes."

Karen: "Is there anything I'm unaware of that I am ready to be aware of now in regards to this blueprint?"

Me: "The time is now; let go of everything. Use my communication skills. These are my gifts. It is all happening in divine timing. I have a healthy, abundant body. I have the means to create a book. I am not in survival mode. I was born into circumstances that will allow me to do this act of love for humanity."

Karen: "Now that your heart is open with that gratitude, drop deeper and deeper into the ocean of SELF, into all that you are. Feeling the vastness of SELF, knowing that you exist across all realms and other densities. Consciously call in all the gifts and codes that are specific to here. Sometimes they come in as other aspects of SELF, sometimes, as you call them in you unlock them in your DNA. They are your unique codes, you do not have to know what they are. Trust and know that you, as the creator, unlock your DNA. These specific gifts are ready to be shared and flow through the book. Acknowledge now that you hold these unique gifts and codes specifically for here, and it's why you came. As you do this, they activate and amplify. Ask SELF, Am I ok with bringing all of SELF here, the entirety of SELF here?"

Me: "Yes."

Karen: "So you are gathering all the gifts of SELF from all incarnations of SELF, all aspects of SELF."

Me; "Which is basically everything because I am everything. So I have access to a lot of knowledge!"

Karen: "Yes it's everything. But you're coalescing all of that to flow through your vehicle into expression here. It will flow through the words in the book, your actions, thoughts, and how your feet touch the ground. This is why there is nothing to do but be all that you are. Just allow it to flow—freely and purely through the vehicle you created just for this purpose. As you feel it all coalescing, consciously anchor your full magnitude into the heart of Mother Earth. From your heart space into her heart space. Consciously, willingly and with an open heart, share all that you are with her, as she shares all that she is with you. You are one with Mother Earth. You exchange codes; imagine your codes merging. This helps create the unified field, it helps stabilize you in all that you are, and in turn, this stabilizes her as she shifts into her sovereignty and unity. Allow this free flow of exchange. Mother Earth is acknowledging the gift of you, the purity of your heart with such gratitude and love for your choice to be and exist here now. She called you forward, and you answered the call. You are here on behalf of love—the love of creation itself. Your existence here invites others to remember they are Source. You reflect that for all through living and being your true SELF. By you being real and authentic, allowing yourself to truly be seen, to be vulnerable, and to be open, you give others permission to do the same. When you truly acknowledge the magnificence that you are, the true beauty, pure love, and grace, when you can truly see that in SELF, you see it in all and reflect it for all. Feel the purity of your original light, before you came into creation, the purity of that light, the purity of that love. You bring this to everything, and it takes care of everything. You know SELF as this, pure loving light, and you allow this to move you, operate through the vehicle, and express through your words spoken and written. You allow this to inspire your actions, for this is your highest, truest expression, completely unified, completely sovereign. You are sitting with higher self. You feel this purity within higher self and your specific blueprint or reason for being—it's all here for this incarnation. As higher self, communicate with Mother Earth, and ask, Is there anything being called forward right now?"

Me: "Love, acceptance, perfection."

Karen: "When you are ready, remaining as that true SELF, open your eyes."

Me: "I feel so clear. When I am Source, SELF, I don't even need to think about alignment because everything is aligned. Thank you, Karen. I am envisioning leaving my job at the end of the year and opening up to my calling."

Karen: "When your heart says yes, the clarity will just drop in, and higher self will energetically move the pieces around, so gaps open up, you meet the people, the opportunities happen, and the space is created that is perfectly in alignment with what you are saying yes to. It is just taken care of. And then all that is required is following what you are inspired to do, you just follow that, you follow your heart. If there is any feeling of trying to make something happen, then you are not in your heart. You may have an old belief that you, the person, has to make it happen but you don't. Feel how that feels different to—creation is taking place through you, by you, for you and all you have to do is allow creation to move you. So, if you feel drawn to sit and write you sit and write as opposed to 'I have to sit here for six hours and write.' Feel the difference? You follow your heart in every moment."

30

RETURNING TO WORK AFTER A RETREAT SELF

49 years old

Monday, May 4th (25 days before my 49th birthday)

MY SIX-WEEK LOCKDOWN retreat came to an end, and I returned to work. I endeavored to view it as an extension of the retreat by telling myself that my students could teach me curiosity, innocence, and purity—tools I needed to live evolved. I was in constant awe of their wise ways, unabating love, and acceptance.

I continued to meditate daily, but I did not need to meditate as intensely. I did two weekly meditation groups: Karen's Tuesday night Australian group, the Friday morning international group (my day off), and monthly Clan Mothers sessions. My lockdown meditations were relevant and meaningful at the time as they catapulted me into clear-sightedness, but now I had transcended the purpose of meditating. I was remaining in a spacious meditative state all the time. My entire day became a meditation and I was focusing on the joy all around me.

Occasionally I noticed an old Kitty thought pop up, for example, *Sue thinks I jumped ship by working from home during Covid.* I would take a deep breath, remaining neutral. *Oh, there's the old Kitty. That's not me anymore. I have no idea what Sue is thinking, so I don't need to go into a story around it. I am a being of magnitude.* These words zoomed me out into the bigger picture of SELF. Which felt expansive, worthy, meaningful, validated, and loving. I saw each interaction as a perfect opportunity to be present, listen to my internal guidance system, and notice choice points. It would have been easy for me to just slot back into auto-pilot but I diligently stalked myself until I settled in and felt confident I was not going to relapse into old habits.

Goodbye, *inauthentic* self

Monday, May 11th

A WEEK later I started to speak my truth, by sharing my SELF-realization catalysts on social media. Why? Firstly, just before COVID, I made my second Native American Medicine drum with Two Crows, a decade after my first drum. I used a much thicker hoop and a kangaroo skin. It sounded deeper than my first drum, symbolic of my transformation after years of awakenings. I was birthing a drum as a shaman this time, so the process shone a spotlight on my *inauthentic* self. It showed me I was lacking integrity by hiding the real me. It was as if the drum was holding me accountable; speaking my truth was suddenly non-negotiable. Secondly, during Covid, the black-shouldered kite visited me and expressed my potential to guide and lead others. How could I *Be the light* and a messenger if I was too scared to speak up? Lastly, I understood my soul's blueprint and call to action following my BOMs course. There was no way I could inspire others to shine their light if I was too scared to shine my light?

I decided the time had come to show people my spiritual side. I chose Instagram as my platform and called it @honey_heart_by_kitty (now @byKitty1). My first post was a recording I did as a testimonial for Karen's BOMs Course. It was a big deal for me to talk about this aspect of self. I had always disguised myself as mainstream. I was your regular teacher, school mom, neighbor, sports team coach, and community member. I felt like I was taking a considerable risk. Doubts crept in, showing me I had not said goodbye to my *caring what people think* self or *my not wanting to get into trouble* self.

I remembered a quote in *Truth Creates Heaven on Earth* by Karen and the collective of lightworkers, "And the day came when the risk to remain tight in a bud was more painful than the risk it took to blossom." Anais Nin.

Goodbye, *stressing* self

I sensed that my biggest challenge going from lockdown to work would be avoiding identifying with my stressing self. Stressing was my previous persona; I was highly invested in this ingrained worry/fear/rush thought pattern. I was that teacher who ran everywhere, all the time. I was always in a hurry, goal-focused, thinking about the next thing while doing what I was doing. I helped too much and did other people's jobs without being asked. I worked all recess and all lunch. I always appeared to have more to do than everyone else and not enough time to do it. I was in a constant state of emotional overwhelm. After school and on weekends, I would contact parents or coordinate upcoming sporting events. I was constantly lost in thoughts about the future. Most notably, what was on my to-do list. *I don't have enough time; when will I do that? How am I going to get all these things done?* I was like this at school and home, pretty much all the time I was awake. For years, I wondered how anyone lived in the present.

Lockdown created a catalyst point where I could no longer bear that sense of self. I became 100% committed to changing it. It took time to prove to myself that it was a choice worth making, but I had the time and the drive to do it, and it paid off. After decades, I finally broke the insidious stress habit. When I returned to work I assumed everyone would expect me to be the way I used to be, but I realized no one really cared. They accepted the new me and never tried to make me play the old role. My belief *I will let people down if I do not do everything* was simply an illusion, one of my many distorted senses of self.

Hello, *being present* self

During my lockdown retreat, I witnessed true SELF where there is no linear time. Through this experience, I gained a timeless perspective. This made me stop clinging to a false fear that I did not have enough time. Once I knew linear time was not real, I could dwell in the present moment.

How?

Let us say I had an awareness that I needed to do something. I did not need to worry about how I would do it continually. I just needed to trust that my higher self had my back, and it would get done. I surrendered, knowing that everything would be taken care of. Small steps would appear until I reached my goal. This meant I could be present as awareness, free from the conditioned mind's distracting thoughts and running commentaries. I could embody SELF and enter the flow state. When I finished doing what I was doing, I would follow what I was guided to do next. The next most important step would appear and it always felt in alignment. At some point, I found myself organically doing what initially needed to be done, and it got done effortlessly. I replaced stress with trust that everything I needed would show up at the right time, and I would know what I needed to know when I needed to know it (divine timing). This felt like being instead of doing, which is living evolved.

This moment-to-moment existence changed everything in my

life. I still experienced the things we all experience but through a different lens. What previously caused me stress no longer caused me anxiety. Not because they went away but because of my new mindset.

When I returned to working at school rather than working from home, my substantial to-do list put my advanced way of being to the test. Much to my amazement, even in a busy school setting, I was able to mindfully do what I was doing until it was done, then do what I was drawn to do next, and miraculously everything got done. I had supreme confidence that I did not have to worry. I felt joyful, uncluttered, and liberated. Nowhere to go, nothing to do, except be present, right here, right now, and see what happens. I noticed synchronicities, laughter, and doors opening.

Also, when I identified with my creator self, I knew that I could create the time I needed to get things done tapped into universal flow.

31

ACTIVATING SUPERPOWERS SELF

49 years old

Saturday, June 27th

I HAD A DREAM: *I was driving a borrowed car, and there were people of all ages, shapes, and sizes dressed up as superheroes (the Incredibles) walking all over the road. I realized the car had no steering wheel. I was committed to navigating around the people. That was my only thought. I felt no fear, just the automatic problem-solving impulse. I used the dashboard like a scooter handle to maneuver the car. I narrowly missed an old couple crossing the pedestrian crossing. After that, I easily weaved through the people and traffic.*

I tried turning the car around to get back to where I came from and realized the car had no accelerator pedal. I desperately scanned the dashboard and saw a symbol indicating it was on the ground. I moved my foot along the smooth carpet and found the spot where I could apply pressure to make the car accelerate. *When I returned safely, I told the story to one of my colleagues at school.*

When I woke up, I heard the word *genius*.

I had accessed my *genius* self.

How? I got out of my way, letting my *genius* self take over.

Firstly, I 'cut my head off' as Karen advised.

I did not ask:

- What if I hit someone?
- Why is this happening to me?
- Why would anyone design a car like this?
- Where is the manual?
- Have I been in this situation before?
- Who can I ask for help?
- Should I do this or that?

Secondly, I kept the end goal in sight. *Navigate around these people.* From a neurolinguistic programming perspective, my specific, intentional language effectively told my brain what it needed to do. Then I simply followed each instinct as it arose.

Hello, *genius* self

Saturday, July 4th

A WEEK later I unleashed my superpowers.

I was at the local farmers' markets putting fresh vegetables into a Lululemon bag that I picked up years ago in Seattle. The producer said, "Are you going to 'unwrap your super powers' today?" as he read aloud the cartoon on the bag.

"Maybe, I hope so." I smiled keenly.

An hour later, I was at the gym running on a treadmill, minding my own business and reading the safety alert stuck at eye level *Recently, a member was seriously injured when a treadmill was left running without a member on it.* I had read those words hundreds of times and thought about the story and the poor man who had suffered every time.

Suddenly, the man on the treadmill next to me began to trip and fall.

Everything went into slow motion. He was going off the back of the treadmill faster than he could reach the stop button. Sheer fear and terror crossed his face as his arms waved hopelessly in front of him. Then, finally, I heard him in my mind, "NOOOOOOOOO." Our eyes locked, and my survival instincts kicked in.

I dove off my treadmill towards the stop button on the other side of his treadmill. I banged it and then suspended in the air; I realized *Shit, my treadmill is running*. Then, miraculously, I landed back on my treadmill with my feet straddled on either side of the speeding conveyer belt. I was shaking with adrenaline and completely in shock. *How had I done such a thing?*

He was also trembling.

"Are you Ok?" I investigated.

He said, "I'm so embarrassed; you just saved my life. I thought I was gone then." He gasped in appreciation.

"I have no idea how I did that! I am 49 years old!" I exclaimed.

It was one of those moments when humans do extraordinary things when they have to. Tapped into my *genius* self, I dove off a moving treadmill, hit something way out of my reach, and then somehow landed back safely.

Had someone asked me if I could do that, I would have said, "No way." My answer would have been influenced by theories of trajectory, analysis of angles, investigation of probability, risk assessments, and weighing up similar scenarios to ensure compatibility and banter regarding my age and level of coordination. But, after all this thought and discussion, do you honestly think I could have done it? Probably not. It played out differently because of the absence of limiting beliefs like fear and inadequacy.

Diving from my treadmill (with no practical plan) was a risk, but it did not feel like a risk because I was not thinking of myself, I was thinking about someone else. The guy was a total stranger, but when our eyes locked, I saw a fellow human, vulnerable and scared, so I did what I had to do without thinking. I just kept the end goal in sight - firstly, save him, then save me.

I accessed perfect human body technology, universal intelligence, and intuition available to us all, and life unfolded effortlessly.

This story mirrors life. When we focus on the end goal the rest takes care of itself. We do not need to plot each step because some steps are beyond our wildest imaginations. We just need to have faith in something bigger than ourselves. I did not need to know how to save this man's life nor do we need to know how to achieve a mass evolution in human consciousness. The collective just needs to hold the idea of a new world in their vibrational fields until it becomes our reality.

Surrendering to spontaneous creation takes care of everything because it evolves everything to its highest timeline. Living evolved by embodying SELF frees us up to experience the magic we naturally create.

This state of allowance 'unwraps our super powers.'

32

HEALING CHILDHOOD TRAUMA SELF

49 years old

Trigger warning: Story contains potentially triggering content for trauma survivors relating to eating disorders.

Monday, July 6th

STITTY TOOK Gigi and Matilda skiing for a week, and I stayed home to write and keep Ruby company, she was studying for her high school finishing exams. I watched an interview on the Awake TV Network with Drunvalo Melchizedek (one of Karen's teachers). The School Of The Heart conducted the interview, which teaches Heart Imagery, an ancient system originating in Tibetan, Sumerian, and Vedic spiritual mystery schools. It sounded like a valuable tool, so I booked four Zoom sessions with a Heart Imagery practitioner, Chris Cheung.

WRITE HERE WRITE NOW

Friday, July 10th

DURING MY SECOND Zoom session with Chris (from Melbourne, Australia, living in Hawaii). I shared, "Dad had good intentions and loved me very much, but he was tough on me. I was a competitive swimmer from age six and had a wall full of ribbons, certificates, medals, and trophies from State and National Titles. I was training 24 hours a week, four hours a day in my teenage years. My team trained twice a day; the only sessions we had off were Wednesday and Sunday afternoons. Before training, we would do a weights session or run eight kilometers (five miles) around the outside of Randwick Racecourse in the pitch dark. I ran it alone as the slowest, which terrified me because I thought someone would abduct me. I wondered how long it would be before anyone noticed and raised the alarm.

Did I enjoy the training? No. I did it to please Dad. I did enjoy the social aspect of it, though; my friends, the trips away, the camaraderie, racing, psyching everyone up to succeed, the war cries, and being part of the best team in Australia at the time. However, I did not love my years as an elite swimmer because Dad would yell at Mum when I did not improve my times. He would say I did not train hard enough and had not tried during the races.

Mum would say: "Oh Donn, stop putting so much pressure on her; she's a child." I hated the way he took his anger out on her. I felt it was my fault she was in trouble.

By the time I turned 16, my heart was not in competitive swimming anymore. My coach knew I lacked commitment and focus, so he tried to force me to quit by making me do everything butterfly. This included a 1500-meter butterfly on a Sunday morning. Can you even imagine having to swim 1500 meters butterfly? My arms ache now just thinking about it! I may not have been determined to train for gain, but I was determined not to let his bullying succeed in making me give up. I would quit on my terms, not because my coach thought I was distracting his Olympians (Seoul was in two years). So I did my 1500 meter butterfly just to spite him.

Later that year, Mum convinced Dad to let me give up after the Australian National Championships, where I won bronze and silver in the freestyle and the medley relays. When I retired, no one supported my life transition. The coaches were not interested in me anymore, and Mum and Dad did not know what to do. I needed advice about things like diet. I went from burning 2400 calories a day to burning practically nothing. I went from morning runs, weight sessions, and swimming four kilometers daily to just walking 100 meters to and from the bus stop. I would buy potato scallops and chocolate on the way home from school and then sneak them into my bedroom. I had more time but was less motivated to study and never exercised. I went from 52 kilos (115 pounds) to 72 kilos (159 pounds), affecting my confidence and well-being during my final two high school years. Mum loved me unconditionally, but Dad would say in an American accent, "Please, Katie, don't eat that, you don't need that… step away from the peanut butter."

After I gave up swimming, I developed feelings of unworthiness. To fix this feeling of lack, I looked outside myself. Unfortunately, it was a self-love issue that I could not articulate or process, so I just began overeating.

I overate to push down:

- My disappointment, *I've let down my coach and parents*.
- My boredom, *What do I do with these countless unoccupied hours?*
- My loneliness, *I miss my swimming friends*.
- My guilt, *Why did I give up?*

- My worry, *I've made the wrong choice.*
- My shame, *I'm a quitter.*
- My fear, *I'm fatter than all my school friends.*
- My dread, *No one will love me.*
- My doubts, *Maybe I don't deserve to be happy.*
- My rebellion, *I'll just give up on everything.*
- My panic, *I'll never be accepted.*

Once I was overweight, I felt invisible, so I made up for it by being loud, the center of attention, the funniest girl in the room, and the drunkest. I would binge drink to the point of memory loss, but my friends assured me I was "hilarious." When we went out, I was everyone's best friend. I would drink for the same reasons I overate, but unfortunately, the ramifications were more severe than excess body fat.

When I turned 18, I took up risk-taking behaviors such as drunk driving, smoking cigarettes, and a few one-night stands that involved unprotected sex. I always said I used the boys as much as they used me. But I knew, deep down, that I was throwing myself onto them to fill a void. I wanted to feel needed, approved of, and appreciated. I did not love myself, so I looked for love in all the wrong places. Did they love me back? Did they ask me out? No, never!

When I was 21, I lost 18 kilos (40 pounds) in 24 weeks by starving myself and throwing up. After that, I was skin and bone. I got a boyfriend who made me give up smoking (thank heavens), but I had not fixed my underlying self-love issue, which explains why I forgave this boyfriend after I found out he was unfaithful with seven different women in two years. *Why did I forgive him? What was I thinking? How desperate was I?*

My next boyfriend was Stitty; I was 24 years old. I fell in love with myself as he fell in love with me because he reflected me to me, showing me all the things there were to love, and just like that, food and alcohol stopped being an issue. I have maintained that weight all these years without a single diet. Once I had a healthy relationship with myself, I had a healthy relationship with everything else. Then, when I was 41 years old, on December 12th, I decided to no longer drink alcohol. Why? I knew it did not serve me, and I wanted to be more present to quit other things that did not serve me. I wanted to be more conscious, not less conscious. So, I never had another sip. I no longer need alcohol to have fun because I know SELF is complete and needs nothing to improve it. Giving up alcohol was effortless and I did not replace it with another vice which means I had done sufficient work to stop addictions in their tracks."

Chris asked, "Did you ever tell your Dad how you felt when he yelled at your Mum when you didn't improve your times?"

I replied, "No."

He asked, "Would you like me to teach you a Heart Imaging technique, used by the Buddhist monks and adapted by me, to clear, heal and reverse past pain?"

I replied, "Yes, please."

He led me through a visualization technique where I returned to myself as a child. Chris instructed me to view my parents interacting with each other and notice what they paid attention to. Then, observe the times they felt most proud of me and most proud of other people. I saw my reactions and feelings when they gave me attention and withdrew their attention. Next, I zoomed forward to my teenage years and examined how witnessing those moments had shaped how I approached life, my priorities, and where I put my energy. Chris asked if I would have spent my energy doing those things if I had been conditioned differently. I zoomed forward to my 20s and beyond and noticed how this mold shaped my behaviors and decisions. Then, Chris invited me to go back to a time in my childhood when I felt lonely and vulnerable. A time when my parents could not hear, see or understand me. Chris asked me, as the adult, to wrap my arms around the neglected me. He invited me to say, "I love you, you are safe, you are held, and you are heard. I will protect you. I am here for you always." I felt how the little wounded child enjoyed this warm embrace. Chris added, "Your inner child does not need the approval of your parents anymore because her adult self loves her and will protect her, as will Mother Earth and Father Sun. You can do what the Tibetan monks do and reverse the suffering (being hurt or hurting others) by detaching from it and bringing the energy from that moment into your heart. This means the painful emotion is integrated, reclaimed, owned, and loved. You can try it now and feel how the trauma transmutes itself."

After the meditation, Chris and I reflected on how we parent our children. The Buddhist clearing, healing, and reversing pain visualization allowed me to see my children's experiences. They are growing up in a household with expectations. They watch and listen to Stitty and me to see what we value. Going back to myself as a child gave me firsthand insight into my daughters' feelings as they navigate their lives.

Chris encouraged me to share my story of finding myself with my daughters. I told him, "I want to be brave enough to openly tell them the process I went through to find my voice. This honesty will require me to show my fragility and say, "This caused me pain, and I don't want you to suffer the same pain." Sometimes I think I have to be infallible, invincible, and flawless as a mum, but thanks to you and this technique, I realize there is a way to connect more authentically. Instead of being stoic, I can tell them that growing up in a mold made me feel trapped and voiceless, especially when I chose to go along with the status quo and do as I was told to keep the peace. By explaining how this impacted me, I open the door for them to explore their motivations and choices. Talking about why I played a role to please people might encourage them to examine any roles they might be unknowingly playing to gain approval. Maybe they have a fear of doing the wrong thing and getting into trouble as I did, and I would prefer to address it now before it becomes a more significant issue. The more transparent I am, the more transparent they will be. If they think I am perfect and never do anything wrong, they might keep secrets, fearing they will disappoint me. I hope my sharing creates intimacy and develops their emotional literacy, which is their capacity to talk about their feelings.

The fact that I can recount my promiscuity in a neutral, matter-of-fact way demonstrates I am not emotionally tied to that aspect of me. I can speak about that false self the same way I talk about a character in a movie because it is not SELF. That self was wounded, but now I have healed, and now, *I am whole*. When I started writing the book, I did not think I would be able to write about this period of my life, but my actions no longer trigger disgust and shame. I have cleared, healed, and reversed that pain, and now I can maintain a love frequency when I think and talk about those times. Thus, creating the new in the now.

Over the years, I have realized that helping my children navigate their experiences helps them to re-frame childhood trauma. Sometimes how we tell our children's stories has more impact on them than the story itself. Why? Hearing us recount stories shapes children's lives because they retell that version over and over in their minds until it solidifies into a memory. Eventually, they identify with these aspects of self. So if you portray them as hopeless, that's what they believe about themselves. By celebrating their resilience instead of their trauma, we move them from a powerless victim to an empowered creator. By telling their story from a positive perspective—we highlight their optimism, resourcefulness, and a strength-based mentality. We show our children that just because an event seemed negative, it does not have to be negative. Instead, it can be an opportunity to develop problem-solving skills."

Chris said, "If you want to, this week, you could go into your heart and call up your Dad, in spirit, and tell him how you felt when he yelled at your Mum. Maybe if he knew how his behavior made you feel, he might have something to say to you."

Saturday, July 11th

The next day I wrote

> Firstly, Dad, as one of my closest karmic teachers, I want to thank you for agreeing to a soul contract to advance me on my path so that I could bring my gift to humanity. You taught me the skills I needed by:
> 1. Being an overachiever with extrinsic goals around money and status invertedly motivated me to pursue different values. I developed intrinsic values like becoming self-realized to serve others for the greater good. Through contrast, you taught me not to prioritize material gain.
> 2. Showing me how conditional love feels taught me to love my children unconditionally.
> 3. Being tough on me taught me how to forgive. I had to accept that you were doing the best you could with what you knew. You wanted the best for me and believed that being a successful swimmer would make me happy.
> 4. Yelling at Mum made me feel unloved. I had to overcome this false self to discover my true SELF. As a result, I can guide others to love themselves.
> 5. Having dedication, perseverance, and reliability

showed me the traits I needed to succeed at school/university, work, relationships, parenting, and as a writer!

I wanted to take the time today, Dad, to let you know that I appreciate you. You could have reincarnated to a stress-free life and lived a ripe old age, but instead, you chose to come back to a stressful life and early-onset cancer. Even though I would give anything to have you in my life, I know Janet, Judy, Bill, Patrick, and I would not be the people we are today without the lessons you gave us. So I know you dying young was perfect for me on some level, but it still hurts!

I went into meditation and intuited unity consciousness. As soon as I focused on Dad, I experienced Dad as an individuated consciousness which took me from non-duality to duality. Then I returned to the oneness again. At that moment I knew that asking Dad if he wanted to converse with me was unnecessary because there was no separate Dad to ask. When I viewed my childhood trauma from the perspective of SELF, the trauma did not exist. I remembered that my painful memories have no inherent existence and only arise dependent on causes and conditions. This allowed me to know mySELF beyond the self that had that life experience. It let me know my potential—as SELF there is only light, no reflections or shadows. So, I am whole even with my childhood trauma. I am SELF manifested in physical form. Going back over past pain and trying to purify puts me in the feeling state of separation. I have evolved beyond this into resting in the now where past pains do not exist. When I am here, being SELF, I feel nothing but acceptance for everything Dad did. Why? Because each individuated consciousness that causes me trauma is still part of me.

This month's Clan Mother is Loves All Things, and after years of journeying with her, I finally understand her message, *To love all things is to love every reflection of who and what you are.* If I am experiencing a reflection/shadow (memory, future fear, present person/situation) that is misaligned to SELF, I know I created it as an opportunity to choose how I respond to it. So we may as well love it to create love instead of more of what's being reflected.

33

BREAKING SOCIETY'S MOLDS SELF

49 years old

Friday, July 31st

AT OUR REGULAR Friday morning meditation Zoom call with Karen's International group, Amana, an Indian woman, shared her anguish. She had disappointed her mother by standing in her power, moving out before she was married, and starting a progressive career as a female embodiment therapist. I had quietly wished I could understand her plight well enough to write a chapter in my book about the challenges people face when choosing to speak their truth and go against their culture. Having spent 12 months traveling through India/Nepal, I knew her story vicariously. I had met women like Amana who desperately wanted to follow their hearts but were shamed by their community. They had family members voice their disgust for them for trying to do things differently. They did not want an arranged marriage, they wanted a love marriage, but their parents could not accept this. As a result, they kicked them out of the house, turned their backs on them, and sometimes cut them off completely. These brave women were shunned and rejected. These heavy emotions were challenging to navigate without any support, and it was often easier to give up and go back to conforming.

Well, as soon as I asked for the insight, it appeared. I got an opportunity to go through a similar experience to authentically write about it.

That afternoon, after only three months of sharing my spiritual writing on Instagram, I decided to be brave and go broader. I posted on Facebook, inviting people to check out my Instagram account. At 10:00 pm, I realized a colleague of mine from the primary school shared the post with parents.

My *caring what people think* false self grabbed hold of my neck, strangling me.

My heart contracted as my body was overwhelmed with fear sensations.

My troubled, tortuous, tormenting mind kicked in.

- I imagined parents analyzing my shares and misinterpreting them.
- I worried they would go to my principal and say they did not want me to teach their children because I was weird.
- I was scared of getting into trouble.
- I imagined people looking at me differently.
- I was convinced I was too much.
- I felt terrified of being judged and talked about.
- I yearned to go back into my shell and become more mainstream and inconspicuous.
- I considered calling the teacher and asking her to remove her post.

- I longed to curl up and hide with the words *What have I done* on my muttering lips.
- I was uncomfortably vulnerable now that my professional world collided with my personal world.

I rang my mum to hear her voice, but I did not tell her I was upset. I did not want to concern her. Instead, I applied my Advanced S Method.

S— Stop. *Ctrl Alt Delete. Whatever I am thinking, saying, or doing feels out of alignment with SELF.*

This technique did not curb my thoughts rooted in anticipation of an unknown future moment. I knew my irrational thoughts were unproductive, but my mind raced. I felt myself thinking about the post's ramifications over and over again. I felt sick.

I needed to apply the Standard STORY method.

S—Stop you're out of alignment. *Ctrl Alt Delete.*

T—Triggered that *Caring what people think* false self.

O—Own it. You're the only one who can shift the misalignment.

R—Realign. Take action. *I'll do one of Karen's recorded meditations.*

Y—You are here embodying SELF.

———

AT 7:00 A.M., I had my last scheduled Heart Imagery Zoom meeting with Chris Cheung. As I waited for our Zoom appointment I read Chris's Kind Trainer website:

- Chris teaches Heart Imagery that can be used to balance our mental, emotional, and physical bodies to harmonize energy.
- Chris teaches techniques to effectively break emotional

- loops, shame, Inner Critics, Self Saboteurs, overthinking minds, and even physical dis-ease.
- Chris teaches the tools to connect the heart with the inner world to reach enlightenment thus, freeing the mind from its slavery to the ego.

It is incredible how divine timing works. I felt imprisoned by my ego, cornered by my crazy Inner Critic, and pursued by my psycho Self Saboteur, and I just happened to have an appointment with an expert in the field! Coincidence? I do not think so! But, wait for it, there is more. We had tried to do this final session a week earlier, but Hurricane Douglas had other plans and ripped up Wi-Fi cables in Hawaii, where Chris lives. It was clear to me that I created the whole thing because I learn best from direct experience. Incredibly I brought a direct experience to our last session, making his teachings palpable, relatable, and potent.

I first said to Chris, "During the last nine hours, I've experienced what it feels like to come out of the spiritual closet. Why does choosing to stand in my truth and be my authentic self feel so scary?"

Chris explained that we are shown molds from childhood that our society expects us to fit into. We conform to these molds because they make us feel safe and accepted. We believe that if we break away from other people's expectations, we will disappoint those attached to them. We learn which molds go with which groups, and we carefully adhere to the list of required characteristics depending on which group we find ourselves. Whether the group is for sport, work, school, or hobbies. We talk about different things in each situation. We play different roles at different times. We become experts in compartmentalizing our lives so that there is no crossover or opportunity to be exposed.

Chris's explanation resonated with me. I shared, "That is true for me. Only the people in my meditation groups knew the real me until I posted on social media after finishing my BOMs course.

Everyone else was seeing an actor wearing a metaphorical mask and playing a role. I played the good girl, who felt secure, and avoided risks by being a conservative conformer who blended in and nodded to common opinions. I was a skillful Gemini, the best in the Zodiac business at adapting to whichever group I found myself in. I was an accomplished master at wearing the required mask at the required time. Whenever I wear a mask and identify with false selves, I deny my sovereignty and stay trapped in the closet. Last night, I experienced how painful it feels coming out of the closet about my spiritual beliefs. It gave me empathy and understanding for others trying to come out about their sexual preferences, how they identify, making choices that go against their community's traditions, or having passions that do not align with their parents' mold. I realized that the tighter the mold, the more challenging the coming out is. For example, in Amana's case, the Indian cultural/religious mold was practically tattooed on her at birth, so I appreciate her anguish. I felt immense compassion for myself as I removed redundant masks to reveal my true SELF to myself and, ultimately, to everyone. Commitment and focus are required to change our ingrained, habitual thoughts that feel automatic. Courage is needed to step up and show the world our vulnerabilities. I believe, however, that if everyone does this, society will accept these vulnerabilities as normal and natural. Therefore, people everywhere will feel respected to speak their truth to discover their unique strengths, passions, and talents. This is the level of teamwork required on Earth now. People need to rip off their masks, reveal their radiant SELF, be comfortable in their skin, and trust and follow their internal guidance system. This raises our frequency and awakens human consciousness."

Chris and I discussed how my Inner Critic and Self Saboteur reared their ugly heads when I tried to remove my *good girl* mask. As soon as I chose to be authentic, they attacked me. Chris felt that the best way to deal with my Inner Critic and Self Saboteur was to learn a powerful Heart Imagery technique that he had adapted and made his own.

Chris led me through a guided meditation where I connected to my heart space, and he took me to a beautiful place where I became a bubble of love with Mother Earth and Father Sun. He said, "No matter what you do and what you share and who you are, Mother Earth and Father Sun love you always. And just feel these words, *I am safe, I am safe.* Feel how Mother Earth and Father Sun keep you safe always. Feel that flowing through your body. Then imagine and feel *I am wanted, so wanted, I am appreciated, I am needed.* Feel Mother Earth and Father Sun expressing that towards you, how much they need you. *I am not defective. I am perfect the way I am, exactly the way I am.* Just feel how Mother Earth and Father Sun love you exactly the way you are. Feeling all three of those elements (yourself, Mother Earth, and Father Sun) as a fiery bubble of love blasting through fear, that made you feel unsafe; shame, that made you feel defective; disgust, that made you feel unwanted. Just feeling that natural, beautiful, unlimited, unconditional love from the Earth and the sun. Imagine this bubble burning away not just negativity coming towards you but also negativity coming from within you. Etched in via a mold, a template, that your family, school, and society etched into your body and just feel how this love energy from Mother Earth and Father Sun can burn through this mold like a bushfire. Setting on fire the mold that powers thoughts that make you feel that if you share your truth you won't be safe, you will be defective and unwanted by your peers, the school, the parents, and by the hierarchical system. Feel into this love energy as it burns away these inner voices and know that should these voices come up in the future, you can burn them away.

The energy is fiery; it has boundaries, it can say NO, it can say STOP! *I am my truth, and I choose to express my truth and share it. Accept me or not, that is not my decision, and that is ok because the only person who matters in accepting who I am is me.* Imagine hugging yourself and saying to your inner child; *I love myself exactly as I am, I am safe, I love you, I see you, I hear you.* Feel this embrace of yourself flowing through your body and feel this love co-mingling with the love of Mother Earth and Father Sun and how they embrace you no matter what. Noticing how the voices of your past, inside of you, have perhaps stopped you from sharing all of your truth before this moment, perhaps working quite slyly in the background like undercover agents. The Inner Critic and Self Saboteur who like to give excuses for not sharing your truth or perhaps enjoy delaying expressing who you are, perhaps are a bit deceptive towards you by saying, *Oh no, I will share myself some other time.* Now feel the love of Mother Earth and Father Sun burning these residual Inner Critics and Self Saboteurs away and burning the mold away like a bushfire. Burning any procrastination vibes, delay vibes, and burning perfection vibes, needs for acceptance vibes.

Now imagine that embrace again and say, *I am safe, I am wanted, I am loved, I am perfect the way I am. The only person I need to be embraced by is myself.* Feel that trinity of the love of yourself, Mother Earth, and Father Sun mingling together in this bubble of love around you and knowing that if these thoughts come in the future, if comments are made, it is not your stuff. Comments made by other people are their stuff to deal with. If comments come from inside of you, know that those comments were powered by projections from others, society, school, family, and parents. The true you has none of these limitations; it is all other people's stuff. So allow them to be burnt by the power of the love of yourself, Mother Earth, and Father Sun. And as you watch the residual mold that limited you from expressing the true you, the authentic, honest, raw, beautiful you turning to ash, imagine yourself rising like a phoenix, a golden phoenix from the ashes, reborn, no limitations, true expression of who you are, unhindered, untethered, unattached. Now beginning to spread your wings, coughing out any residual dust, shaking off any dust from your wings. Knowing that you are free to do whatever you choose to do. Anything or anyone that stands in your way can be burnt away by the love of yourself, Mother Earth, and the Father Sun. Now just seeing yourself flying off to the horizon."

When I opened my eyes, I felt as free as a bird. I told Chris, "Thank you so much. I feel empowered to stand up to my Inner Critic and Self Saboteur. I imagine them in dark sunglasses and overcoats, calling themselves Special Agents, lurking in the shadows, waiting for an opportunity to pull me back into a mold. Knowing they are working for the ego motivates me to stop listening to them. I'm not going to take any more shit from them; instead, I'll silence them with my love blaster!"

34

LEAVING MY JOB SELF

49 years old

I WAS HUMMING ALONG WELL at work because Australian schools adhered to COVID-19 restrictions, so organized sport was banned. Therefore, I only had to teach my classes. This meant I could easily juggle work and writing. To do this, I got up at 4:50 am every morning and wrote for two hours before school.

Soon though, that luxury came to a grinding halt. As restrictions lifted, my workload as a Personal Development/Health/Physical Education (PDHPE) teacher returned to normal. I needed to stay back after work to organize sports. As a result, I prioritized work over writing and writing over exercise. I tried justifying this decision by telling myself I could exercise once I finished the book. But I felt terrible. I missed my daily walks and began feeling out of balance. Soon work commitments got so demanding that I could not physically get to my desk, let alone be in the vibrational headspace to create content. All my energy went to my job and caring for my children and Stitty. I began to feel worse than terrible! My body became stiff, and my neck hurt.

Stitty and I talked about writing the book after Matilda finished high school in six years. However, after answering the call to write during my BOMs course, I felt incapable of waiting one minute, let alone six years! Whenever I saw, heard, or experienced an author doing what they loved doing, like Brene Brown or Elizabeth Gilbert, my whole body would light up. *I could be doing that. So why aren't I doing that? Why aren't I following my dream? What's stopping me?*

The answer was always the same *FEAR!*

Then one day I thought *Doing this job is out of alignment with my higher purpose. It is time to start making a bigger difference in the world.*

This calling tugged harder and harder, and my evolved self's nagging voice got louder and louder *There is no way you can do your job and write this book.* Soon, it got too loud to ignore. *Something will have to give, and it will not be the thing that lights me up.*

Then I got smacked in the face with a wake-up call.

Friday, October 30th

I had a massage that wiped me out. I went so deep that I could barely lift my head at the end. I said to Kathy, "I do not know what happened, but I just shifted some heavy stuff."

Saturday, October 31st

I woke up with a sore throat and a shocking cold.

LIVING EVOLVED

. . .

Sunday, November 1st

FULL MOON CLAN MOTHERS. Two Crows and I had been journeying with *The 13 Original Clan Mothers* by Jamie Sams for seven years as we were in our fourth cycle. As we read about the November Clan Mother, Walks Tall Woman, so much resonated with my predicament, *...actions always speak louder than words and...when we are living examples of our philosophies, we are walking our personal truths. When we walk with truth, there is no need to fear what others think of us... The eleventh Clan Mother is the Guardian of Leadership and the Keeper of New Pathways. She shows us the value of leading through example, being our personal best, exploring all our options, and the importance of innovation. If there is a more appropriate or more efficient way to do something, Walks Tall Woman will apply those new ideas to her Earth Walk to see if the new way will assist her in Walking Her Truth.*

I felt it was time to apply some new ideas to assist me in walking my truth. During the drumming session, I visualized Walks Tall Woman bursting into the circle on a mission. I had a feeling she was not going to let me get away with staying in my job. Instead, I sensed she wanted immediate action. I heard her say, *It is time to start walking the talk, Kitty.* After the meditation, I went home and talked to Stitty about leaving my job to follow my dream.

As I told Stitty my plan, I realized that I had been institutionalized my whole life. Being in a system with a teacher/supervisor, a principal/dean, and an organizing body required me to be accountable and compliant 24/7. It occurred to me that I had spent 47 years in various types of educational institutions: the Montessori School, Paris, a private co-educational school in Indianapolis, Indiana, USA;

private all-girls schools in Sydney (as a student and as a teacher), the University of Sydney as an undergraduate student and as a lecture, WA government school teacher, U.K. government school teacher, Nepal not-for-profit school teacher, Forbes government and Catholic school teacher.

I have always had a desire to serve humanity. Dad sensed this and recommended the teaching profession because it is a service-to-others career. But now, I knew I was ready to reach a larger community. I knew I could still utilize my passion for teaching in a new way. These institutions felt like the old way, and I was here to create the new way.

Stitty agreed with my observations but questioned the timing. He is an incredible provider who is constantly planning our retirement phase, so he suggested I wait and write the book when I was older, "I feel like you should work while you can and then write while you can't." I told him I could still do substitute teaching, which is less demanding. He trusted me and said he would give me his support if I wanted to leave my job.

I decided to leave at the end of the year and planned to tell the principal after my whole-school presentation on Tuesday afternoon. But, as the time drew closer, my mind filled with fears which triggered my *lack* false self. My thoughts went on loop: *What if I can't make enough money? What if we miss my steady income? What if I am lonely without the staff's camaraderie?* Then the unworthy self turned up *What if no one wants to read my book? What if this is a luxury we can't afford?* Then my *guilty* self crept in *If I leave, I'm letting the team down. No one can do my job with as much enthusiasm and dedication as me.*

Monday, November 2nd

I WOKE with an uncharacteristically heavy menstrual flow to add to my sore throat and shocking cold. I had not had a cold like this for 12 years, so I knew it was a sign showing me I was fearful of following my calling. I needed to stay home and recuperate, but I pushed myself to go to work to finish planning my presentation. Then, unfortunately, I ignored my symptoms as they worsened during the day and burned the candle at both ends by working late.

At 6:00 pm, I walked out of the staff room and fell over a large orange cone, left in the middle of the path by a tradesman. I landed flat on my face, sending the 40 workshop participants' kits (all perfectly ordered in plastic sleeves) fanning across the concrete.

Boom! Wake up, Kitty! Accidents and sickness show me when I am out of alignment.

My knees ached, my elbow dripped, and my legs shook. Despite the intense pain, I tried to get up but fell again. By now, two tradesmen were lifting me like a prima ballerina.

"Miss, oh no! You're bleeding, Miss. Please sit down." said one as the other scooped up my intellectual property along with my pride.

"I'm fine, really. It's ok. I'm fine," my voice wobbled as I brushed at the rocks embedded in my knee.

I flashed an *It's ok, don't feel bad* smile, but my eyes lacked luster. I was tearing up with disappointment.

I headed for the toilet—to be alone.

I sat down *I haven't stopped all day.*

Then to add salt to the wound *Shit, I leaked blood all through my pants.*

During my presentation the next afternoon, I forgot about my sickness as soon as I started drumming and talking about our student's well-being. Afterward, I planned to tell the principal I was leaving, but she rushed off to another meeting. So I went to the supermarket, where I felt incredibly depleted and physically shattered. I was also picking up on the world's uneasiness associated with the US Presidential election that day. Instinctively I knew I needed to get into nature to recalibrate with Mother Earth, but I thought I was too tired. As a result, my cold was exacerbated, my nervous system heightened, my blood pressure elevated, my heart raced, and my muscles ached. This was dis-ease at its finest, and it was my body. *How had I let this happen?* It was so far removed from my vibrant state during lockdown that it was almost comical.

Even though I was still suffering the next day, I went to work because I had a Regional Sports Coordinators meeting on Zoom after school, and I wanted to tell the principal I was leaving in person. So when the coordinator's meeting finished, I dragged myself to the principal's office. The door swung open to reveal the whole executive team but no principal.

"Sorry Katie, she's off-site at another meeting," announced an Assistant Principal. "Is there anything we can help you with?"

My mouth dropped, and they stared at me, "No, it's ok. I'm fine. I'll catch up with her tomorrow."

I limped out the school gates at 6:00 pm for the third day. *What am I doing?*

The following morning I had a throbbing headache and pain across my back. My body shouted *Enough is enough. You have to stop. What do you want, a louder wake-up call than falling on your face?*

I called in sick and then meditated. Afterward, I reread the month's 13 Original Clan Mothers. *The eleventh Clan Mother is also the Mother of Perseverance and Stamina, who teaches us the value of health. The needs of our physical bodies and the use of exercise to make them strong are part of her teaching... A healthy mind will support the body's health. A mind riddled with half-truths and negativity can thwart the body to the point where disease is created. Walks Tall Woman shows us how to honor the body's needs by balancing physical activity, proper attitudes, good eating and sleeping habits, and hygiene... Walks Tall Woman also teaches us that we can persevere, meeting our goals when the body is healthy. Stamina comes from treating the body with care... Walks Tall shows us to keep our eyes on the goal, our feet on the path, and the truth in our hearts, never waiting for another to do it for us. Leading through example by being personally responsible in thought, action, and deed is the way we find the Medicine of Walking Our Talk. Our challenges are to be willing to drop our fears of taking action and to balance our work activities with rest, relaxation, and retreat.*

Have I looked after my health? No!

Have I done physical exercise? No!

Have I had good nutrition? No!

Have I had enough sleep? No!

Have I had good hygiene? No way - I was too busy to change my tampon.

Have I balanced my work activities with rest, relaxation, and retreat? No!

Have my thoughts been healthy? No!

Have I treated my body with care? No!

Have I kept my eyes on my goal? Unfortunately, no—I have not written the book in days.

Have I kept my feet on the path? Hell no, I smashed my face on the path instead!

Have I led through example by being personally responsible in thought, action, and deed? No!

THEN I READ the next section of the chapter that tells the story of Walks Tall Woman's journey as a two-legged, learning the necessary lessons to eventually guide the sisterhood from the star realm. *Mountain Lion said, "You have been so busy doing, you have forgotten to take the time you need to reflect and regroup your thoughts, dreams,* and energy... In the present world of time, women have come to take the role of nurturing others. A balance must be found... For females, that space is the womb. As Mothers of Creative Force, women must understand their role of nurturing the seeds of all of tomorrow's dreams for the Planetary Family as well as birthing new generations of children. To accomplish this task, every woman must commit to herself to take the time she needs to retreat during her menstrual flow, when her womb is open to the light. This special Moontime is when the Earth Mother feeds all women if they are willing to spend three suns and Sleeps during their flows in total silence, becoming the receptive vessels of love created by the Great Mystery. During the other days of their flows, they can be with their sisters, sharing experiences, handicrafts, and inner thoughts. During their Moontimes, women have the power to claim any available energy in their midst because their wombs are open to receiving. This is one new Tradition that you can start for the Human Tribe that will also serve you in discovering your own humanness.

Donkey said, "You have set an example that would break the back of any beast of burden... There is great inner strength to be found in showing mercy to yourself and in allowing yourself to be an example to other women by showing them that all humans are worthy of rest and pleasure. The example you set through making time for your needs will liberate you and every other woman who looks to you for guidance. The excuse that you do not have the time or the space to be nurtured will harm more people than yourself, giving the Shadow the upper hand."

Quetzal (bird) carries the medicine of the totally free, uninhibited spirit who is willing to express all aspects of the Self. If caught and caged Quetzal dies.

I KNEW in my heart that I could not express all aspects of SELF in a free and uninhibited way while doing my job. I had slipped into an old program where I played the role of a perfect, overachieving, good girl.

I had to call my principal.

When I told her I was leaving my job at the end of the school year (December), she exclaimed, "We haven't burnt you out, have we?"

I replied, "It's not the job. It's me, I do everything 100%, and I just need to focus my attention on the book now."

As soon as I spoke to her, a huge weight was lifted from my shoulders. I remembered a line in *Dancing The Dream* by Jamie Sams, *...everytime we eliminate a fixed idea that was created by hidden fear or judgments, we break through a ridge of stuck energy... When we go beyond any self-imposed limitation, we experience a profound sense of relief, accompanied by a flood of new life force... [breaking a] type of dam that disallowed potential growth.*

FIVE YEARS AGO, *I birthed the vision to leave my job to write the book, and today I manifested it.*

I rolled over with a big grin and slept for four hours, dreaming my way into a new chapter of my evolution.

35

ACCESSING MULTIDIMENSIONAL ME SELF

49 years old

"IF YOU WANT to find the secrets of the universe, think in terms of energy, frequency and vibration." Nikola Tesla

Sunday, January 3rd

We were staying at Stitty's family beach house on the South Coast of NSW. For days, I wrote about and explored myself as a multidimensional being. I contacted my space babies (Chapter 8) and asked them to connect with me. Every day I thought about ways to access my 12-Dimensional (12-D) self, the aspect of SELF that exists as light on a higher timeline.

Tom, one of Karen's BOMs students, offered to run a Healy Frequency device on me. I prepared for the Healy session by listening to solfeggio frequencies on YouTube (396hz – 417hz –

528hz – 639hz – 741hz – 852hz) used by Gregorian monks in their meditation chants in the 11th Century. Each frequency correlates with a chakra, so I chose 528 Hz, which is the frequency of the heart. I had researched the positive effects sound can have on the body and knew that these meditations would activate healing and balance my system.

Tom arrived, and I registered my details in the Healy program. I put my finger on the sensor and allowed the Healy device to measure the frequency of energy wavelengths coming from my body. The machine suggested some programs to provide a bioresonance type remedy to balance out the frequencies detected. The Healy fits in the palm of your hand. It acts as a radioreceptor, and its hardware is basic and inexpensive. The $4000 US price tag is the exchange for 100 years of scientific progression researched by a German team headed up by Markus Schmieke (physicist, author, and founder of the Institute for Applied Consciousness Research). The group initially developed the TimeWaver technology in 2007 when they put Information Field technology into practical application for the first time (I used a similar machine in Dr. Chan's office after I was diagnosed with Hashimotos). Healy is a U.S. Food and Drug Administration-approved medical device that heals on a cellular, bio-energetic, and quantum energetic level. It uses Individualized Microcurrent Frequencies to harmonize your Bioenergetic Field. The microcurrents transmitted through the Healy help boost ATP (Adenosine Triphosphate) production in the cells (mitochondria) and balance cell membrane voltage. Put simply, cells have more energy to carry out everything they do.

According to Albert Einstein, all matter is energy made up of light and sound that has slowed down enough for the senses to perceive it. This means the body is made up of energy too. So to cure our body, we need to do a combination of emotional, physical, and energy work. It is challenging to fathom our bodies as energy because we can not see it with the naked eye. We know from Einstein and

Tesla that matter equals energy, but we have grown up believing that a chair, for example, is solid matter when in fact it is made up of atoms vibrating at a low enough frequency to be perceivable by the eye. If those same atoms somehow moved into an excited state and began vibrating at a higher frequency, then we would no longer be able to perceive the chair. Therefore, understanding quantum physics requires us to re-train our brains or take a leap of faith! To illustrate the wide range of frequencies available to us throughout the universe, we can look at a dog that hears sound waves that we can not detect. Just because we can not hear those sound waves does not mean they do not exist. We can also look at a snake that can detect infrared light frequencies not seen by human eyes. Again, just because we can not see this light does not mean it does not exist. So to understand how bioresonance healing works, we have to let go of our limiting beliefs. Ancient philosophers and medicine people have always studied chakras/energy centers and meridians, so the Healy machine is East meets West technology.

 I looked at the list of programs the device identified as beneficial for me and chose one that resonated. It was the physical and psyche program frequency, targeting the thyroid, nervous system, and stomach. I lay down on the bed and selected the 5 minutes and 59 second program. I felt the energy moving throughout my body. While the program ran, a colossal thunderstorm raged. The gauzed-in porch allowed torrential rain and gusting wind to rip across my body. It was the middle of summer, so I was not cold. The sound of the pelting rain on the tin roof was deafening and sounded like a frequency cleanse, cleaning and purifying my physical body. It felt like I became the molecules of energy in my environment: the room, the backyard, the entire planet, near and far galaxies, and the whole universe. My left kidney twitched repeatedly, and my hands went totally numb. I continued meditating for 27 minutes, long after the Healy machine switched off. Tom said while I was meditating, he invited me into an aspect of himself that he had only recently discovered. In that space, he intuited blockages which he released. He said he knew before he arrived that he would be working with my energy centers through accessing this higher dimensional version of himself.

Next I chose a program to strengthen my connection to my truth because I had been doubting myself. I wanted to clear my *too out there/too much* false self.

Tom said he would run a mental balance program on me. Again I chose 5 minutes and 59 seconds, but we meditated together for around 45 minutes. Immediately the frequency felt different from the physical and psyche program. It felt mental instead of physical. All the sensations centered around my head. I could feel my third eye activating, and I got a tickle in my throat, which I knew was my throat chakra opening. I had the most unbelievable amount of pressure over the bridge of my nose. I had never felt this way before. It was the most bizarre sensation imaginable because my skull and head felt transformed into a new shape. I felt like I became an insect *Am I shapeshifting?* Somehow I knew I was accessing an aspect of myself on a parallel timeline, the 12-D version of mySELF. I felt utterly nauseous because the frequency was so much higher than anything I had ever experienced. It occurred to me that if I were a 12-D being, I would have direct access to SELF. I smiled as a wave of expansive bliss washed over my entire body. It was euphoric, and I was overcome with ecstasy. I felt whole, limitless, unconditional love, expansive, omnipresent, peaceful, and all-encompassing. It felt like I imagined heaven when I was a child, and it reminded me of my rebirth in Kalgoorlie when my body dissolved into pure light (just a head on the bed).

This feels as blissful as my rebirth in Kalgoorlie just before the other-dimensional beings examined my DNA, but this time the other-dimensional being is not separate from me. It is me; I am a 12-D light being.

My smile was so enormous *I wonder if I am physically smiling or just smiling on the inside?* So I smiled harder and was assured that my teeth were exposed, very exposed. The whole time I had severe pressure over the bridge of my nose, it felt surreal.

Then the rain stopped, and stillness returned to the room. The kookaburras began laughing with joy. Other birds joined the chorus. At this point, I felt myself starting to contract back through dimensions. It was very distinctive and graduated. I could feel every step in the contraction as if I was a balloon having air let out in stages. I physically and energetically experienced each shift from 12-D, to 11-D, to 10-D, to 9-D, to 8-D, to 7-D, to 6-D, to 5-D, to 4-D, and finally, the exact moment I came into my physical body lying on the bed in the gauzed-in porch.

I wiggled my fingers and toes, and Tom said, "Are you OK? Are you back now?"

I replied, "That was insane. Were you experiencing what I was experiencing?"

Tom explained that he did not know exactly what I was experiencing, but he was there as a guide because some people find exploring other states of consciousness overwhelming.

I laughed, "I am not one of those people; I love it. It's been decades since I experienced that blissful state. Last time, in Kalgoorlie, the other-dimensional beings felt separate to me but this time they were me. Originally, I thought they visited me, but now I know they are aspects of me/individuations of SELF/expressions of unity consciousness. This is what being multidimensional means—we have access to ourSELF on all dimensions, realms, and timelines. Which is why I experienced mySELF as a 12-D light being.

Tom asked, "Tell me about the 12-D aspect of yourself?"

I replied, "12-D is the highest known dimension where everything in the universe merges into one. It's the zero point where all possible timelines that have ever existed coalesce into a single point. This is universal consciousness. When I experience my 12-D self, everything that has ever existed is known to me at a profound level beyond language. At that moment, I know God is not something outside of us; we are God.

While we are in our body, SELF is expressing itSELF separately from the whole which causes us suffering because we innately know we are one consciousness. This suffering motivates us to find ways to be whole. Our humanness will always feel separate, but the more we intuit the whole, the more we feel at home. Wow, Tom, I have just physically experienced the Buddha's first Noble Truth: there is suffering in life and it is to be understood. I have not studied enough Buddhism to know if the Buddha had a similar experience to mine, but when I accessed myself as pure light without a physical vehicle I had an awakening: we suffer because we are separate from SELF."

After the session, we talked for hours about our shared experiences navigating the unseen world. We discussed the Healy machine's incredible potential. We imagined it supporting mainstream health practitioners, enabling patients to heal themselves using frequency and freeing them from dependence on pharmaceutical medications and invasive practices such as diagnostic procedures and surgeries. We also acknowledged that humans do not need a Healy machine to do these things. If it helps, then great, but the truth is we can tap into these frequencies any time we choose and heal our bodies. We just need to believe it is possible.

That night, when Stitty and I made love, I deliberately dropped into the feeling state of my body as energy. Just before I orgasmed. I said to myself *I am the frequency of orgasm. Boom.* That was it, so simple. Mastering our body's frequency is living evolved on our highest timeline. Living this way raises the planet's vibration and puts Earth on its highest timeline.

Sunday, January 17th

I JOINED Two Crows and the other women's circle sisters via Zoom to welcome in the 13th and final Clan Mother, *Becomes Her Vision* (a combination of all the clan mothers). I met her at 43, 45, 47 and 49 years of age. This time she felt different because I was finally able to embody her. It was as if I had become the butterfly ...*who signaled the final stages of the Clan Mother's Rite of Passage.* I felt transformed physically, emotionally, and spiritually. I felt luminous and pure with an all-pervading gentleness, unrecognizable compared to the woman lying on the laundry floor having a screaming temper tantrum seven years earlier. *Was it an easy journey?* No, it was very confronting and required one hundred percent commitment and determination. But what choice did I have? It was too painful to remain out of alignment with my truth/true SELF.

The Clan Mothers taught me how to live on Earth, in the traditional way instead of the modern way. Living in Forbes in the bend of the Galari (Lachlan River) I formed a connection with Mother Earth. She taught me through the clan mothers how to enter the stillness to discover how to dance with nature to celebrate Earth's sacredness. By experiencing Spirit in all things, I realized we are all one family. I had passed through the initiations by practicing and mastering each Clan Mother's advice. I had been vulnerable, humble, and willing to try anything.

This time I cried when I read the end of *Becomes Her Vision*'s chapter because I understood, on a cellular level, how interconnected we all are. Everyone is a reflection of me. The Native American Whirling Rainbow Dream for world peace and spiritual illumination, referred to by *Becomes Her Vision,* is prophesied by many Indigenous cultures. For eons, our ancestors have had a vision of oneness–just like mine.

Becomes Her Vision's song of wholeness reminds us: "You are—the moment you decide to BE."'

Finally, I understood this profound quote. BE what we already are. When we identify with our expanded true SELF, we honor and respect everyone and everything to bring balance to the present moment. We embody SELF with a vibration of unconditional love and dwell in true reality: free from limiting beliefs, stories, or constructs. From this love frequency, we spontaneously and naturally accept the now as perfect and BE whatever is required at that moment, tapping into infinite intelligence and universal creative power.

This is creation.

Indigenous people were abundant and Earth sustaining before the white man changed creation and went against natural law. It is time to return to natural law and reclaim creation. The future depends on it.

36

ACKNOWLEDGING I'M FREQUENCY SELF

49 years old

Wednesday, 22nd April

I WAS BACK at the Stitt family's South Coast beach house giving myself eight days of solitude to write the book. I read over my Accessing multidimensional me self chapter about my Healy experience. Who should turn up? My ego's Special Agent Inner Critic *Kitty, you can't include this story in the book.* Then Special Agent Self Saboteur, chimed in *If you even mention other-dimensional beings, you'll lose half your readers.* So I applied the STORY Method, and when I got to **R**—Realign. Take action, I chose to reset my internal state of being by writing a more mainstream, 3-Dimensional (3-D) type story about New York City.

Matching New York City vibes self

28 AND 46

I can not write a book about frequency without a story about New York City. The first time I visited, I was 28 years old. It was September. Fresh from Kalgoorlie and accompanied by my younger brother Patrick. I had never been in a place so vibrant, I had met my energetically matched city. The atmosphere was electrifying. I felt my vibration mirrored everywhere I went. The sidewalks, the buildings, the bars, the people, everything hummed. A day in Central Park, people watching, was better than any movie. For example, a man zigzagging on rollerblades narrowly avoiding cone after cone in mesmerizing fashion. A funky roller skater joined him with a ghetto blaster blaring disco music. At the Tavern on the Green, friendly and inquisitive staff shared their unique NYC back story. We lay in the sun on the Great Lawn and watched local personalities and tourists going about their day. In a city of 7.4 million dominated by urban high rises, lawn is scarce, so the park is everyone's backyard. I grew up sunbaking on Bondi Beach, so I had the subtle art of squeezing in between fellow park-goers and the odd dog to secure a small piece of lawn. I loved the feeling of community brought about by proximity. No one spoke, but there was a feeling of camaraderie. A silent nod *How incredible is this scene? How cool is Manhattan?*

Patrick's friend Josh and his then-girlfriend/now wife, Patricia, met us at their apartment. We were buzzing. We got changed (black or charcoal, of course), knocked back a martini, and headed to the Downtown Manhattan Heliport at Pier 6 East River. Not sure why but there was no safety briefing; we just walked straight onto the helipad and into the chartered sunset chopper. I was lucky enough to ride up front. I grinned like a Cheshire cat. It was the most exhilarating ride imaginable. We flew around the Statue of Liberty, down

Wall Street, and looped the Twin Towers. After about 15 minutes, the sun went down, and the lights came on. Every color imaginable twinkled and reflected off the Atlantic Ocean and surrounding rivers. The city pumped to the beat of the helicopter's rotors' "chuff, chuff, chuff, chuff." The pilot sounded like Tom Cruise and gave me a breathy commentary through my headphones!

When we landed, we were on a high. I rang Stitty back in Kalgoorlie, but he did not answer. So, I rang Nikki, who did answer. She still tells the story of my exuberance that day. She could feel me rushing through the phone. It was apparent I had fallen in love with NYC.

Afterward, we went to a hip restaurant called Mercer Kitchen in SoHo and ran into someone we knew from Sydney. I asked him to recommend a club. He replied, "They're opening a new nightclub *Exit* at 610 West 56th Street; you could try and get in."

When the four of us emerged from the restaurant, a random limousine pulled up, and we hopped in. I did not think the night could get any better. But it did. The limo driver dropped us around the side at *Exit*'s exit. As I got out of the limo, I saw a security guard and walked straight up to him with an extended hand, "Hi, I'm Kitty from Australia."

"Well, hello, Miss Kitty from Australia. I'm Leon." His sentence went down in pitch in typical New York City fashion. His enormous palms gently engulfed my tiny hand as we shared warm smiles, and lingering eye contact before I went on my way. As we rounded the quiet corner, we were hit with noise, flashing paparazzi cameras, a red carpet, and hundreds of people lined up in an orderly line that snaked backward. Unbeknownst to us, New York City celebrities Michael Douglas, Jennifer Lopez, and Puff Daddy had just walked in.

I have no idea what came over me, but I walked straight up to a security guard at the front of the long line and assertively said, "Hi, I'm Kitty, I'm a friend of Leon's, he told us to go straight through."

My whole body exuded the city's personality; my mood was New York City at its finest, my frequency was as high as the Empire State Building, and I was lit up like Times Square. Nothing was stopping me.

Click went the first velvet rope with a holler, "Yo, friends of Leon's let dem drew," with the sharp musicality of a Bronx dialect.

Click went the second velvet rope with a shout, "Coming through friends of Leon," with a Queens monotonal drawl.

Click went the third velvet rope with a relaxed yell, "Hey, my guy no cover charge, 'fuhgeddaboudit,' (with a lot of jaw action, forward and down tongue Brooklyn accent), they're Leon's friends."

Lastly, the door girl waved us by, "Welcome to Club Exit, thanks for joining us."

As each barrier lifted, my gait slowed to a strut, my mouth curled upwards, and I could sense staring with disbelieving eyes, mostly drilling into the back of my head from Patrick and his two local friends. They were as shocked as I was by what they were witnessing. We could not have pulled this off if we tried. The fact that it was innocent and spontaneous made it possible. Still, I wonder how I did it!. Did I think *Maybe I'll pretend I'm a friend of Leon's*. No! Perhaps my evolved self guided me, the supremely confident one. It felt like I followed an invisible New York City impulse or surrendered to that distinct flow that propels so many outstanding New Yorkers to do great things. All I had to do was tap into that frequency then get out of my own way. Maybe I channeled the groovy Studio 54 disco queen version of mySELF on a parallel timeline sauntering into the uber-cool Studio 54, a seven-minute walk along West 55th Street.

Once inside, we hit the dancefloor on the lower level and danced there until sunrise. Deep house music shook the walls as 4,000 people lost themselves in the tunes, the euphoria, and the energy of a New York City dance club on opening night.

THE SECOND TIME I visited NYC, I was 46 years old. Fresh from Forbes and accompanied by Stitty. I felt the collective trauma of 9/11 deep, deep in my heart. But the people were resilient, creative, and innovative. They had bounced back. We went to Broadway shows, stand-up comedy, fantastic restaurants, cool bars, speakeasies, a Yankees game, The House of Yes Nightclub, The Brooklyn Mirage Nightclub, and Cielo Nightclub (DJ Tasha Blank *The Get Down*).

The frequency was still high, especially among the people I met on the dance floor. For example at The Brooklyn Mirage, we met a gorgeous local girl and her French fiancé. She was studying to be a doctor, and they were about to fly to the south of France to be married in his hometown.

I told her, "We have been together for over 21 years and are in New York for three weeks. Tonight we are out with my brother Patrick and our friends Simon, Jami, Jesse, and Lisa to celebrate 15 years of marriage. We have 3 girls, 14, 12, and 8, staying with family in Australia."

She exclaimed, "You two are my idols; I can't stop staring at you both. I hope my fiancé and I can still party like you two when we are your age!"

I asked her, "Where did you grow up?"

She replied, "I grew up in central Siberia."

I joked with her, "Wow, central Syberia. I thought Forbes in central NSW, Australia, was isolated! How did you end up studying medicine in New York?"

"My dad moved here when I was born to work as a taxi driver. When I was eight years old, he saved enough money for Mom, my sister, and me to come and live here," she explained.

I declared, "Your dad proved to you that we can do anything we put our mind to with determination and perseverance. Now you're an example of this: living your dreams in the City of Dreams."

Meeting her confirmed that it does not matter where you grow up or what school you go to, what matters is your spark. Your frequency gives you that *je ne sais quoi* quality and that charisma gene, as Jesse calls it. With this energy you light up the world.

When I finished writing about NYC I was well and truly at **Y** —You are here embodying SELF.

———

I ENJOYED WRITING the NYC story because it did not challenge me. I felt at ease writing about common phenomena. I noticed my ego's Special Agents *Inner Critic* and *Self Saboteur* were nowhere in sight because I was toeing the line, doing what I was told, and conforming to society's mold.

I reread my Accessing multidimensional me self chapter about my Healy experience and immediately noticed the secret agents lurking—on a validation mission. I felt anxious about how people would relate to an event potentially foreign to them.

Why am I so scared of being judged?

I went to sleep contemplating this question.

Thursday, 22nd April

When I awoke, I recalled my dream in which I was pregnant. I wrote the following in my journal

Writing the book is like being pregnant. I can't be a little bit pregnant; I am either pregnant or I'm not. In the same way, I'm either writing my truth or I'm not writing at all. The book has to be the whole truth, not just part of the truth. So I'm leaving my Accessing multidimensional me chapter in the book.

When I was pregnant with my daughters, I trusted them to guide me through the pregnancy and birth. I respected them during the pregnancy and birth. I realize now that I am pregnant with a book and I

have to trust and respect it during its incubation and birth. While pregnant I could not wish the baby had a certain hair color, eye shape, height, body shape, and personality. No, the baby was going to be what the baby was. It would forge its unique path despite my worrying. It is the same with the book, the book will be what it is, and no amount of worrying will change that.

I know my calling in this lifetime is to birth the book being called forth by humanity for humanity to raise human consciousness to evolve our species and Earth itself. Therefore, I do not need to control the book's content. Instead, I can simply allow the words to be written through my vehicle by taking a leap of faith.

I dropped into gratitude for my support team: my trusty laptop Birtha, my family, friends, teachers, other inspiring authors, and my privileges: my freedom, the means to write, and the places I can write.

When the time comes to birth the book, the book's creative doulas will turn up.

As I wrote this creative vision, tears flowed, sending my dream out into the universe to find its energetic match. The joy this activated was a SELF-realization catalyst: my internal guidance system shows me when I am expressing my purpose for being. Interestingly, these alignment symptoms feel as intense as my misalignment symptoms.

How does your body show you when you have hit that flow state? How do you know when you are aligned to the love frequency? Does this feeling signal you are on the right track? Does it feel like happiness?

Friday, 22nd of April

THE FOLLOWING day I was on a late morning walk. The beach was empty because it was term time. The sun was beating down on my face *I am feeling supremely blissful right now. I can't believe I wrote for 15 hours a day?" I can't believe I wrote 30,000 words in six days?" I can't believe my body and mind are capable of doing this! It's incredible how the stories simply poured onto the keyboard.* SHIT, *I'm burning right now! I really need a hat!*

I looked ahead of me on the deserted beach and saw a hat to my astonishment. I laughed *You've got to be kidding me. This is too much! Not a person anywhere.* As I put the dry hat on my head, I said, "Thank you! I manifested this!"

When we embody SELF we are taken care of. We create things that seem intangible, impossible, and unbelievable. The more I live this way, the more I know: *I do not have to try and make things happen or consciously write my story. That was the old way. The new way says—when I know myself as SELF my highest potential timeline writes through me allowing me to create things beyond my known reality. These creations are hard to claim but I am learning to claim everything I experience, even this random hat!*

As Macey said in Kalgoorlie, twenty years ago, "Don't dismiss these occurrences—own them… People tell us that we can't do these things so we don't believe we can. So much so that when they occur we either don't notice them or we write them off as coincidences. The only reason these supernatural skills remain dormant in most people is that no one is encouraging them. By owning and celebrating these experiences, we bring them into mainstream consciousness, normalize them, and shift into a new paradigm."

The frequency we chose attracts everything in our reality.

Creating that hat was a SELF-realization catalyst reminding me *I am the creator, NOT THE VICTIM. When I am living my truth aligned to the love frequency the rest takes care of itself.*

37

BEING SELF

50 years old

Saturday, July 3rd

STITTY TOOK the three girls away and left me to write, uninterrupted, for eight days. I did my usual thing and did not see another person the whole time. On Wednesday night, I was doing a recorded meditation by one of my online spiritual teachers, Mooji, who trained with the great Indian gurus. The guided meditation is called *Sit inside your own radiance* (Insight Timer App). I had done it often over the last few months. I loved it because Mooji is in Rishikesh, in northern India, near the source of the holy Ganga. In typical Indian fashion, there are constant distractions like coughing, smashing plates, and a thunderstorm accompanied by exuberant squealing. The backdrop perfectly suits his meditation pointers that invite us to notice that we are not our sense perceptions. We are not our body, our breath, our thoughts, we are not even our noticing. Mooji says, "Never mind the mind: there is nothing to fix or change. You are already the Self—for a long time dreaming, you were separate from the Self. Now you rest inside your own splendor. Sit inside your own radiance." I felt a strange phenomenon occurring around my mouth, and then I felt my whole face dissolve. This seems to be my cue that I am slipping into a deeper state of consciousness. Then pop. I was in the formless, indescribable, empty but full of unlimited possibilities place. I was resting in the space that is before the first manifestation of consciousness. I call this SELF.

I had the same knowing that everything was about to happen (infinite expressions) and then return to this feeling of interconnectedness again. The same question came to me *Could I live in my world as SELF?*

Stop thinking about it and just be it. Be SELF. My thoughts ceased.

Then one more little thought crept in *I have come full circle to this unfathomable place. It is time to finish the book and let it ripple out to ignite a global shift in consciousness. It is done, it is done, it is done.*

Thursday, July 8th

What did being SELF allow me to realize about SELF?

The more we realize SELF, the more we realize there is no-thing to realize.

Being SELF feels like we are the origin of everything. This means SELF-realization can never occur. We can never realize SELF because it will never appear to us—we are before it. Therefore, SELF can never be realized; it can only be intuited. This was a very subtle catalyst and perhaps my most profound. Everything is us, and we are everything, but at our core, we are no-thing because SELF is formless. So everything is nothing. This is why being SELF feels expansive, all-encompassing, all-pervasive, omnipresent, vast, and peaceful.

When we are being SELF, our person self feels like it is experiencing a foreign phenomenon. But it is paradoxical because it also feels oddly familiar. Why? Because we intuitively remember being SELF before we took human form. So it feels like going home to a place we remember but not from this lifetime. Hence, the paradox: *We know it but we do not know how we know it.*

When we are being SELF it is like we are witnessing the moment before creation. *It still blows my mind that I somehow knew all this on the meditation cushion two decades ago with no knowledge of the subject. Still, I struggle to put words to the experience of being SELF because it is a rare opportunity to dwell in non-dual reality and feel the fullness of emptiness. I have done my best to describe it, but it is indescribable. I believe witnessing my potential 20 years ago sent me on a mission to discover how to live in this world of separation while maintaining our innate wholeness. Modern western society perpetuates lack, but lack can not exist if everything is one interconnected SELF.*

Could we live in this 3-Dimensional (3-D) world as SELF?

The answer is *No* because as soon as we individuate in a vehicle (body), we are no longer unity consciousness/SELF because we have a physical body separate from the whole. Yes we are made of SELF, but we are not SELF, because SELF is formless. All we can do in our 3-D world is express our unique version of SELF (ourSELF), and occasionally we get to be SELF. Imagine my vehicle as the whirlpool above the drain in the bathtub to provide an analogy. Even though this whirlpool is a complete package, it is still water. If I stir up the whirlpool, it returns to water, losing its unique whirlpool vehicle. It is the same with being human. We are ultimately SELF, but if you take away our humanness (our form) and return us to SELF you destroy our vehicle. So humans are SELF individuated, they are not SELF because SELF is unity consciousness and has no vehicle/form.

SO HOW DOES SELF INDIVIDUATE?

There are infinite individuations of SELF as matter and energy from a dense book to less dense air.

- Everything is SELF, just in different forms.
- Everything is happening by itSELF.
- I express my version of SELF through my unique human body vehicle, which I call mySELF. Only I can express my version of SELF.
- You express your version of SELF through your unique human body vehicle, which you call yourSELF. Only you can express your version of SELF.

SELF is everything
Including:

- Humans: all eight billion.
- Animals, stones, trees, flora and fauna, creatures, birds.
- Things: books, houses, bridges, rainbows, snow.
- Beliefs: religion, gravity, rules.
- Feeling states: unity, mind, memories, ego.
- Realities: 3-D, dreams, other dimensions, ghosts, physical, non-physical.
- Time concepts: now, before, after, age, dates.
- Stories: Bible, Koran, Heaven, history, Dreamtime.
- Constructs: personal identity, politics, family, governments.

If I am an individuation of SELF (like the whirlpool over the drain), then I am also all the other individuations of SELF mentioned above (the water). So each of us is everything because everything is SELF. Some individuations of SELF possess consciousness and can perceive/cognize (humans), and some can not (inanimate objects).

If everyone is SELF, why would we judge another human being? They are us.

When we are being SELF we realize we are all equal. The SELF in me is the same as the SELF in you, which is the same as the SELF in others. We cultivate equanimity by knowing that each expression of SELF possesses the same potential to return to oneness regardless of the form it has taken. We foster compassion by knowing that all humans are trying to express SELF through their vehicle, but some have trouble intuiting SELF due to their unresolved trauma.

Can we embody SELF and unconditionally love others despite their misaligned choices. Can we view their misalignments as perfect catalysts for their SELF-realization which have the potential to create individual and collective evolution?

Can we want peace for every expression of SELF as much as we want peace for ourSELFs? After all, we are all one consciousness.

Labels are illusions

Being SELF shows us that we could call everything SELF. But we label things to organize our world. For example, I am an individuation/expression/aspect of SELF whose senses experience matter and energy through a human body vehicle. So, I label my existence—me, I, myself. Others label my existence as I enter their awareness—human, Katherine Sarah Joyce, Katie, Darling, Katie Pops, Kitty J, Kits, Kitty and Stitty, Babe, Katie Stitt, Mum, Mrs. Stitt, Thubten Pema, Junu, Radha, Sunshine Kitty Hawk, Hallelujah. These names are practical tools for communicating, but they could all be called SELF.

Maybe SELF should be our universal pronoun to replace she/he/they. So instead of "Pass Jenny her pen," we would say, "Pass Jenny SELF's pen."

Fluid SELF-expression is the new way of being

Being SELF proves that SELF is formless, Because we have access to all expressions of consciousness on all timelines we can access other multidimensional aspects of SELF anytime we choose. Therefore, we can use our free will to express ourSELF in any vehicle that is relevant in the now. For example, we can express through a non-binary human vehicle, higher dimensional being vehicle, spoon-bending vehicle, superhuman strength vehicle, animal vehicle, sacred geometry-shaped vehicle, self-healer vehicle or dream-runner vehicle.

Being SELF lets us know SELF is sovereign, so we can show up how and when we choose. We can shapeshift into any vehicle we choose to do what we need to do to best express SELF. There are no limits to our capabilities, skills, and powers.

Unity consciousness and non-attachment

Being SELF feels like a universal awareness—in which everything appears and then disappears, returning to unity consciousness again. Each expression is dependent on a set of causes and effects that do not exist independently. So, everything is interdependent, but nothing is real or solid and can be seen through. Experiencing this reality releases the need to be attached to what happens because everything that appears is inherently perfect. It comes from the whole and returns to the whole in the next moment. There is nothing to cling to. Here we feel a sense of complete acceptance for whatever happens. *We could think or not think, and both would be perfect. We could act or not act, and both would be perfect. We could speak or not speak, and both would be perfect. We could be here or there, and both would be perfect.*

Being SELF shows us that our sense of self (ego) is no more real than the things we perceive. Therefore, it is not to be taken seriously or empowered with attention. There is no permanent self sitting behind our experiences—our sense of self is just another dependent arising that we can easily laugh at. Thus, we can lighten up and be enlightened.

SELF is invincible

Being SELF gives us a sense of steadfast confidence. No matter what happens to us, our loved ones, pets, or things, nothing can affect our core existence because it is uncreated, therefore can not be destroyed. Nothing we experience impairs or improves what we truly are, just as the storm clouds and the rainbows do not impair or improve the radiance of the sun. This does not mean we refrain from making changes in our life, we still strive for alignment but we unequivocally know that whatever is arising has no power over our expanded SELF. Therefore, we can be at peace even when we are suffering; *It is what it is, and it is happening to the character called Kitty in the play called life.* Does this knowing shield us from grief? No, we are having a human experience, so we feel emotions, trauma, and pain that we must process. However, knowing SELF is invincible is a protective factor that builds the resilience necessary to bounce back.

Knowing everything is SELF

When we truly know everything is one consciousness, we can remain in a state of alignment most of the time. This means, my alignment tools, STORY Method (Standard or Advanced) are needed less and less. Why? The need to get back into alignment is only felt when we are identifying with a separate self who is out of alignment. Eventually we evolve into a unified being who is part of everything and everyone. With this awareness, there is nothing to align; we simply live evolved most of the time. To do this I invented a third method.

Inventing the Evolved STORY Method—The Y Method

The Y Method involved just doing the Y part of the STORY Method.

Y—You are here embodying SELF.

Inventing a breathing technique to go with the Evolved Y Method

Breathe in—*I accept every individuation, expression, and aspect of SELF that appears.*

Hold—*I am here being SELF.*

Breathe out—*Expressing mySELF by embodying SELF's love frequency.*

AS WE BREATHE in we may notice a triggered thought rising, we simply acknowledge *There's that which is not love leaving the body.* We rest in SELF's void of infinite possibilities. Then we exhale the love frequency and attract that which matches that coherence.

This method recognizes that we are before it all, untriggered, formless, and timeless, affected by nothing. We still perceive through our body's senses but with acceptance, knowing that we are always in alignment. Therefore, we live in a flow state where doubts and wake-up calls occur less and less, and synchronicities arise more and more. Why? Because we start to view wake-up calls as synchronicities because they are part of SELF instead of separate—they are still in alignment even though they feel out of alignment. For example, I can fall flat on my face and not make it mean anything at all. I can welcome the fall as perfect for me in the now without creating a story around it. Instead, I live evolved as mySELF experiencing SELF. Trusting that I am taken care of even when I fall. There is nothing to do, nothing to say, nowhere to go, nothing to heal. I simply remain in the love frequency by accepting the fall as perfect. *Everything is happening by itSELF. I can surrender to spontaneous creation no matter how it feels to my person self.*

Methods Summary

The Standard STORY Method: The solution comes soon after the problem when I use the STORY method.

The Advanced STORY Method: The solution comes before the problem when I use the S Method.

The Evolved STORY Method: There is no problem when I use the Y Method because this method is beyond stories, it transcends the mind entirely. It becomes as natural as breathing.

See Appendix 2 for STORY Method examples.

How do we embody SELF?
It is a feeling state unique to each individual.
I felt SELF when:

- My heart exploded in love for Dad in St. Nicholas Cathedral.
- My body blissfully dissolved into pure light during my Kalgoorlie rebirth.
- I locked eyes with an endangered snow leopard.
- I had an orgasmic birth.
- I visioned the void on Vision Quest.
- My base chakra exploded outwards during my Kundalini awakening.
- I put someone else's life before my own on the treadmill.
- I accessed my 12-D light body.

I also felt SELF when:

- I was terrified and promised Lysa's dad I would protect her.
- I cried out in compassion for Stitty on the Warchok hilltop.
- I pleaded with the universe to help me get out of Newtown.
- I grieved my lost son.
- I wept for Lou and vowed to look after her children.
- I held Melissa after Kellen transitioned to the spirit world.
- I disgusted myself while raking the cow dung during my lockdown retreat.

Sometimes SELF feels like love, compassion, joy, and bliss, and sometimes SELF feels like fear, desperation, anguish, and despair.

Each experience of SELF is a catalyst for profound transformation. And every time we are taken care of. It may not be evident at the time, but later we see its significance. Feeling our wholeness is our birthright. We can not feel this wholeness when we are numb, busy, or distracting ourselves. So let's take that risk, give up that addiction, leave that unsatisfying job, and end that toxic relationship. Because the more we experience the wholeness, the more we realize our purpose for being, which contributes to our new world vision. *Each of us will express ourSELF by embodying SELF, living evolved, and creating our dreams, thereby raising the frequency of the planet and igniting humanity's vision to awaken human consciousness. The collective will hold the idea of a new world in their vibrational fields until it becomes our reality.*

What can you do to make the new world vision a reality? How can you express yourSELF by embodying SELF, living evolved, and creating your dreams?

―――

THAT NIGHT I HAD A DREAM. *I was floating on my back, traveling feet first, along a river. It felt like Galari (Lachlan River) that runs through our farm. At times the river was treacherous, but I remained floppy. I surrendered to the flow without fear, accepting that I was out of control and being thrashed around in a dangerous current. I trusted the not knowing by believing I was where I needed to be. I traveled for a long time through different conditions. My view was always the same; clear, wide-open, blue sky. But my heightened kinesthetic sense allowed me to detect the river's status. My ears were below the water, so all I could hear was a constant hum, pounding, at times soothing. I focused on the underlying "Om" sound to anchor me. I could smell the river and the Australian bush. Finally, after a long expedition, I arrived at a lush green meadow. I emerged from the water effortlessly and walked up the bank and onto long, green, soft grass.*

The sun was shining, and I was instantly dry. I began walking peacefully towards the light.

I contemplated my dream. I felt as though my false selves died during Mooji's guided visualization and my dream represented my rebirth. In the dream I had bounced around, immersed in embryonic fluid surrendering to the flow/process before being birthed onto dry land in a physical body vehicle capable of living the same way. We can all utilize our senses to stay present instead of being lost in the past or consumed by plans for the future. We can all experience things without adding commentary, labels, comparisons, or expectations. We can all trust we are being taken care of. My dream's final prophetic scene symbolized life as a journey towards the clear light of death. Accepting our imminent death forces us to live in the now, knowing it could be our last moment. Each step on the path is an opportunity to embody SELF and be the light which adds to the collective light.

The dream prompted an awakening. *To live evolved, I do not need to be a fully realized being who has transcended human emotions. I just need to let SELF shine through me.*

38

EXPRESSING MYSELF

50 years old

I FINISHED WRITING *LIVING EVOLVED: Write Here, Write Now* on October 8th, and in November I privately welcomed Walks Tall Woman (one year after resigning from my job as a school teacher). Two Crow's attuned me to Isis Seichim (pronounced say-sheem), another healing modality in which living light energy made up of unconditional love is transmitted through the hands, using powerful symbols of ancient mystery schools. Shin Yon Buddhists traveled to Egypt to be initiated into the temples to learn this technique. Again, I could trust the Seichim lineage because Reiki Master Patrick Zeigler was given the Sekhem (pronounced say-kem) Egyptian system in the same way Dr. Usui had received Reiki. Patrick initiated Grandmother Mary Stewart who initiated Rosemary Dan who initiated our teacher Medicine Crow. The living light energy flowed easily through my hands. I think this was because my system was pure. I had not had a drink for a decade, no meat or seafood for two years, no gluten for nine years, and minimal dairy. I consistently practiced daily bodywork such as 10 minutes of yoga or kundalini breathwork, walks in nature, and monthly massages. This intentional purifying makes my connection to source feel strong. I felt like a clear conduit.

During Two Crow's Seichim retreat she told us that she and her family were leaving Forbes to live off the grid. She encouraged me to host the next 13 Full Moon Clan Mothers Women's Circles cycle, beginning in January. It was time for me to step up and start walking the talk. My 12-year Native American Apprenticeship was over, it was time to be the shaman.

In December, a school colleague said to me, "I'm fried; I need to be Stittyfied!" so I booked her in for a one-on-one healing/clarity session. I transformed the living room in the old cottage into my treatment room. As soon as I opened the door to the first woman, I stepped into a new evolved chapter and onto my highest potential timeline.

The one-on-one was a huge success. I loved it, and so did she. I was in my element. I took her on a deep shamanic Native American Medicine Drum journey and rebirth. Then I gifted her with some Reiki and Seichim healing. Followed by a card reading and some intention setting.

The second woman I supported, another colleague, told me after my guided meditation, "My grandfather, in spirit, gave me a message, and I went to a place I'd never been before that felt strange—like there was no atmosphere." I told her it sounded like the place I went on the insight meditation cushion. I felt so excited to be guiding people to this no-thing place that seems to ignite mystical experiences because the thinking brain switches off.

Soon more people booked in. As soon as a woman or man booked in, their guides started communicating with me. For example, vivid dreams, headaches, messages via animals, signs, and symbols. I started thinking about the healing tools in my toolbox and when they arrived I reached for the most appropriate tool for the job and the session flowed in perfect synchronicity.

I loved helping others to rewrite their stories. First they stalked themselves by catching their thoughts (Karen's CYT method) to see where they were out of alignment, identifying with false selves, believing untruths and limiting beliefs. They would practice the STORY methods until they became less triggered and old addictive habits (drinking, negative self-talk, over-eating, self-sabotage, avoidance) became irrelevant because they were no longer trying to escape painful thoughts. Soon false selves fell away revealing their true SELF. Over time they mastered remaining untriggered as they effortlessly expressed the love frequency. This evolved way of being allowed them to observe *that which is not love* rising and leaving the body. They also worked on rewriting their old stories. When they expanded their perspective about past events it changed the memory's vibration in the now. Therefore, attracting thoughts, people, and experiences that matched that higher frequency. In essence they wrote the past, present and future their way instead of the old programmed way. Once they were living their truth, the rest took care of itself and they began creating their dreams as well as dreams they never imagined.

In January I started hosting monthly women's circles, supporting people weekly and running my *Light Up and Stay Ignited* workshops locally.

I am doing what I was called to do.

LEGEND HAS it that Mother Earth sent a call into the universe for assistance to evolve consciousness. I believe I was one of those that answered the call.

You were too. That is why you sometimes think:

- *Life should be easier and more joyful.*
- *There must be more to life and more to my relationships.*
- *Am I more than just this physical body?*
- *Maybe I am here for a reason?*

You are right, you are here for a reason.

This book is you, calling you home to you—to yourSELF.

What are you going to do about it?

I can feel you lighting up as you read these words, can you?

My vow

I will express mySELF by utilizing my unique teaching, writing, and storytelling gifts to inspire others to serve the greater good on behalf of all.

Your vow

What is your vow: how will you express yourSELF by embodying SELF, living evolved, and creating your dreams to answer the call to action?

Our vow

Together we raise human consciousness and evolve as a species to support Mother Earth and preserve our planet.

The universe's vow

Each of us is pre-programmed to remember ourselves as SELF. At the same time, the whole of existence is pre-programmed to recognize itself as SELF. So together, we strive, moment after moment, to return to our origin—to wholeness which is the frequency of love.

We write the new in the now. So what story will we write—*write here, write now?*

SELF

70 years old
    Imagine a time in the future, April 2042.

ACCORDING TO THE MAYAN TEACHINGS, sun portals opened up in 2012, allowing children to be born as new souls with no karma. Imagine that these post-2012 high-frequency babies are now our empathetic, compassionate, and future-focused world leaders. They came as evolved beings, remembering their multi-dimensionality, free from unresolved trauma, blockages, and debilitating patterns. They incarnated to help us evolve. They embody peace, surrender, and creativity. We have been watching, listening, and imitating them for three decades to discover our true potential and end our karmic cycles.

    Over the two past decades, millions read *Living Evolved: Write Here, Write Now*. We trust the perfection of each moment, utilize our perfect body technology, and sustain Earth. We live aligned to our natural magnificence, knowing we came to benefit humanity and Mother Earth. We express ourSELF by embodying SELF, living evolved, and creating our dreams by utilizing our unique strengths. Millions of us feel satisfied, engaged, and fulfilled doing what we love to do and sharing our abilities for the good of all. As evolved Homoluminous Ones, we dwell on our highest timeline, which places Earth on its highest timeline. Thus, raising the frequency of the planet and evolving consciousness.

I approached the world's spiritual leaders and suggested a mass meditation. I explained the vision that came to me when I was 38 years old. I described the moment that changed the world and the evolution of human consciousness. I knew a proportion of the population was not living evolved, but I also knew the collective consciousness contained enough light for all to evolve. Nobody would be left behind because everyone is SELF. I told the spiritual leaders that if we pool our positive energy, a tipping point (assisted by unseen helpers) will create our new world vision here on Earth.

The spiritual leaders agreed to coordinate a global meditation. We asked everyone to gather with their community members, be still and hum *Om* at a specific time while focusing on unconditional love.

The moment arrived, and a hush fell over the planet.

We waited, sensing the enormity of what would unfold.

As millions began to hum *Om*, they witnessed being at the moment before creation because they had been there before (on a parallel timeline). They instinctively knew they were about to witness another creation, a new creation. Overwhelming excitement welled up, followed by joy, abundant bliss, and gratitude.

Click, click, click. All timelines converged.

A tear fell down my cheek. Time stood still.

Together we breathed in—*Accepting every individuation, expression, and aspect of SELF.* Together we held our breaths—*We are here being SELF.* Together we breathed out—*Expressing ourSELF by embodying SELF's love frequency.*

Millions embodied SELF in unison for the first time.

The veil of separation lifted, allowing all to experience wholeness.

Firstly, every human's pure essence became a rainbow and began swirling with the rainbow of everything else's pure essence. This coalesced into one rainbow Earth consciousness.

Secondly, this Earth consciousness merged with the consciousness of everything in the universe, forming the Whirling Rainbow Dreams of Wholeness (prophesied by Native Americans in *The 13 Original Clan Mothers* by Jamie Sams), which swirled together, forming a whirlpool of pure light.

Everything took a leap of faith and jumped into this whirlpool and onto the highest potential timeline of all. They marinated in the currents containing evolution codes as they tumbled and twirled. Each code deleted, upgraded, and purified each individuation/expression/aspect of SELF to the purest form of love. Their collective vibrations made a deep hum *OM*.

At that moment, everything that had ever been created began being SELF.

SELF's in-breath was now the same as SELF's out-breath, which was the same as SELF's in-between breaths. It was all SELF. There were no infinite timelines, individuated consciousnesses, or aspects of SELF. The whole of existence recognized itself as SELF and became unity consciousness expressing itself as one harmonized vibration, *Om* (the primordial sound of creation).

This sound caused a universal orgasm, and all of existence had a Kundalini awakening erupting our universal creative power triggering the universe's vow to return to our origin—to wholeness. This power set off a solar flash that traveled at the speed of light sending waves and waves of love frequency throughout the universe (billions of galaxies). Everything evolved from separation (individuated consciousnesses) to unity (one consciousness) igniting a global shift in consciousness.

Beyond Evolved: Write Here, Write Now

The vision that came to me when I was 38 years old, the one I shared with the world, the one we held in the collective's vibrational field, was now our reality.

A new creation story began.

What happened to us all?

We will find out when we create it.

APPENDIX 1

Glossary of Terms

SELF—your word for God

mySELF—my individuated consciousness expressing
aligned to SELF (mySELF Expressing Love Frequency) or
misaligned to SELF (mySELF Expressing Low Frequency)

yourSELF—your individuated consciousness expressing yourSELF aligned to SELF (yourSELF Expressing Love Frequency) or misaligned to SELF (yourSELF Expressing Low Frequency)

himSELF—his individuated consciousness expressing
himSELF aligned to SELF (himSELF Expressing Love Frequency)
or misaligned to SELF (himSELF Expressing Low Frequency)

herSELF—her individuated consciousness expressing herSELF aligned to SELF (herSELF Expressing Love Frequency) or misaligned to SELF (herSELF Expressing Low Frequency)

themSELF—their individuated consciousness expressing themSELF aligned to SELF (themSELF Expressing Love Frequency) or misaligned to SELF (themSELF Expressing Low Frequency)

New world vision—*Each of us will express ourSELF by embodying SELF, living evolved, and creating our dreams, thereby raising the frequency of the planet and igniting humanity's vision to awaken human consciousness. The collective will hold the idea of a new world in their vibrational fields until it becomes our reality.*

Ask ourselves—*What can I do to make the new world vision a reality? How can I express mySELF by embodying SELF, living evolved, and creating my dreams?*

My vow—I will express mySELF by utilizing my unique teaching, writing, and storytelling gifts to inspire others to serve the greater good on behalf of all.

Your vow—What is your vow: how will you express yourSELF by embodying SELF, living evolved, and creating your dreams to answer the call to action?

Our vow—Together we raise human consciousness and evolve as a species to support Mother Earth and preserve our planet.

APPENDIX 1

The universe's vow—Each of us is pre-programmed to remember ourselves as SELF. At the same time, the whole of existence is pre-programmed to recognize itself as SELF. So together, we strive, moment after moment, to return to our origin—to wholeness which is the frequency of love.

Mantra—*Thank you for this opportunity to be an enlightened being in this now moment.*

APPENDIX 2

STORY Method Examples

STORY Method

S—*Stop you're out of alignment.* Ctrl Alt Delete.
T—*Triggered. Name the false self.*
O—*Own it. You're the only one who can shift the misalignment.*
R—*Realign. Take action.*
Y—*You are here embodying SELF.*

Example: I feel insecure at a party.
    <u>Awkwardness</u>

S—Stop you're out of alignment. *Ctrl Alt Delete.*
    T—Triggered that *I'm not enough* false self.
    <u>Looks like:</u> shyness

APPENDIX 2

Sounds like: insecurity narrative, *Everyone fits in but me. I might say the wrong thing. Everyone is looking at me.*

Feels like: exclusion, heart racing.

O—Own it. You're the only one who can shift the misalignment. Take some deep breaths.

R—Realign. Take action. Flip it—*Everyone is worried about themselves, not me. If I go and make someone feel good I will stop focusing on my insecurities. The more I expand and help others shine, the less focussed I will be on my small self. The bigger I go the less I will worry. Be mySELF Expressing Love Frequency*—make someone feel interesting, ask others questions, talk about a global issue, introduce yourself to someone, help the host.

Y—You are here embodying SELF.

Looks like: socializing

Sounds like: connecting

Feels like: calm

Example: My teacher said I received a lower than expected exam result.

Negativity

S—Stop you're out of alignment. *Ctrl Alt Delete.*

T—Triggered that *I'm no good* false self.

Looks like: disappointment

Sounds like: negative narrative, "My teacher is crap. I had a headache that day. I won't get into University now. I knew I wouldn't go well. Why did I even bother studying."

Feels like: failure, tight shoulders.

O—Own it. You're the only one who can shift the misalignment. Take some deep breaths.

R—Realign. Take action. Flip it–*I take full responsibility for my* result. This is not the end of the world, it's only one exam. I can bounce back. There are many avenues into my career—I will do better next exam. Be mySELF Expressing Love Frequency. I will identify areas for improvement. I will set up a study timetable. I will seek help from teachers/online. I will chat with ex-students.

Y—You are here embodying SELF.
<u>Looks like:</u> commitment
<u>Sounds like:</u> ownership
<u>Feels like:</u> hopeful

Example: I told my partner I loved them and they didn't reply. I expected a different outcome.
<u>Expectations</u>

S—Stop you're out of alignment. *Ctrl Alt Delete.*

T—Triggered that *clinging* false self.
<u>Looks like</u>: desperation
<u>Sounds like:</u> expectations narrative, *I thought you would say "I love you" back. You should say it if I said it. Why don't you love me?*
<u>Feels like:</u> control, sweating.

O—Own it. You're the only one who can shift the misalignment. Take some deep breaths.

R—Realign. Take action. Flip it—*I am content with my feelings right now. I am proud of myself for being brave and saying 'I love you'. He/she/they will say it when they are ready or not. If not, I will either be content with non-commitment or I will leave and find a partner who is more emotionally available. Right now, I choose to remain silent because anything I say will sound needy and controlling and will have no impact on their feelings anyway. I will observe our relationship in the future and make my decision.* Be mySELF Expressing Love Frequency—lead by example, be the change I want to see, model

APPENDIX 2

a committed relationship style, communicate honestly, be vulnerable and authentic. Set a definitive date, if he/she/they has not committed to me by that date and I want commitment then I must leave. This is non-negotiable. I can not change someone.

Y—You are here embodying SELF.
<u>Looks like:</u> trust
<u>Sounds like:</u> boundaries
<u>Feels like:</u> surrender

Example: I need a cigarette/overeat/drink/drugs/screentime.
<u>Craving</u>

S—Stop you're out of alignment. *Ctrl Alt Delete.*
T—Triggered that *addicted* false self.
<u>Looks like:</u> preoccupation
<u>Sounds like:</u> addiction narrative *I need something outside me to be happy, block out the pain and memories or to feel worthy. If I do this I can avoid feeling or doing things that are uncomfortable.*
<u>Feels like:</u> out of control, panicked
O—Own it. You're the only one who can shift the misalignment. Take some deep breaths.
R—Realign. Take action. Flip it—*I have everything I need, the craving will pass. I don't need this to numb my trauma. I know that what happened to me happened to the character in the play called 'life'. I exist before it all. In this new moment, I can return to that awareness where there is no craving, just bliss. I am a non-smoker. Be mySELF Expressing Love Frequency*—I will punch a bag, have a shower, put my hand in ice, exercise until the craving subsides.
Y—You are here embodying SELF.
<u>Looks like:</u> self-control
<u>Sounds like:</u> quiet

APPENDIX 2

<u>Feels like:</u> triumph, pride

———

Example: I feel bored.
   <u>Boredom</u>

S—Stop you're out of alignment. *Ctrl Alt Delete.*
   T—Triggered that *lack* false self.
   <u>Looks like:</u> fidgeting
   <u>Sounds like:</u> scarcity narrative I am bored. There is nothing to do. The grass is greener over there.
   <u>Feels like:</u> stagnation, aversion
   O—Own it. You're the only one who can shift the misalignment. Take some deep breaths.
   R—Realign. Take action. Flip it—*I am grateful for the things I am doing. Be mySELF Expressing Love Frequency*—list everything I am grateful for, fully connect to the task at hand, give it your full focus and attention.
   Y—You are here embodying SELF.
   <u>Looks like:</u> contentment
   <u>Sounds like:</u> gratitude
   <u>Feels like:</u> bliss

———

Example: I am angry because my family packed the dishwasher incorrectly and the plates are still dirty.
   <u>Control</u>

S—Stop you're out of alignment. *Ctrl Alt Delete.*
   T—Triggered that *angry* false self.
   <u>Looks like:</u> banging the plates down

APPENDIX 2

<u>Sounds like:</u> criticism/resentment/victim narrative, "Why can't you just pack it the right way. You guys make me so angry. How many times have I told you this? Why can't you just do as you're told?

<u>Feels like:</u> separation, them versus me

O—Own it. You're the only one who can shift the misalignment. Take some deep breaths.

R—Realign. Take action. Flip it—I am grateful to have a family who wants to help me. I am grateful to have a dishwasher. I have all the time I need to rewash this plate. I am choosing to be present. They did the best they could, maybe I will show them again. Does it really matter in the end? *Be mySELF Expressing Love Frequency*—come into my body by feeling the water on my hands and watching the soap bubbles. Drop into my heart. Feel my love for them.

Y—You are here embodying SELF.

<u>Looks like:</u> serenity

<u>Sounds like:</u> non-judgement

<u>Feels like:</u> presence

Example: My new, kind partner pours a beer and I feel unsafe.

<u>Anxiety</u>

S—Stop you're out of alignment. *Ctrl Alt Delete.*

T—Triggered that *traumatized* false self.

<u>Looks like:</u> stress

<u>Sounds like:</u> controlling narrative, *Why do they have to drink?*

<u>Feels like:</u> fear, can't breath

O—Own it. You're the only one who can shift the misalignment. Take some deep breaths.

R—Realign. Take action. Flip it—*This is an old trigger. My partner is not my ex-partner/parent/carer. I am not a child or my past self. They can drink without me being unsafe. Nothing bad is going to* *happen to me if they drink. I am safe. Be mySELF Expressing Love Frequency—hug them and say how much I appreciate them.*

Y—You are here embodying SELF.

Looks like: love

Sounds like: realistic

Feels like: relaxed

Example: I think someone is having a go at me.

Insecurity

S—Stop you're out of alignment. *Ctrl Alt Delete.*

T—Triggered that *paranoid* false self.

Looks like: shame

Sounds like: judged narrative, *I am getting into trouble. I need to defend and justify. They are accusing me.*

Feels like: fear, defensiveness

O—Own it. You're the only one who can shift the misalignment. Take some deep breaths.

R—Realign. Take action. Flip it—*I am safe. This reminds me of how I felt in the past. This person may not be having a go at me. Give them the benefit of the doubt. We are just discussing. Share openly from the heart. All is as it should be. I am respected and honored. Be mySELF Expressing Love Frequency*—feel at ease, picture you both as love.

Y—You are here embodying SELF.

Looks like: openness

Sounds like: communication

Feels like: togetherness

APPENDIX 2

Example: I feel guilty for a decision I made concerning my child/partner/friend/family member.
<u>Guilt</u>

S—Stop you're out of alignment. *Ctrl Alt Delete.*
T—Triggered that *guilty* false self.
<u>Looks like:</u> ruminating
<u>Sounds like:</u> guilt narrative, *I made the wrong decision. It's all my fault. Because of me this has happened.*
<u>Feels like:</u> constriction, nausea
O—Own it. You're the only one who can shift the misalignment. Take some deep breaths.
R—Realign. Take action. Flip it—*I did the best I could at the time with what I knew then. Now that I know better I will do better. My child chose me for all the decisions I will make. Even this decision was perfect on some level.* Be mySELF Expressing Love Frequency—do something I love to do, play the solitude card game, hug someone, watch my favorite movie, write a poem about how much I love them.
Y—You are here embodying SELF.
<u>Looks like:</u> peace
<u>Sounds like:</u> forgiveness
<u>Feels like:</u> compassion

Example: I feel intimidated.
<u>Unworthy</u>

S—Stop you're out of alignment. *Ctrl Alt Delete.*
T—Triggered that *inferior* false self.
<u>Looks like:</u> self-doubt
<u>Sounds like:</u> inferiority narrative, *They think they are better than me. They wouldn't talk to me because I'm not rich/smart/cool enough.*

APPENDIX 2

I wouldn't know what to say to them anyway. They are snobs. Maybe they are better than me.

Feels like: competition, hypervigilance

O—Own it. You're the only one who can shift the misalignment. Take some deep breaths.

R—Realign. Take action. Flip it—*I am equal to them. We are both aspects of SELF. We both have unique codes, strengths, abilities and talents that we contribute to humanity. I trust that whatever I say will be in perfect alignment. Be mySELF Expressing Love Frequency*—ask questions, share your opinion, give a compliment.

Y—You are here embodying SELF.

Looks like: self-assured

Sounds like: confidence

Feels like: unity

Example: I feel irritated because I am stuck in traffic.

Annoyance

S—Stop you're out of alignment. *Ctrl Alt Delete.*

T—Triggered that *agitated* false self.

Looks like: road-rage

Sounds like: poor me narrative, *Typical, just when I need to be somewhere I get stuck behind a 100-year-old. My colleagues are going to think I'm useless if I'm late. Why does this always happen to me?*

Feels like: increased cortisol levels, gripping the wheel

O—Own it. You're the only one who can shift the misalignment. Take some deep breaths.

R—Realign. Take action. Flip it—*I can warp time. By being fully present in the moment I can practice patience, surrender and acceptance. I know I will arrive at the perfect time and that right now I am exactly where I need to be, doing exactly what I need to be doing,*

APPENDIX 2

breathing. Thank you for the opportunity to be an enlightened being in this now moment. Be mySELF Expressing Love Frequency—hum, sing, drum, smile at other drivers, laugh and dance to the playlist.

Y—You are here embodying SELF.
<u>Looks like:</u> chilling
<u>Sounds like:</u> positive self-talk
<u>Feels like:</u> tranquility

Example: I am breaking up with my partner when there is nothing wrong because I fear being abandoned in the future.
<u>Avoidance</u>

S—Stop you're out of alignment. *Ctrl Alt Delete.*
T—Triggered that *abandoned* false self.
<u>Looks like:</u> irrational behavior
<u>Sounds like:</u> abandonment narrative, *I don't deserve devotion. It is too good to be true. Something bad will probably happen anyway. I can't bear to feel abandoned again so I'll end it before you do. I am terrified you are going to leave me. I need to protect myself.* "It's not you, it's me. I have been with someone else. It's not the right time for us. I need some space."
<u>Feels like:</u> nervousness, stiff neck
O—Own it. You're the only one who can shift the misalignment. Take some deep breaths.
R—Realign. Take action. Flip it—*This is my childhood/past relationship trauma playing out. I may have been abandoned (physically or emotionally) but I am worthy of love. I am loveable. He/she/they may not leave me and if he/she/they does I will be ok. I choose to give this relationship 100%. I choose to be vulnerable and honest about my fear and how it affects what I think, say and do. I refuse to let my childhood/past relationship trauma sabotage my happiness. I'm sorry,*

Please forgive me, I love you, Thank you. Be mySELF Expressing Love Frequency—Don't push them away. Take a risk, love freely and unapologetically and see what happens. Trust that whatever happens, I will be ok. Surrender to the process.

Y—You are here embodying SELF.
<u>Looks like:</u> staying together
<u>Sounds like:</u> honesty
<u>Feels like:</u> vulnerability

Example: I feel dumb in a social situation.
<u>Ego/imposter syndrome/inner critic</u>

S—Stop you're out of alignment. *Ctrl Alt Delete.*
T—Triggered that *disregarded* false self.
<u>Looks like:</u> embarrassment
<u>Sounds like:</u> insecurity narrative, *I am not going to contribute, I've been shut down.*
<u>Feels like:</u> blushed, lump in throat.
O—Own it. You're the only one who can shift the misalignment. Take some deep breaths.
R—Realign. Take action. Flip it—*No one is judging me right now. My opinions are valid. It only matters what I think about myself. I know my self worth. This interaction doesn't define me.*
Y—You are here embodying SELF.
<u>Looks like:</u> friendly banter
<u>Sounds like:</u> humor by developing a repertoire of witty comebacks that make you bounce back instantly.
<u>Feels like:</u> empowered.

APPENDIX 2

The Advanced STORY Method—The S Method

Sometimes, for day-to-day slip-ups, we do not need to use the whole STORY Method. We know what story our programmed brain will write, so by doing the S part of the STORY method we stop it in its tracks and course-correct.

S— Stop you're out of alignment. *Ctrl Alt Delete.*

Stopping and thinking *Ctrl, Alt, Delete* intercepts a triggering thought and takes us straight to *Y* —You are here embodying SELF. This method requires us to sense the possibility of an old patterned thought popping up while remaining in alignment. Then shut it down before we're triggered.

The Evolved STORY Method—The Y Method

The Y Method involved just doing the Y part of the STORY Method.
Y—You are here embodying SELF.
The breathing technique to go with the Evolved Y Method
Breathe in—*I accept every individuation, expression, and aspect of SELF that appears.*
Hold—*I am here being SELF.*
Breathe out—*Expressing mySELF by embodying SELF's love frequency.*

As we breathe in we may notice a triggered thought rising, we simply acknowledge *There's that which is not love leaving the body.* We rest in SELF's void of infinite possibilities. Then we exhale the love frequency and attract what resonates with that coherence.

This method recognizes that we are before it all, untriggered, formless, and timeless, affected by nothing. We still perceive through our body's senses but with acceptance, knowing that we are always in alignment.

Methods Summary

The Standard STORY Method: The solution comes soon after the problem when I use the STORY method.

The Advanced STORY Method: The solution comes before the problem when I use the S Method.

The Evolved STORY Method: There is no problem when I use the Y Method because this method is beyond stories, it transcends the mind entirely. It becomes as natural as breathing.

What about times when we feel out of alignment because our body is alerting us to something that needs our attention. It is important to realize that sometimes signals are not triggered false selves but messages from SELF. Our body is our built-in expert and authority figure. We need to check in and inquire *Are we triggered or is this fight or flight response keeping me safe?* Overt positivity can mask an important cue. The STORY methods are not about flipping everything to the positive. On the contrary, one must practice discernment to ascertain whether or not a warning sign is a triggered false self or intuition giving us a message such as; *my partner is having an affair, I am in danger* or *I have been eating unhealthy food, avoiding exercise and overworking.*

———

A word of warning, the ego sometimes creates smoke and mirrors to stop us ignoring false selves because change is uncomfortable. Sometimes we fall into a trap of giving up on being our highest potential self because we think *There are signs telling me not to change* when in fact it's our ego tricking us because it wants us to remain safe and

APPENDIX 2

secure. The ego's deceit can be subtle, so we must pay attention and not be fooled.

ABOUT THE AUTHOR

Kitty guides others to find their truth, align to it and eventually embody it. She inspires the collective to answer their call to action.

She is an engaging storyteller who grew up in Italy, France, the U.S.A, and Australia. She facilitates monthly Full Moon Women's Circles and provides one-on-one sessions for healing, intention setting, and self-exploration (including trauma resolution) through her business, By Kitty, which is dedicated to inspiring Homoluminous Ones to shine their light.

Kitty's life-long mission is to evolve from chaos to calm. This yearning led her on a path of SELF-discovery, which included practicing the Buddha's teachings, exploring consciousness, and a 12-year Native American shaman apprenticeship.

She has been teaching health and wellbeing for over 30 years, including six years lecturing at the University of Sydney in the Faculty of Education. When she realized her impact could reach further, she left teaching to translate decades of personal development insights into empowering and easy-to-read stories. She shares these in her workshops locally, inter-state and overseas.

Kitty's charisma encourages everyone to create a life aligned to their highest potential. This book is full of Kitty's awakening stories that created the necessary catalysts to live evolved. She hopes her readers will discover their true SELF and purpose.

Be on the lookout for more books in this series:

Beyond Evolved: Write Here, Write Now

Sensually Evolved: Write Here, Write Now

Soberly *Evolved: Write Here, Write Now*

Parenting *Evolved: Write Here, Write Now*

Creating *Evolved: Write Here, Write Now*

Kitty's message to each of her beloved readers is, *As each of us lights up, we evolve as a species to preserve our planet. Together we create peace and raise human consciousness.*

www.ingramcontent.com/pod-product-compliance
Lightning Source LLC
Chambersburg PA
CBHW052130070526
44585CB00017B/1763